The
WRITER'S WAY

Jack Rawlins
California State University at Chico

Stephen Metzger
California State University at Chico

SEVENTH EDITION

Houghton Mifflin Company   Boston   New York

Executive Publisher: Patricia Coryell
Senior Sponsoring Editor: Lisa Kimball
Senior Marketing Manager: Tom Ziolkowski
Development Editor: Meg Botteon
Project Editor: Aimee Chevrette
Art and Design Manager: Jill Haber
Cover Design Director: Tony Saizon
Senior Photo Editor: Jennifer Meyer Dare
Senior Composition Buyer: Chuck Dutton
New Title Project Manager: Susan Peltier
Editorial Assistant: Sarah Truax
Marketing Assistant: Bettina Chiu
Editorial Assistant: Laura Collins

Cover image: © Shaun Egan/Getty Images, Inc.

TEXT CREDITS

Credits and acknowledgments appear on p. 405, which constitutes an extension
of the copyright page.

Printed in the U.S.A.

Library of Congress Control Number: 2007941449

ISBN-10: 0-618-95842-8
ISBN-13: 978-0-618-95842-9

3456789-2007941449 -EB-11   10   09   08

CONTENTS

Part Two

PLANNING AND DRAFTING   35

Chapter 3

Chapter 4

Part Three

REVISING AND EDITING   67

Chapter 5

Chapter 6

Chapter 12

Chapter 13

Chapter 14

Part Five

ACADEMIC WRITING   281

PREFACE

Passing the Baton

In the fall of 1979, I enrolled in a graduate-level seminar in English-language stylistics at California State University, Chico. The professor was Jack Rawlins, a Victorian literature scholar and an expert in composition, and he had quite a reputation. "He's *really, really* hard," my friends said. "And picky! He'll mark you down for not putting your name in the proper place on the title page."

So naturally I was a bit nervous about taking the class. However, I knew Professor Rawlins in another context: we both played on the Pests, a recreational men's softball team made up mostly of English professors and graduate students (originally sponsored by a pest-control company, hence the odd name). So while Rawlins had it all over me in the classroom, out on the field I had, well, the bigger bat and, as a twenty-six-year-old, was still playing a pretty mean shortstop.

The class turned out to be the best class I ever took in college. After a six-week crash course in the history of the English language and the principles of stylistics, each of us had to choose a work of literature on which to do a stylistic analysis; in addition to writing a paper, each of us had to lead a three-hour class discussion on our topic. Rawlins was amazing, both enriching our own understanding of our material and contributing to our presentations in such a way as to make them far more convincing and compelling without stealing any of our own thunder. And yes, he was hard, but I loved being pushed that way, and besides, it was pretty easy to put my name in the right place on the title page. (I presented D. H. Lawrence's *The Rainbow*, the close reading of which, if you'll pardon the cheesy cliché, truly changed my life. . . .)

In fact, I liked the class so much that after I got my M.A. in English I considered staying in school and pursuing a Ph.D. in literature, and while my grades and test scores probably qualified me, I just couldn't bring myself to apply. I just wanted to write. For a living.

As attractive and exotic as that sounded, though, I knew the odds were slim. Like everyone's parents always say: I'd need something to fall back on.

So I fell back on teaching writing parttime at California State University, Chico, where I was assigned an office directly across the hall from Professor Rawlins. One day, he brought over a two-inch-thick, dot-matrix-printed manuscript and dropped it on my desk.

It was the first draft of *The Writer's Way*, and he wanted feedback. I read it, liked it a lot, made some minor suggestions, and kind of forgot about it. A couple of years later he brought the published first edition across the hall and presented me with a copy, thanking me for helping. That would have been about 1984.

By the late 1980s I was beginning to make some headway in my freelance writing career. I was writing regularly for the skiing magazine *Powder*, whose editors were sending me on assignment to ski the Rockies and the French and Italian Alps. I was also writing for several in-flight, health-and-fitness, travel, and other skiing magazines and had written a guidebook on New Mexico and was working on one on Colorado. I tried my best to bring into the classroom what I knew about writing in the real world.

In the early 1990s, our department chair moved me in with Rawlins, his officemate having recently retired. At the same time, I had begun using *The Writer's Way* in my own classes, mostly advanced-composition courses for students pursuing their California teaching credentials. The students who came to my office to discuss their papers were always surprised to learn that their textbook had been written by the guy sitting at the desk next to mine.

Rawlins retired from the Pests shortly after that and from the CSU, Chico, English department in 2003. One day he called me. His retirement was keeping him quite busy—he was taking bicycling trips all over the world, among other things—and he didn't think he could keep giving *The Writer's Way* the attention it deserved. He thought I knew the book, and him as author, as well as anyone. Would I want to revise it for its next edition, the seventh?

What's New

My mandate was pretty straightforward: I was to keep the overall sense of the book—the pedagogy, the philosophy, the tone, the focus on student writing—the same, but I was to update it, in part by replacing model essays that no longer seemed relevant as well as by ensuring that it reflected current classroom strategies and other ideas about learning to write. I was also encouraged to bring to the book what I knew about writing professionally. Ironically, I started by taking out a chapter about publishing, figuring that while that's an important part of writing, it didn't have a whole lot to do with the way writing is taught in schools—though of course most of the principles are the same. I took out the chapter on collaborative writing, combined some of the chapters about organization, and replaced some twenty of the model essays.

When you come across a first-person reference in this edition, it's me. These are my stories—some come from the classroom but more come from my twenty-five-year career as a professional writer.

And while I still play for the Pests, I have moved from shortstop to first base.

What Isn't New

The Writer's Way remains based on two core principles, and it returns again and again: (1) good writing begins when you write for the right reasons; and (2) good reasons to write will teach you everything you need to know about technique. A writer constantly makes choices: Should I do *this*, or *that*? Should I do it *this* way, or *that* way? Real writers don't answer such questions by asking themselves, "What's the rule?" or "What do good essays do?" Instead, they ask, "What am I trying to accomplish here?"; "Will this help me accomplish that?"; and, "Is there another way of doing it that will accomplish it better?" In short, the real writer asks, "Will this *work*?" The goal of *The Writer's Way* is to train you in this new way of thinking.

How the Book Is Laid Out

This book is divided into seven parts. The Prologue is a two-part introduction to the art of going to college. The first part is a list of things good students do in order to get an A. The second part is an instruction manual on how to study. You'll want to have the Prologue down cold before you walk through the classroom door, or as soon thereafter as possible.

Part One is an introduction to the attitude toward learning to write that lies behind the rest of the book. I encourage you to read it before doing anything else.

Parts Two and Three are a step-by-step walk-through of the writing process: from first thoughts through brainstorming, drafting, rethinking, organizing, peer editing, stylistic polishing, and cosmetic editing. Part Two covers all the messy, creative steps from first thoughts through the first draft. Part Three is about ways to take that draft and revise it into something better. It would be lovely if you could know everything in Parts Two and Three before you wrote an essay, but you won't be able to wait, so you will probably find yourself writing essays while reading one chapter after another, and in fact you can read them in almost any order.

Part Four introduces you to the three main essay "modes": personal writing, writing to inform, and argument. You'll want to read these three chapters if your writing course gives assignments by mode ("Write an informative essay") or you're just looking for ways to break out of your old essay-writing rut. For each mode, there is a collection of sample essays in Part Six, A Collection of Good Writing. You'll want to read those samples along with the chapter.

Part Five discusses writing for college courses. Here you'll learn how to approach traditional academic writing assignments and how to perform basic scholastic writing skills: research, documentation, quotation, and the like. If your writing course gives assignments that use these forms and techniques, obviously you'll want to read these chapters, but even if it doesn't, these chapters will help you in every other course you take in college that involves writing. There are sample academic essays in A Collection of Good Writing, and two complete research papers at the end of Chapter 18.

Part Six is the fun part. It's a collection of essays written by students in both Professor Rawlins's and my classes, as well as five published essays about food. You'll want to read them, because they're wonderful, and because the easiest way to help your writing is to read some great writing and fall in love with it. Then the most natural thing in the world is to go out and try to do something like the writing you love.

Unusual Features

The Writer's Way has several features that set it apart from other composition textbooks:

The Prologue addresses questions you need answers to before you can begin any school work: What do good students do that poor students don't do? What does it mean to "study" a chapter in a book? How can I tell if I'm "learning" anything? What do good readers do beyond looking at the words and trying to remember them?

The Writer's Way contains *fifty complete essays*—about half sprinkled throughout the chapters to illustrate principles, and half collected at the end of the book in A Collection of Good Writing (Part Six). Forty-two of these essays are by students, so you can see that your peers can and do write wonderful essays, and you can as well.

Most of the chapters end with *Writer's Workshop* sections. These workshops are similar to the lab sections of a science course: first you watch a hands-on demonstration of one of the concepts presented in the chapter; then you dig in and get your own hands dirty.

Almost all the chapters end with *exercises*. These obey the spirit of the book and the Writer's Workshop sections by avoiding drills and mechanical activities whenever possible and focusing on whole-language activities, in which you are asked to work with entire blocks of text. As often as possible, the text being worked with is your own, since anything one learns about someone else's writing is far less powerful than what one learns about one's own.

Several topics that often are not covered in composition textbooks are covered in this book. In addition to the Prologue, on how to go to school, and Part One, on how writing gets learned and what makes writing work, there are chapters on critical thinking, peer editing (including explicit instruction on how to do it well), titling, and how to make a too-short essay longer. The chapter on first-drafting examines writer's block, explores where it comes from, and offers eighteen strategies for overcoming it.

Acknowledgments

In addition to the students and professional writers whose essays I've included in this edition of *The Writer's Way*, as well as the gracious and insightful editors at Houghton Mifflin, I'd like especially to thank Professor Jack Rawlins, who trusted me to take over this wonderful book as he stepped away from it. I hope I have honored you appropriately and done your book justice. I am grateful to the following reviewers of the seventh edition: Chris Dew, University of North Florida; Christina Fisanick, Xavier University; Liz Kleinfeld, Red Rocks Community College; Mark Leichliter, University of Northern Colorada; Matthew Schmeer, Johnson County Community College; and Rick Walters, New Hampshire Community Technical College. Of course, thanks and love always to three of the best writers I know: Betsy, Hannah, and Gina.

S. M.

PROLOGUE:

HOW TO SUCCEED IN SCHOOL

How to Get a Good Grade

Here's a time-tested list of things good-grade getters do. There's some overlap with the Guide to Studying (p. P-2), since learning and grade getting are related. Suggestion: note which things you already do, mark the ones you don't, then pick two or three of those "don'ts" as personal goals for this semester.

"We hold these truths to be self-evident":

1. Go to class every day.
2. Be on time for class.
3. Study the course syllabus.
4. Do all the assigned reading, by the time it's due.
5. Hand in all assignments, on time.
6. Take part in class discussion.
7. Take notes during class.
8. Rewrite all papers.
9. Use a computer for all essay-style assignments.
10. Print your drafts and proofread from hard copy.
11. Follow directions carefully and precisely.

Less self-evident truths:

12. Sit near the front of the classroom, or where the instructor can see you clearly.
13. Become an expert on the course grading system.
14. Come to each class session with a question about the material.
15. Visit the instructor during office hours.
16. Study for tests over as long a period as possible.
17. Take notes recording your thoughts and reactions as you're doing the course reading—not after.
18. Write in your textbooks—highlight, underline, jot marginal notes.
19. After all assigned readings and all class sessions, write answers to these questions:

> What was the point? What am I supposed to learn from it?
> Why does it matter?

20. Before each class session, remind yourself where the class left off last time.
21. Reflect on assignments off and on, all the time, from the moment they're assigned until they're due.
22. Study by *talking* with classmates, in addition to reading or note taking.
23. Be respectful to your teacher and classmates.

How to (Re)Learn in School: A Guide to Studying

The basic school experience is this: you hear a lecture, read a chapter of a book, or do an exercise in class, and the teacher says, "Go learn that." If you're like most students, despite having been in school for umpteen thousand years, you don't have a very clear notion of how to go about it. To help, here's an introduction to the art of studying. The first ten principles are about the attitude you bring to the task, and the next six are about what you actually do.

1. You learn by reflecting. You begin by having an experience—you read, see, hear, or do something—and then you think about it. No reflecting means no learning. No one can reflect for you, which means no teacher can hand you the understanding or the insight or force you to have it. Learning goes on inside you, and it takes place in the quiet moment after the activity (or, less often, during the activity). You ride your mountain bike over a rocky spot; you fall; you stop and ask, "What went wrong?" You read a book; you stop and ask, "What did that mean? What are the consequences of accepting it as true?"

School rarely gives us time to reflect. It's always rushing on to the next activity. So the most difficult and most necessary part of learning is to *make time for reflection.*

Don't fall for the trap of performing actions that substitute for reflecting and calling them learning. For instance, taking notes in class, making up flash cards, or outlining assigned readings all *look* like learning, but if you aren't reflecting while you do those things, they're just more pointless motion.

2. Learning equals changing. Experiencing and reflecting are merely the first two in a series of five steps to learning: (1) you experience something; (2) you reflect on the experience; (3) you arrive at an insight ("Now I see what I did wrong!"); (4) you resolve to be different ("Next time I'll take water before I go into the desert"); and (5) you implement the change—you do it differently next time. Going through just some of the steps and stopping short of number 5 equals learning nothing. If you want to assess how much you've learned at the end of a lecture, book, or class, ask yourself, "How different am I from when I started?"

3. All learning is self-teaching. The five-step program goes on in your head, where no one but you can get at it. A teacher or textbook can encourage, guide, inspire, or bribe, but that's all in *support* of the teaching; it isn't the teaching itself. And self-teaching can't fail, if you stick with it. Let's assume you act, reflect, and come to an erroneous conclusion. You act on that conclusion and reflect on the outcome. You conclude that your first resolution was misguided. So you conclude that you should try something else. Then all you have to do is continue running the five-step program until by trial and error you've figured things out.

4. Learning in school is relearning. Learning when you're little is easy because you're writing on a blank slate. But by the time a person gets to age sixteen or so, her worldview is complete and any teaching is reprogramming. You "know" what writing an essay is like, and you have to unlearn what you know and replace it with a new model.

Relearning is harder than learning. Breaking an entrenched habit is much harder than picking up a new one. I started taking piano lessons in my early forties, after "teaching" myself and playing for about ten years. At my first lesson, I sat down at my instructor's gorgeous Steinway grand and played what I thought was a pretty decent rendition of the Beatles' "Let It Be." My teacher shook her head. "You're not paying attention to your fingering, are you?" she asked. I wasn't. "I think the best thing for you to do," she continued, "is to start over." She went to a cabinet and pulled out a first-time beginner's book. "I want you to take this home and do the exercises on pages one to five." I was heartbroken, but I also figured it would be easy to relearn, since I thought I could already play pretty well.

Well, it might have been if I hadn't already learned the "wrong" way. But you know what? I stuck with it, and with time it did get easier, and now not only does she compliment me on my fingering, but the songs sound *much* better as well.

5. Relearning is uncomfortable. Change is momentarily destabilizing. You feel like your feet aren't firmly on the ground. And they aren't: change is like stepping off a ledge into the dark. You can't be sure where the new path will take you, and it only makes sense to feel uneasy. Teachers or classrooms or textbooks lessen the discomfort but can't make it disappear. When I was first trying to learn correct piano fingering, I got extremely frustrated. I was afraid that I wouldn't be able to "relearn" and that I'd fail. I even got angry. "Why do I have to do it like this?" I thought. "I already play pretty well." But once I got past the discomfort—and the anger—everything started to fall into place, and the change was remarkable. That's because the discomfort is in proportion to the potential for change. There needs to be some risk, at least some potential for failure. Remember that the more comfortable you are, the less likely you are to learn anything—that matters.

You must learn this lesson well, because if you don't, every time you get close to important learning, you'll feel discomfort, assume something is wrong, and run away.

6. Relearning feels wrong. The old way feels "right" because it's familiar. We are so committed to the familiar that people will let their lives be ruined by alcohol or spousal abuse simply because that's what they're used to. You have to accept that period when the new feels wrong, wait it out, and give the new time to become the familiar.

7. You have to want to be different. Relearning means becoming a different person, and you have to be willing to let the old person die so the new can be born.

The ego defines change in one of two ways. In the first, change is defined as a condemnation of the self: "I need to change because there's something wrong with the old me." The ego's only healthy response to that is to fight off the learning to avoid adopting the toxic message that comes with it. That's why dieting because you're fat and feel disgusting doesn't work. In the second way, change is defined as growth: "I want to change because I see a way to become a more enriched, more complete person." Now the ego can embrace the learning.

8. Learning can't be scheduled. You can't know when insight will come or how to make it come. So don't schedule a time to study—"I'm going to have insights about my composition assignment between 6:00 p.m. and 7:00 p.m. tonight." Instead, *reflect all the time*—muse on the assignment or the course material constantly, with a part of your brain, while you go through your day.

Reflecting all the time sounds like work, but it isn't. Your mind works all the time whether you want it to or not, as we discover when something is worrying us. Any yogi will tell you that it takes years of practice to learn to turn the mind *off*, even for a minute or two. And it's physiologically impossible for your brain to get tired, which is why you can study or write all day, go to bed, and find your mind still racing while your body cries out for rest. With practice, keeping a part of your mind on a task becomes effortless—you just tell your brain to call you when something pops into it (like the chime that says, "You've got mail"), and it does.

9. Learn by joining the club. For every skill or body of knowledge, there is a club of people who practice or study it. Sometimes the club is a physical group of people with a clubhouse and dues—the Garden Club, the Chess Club. Just as often, the club is virtual—the club of writers or the club of fans of Stephen Colbert. In either case, you must join up. You can join literally, by paying dues and attending meetings, or you can sign up mentally, by calling yourself a writer and acting like one.

This act of joining is very powerful. Notice the difference between "I'm taking piano lessons" and "I'm a pianist"—wow! Joining means you stop defining yourself as a "student" and start defining yourself as a "doer." All doers are learners—Tiger Woods is still learning how to play golf.

A member of a club flaunts membership—by wearing the uniform, talking the talk, reading the magazines devoted to the discipline, hanging with other members, talking shop, sharing work with colleagues, going to meetings. Writers' "clubs" tend to be more private and personal, but they still exist. Members pass around favorite essays they've come across and discuss new authors they've discovered. They also share drafts of their own work.

10. Learn by imitating. Learning is done by imitating the mentors, the older and wiser members of the club—every young golfer imagines she is Michelle Wie—and mentors are all around you. Every time you read a CD review in *Rolling Stone*, the op-ed page of the newspaper, or good writing on a website, there's a potential mentor at work—and lots for you to learn.

So much for the learning attitude. Now let's talk nuts and bolts. Let's say you just read a chapter or heard a lecture and are setting out to "learn it." What does that actually mean?

11. Learning means understanding. If I know that $E=mc^2$, I know nothing unless I understand what that means. Let's divide understanding into three rounds. Round One consists of five basic questions about the experience you just had:

a. *What just happened?* (What did I/we do?) Answers sound like "We practiced outlining essays." Don't think this question is somehow beneath you or irrelevant. Frequently, when students are asked what happened in their last class meetings, they can't say. It's important to know—and remember—what your instructor decided to spend class time doing.

b. *What was the purpose?* (Why did I/we do it?) Answers sound like "We did it to understand how essay titles work." In school, "Why?" can be a threatening question because it's so powerful, which is why you need to ask it.

c. *What did it say?* (What was the content?) This question only works with texts (books, lectures, movies). What you're seeking is a *paraphrase*, a brief rewording of the content in your own words. *Don't react yet.* Reacting is a way of skipping over this step.

d. *What was the point?* What did it mean? What was the message? What lesson was I supposed to learn from it? Never do anything that's pointless, and never do anything until you're clear on what the point is. In school, the teacher typically has a point in mind. Know what his intended lesson is, but feel free to draw as many lessons of your own as possible.

Because "point" is scary, people often want to substitute purpose. When I ask my students to explain the point of a previous exercise to me, they typically give me verbs: "The point was *to learn* how to outline." A verb is a purpose; a point must be *a sentence:* "The *point* was, you should outline your essays."

e. *How can I use this?* Learning something is meaningless unless you can do something with it. How can you use the things you learn in school? However tricky a question that may be, you must answer it.

Round One is the groundwork for understanding. Round Two is about bringing order to the material. If you're learning material that has no structural logic, such as the alphabet, you have to pound it into your brain via jingles, mnemonic gimmicks, or massive repetition. But that won't work with college lessons (chapters in a book or class lectures) because just one of them consists of literally thousands of parts: sentences, points, examples, explanations, statistics, formulas. No one is smart enough to make up a jingle for all that. But the thousands of bits have logical structure. Here are four ways to use that fact to your advantage:

12. Reduce the material to something you can see at a glance. In other words, make a *summary.* If you wrote a paraphrase for a basic question, you may already have done this. *The Writer's Way* offers you two concrete ways to do it on paper, the outline and the abstract (Chapter 6).

How small is small enough? Psychologists have an answer: seven items. Seven is the number of items a normal human mind can hold at one time. So shoot for a summary that's seven normal-size sentences or fewer. The Magic Number Seven never changes, so don't make the summary bigger if the original text is bigger. A summary of an essay is as long as the summary of a book.

13. See the pattern. The pattern, also known as the design, structure, organization, governing principle, logic, paradigm, system, map, model, template, outline, or algorithm, is the idea that arranges the pieces, explains why they're all there and arranged just so, and lets us see the whole thing at a glance.

Since most of us can hold only seven things in our brains at once, the only way we can master material larger than seven sentences is to see the structure—the organizing principle that makes a book, for instance, be *one* thing, made out of a certain number of chapters, thousands of paragraphs, and tens of thousands of sentences.

Everything that makes sense has a pattern. If I ask you to remember the following:

123456789

it's easy, because you see the pattern and therefore only have to remember one thing. If I ask you to remember this sequence of numbers:

112358132134

it's brutal slogging beyond seven numbers or so, until you see the pattern: Each number is the sum of the previous two numbers (what mathematicians call a Fibonacci series). Now there's only one thing to remember, and it's easy. And notice how size doesn't affect learning difficulty—if I add numbers to either series, the series doesn't get harder to learn as long as its generating principle remains the same.

Often the pattern is spelled out for you. Books have tables of contents, meetings have agendas, theme parks have maps, car manuals have wiring diagrams, houses have blueprints. When the pattern isn't handed to you, you have to figure it out.

14. Connect the new to the old. When you learn something new, it needs a place to attach itself on the network of knowledge in your head, like a mollusk that settles on the hull of an ocean liner. The more links you can find between new knowledge and old, the more you'll understand and the better you'll remember. If I ask you to remember a random number, that would take some mental work; but if I ask you to remember your age, which is also a number, you can remember it effortlessly.

The links are for you to invent, and you can construct a personal connection to anything. When I talk about learning by imitating your teacher, connect it to your mental map by imagining yourself imitating horrid Mr. Roarer in fifth grade.

15. Consider the implications. To understand something is to be aware of its logical consequences: "If X is true, then Y must be true." All ideas have implications. A lesson will lay down a principle, such as "Read for the bigger issues first"; you make it real by deducing the logical consequences: "If you're having trouble reading a text, read faster, not slower." Understanding isn't about whether you like an idea or think it's true; it's about whether you can live with its consequences. In the 1950s America committed itself to the idea that African Americans should have social and legal rights equal to those of whites. We've spent the last fifty-plus years working out the implications of that decision, and we haven't finished yet. Einstein said "$E=mc^2$," and most of the scientific and technological advances of the last century have resulted from exploring the practical applications of that simple equation. We'll talk about ideas and their consequences in detail in Chapter 14.

16. Test your learning by talking. When the learning process is over, how do you know it worked? That's easy; *say* what you've learned to someone. Tell the material to a classmate, partner, or friend. With knowledge, the proof of ownership isn't being able to write it or think it. Writing is too passive—it's too easy to transcribe without comprehension. And thinking is so insubstantial that we can always tell ourselves we think well. The proof of learning is being able to teach it. This is why generations of teachers have said, "The person who's really learning a lot in the classroom is the teacher."

Part One

INTRODUCTION TO WRITING

Chapter 1

LEARNING TO WRITE

In the rest of this book, we'll talk about what to do at the moment you're writing. But here in the beginning let's think about what you do *in your life* to learn to write well. Here's a lifelong approach to writing, one that makes good writers.

Learn Like a Child

As far as we know, the way a baby teaches itself to talk is an excellent way to learn language skills. Generally, people learn to speak effortlessly, happily, and voluminously in seven years or so, starting from nothing. And everyone gets it right; have you ever met a grownup who didn't know where the adjectives go or hadn't mastered his interrogatives?

Here's what we know about how children learn to talk:

1. It takes a long time—years. *Learning to write also takes a while. There is no trick or device or weekend workshop that will hand good writing to you.*
2. They practice constantly—not fifteen minutes a day, not an hour a day, but all the time, as an ongoing part of living. *In the same way, writing must be a part of your daily life—you can't just write once a week or when an assignment is due.*
3. Children work hard, but the work doesn't hurt, and it doesn't leave them exhausted, resentful, or hostile to talking. *Writing also takes work to learn, but the work shouldn't hurt.*

4. Children need constant exposure to models. They must be surrounded by adult speech, and the more they hear the easier it is to learn. There's no alternative to listening: If children don't hear English, they can't learn to speak English. *Thus you need constant exposure to examples of good writing. The more you've read, the easier it is to learn to write. There's no alternative to reading: if you haven't read essays, you can't write an essay.*

5. Children want speech desperately. You don't have to make them talk, and bribing them doesn't help much. They want to learn for two reasons. First, language is powerful: if you can talk, you can get things you want. When my younger daughter, Gina, was learning to talk, she had a terrible speech impediment, due to chronic ear infections—she was repeating what she was hearing, but it sounded like she was talking underwater. We literally couldn't understand her. Finally, when she was three, a doctor recommended she have tubes inserted in her ears. Voilà! She could hear . . . and talk, clearly. And, naturally, this empowered her: she was now understood when she asked for things—Cheerios, quesadillas, hot dogs, all her favorite foods—and so the chances of her getting them were greatly increased.

    Second, language is a primal joy, like music. Babies babble long before they know sounds can "mean" things, just because it's fun. *So you have to want to write, and the only reasons to write that work are to get something you want and to have fun.*

6. The whole world expects children to learn. Not talking is a sign of a disability or severe psychological trauma. A child is treated as a *talker* from before he utters his first word, not as a *person learning to someday talk. So the world must expect you to write and treat writing as an expected, normal human activity. You must call yourself a writer, not a person trying to learn how to write.* (See joining the club, in the Prologue.)

7. It's easy to try too hard or care in the wrong way. If we tell a child to try hard and to watch his speech carefully, he won't speak better; he'll become tongue-tied. *If you try too hard, you probably won't write better and you may give yourself writer's block. The more you write in fear or write to avoid error, the worse you'll write.*

8. Nobody tells children how to do it; children teach themselves. *You'll teach yourself to write. Teachers can encourage, but they can't explain how to do it.*

9. Children practice all aspects of talking at once, holistically. They never break language into pieces or steps. No child ever

said, "First I'll master nouns, then move on to verbs; first I'll learn declarative sentences, then work on interrogatives." Instead, the child starts out trying to say the whole messages that matter to him the most. *Don't break writing into pieces or "work up to" writing with drills or mechanical exercises. If you want to learn to write essays, write whole essays.*

The Four Basics

To learn any language—Vietnamese or formal essay English—you need four things: exposure to models, motivation, practice, and feedback. But in each case you need the right sort—not just any kind of exposure, motivation, practice, or feedback will do.

Exposure

Exposure, all by itself, will teach you most of what you need to write. Children learn to talk by listening, not by talking. If you went to live in England for a year, you'd come back speaking with a British accent and using British vocabulary without consciously practicing, doing drills, or being corrected. Saturate yourself with eighteenth-century prose for a couple of months and you'll come out thinking in eighteenth-century prose.

We make language the way we see it made. We have no other choice. That's why we should expose ourselves to models that are written the way we want to write. And being exposed to one thing doesn't teach us to do another, so we must expose ourselves to exactly what we want to write. A lifetime of reading cartoons won't teach us how to write formal essays. If you want to write essays, read essays.

Exposure works faster than you'd imagine. It only takes a Western movie or two to catch on to how Western movies "go." If you read Steve Martin essays for twenty minutes every evening for three weeks, afterward you could probably write a pretty good Martinian essay.

Ordinary reading will work, but a special kind of reading works better: *reading for the craft.* If someone loved to watch dance and went to a ballet, how much would she learn about dance by watching? A little. But if a practicing dancer went to the ballet, how much would she learn? A lot. The difference is in the way the two people watch. The first watches like an audience. The second watches like an apprentice. Experiencing art doesn't teach you to make art well by itself. Watching movies doesn't make you a director. But once you decide to study directing, you watch every movie differently and learn from it.

To write, you must read the way the dancer watches dance and the director watches movies: for the craft, not merely to experience the *effect* of the art, but to see how the effect is wrought. The masses see a movie like *Borat* and laugh; the artist sees *Borat* and, while laughing, studies how the director makes us laugh. How do essays end? Most people have seen it done hundreds of times but haven't noticed how. To learn, as you go on with your reading life, notice with a small part of your mind how each writer you read solves the problem of ending. After a while, you still might not be able to say how endings go, but you'll know, and when you write you'll be more likely to do it like that.

You need a second kind of exposure as well: besides exposure to the finished product, you need exposure to the writing process. If you were in a band and wanted to learn how to record a CD, you'd need to do more than just listen to finished CDs. You'd have to go into a recording studio and watch an engineer working with the different tracks, adjusting volume levels, and listening closely to playbacks. Writing is the only complex skill we're asked to master without spending a lot of time seeing someone do it.

This second kind of exposure is hard to get. When was the last time you watched a skilled writer rewrite a draft? For most of us, the answer is "Never." Where can you go to get such exposure? To a writer's colony. There's probably one meeting in your composition classroom.

Motivation

To write well, you have to want to. How obvious. If someone hates tennis and plays only when he's forced to, he probably won't play well. Yet in our world we usually accept hating to write and try to work around it: of course you hate to write—doesn't everyone?—but we'll force you to write with grades or convince you to care by telling you no one will hire you if you can't write. That doesn't work. If you can't find real, personal reasons to write, you won't write well. Period.

Luckily, those reasons aren't hard to find. All humans love writing, the way we love music, dancing, or talking. All children are dying to write, and they scribble long before they can make letters. We even love the supposedly unrewarding parts of writing, like spelling—as you know if you've ever done crossword puzzles or jumbles, or played Hangman, Scrabble, Word Search, Boggle, Perquacky, Spill and Spell, Four Letter Words, or any of the other spelling games that fascinate schoolkids and make game manufacturers rich. We love language as stuff and love to play with it like clay; we love puns, word games, tongue twisters, the latest slang phrase, rhymes, and secret codes like Pig Latin. Even the people who "hate English" in school write secret notes to each other in class the minute the teacher's back is turned and rush off to read the latest X-Men comic book or see a movie or listen to a rap album, all of which are forms of literature and are made out of "English."

Nor do we have to work hard to develop high standards. Children, when they begin writing, have to be taught to *lower* their standards, or they'll fuss over and polish every letter and every punctuation mark and never get beyond the first word or two.

But something gets in the way of all that natural love of language, because most people, by the time they're grown up, say they don't like to write. And when they try to motivate themselves, things get worse. They try harder and hate writing more. People usually write poorly not because they don't care enough, but because they care too much. Most people who "hate to write" care so much that they dare not do it—the chance of failure and pain is too high. Example: You're at a party and find out the person you're talking to is an English major or, even worse, an English teacher. Suddenly you realize that the way you use English "matters." Does that make you speak better, or worse?

We let fear of criticism and failure kill a lot of things we once loved. We all love to dance and sing as children, but when we grow up we learn to raise our standards, critique our dancing and singing sternly, and think about how we sound or look to others. As a result, we decide we "don't like" dancing and singing, and never do it where anyone can watch. But it's not the dancing and singing we don't like; it's the value system we've learned to impose on it.

So what can you do? First, relax. Write the way you used to paint or play with clay. Pablo Picasso said, "Every child is an artist. The problem is how to remain an artist once he grows up." (Of course, you'll have to polish the writing before you submit it to your teacher or an editor.)

Second, use writing to accomplish something you passionately want to do. A former student of mine—a nice guy and a good but not great writer—got in a minor scrape with the law a few years ago and had to write a letter to the judge explaining his actions and what he had learned from the experience—that is, from getting arrested. The letter would determine in part the severity of his punishment. He brought a draft by my office, and you know what? That was the best piece of writing he'd ever done—because it mattered to him. He had purpose, and he had an audience (much more on that later).

Practice

Of course, you have to write to learn how to write, and the more you write the better. But practice is vastly overrated as a teaching device. Children will never learn to speak French, however much they "practice," if they never hear it spoken, and doing something over and over again won't make you remember it if you don't care, as every generation of sentence diagrammers has proved.

Additionally, you need to believe in yourself as you're practicing. If you're practicing free throws and you're standing there at the line saying to yourself, "This one won't go in," guess what? It won't—or at least it's not very likely to. On the other hand, tell yourself that "This one's goin' in! Nothin' but net," and you greatly increase your odds. Same idea if you're standing in skis or on a snowboard at the top of a run. Tell yourself you're going to fall, and you probably will. Tell yourself it's a piece of cake, and you greatly increase the chances of making it to the bottom not only without falling but in pretty darn good form as well. Oh, and don't forget how great you can really sing . . . in the shower or all alone in your car!

Feedback

When you're learning, you try something and see what happens. You hit the tennis ball and watch where it lands. Where it lands tells you if the shot worked or not. That's feedback. Writing has no built-in feedback system. You write the essay and hand it in, and it's like playing tennis in the dark: you hit the ball, it flies off into the blackness, and you learn nothing. You need to know where the ball went. You need readers who will tell you: Were they convinced? Was the explanation clear? Did the opening paragraph capture their interest? Did they like the writer's voice? Were the jokes funny?

Feedback can go horribly wrong and maim the user. If you ask someone who "hates to write" where she learned to hate it, she'll probably say, "My Xth-grade teacher ripped every paper I wrote to shreds, covered every page in red ink, and I've been afraid to write ever since." We know the damage it does, yet against all evidence people remain convinced that mechanical error marking is the single most necessary element in a successful writing program. Many students demand that I mark their writing up, like patients who demand that the dentist's drill hurt so they know they're getting their money's worth.

Here are four reasons that error marking won't teach you much about writing. First, it equates good writing with error-free writing, yet we all know that just because a piece of writing has no "mistakes" doesn't necessarily make it effective. Second, because error marking works best on minor mechanical features (e.g., spelling, noun-pronoun agreement) and worst on big issues (e.g., thesis, structure, intention, tone), it implies that minor mechanical features are the most important aspects of writing. Third, it overloads the writer: the essay comes back a blur of red, and the writer doesn't know where to begin. Fourth, it speaks to the what and not the how: it labels what's wrong but doesn't tell you why or how to prevent it. It's as if a snowboard instructor watched you come down the mountain and said, "You fell, there and there." You know that. You want to know what to do to *avoid* falling.

So what kind of feedback helps? Chapter 9 is all about that, and writers will tell you later in this chapter, but briefly, feedback helps when it is offered as suggestions (instead of orders) given to help accomplish what the writer wants to do (instead of to correct errors or follow rules or do what the teacher wants). Ideally, the writer says to the reader, "I'm trying to do *this*; how could I accomplish that better?" And the reader says, "Maybe if you did a little of *that* it would work better."

The Purpose of a Composition Class

In your pursuit of the Four Basics, a composition class can help:

Exposure

A class can't give you the thousands of hours of reading you need, but it can help by exposing you to a world of great writing you might never encounter otherwise. And it can help you practice the art of reading for the craft, so the reading you do for the rest of your life will be writer's training. More important, it can expose you to models of the writing process. A writing class will surround you with other writers writing, so you can see how they do it.

Motivation

A writing class can help you find real reasons to write, by introducing you to the great writers who inspire you and make you say, "Hey, I wish I could do that!" And it can help by giving you a real audience of classmates who will react enthusiastically and thoughtfully to your work—and by surrounding you with working writers who are excited by language and reading and writing and who will quicken your excitement for these things.

Practice

A writing course may be the one time in your life when you can treat writing the way it should be treated, as an ever-present, integral part of your thinking, reading, and conversing. You'll never have it so good again, believe me.

Feedback

Feedback is the greatest thing a writing course has to offer. A writer's most precious possession is a thoughtful colleague willing to read her writing carefully and offer considered advice. In life, you're lucky to find two; in a writing class, you should be surrounded by them. Think of it: the university goes to all the trouble of rounding up twenty-five people whose job it is for four months to help you write.

How Can I Write Well Right Now?

What if you have an essay due this Friday? We can use the principles of exposure, motivation, and feedback to find a way to write well today.

Since you need exposure, write in a language you already know—your speaking language, or close to it. Most writing situations allow for—and most readers appreciate—a less formal language than you might expect. In fact, you'd be surprised how many student writers get in trouble by trying too hard to "sound like writers" and use big words just for the sake of using big words. Use big words when they're the right words, not to impress your reader.

Since you need motivation, write something you want to write; say something that matters to you; write to people you want to talk to; write something you'd love to read. Naturally, some assignments allow you more freedom in this area than do others, but keep in mind that most instructors also want you to write about something that interests you. Try to take the assignment in a direction that will make the material important to you. And remember, from How to Succeed in School, that your instructor will probably be very happy to talk with you about how to approach the assignment. After all, she'll be reading your paper in the end.

Since you need feedback, find a classmate—a fellow member of the club of writers—and two days before the essay is due spend an hour kicking a rough draft around. Ask your classmate what he thinks in response to what you said. Ask him how the essay could be made to work better. Pay him back by doing the same for his rough draft or take him out for pizza.

Sometimes you only have to do the first of these three. Here's a writer who learned to write well overnight by using the language she spoke. Her first draft began like this:

> The use of phonics as we discussed after reading Weller's book is like starting at the end of learning to read in which no meaning or insight is given to the context of the concept of reading.

In conference, she described, in plain English, what she meant. When she realized that it was okay to write like that, she went home and tried again. Her next essay (on how to teach spelling) began

> Spelling should be taught as a subject separate from reading. Good reading skills do not mean good spelling skills. Spelling is learned by writing.

Beautiful!

Now here's a writer who learned to write well overnight by writing in a form she knew well. Her first essay began like this:

> As a teacher of young children the act of censoring literature is an important task. This prevents bad material from entering the classroom. On the other hand, who has the right to judge what is considered "bad material"? However, our society has a set of basic human values and it is necessary to protect these morals through the act of censorship in regards to textbooks and other various forms of reading material.

That's in trouble. Her second essay was a narrative, and she wrote like this:

> Finally, the moment had arrived. Summer was over and the first day of school was just three days away. Jennifer was so eager and anxious to go to school. She got up bright and early, put on her favorite jeans, her new tee-shirt, and her new blue tennis shoes. Her mom and dad were still asleep, so she made her own lunch and left a note telling them she went to school early because she did not want to be late for her first day. With her lunch pail in one hand, and her Pee-Chee folder in the other, she set out for her little journey to the bus stop alone.

WRITER'S WORKSHOP

What Helps, What Doesn't

Many of the chapters in this book end with Writer's Workshop sections like this one. If you would like a word on how they work and how you might read them, see the Preface.

When I was a sophomore in college, I took a beginning creative writing class from Dr. Clark Brown, a highly regarded author. In addition to having published countless essays and short stories, he had actually published a novel, which I had finished by about the third week of class. I was in awe—taking a writing class from a real novelist!

By midsemester we had submitted several pieces of work, and he had returned mine with mildly encouraging comments. After class one day, I gathered up the courage to take his book, *The Disciple*, up to the lectern at which he was standing and ask him to sign it, which he did, graciously, before handing it back.

As I walked down the hall afterward, I opened the book to the page he had signed, and there it was, scrawled beneath the title but clear as day, "Steve, Be a writer." I was ecstatic. The novelist had recognized the student's talent. It fueled the fire. From then on, I could hardly keep from writing. I wrote, and wrote, and wrote. It was largely why I became a professional writer. For more than twenty years, I kept that book on a prominent shelf in our living room and brought it down from time to time to show friends. "See, Clark Brown told me I should be a writer, way back then."

Except for one minor problem: a couple of years ago, I took the book down and looked again at the inscription, looked hard and closely, from every angle. Oh no! It didn't say "Be a writer" at all. It said, "Best wishes."

I was crushed. Brown hadn't been inscribing the book in response to any talent he had seen in me. It was just a generic inscription. But you know what, because I *thought* it said "Be a writer" and because I *thought* Brown had written it to encourage me to continue writing, I did. And frankly, that little misreading— at an impressionable age—played a huge role in how I saw and defined myself. In fact, had I not had an image in my head of myself as a writer, I'd most likely be pounding nails this very moment instead of sitting at a computer keyboard talking to you about how to become a writer.

Chapter 1 is about the model for "good writing" and the image of ourselves as writers we carry around with us. We construct that model and that image from lessons learned in experiences like mine. Some of the lessons are good, and we should keep them. Sometimes they're poisonous and keep us from writing well, and we have to unlearn them. Every term I ask my students to examine their past for the events that shaped their attitudes toward writing, then turn the responses into conclusions: What works, what doesn't? What experiences make for strong, happy writers and what make for frightened, weak ones? Here are some typical responses:

In elementary school, I was very proud of all forms of my writing, including my speeches, especially with so much support I received. I would spend countless hours on my writing and practice my speeches for my family again and again, taking advice from my mother on being enthusiastic and varying my hand gestures and facial expressions. She would also act as my guide through essay writing as well, helping me improve my papers as a whole and focusing on more than just syntax errors.

However, I will never forget a remark one of my fellow classmates in my tenth grade English class made to me after I made one of my speeches on which I had worked so hard. All he had to say was, "You look so fake up there." This is all it took for me to second-guess everything I did from then on. Ever since then, I have hated speaking in public, and even writing essays, in fear of sounding "fake" to the readers and listeners. My main focus has been on not smiling the entire time and not sounding too sophisticated. I would only let my mom correct grammatical errors in my essays to ensure my writings would sound exactly how I intended them in the first place. Otherwise I felt it would not be what first came to my mind, and therefore not "me." It may sound ridiculous, but anyone could compare my first and final drafts and see that the only corrections I truly made were ones that spell check had searched out and fixed for me.

I have been extremely lazy and dread every time I have to write an essay. But even as recently as a few days ago, during my first week as a sophomore in college, my views on writing changed yet again. I realized that you should not fear the idea of writing an essay; you have to want to do it. That is what makes a good essay, not the grammar, not the length, but truly expressing yourself and not always worrying about impressing everyone. Many times this takes more than one draft. The best way to communicate to someone is not necessarily the first phrasing that you may think of. You have to constantly be thinking about ways to improve, and look forward to writing your thoughts down on paper. So for the first time in a long time, I am going to take on a new perspective for writing, a more optimistic one, for fun. ❖

(Katrina Nelson)

My love for capturing my imagination in ink was encouraged from a very early age beginning, perhaps, in my toddler years. My parents used to keep my room stocked with picture books. My sister and I would spend hours flipping through them, making up the story line. When we were old enough, we wrote our own books. I remember one of my sister's about a zebra called Lacey. (I told her that was a dumb name. She cried.)

My development as a writer can be accredited largely to *The Hawk's Eye*. This annual publication of poetry, short stories, and drawings submitted by my home town's primary and middle school students, accepted and printed my submissions as early as my second grade year. *The Hawk's Eye* was reason for me to write; it gave me an audience and motivation to improve, and most importantly it gave my writing value.

The opportunity and experience of being published (in a loose sense of the term) was great, but it was nothing compared to the experience of *being* a publisher. In sixth grade I was in Pam Guliano's class. Ms. Guliano was queen of all things literature in the middle school and the woman responsible for the birth and life of *The Hawk's Eye*. Sixth grade offered me the chance to be a part of the team that critiqued, chose, and then compiled all the submitted works to be published in the small literary magazine. *The Hawk's Eye* placed value on unstructured creativity throughout my grade school years. Not only was I able to exercise imaginative writing, but I was also exposed to other students' writing, and challenged to think about what was good writing. ❖

(Laura Kate James)

Before my second year of high school, my teachers, peers and parents encouraged me to write. I remember in the sixth grade, my class had a writing assignment in which we were supposed to write a thirty-page story, and most people chose to write with few words, in the format of a children's book. My story was a solid thirty pages of text, not including the illustrations. By freshman year of high school, I had started a few books out of boredom, and had gotten past the one-hundred-page mark in one of them. However, sophomore year stopped me cold when it came to writing.

In the first place, my sophomore teacher was mainly into theater and drama. What he was doing teaching English, I have no idea. As a director of our school plays, he had to pick his favorite actors all the time to play lead roles, and this policy carried over into his English class. I found myself unable to get above a C in his class on written assignments—not because my papers were particularly "average." My friend, one of the aforementioned favorites, had papers that seemed about the same quality as mine and she consistently received As. We believed he took the score from the first essay and just carried it over without reading and seeing how much we had improved, especially since he wrote few comments on our essays besides those concerning spelling. I found myself frustrated with that class and infuriated time and time again with the teacher; worse yet, I found myself growing to believe that I was truly a bad writer. If anything, that class lowered my writing ability, something I am as of yet trying to recover from. That year, I stopped writing my stories, even though I still believe their plots and characters had merit. Those books are still sitting, dead, on my laptop.

My junior and senior year I spent with another English teacher, who was much more helpful in showing me how to organize formal essays and much more encouraging. After those two years, I got back into the habit of jotting down story ideas and maybe expanding on them later; I even wrote a short screenplay as my senior project, something I got full credit on. Although I write more often, I do not have the love of writing that I once possessed. Sadly, after that one bad year, I will spend a lifetime trying to regain that passion. ❖

(Daniele Smith)

Throughout junior high school, my papers always came back to me with a large A up on the top. However, my first high school paper had so many red marks on it that I thought a pen had exploded on my paper. I rewrote that paper three times; I am proud to say that I finally ended up with a B+ for my effort. Since then my papers have had a kind of hit-and-miss effect. I either just do average or I hit a home run. Topics that were inspiring or gave me a cause to fight for always brought about my best work.

I may never have a book that is on the *New York Times* bestseller list, or make millions writing for a famous magazine, but writing is a passion of mine. Truth be told, one could even say that it is all I have ever known. ❖

(Nicole Benbow)

I had always loved writing when I was in school; I considered English to be my best class. During my sophomore year of high school that changed. Whenever I would write an essay it would return to me with the text barely legible. My teacher would mark up my entire essay with a series of "whys," "hows," and "explains." It seemed that however detailed I thought the paper was, it wasn't detailed enough for her.

After receiving a few less than desirable grades on my essays, I came up with a new plan. I decided that I would write the essay early, have her edit it and then I would revise it. I thought that surely with this new plan I would be able to revise the paper to her specifications and receive the grade I believed I had deserved all along, an A. Suffice it say, my plan failed.

My revised essay came back with just as many pencil marks as before, if not more. For the rest of the year I was completely shut off to writing. I didn't know what my teacher wanted and I was so focused on trying to please her that it wasn't fun anymore. I felt that I didn't grow as a writer that year because I was so preoccupied with what my teacher wanted that I didn't really focus on my writing. ❖

(Ashley Yates)

At the age of ten I was turned on to writing by my fourth grade teacher. Early in the year, she assigned us the task of writing a paper using animals. One stipulation was that each student had to incorporate a myth into his/her paper. I chose to write "How Turtles Got Their Shells." I wove my story around a turtle named Shelly. Original, I know. The tale told of how defenseless turtles were constantly plagued with birds that would peck at their backs. Alas, the dutiful Shelly took it upon himself to go in search of protection. As the tale unfolded, our hero accidentally had cement poured onto his back, which the birds couldn't penetrate.

I had an enjoyable time writing my paper, but I was even more thrilled at what happened after I turned it in. The teacher announced to the class that out of all the papers, one was exceptionally good. She then proceeded to read that paper aloud. My anxiety grew when the story commenced and I realized she was reading about a turtle named Shelly. When she was done, she told the class that the author was Tommy Parker, as my face turned a color of crimson that Crayola "ain't got nothin' on."

Ever since that day, thanks to Shelly and a nurturing elementary teacher, I have counted writing as one of the joys in life. ❖

(Tom Parker)

By the time I entered junior high, I had learned that "school writing" was far different than the creative story writing I enjoyed doing with my spare time. Bland essay assignments on wars and presidents eventually led me to dread the sight of pen and paper. When I stepped into my eighth grade English class, my entire view changed. With her personal passion and enthusiasm, my teacher restored a love for writing within me that had dimmed over time. I learned in that small classroom that with imagination and interest, a writer can make any type of work exciting.

There is no strict pathway I followed to become the writer I am today. Many essays, journals, experiences, and teachers played a part in shaping me, no matter how subtly. In all honesty, a writer cannot be a writer unless they enjoy their work, and the drive and inspiration that dwells within me truly created my writing skills. ❖

(Katie Brown)

Obviously, many people are feeling a lot of pain about their writing. And the people in these histories are the system's *successes*, those who thrived and went to college, most of them intending to become teachers! But there's comfort to be taken here, too. All of us writers are having the same experiences, reacting the same way, thriving on the same things, and being curdled by the same things. We're all in this together, and we agree on what helps and what doesn't. For instance, being read to a lot by your parents helps; being forced to push your personal message into cookie-cutter patterns like five-paragraph essay paradigms doesn't. Critical feedback in the form of conversation with a mentor making suggestions about alternatives helps; critical feedback in the form of red-pen corrections doesn't. All we have to do is do the things that help and avoid the things that don't.

So what should you do to become a healthy writer? First, tell your own story. Get clear on what assumptions about writing you now own and where you got them. Second, using the histories in this section and your own experience, make a list of things that work and things that hurt. Third, reject the poisonous messages you've been fed. Finally, create for yourself a writing environment that nourishes you as a writer.

Now it's your turn. In this chapter you've been listening to a conversation about how people learn to write. It's time to join the conversation.

Step 1: Make your own contribution to the collection of tales in Writer's Workshop. Write a two-page narrative detailing everything you've done or had done to you that has helped form your writing or your view of yourself as a writer. Remember to go back to the beginning—most people's attitudes toward reading and writing are formed long before they get to school. And think about what isn't in your life as well as what is— sometimes what's lacking is profoundly educational, like never seeing your parents reading for pleasure.

Step 2: Make a list of experiences that promote writing and a list of experiences that obstruct it. For instance, you might have "Mom puts sample of my writing on the fridge" in the plus list.

Step 3: As a class, pool your anecdotes and your lists, until you have answered this question: What would a person do if she were setting out to create for herself the writer's perfect upbringing and environment?

EXERCISES

1. Write a two-page essay exploring how well your writing career up to now has provided you with each of the Four Basics. List changes you could make to improve the amount and type of each you're getting now.

2. For each of the nine principles in Learn Like a Child, write a paragraph discussing how well your writing program up to this point in your life has followed that principle. List changes you could make to follow it better.

3. Write an essay discussing the kinds of feedback your writing has received throughout your life. Begin with your earliest memories of writing, and continue through recent school experiences. Rate each kind of feedback for effectiveness: Did it help, or did it hurt? How much healthy feedback have you received in school?

Chapter 2

WHAT MAKES WRITING EFFECTIVE?

In Chapter 1 we talked about how the bulk of your writing skills are acquired. Now let's talk about what the goal of writing is. When you set out to "write well," what exactly are you trying to accomplish? You can't write well until you know the answer, just as you can't play baseball well until you know that the objective is to run around the bases and reach home plate. The bad news is, many students are trying to "write well" by trying to accomplish the wrong things. The good news is, what makes writing good is something simple, something you already have.

Let's look at a piece of the real stuff and see what it's got. Here's a professional essay. What does it have that bad essays don't have?

NOTHIN' BUT A TWEEN THANG
NEVA CHONIN

I live in a blessed bubble. My local cafes have free wireless, two green grocers grace the neighborhood, my landlords babysit my pet mouse and I have never seen a Club Libby Lu.

If you, like me, knew nothing of Club Libby Lu until recently, lemme tell ya, they're all the rage. Club Libby Lu is a chain of more than 80 stores targeting girls ages 5 to 12, known by marketers as the "tween" demographic. This is the age where girls grow tired of toddling but haven't yet decided to hate their parents.

According to www.clublibbylu.com, their stores aren't just retail outlets, but "something special!" They offer "a fun, funky place to hang out," where girls can "dress up like a princess, rock star or drama queen" in a "famous Style Studio." They can get a manicure. They can "sing and dance to the latest club beat" with Libby's "inspiring Club Counselors." At Libby Lu, "every girl is treated like a VIP—Very Important Princess! It's totally a girl thing!"

Totally! Libby Lu is one reason I'll never have children. The thought of sharing my home with a preening little monster in drama-queen drag is enough to make me . . . oh, do something that would qualify me as an unfit mother. Like engaging said child in endless games of "Make the Princess Cry" and "Destroy the Drama Queen's Self-Esteem—Forever." Besides encouraging kids to be egotistical brats, Libby Lu and other kiddie stores like Monkey Dooz reinforce annoying stereotypes—as opposed to legitimate sexual differences—and transform children into tiny grotesques destined for an adulthood as gender-polarized as their parents'. Do all little girls long to be pretty in pink? Really? Because by age 6, I was eating dirt and wanting to be a Japanese robot. I pulled my Barbie dolls apart limb by limb and reassembled them into hybrid monsters. I did the usual sick stuff all kids, regardless of sex, love to do as they explore their world's boundaries.

There are no Japanese robots at Club Libby Lu. Instead, tweenies are treated to makeovers—hair extensions, makeup, the whole shebang—and then, according to a March *Washington Post* article, led in a dance by club counselors who urge them to "shimmy down" and "shake it" while a soundtrack instructs, "Wet your lips/And smile to the camera."

That done, the tots visit the Pooch Parlor to select a miniature stuffed dog, complete with couture carrier and a doggie T-shirt sloganed with something like "The Royal Heiress."

I'm sorry, did my projectile vomit just splash your coffee mug? Such is the risk of reading me in the morning. Because, I mean, dude. Just . . . dude. I'll say it plainly: LIBBY LU IS BREEDING MONSTERS. GOD HELP US. GRAB THE KIDS. TAKE THE DOG AND HEAD FOR THE BOMB SHELTER. GO NOW. Does the world need more vapid idiots? Does it? Look at the White House. Look at Britney Spears and K-Fed. And it gets worse. Worse! From the *Post*, a description of Libby Lu's interior:

"The store is pink. There are pink ruffles around the light fixtures. The walls and stools are blue and pink. The staff wears pink. There are pink cowboy hats for sale, pink Ugg-like boots, pink phones decorated with pink feathers. There are rings with huge diamonds, like J.Lo might wear (only fake), with pink packaging that reads 'Bling! Bling!' "

Bling. Bling. Pass me an airsickness bag, cover your cup and tell me what you think of this: Libby Lu stores are all the rage for birthday parties. So what if a little girl's circle of friends includes little boys? Are little boys allowed to explore their inner drama queens, too? The question is rhetorical. Of course they're not. Libby Lu likes to keep the sexes segregated, Taliban-style. Libby Lu isn't regressive, it's revolutionary, proposing a level of male-female isolation that this country hasn't seen since Puritanism waned four centuries ago. Sayonara, childhood friendship between the sexes. Hello, tween-boy frat parties with ginger-ale kegs. This is what really irks me, but what bothers many anti-Libby parents the most is something hinted at in yet another *Post* outtake (hey, I enjoy my newspapers). "Sometimes people walking through the mall gather by the windows at Club Libby Lu to watch the spectacle of little girls," the article observes. "All that pink and glitter. All that flesh, too."

Mmmm. All that girl flesh. Tastes like chicken. Now, while my thoughts turn to cannibalism, others have less savory minds. For many moms, the thought of adults watching kids parade in skimpy outfits raises the specter of—what else?—pedophilia. Yow! Perverts in the mall!

To that, I say, hush. I do think it's wretched for Libby Lu to train tots for lives as gold-digging sex-bots, but I don't think it necessarily inspires men in trench coats to abscond with the foul little princesses. Some mothers disagree. They disagree to the point where they're ready to picket, say, Kenneth Cole for dressing kids in any kind of adult attire, even suits and ties.

Where does this leave us?

On one side, the pink vacuum of Libby Lu; on the other, the repressive hysteria of neo-Puritans. Stuck in between on an ever-shrinking field of sanity, the rest of us.

I've said it before, so I might as well say it again: Procreation is vastly overrated. ❖

(San Francisco Chronicle, Datebooks, July 23, 2006)

What Good Writing Isn't

Let's list the things that a good essay *doesn't* need:

A large vocabulary. We know all or almost all of Chonin's words.
Complex sentences.

A brand new idea. Chonin isn't saying anything that hasn't been said before. (She even admits that in her last paragraph.)

An argument that's absolutely and exclusively true. The essay has a nice thesis, but the opposite—that Club Libby Lu is completely harmless and raising children is full of joyful surprises—is just as true.

The last word on its topic. The essay doesn't end discussion of children in our society; it just adds a little something to it.

Profound thinking. The ideas in the essay aren't subtle or brainy.

Extensive research or expertise. Chonin's only "research" she got from the newspaper.

Extraordinary experience. Lots of people have had experiences like Chonin's; it's not at all extraordinary or unusual.

Since Chonin's essay doesn't have these things, they can't be what makes good writing good, and you don't need to have them either.

There are things Chonin's essay does have that make it *better* but that won't make the essay good by themselves: transition between ideas, overall organization, thesis, examples, conclusion, unambiguous language. They're not the heart of writing, the way reaching home is the heart of baseball—they won't make your writing good unless you have the "other thing" too.

There are also things the essay *must* have but for which it gets no credit at all: spelling, punctuation, sound usage, and the other mechanical aspects of writing. You'd never say to a friend, "Oh, I read the most wonderful article in the paper yesterday. Such comma placement! And every word spelled just right!" These things don't make your writing "good"—only legal.

What Good Writing Is: The Sense of Audience

The key that separates good writing from bad is a sense of *audience*. Writers who write for the wrong reasons think of writing as a mechanical act with certain "good" surface features, and when they write, they try to make an essay that includes them: correct spelling, an outlineable structure, a thesis statement, a large vocabulary, complete documentation of sources, and so on. That approach produces essays like Dr. Frankenstein's early experiments: however meticulously you sew the bits and pieces together, it's never going to get up off the operating table and walk. The alternative, the only approach to writing that works, is to set out to do *something to the reader*.

You can do anything to your reader you want—move him to tears, bug him, convince him to vote for your candidate, convince him you're right, teach him how to make jambalaya, make him feel what growing up with your big brother was like. And you know you've succeeded when you get what you set out to get: he cries, he feels bugged, he votes your way, he thinks you're right, he learns how to make jambalaya, or he knows what growing up with your big brother was like.

You already know all this. And (here is the really wonderful thing) you already know how to do it, too. All children begin their writing careers by writing the messages they think will pack the biggest wallop for their readers: "I love you." "I am Ericka." "Come to my party." But somewhere along the line we forget we know it. A friend of mine once asked his students to write dialogues. He suggested to one student that if she had the speakers say less than the whole truth the scene might get more dramatically interesting, because the reader would then have to look behind the words. The writer replied, "But you didn't say we had to make the dialogues interesting." All we have to do is remind ourselves of the secret that writer forgot.

Once you get the secret of good writing firmly in your mind, you think in a different way about writers' decisions. Instead of saying, "What's the rule?" when a question arises, you say, "What works? What does my reader want? What will be most effective here?" For instance, let's say you're writing your way through an essay and you approach the conclusion. You have a decision to make: should you summarize the essay in the final paragraph? With the old attitude, you recall someone telling you that in an essay you should "tell them what you're going to tell them, tell them, then tell them what you told them." So you summarize. With the new attitude, you ask yourself, "Does my reader want or need a summary? Will a summary conclusion be effective?" For most essays the answer to both questions is no. Readers can remember what they've read and usually don't need to be told again. In other words, summary conclusions usually *don't work*.

Having a Reader in Your Head

All writers have colleagues read their work and tell them how it reads. But no reader has the time to tell you how every line you write works, and you need to know, so you need an imaginary reader in your head. As you write every line, you imagine a first-time reader reading it and guess how she responds. The more you hear the reader's responses, the better you can decide how to react to and control them, and the better you'll write.

When you think about hearing the writer's responses in your head, think literally. If you're writing a recipe for novice cooks and you write, "Then add a tablespoon of oregano," you should hear your reader responding, "What's oregano? Where can I get some? What if

I used *two* tablespoons?" If you write, "All U.S. presidents in this century have been owned by the oil companies," you should hear the reader responding, "How do you know? Can you prove it? That sounds awfully wild to me. Are you putting me on?" and so on. If you write, "Cleaning up our environment is a humongous task," you had better realize that some readers will respond, "This person talks like a kid," or "This guy doesn't speak my language."

You can never be sure how your reader is responding, because people are unpredictable and different readers have different values and knowledge. If you write, "Gun control violates the right to bear arms guaranteed by the Constitution," you'll evoke a firestorm of reactions:

> Right on!
> Just another gun nut.
> Not that old cliché!
> What does the Constitution say?
> Is that what the Constitution really means?
> So we can't control guns at all?
> Can't we change the Constitution?
> What's "the Constitution"? That old sailing ship?

You can't speak to all these voices, but you don't have to—as long as you're imagining your reader responding *in any way at all*, you're being a writer.

Nor does this mean you have to do what the reader wants. You may want to frustrate him, make him mad, trick him—but you have to know he's feeling frustrated, angered, or tricked, and you must be doing it to him for a reason. And the reader doesn't need to be *pleased* all the time; he just needs to be able to look back, when the reading is over, at what was done to him and see the reason for it—he says, "I see now why the writer refused to tell me what was going on until the end—he had his reasons."

So the good writer doesn't write and then ask herself what she wants to say next; she writes, asks herself what her reader says in response, then asks herself what she wants to say in response to that. The text becomes a dialogue.

We depend on the dialogue more than we know, and writing is harder than speaking, largely because the other participant has to be made up. When we talk, we know the listener is involved even when she's silent, because the body language tells us so. But to get in touch with how crucial the listener's response is to us, try talking to someone who seems to be asleep, or try talking to someone who is utterly quiet on the telephone. We become tongue-tied and have to prod the listener for assurance: "Are you still there? You listening to me?" When we write, we need the same assurance, but we have to construct a listener who gives it to us.

This does *not* mean that writing is good if it causes a reaction in the reader. Any and all writing causes readers to react—lousy writing often causes readers to react with confusion, frustration, boredom, and anger, for instance. The true principle is, Writing is good if it causes the reaction *the author set out to cause* in the reader, and then *works with* that reaction—hears it, reacts to it, addresses it, honors it.

Giving the Readers What They Need

Good writers give readers everything they need to read them well. Good readers are busy doing lots of jobs; it's your job to assist them. For example,

> *They're summarizing,* so you must give them an essay that's summarizable.
> *They're trying to put what they're reading to personal use—* "What good is this to me?"—so you must give them something they can use.
> *They're trying to understand how you got to your conclusion,* so you must include the evidence and reasoning that took you there.
> *They're trying to understand,* so you have to explain.
> *They're trying to connect with you,* so you have to be human on the page.
> *They're trying to connect to something else,* so you have to show how your topic fits into a bigger picture.

The clearer you are on what a reader's jobs are, the more you can help him do them and the better you'll write.

Seeing Writing as Performance

Good writing knows it's a performance. Good writers are hams on the page. They feel the presence of the audience the way a stage actor does. The only difference is that the writer's audience must be imagined. People who read aloud well are usually good writers, and a simple way to write well is to *write something you'd love to read out loud.*

It Really Works: Two Proofs

If good writing is all about having a reader firmly in mind, we should be able to take writers who are trying to "make essays" and tell them to write to real people instead, and their writing should get better instantly. And it works. Here's a passage from an essay on hypnotism, written by someone with no sense of humans reading him:

> For some types of material, learning while in an actual state of hypnosis is best, while for other types of material, it is better to study in a waking state with post-hypnotic suggestions providing the improvement. Rote memorization is best done in a hypnotic state, but material of a technical nature which requires integration into one's present knowledge of the subject area should be done in the waking state. The reason that technical material can't be effectively learned while under hypnosis is because the subconscious mind lacks the ability for critical and inductive reasoning. Only the conscious mind has this ability. However, post-hypnotic suggestions can help to improve the learning of technical material.

The writer was asked to rewrite it as if he were talking to real people, and he produced this lovely stuff:

> If you're trying to learn a foreign language, memorize a definition or a speech, or anything that requires rote memorization, then it is best to do it in an actual hypnotic state. However, technical material is another matter. You can memorize the material easily enough, but all you can do with it is repeat it, just like a parrot. With post-hypnotic suggestions, you can improve your ability to concentrate, retain, and recall the technical material.

We should also be able to find good writing that "breaks the rules" when breaking the rules does what the writer wants to do to the reader. Here are two examples. The first is a paragraph from *The Right Stuff* by Tom Wolfe, describing how navy pilots feel the first time they have to land on an aircraft carrier:

> This was a *skillet!*—a frying pan!—a short-order grill!—not gray but black, smeared with skid marks from one end to the other and glistening with pools of hydraulic fluid and the occasional jet-fuel slick, all of it still hot, sticky, greasy, runny, virulent from God knows what traumas—still ablaze!—consumed in detonations, explosions, flames, combustion, roars, shrieks, whines, blasts, horrible shudders, fracturing impacts, as little men in screaming red and yellow and purple and green shirts with black Mickey Mouse helmets over their ears skittered about on the surface as if for their very lives (You've said it now!), hooking fighter planes onto the catapault shuttles so that they can explode their afterburners and be slung off the deck in a red-mad fury with a *kaboom!* that pounds through the entire deck—a procedure that seems absolutely controlled, orderly, sublime, however, compared to what he is

about to watch as aircraft return to the ship for what is known in the engineering stoicisms of the military as "recovery and arrest." . . . As the aircraft came closer and the carrier heaved on into the waves and the plane's speed did not diminish and the deck did not grow steady—indeed, it pitched up and down five or ten feet per greasy heave—one experienced a neural alarm that no lecture could have prepared him for: this is not an *airplane* coming toward me, it is a brick with some poor sonofabitch riding it (*someone much like myself!*), and it is not *gliding*, it is *falling*, a thirty-thousand-pound brick, headed not for a stripe on the deck but for *me*—and with a horrible *smash!* it hits the skillet, and with a blur of momentum as big as a freight train's it hurtles toward the far end of the deck—another blinding storm!—another roar as the pilot pushes the throttle up to full military power and another smear of rubber screams out over the skillet—and this is nominal!—quite okay!—for a wire stretched across the deck has grabbed the hook on the end of the plane as it hit the deck tail down, and the smash was the rest of the fifteen-ton brute slamming onto the deck, as it tripped up, so that it is now straining against the wire at full throttle, in case it hadn't held and the plane had "boltered" off the end of the deck and had to struggle up into the air again. ❖

(Tom Wolfe, The Right Stuff, pp. 20–22)

Here are some of the conventional essay-making rules Wolfe breaks:

Avoid run-on sentences.
Avoid long paragraphs.
Have a thesis statement.
Avoid redundancy.
Avoid exclamation points.
Avoid parentheses.

Now here's a rule-breaking essay by Jon Carroll:

I hold no brief for bullfighting. I know people who have been to bullfights, and they have been impressed by the vigor of the culture and the operatic nature of the spectacle, but to me, it's just cow killing. It could be argued that it's a mindful kind of cow killing and that maybe if we understood that cows were actual animals that experience pain rather than steaks wrapped in plastic, we might at least consider the life that is being sacrificed for our nourishment and our pleasure.

But I don't really think bullfighting is about that. I think it's about guys proving their guyhood. A lot of the cruel practices in the world boil down to guys proving their guyhood. There are plenty of opportunities for guys to demonstrate their manliness in real-world situations—lifting streetcars off trapped pedestrians, beating up bullies who threaten the elderly, plus the whole 60-minute man thing, not referring to the news-based television program—without creating an artificial guy-affirming infrastructure.

Besides, there's football, or, as the Europeans call it, football.

Nevertheless, I was saddened to learn about the fate of the Hotel Reina Victoria in Madrid. For a very long time, the hotel was the place where matadors dressed for their fights. Manolete dressed there, as did El Cordobes. After the bullfight, all the participants, from matadors to picadors, drank in the lobby bar, along with the men who owned the ranches where the bulls were trained. It was one of those places, like the Chelsea Hotel in New York or the Chateau Marmont in Hollywood. Things happened there.

Lately, things haven't been happening there as much. The neighborhood has changed. Bullfighting is not as popular as it used to be—although, according to the *New York Times*, Spaniards spend an estimated $1 billion a year to watch an estimated 17,000 bullfights.

The Hotel Reina Victoria has closed down for the offseason. When it reopens, it will be the Madrid branch of the Hard Rock Hotel, which promises an atmosphere of "pure, unadulterated rock and roll." And that's pretty much everything I hate about cultural imperialism right there.

A rock 'n' roll hotel? Hotel rooms are to rockers what feudal villages were to the Visigoths. For a chain hotel to be "pure rock and roll," it would have to replace the windows and furniture every morning. It would have to encourage licentious behavior, perhaps with a starter kit of recreational drugs. And musicians would stay free, always. Rock 'n' roll is (or, I can face it now, was) a freeing of the id, a way of making the animal instincts inside all of us into art—and a way of uniting, at least musically, African American culture and European American culture. It was the robust child of integration.

But now it's a franchise. It's a lifestyle. It's a hyphenate—country-rock, folk-rock, eclecto-trance-house-hip-hop-mental rock. It's a niche market, except it owns all the niches. It's a hotel where tourists stay. It's a guitar inside a Plexiglas case.

As anyone who travels knows, the steady backbeat of American rock 'n' roll is the music of the world. It exists in every language, blasts out of every taxicab, invades every dance spot. It sells whiskey and diapers and political candidates. I have no idea which of the 1,900 kinds of international rock 'n' roll are "good"; I don't think "good" is the point anymore. It's musical monoculture; it's high-fructose corn syrup for the ears.

I love rock 'n' roll; I grew up on rock 'n' roll. When I hear the phrase "let's rock and roll" used today, it usually means "Let's go rob a bank" or "Let's gather the ingredients together for a barbecue" or "Let's start the entertainment for the Pepsi/ Delco Battery 2006 Charged Up Tour." And it could be a bicycle tour or a musical tour; doesn't matter. There's a big stage with lots of logos, and people carrying musical instruments playing . . . who knows? Maybe they're lip-syncing. Too much distortion anyway. Have a tequila beverage.

So on this side, you've got short, thin guys in dancing slippers and black stockings and matador suits of red and blue and orange with roses worked into the stitchery going out to kill bulls, and on the other side you've got big hairy guys in T-shirts and jeans going out to kill the audience. "We killed," they'll say later, and they will be so, so right.

Yes, I'd like the Keith Moon Suite—that comes with the breakaway furniture, yes? And the swimming pool is directly beneath the window? And we'll need about five room carts with wobbly wheels. Can we order the groupies later? ❖

(*Jon Carroll, San Francisco Chronicle, April 17, 2006*)

Here are some of the essay-making rules Carroll breaks:

Avoid redundancy.
Add short sentences together to avoid choppiness.
Reveal topic, thesis, and purpose in the opener.
Don't start sentences with "And."

Wolfe and Carroll break the rules because breaking the rules "works." Wolfe wants to overload the reader and make her slightly hysterical, to re-create the pilot's sensation of nightmare bewilderment. Carroll breaks rules to create a tone and style that shows just how flabbergasted he is. Besides, he's writing about rock 'n' roll, which itself is about breaking rules.

The rest of this book will offer you scads of rules for good writing. They're good rules, and your writing will usually get better if you follow them. But trying to write well by following the rules is the long, hard road, and I'll keep encouraging you to take the shortcut: ask, "What works?" And there is no answer to that question until you know what you're trying to *do* with your writing.

WRITER'S WORKSHOP

The Reader's Dialogue

Readers typically keep their reactions to themselves as they read, but if we ask them to speak those reactions out loud, they will. In a recent class, students were asked to read one sentence of an essay at a time and then to say out loud everything they were thinking after each sentence. Here's the passage, beginning with the title, with some of their reactions in italics.

Writing Outside Oneself

What does "writing outside oneself" mean?
Must be some kind of teacher's manual.
Is there "inside" and "outside" writing?

In order to make beginning writing students feel comfortable about their writing, we encourage essays that are very egocentric.

This isn't for me—I'm not going to be a teacher.
What does "egocentric" mean?
I'm not sure what an egocentric essay is—got any examples?
Isn't "egocentric" a bad thing to be? It has very negative
*   connotations for me.*

We ask them to write about their own lives, to describe a favorite place or best friend, to write about a favorite holiday, or to tell a story about something that happened to them.

I know what he means by "egocentric" now.
That's "inside writing" I suppose—so "outside writing"
*   must be nonpersonal, objective writing?*
Is he in favor of doing this or against it?
Why do "we" do this?

These essays allow the students to loosen up.

He's telling us why now.
He thinks it's a good thing.
How does egocentric writing make people "loose"?
I thought the problem with most writing was it was TOO
*   loose.*

They write more freely and with greater confidence when they discover that it's OK to write about themselves.

> *He's giving us more reasons for doing it.*
> *I've been writing personal essays since kindergarten—I'm sick of it.*
> *Why is he telling us this? What does he want?*

When one of their fellow students laughs at their funny story about getting caught toilet-papering a friend's house, they know that they can write this way and have an effect on someone.

> *More examples of how personal writing does good things.*
> *I bet he's going to say there's a problem with doing it that way.*
> *He's going to say "but" sooner or later.*

Helping writers understand this, however, can be both a blessing and a curse.

> *There's the "but."*
> *I knew it—he's going to say there's something wrong with doing that.*
> *He's told us about the blessing; what's the curse?*
> *He's either going to tell us not to do personal writing or he's going to suggest a way to keep the virtues of personal writing and avoid the "curse."*

As you can see, readers in a crowd are busy folk, generating a messy blizzard of responses. From that blizzard, Bob, the writer, has to choose which responses to address. He can't address them all, and he wouldn't want to. He decides to talk only to writing teachers who are interested in teaching personal writing; to everyone else in the world he says, "Goodbye." And he can't please all tastes: Some readers will be scared off by words like *egocentric*; some will be repulsed by the mention of toilet paper. And he can't respond to all legitimate demands at once. While some readers are saying, "What does that mean?" others are saying, "Like what, for example?" and others are asking, "Why?" Bob can only answer one at a time and put the other questioners on hold. So Bob defines his chosen audience and imagines a likely scenario, a set of responses the bulk of his chosen audience is likely to share, whatever additional personal axes they may be grinding. Here's the text again, with the single audience response Bob chose to imagine after each sentence.

A Lesson Plan

What does "writing outside oneself" mean?

In order to make beginning writing students feel comfortable about their writing, we encourage essays that are very egocentric.

What's an "egocentric" essay?

We ask them to write about their own lives, to describe a favorite place or best friend, to write about a favorite holiday, or to tell a story about something that happened to them.

Why do teachers do this?

These essays allow the students to loosen up.

Why is that?

They write more freely and with greater confidence when they discover that it's OK to write about themselves.

Got any examples?

When one of their fellow students laughs at their funny story about getting caught toilet-papering a friend's house, they know that they can write this way and have an effect on someone.

So what's the problem?

Helping writers understand this, however, can be both a blessing and a curse.

What's the curse?

Bob has in fact composed a *dialogue* between himself and the reader. He's composed both parts, but he's printed out only one—his own lines—and expects the reader to know her part and speak hers.

Bob's dialogue helps us solve one of the great mysteries of writing: *What makes one thing follow another?* Why do we read one sequence of sentences and say, "That flows" or "That has transition," and we read another and say, "That's choppy"? The flowing text shows awareness of the invisible dialogue; the choppy text doesn't. See Chapter 6 for more on that.

Now it's your turn. Here are the opening lines of an essay. Cover them with a piece of paper and pull the paper down slowly to reveal one line at a time. (If you read the whole text at once, this game doesn't work.) After exposing each line, write down one or two responses you have to the line—questions you want to ask, feelings you want to express, desires you want met. When you've gone through the text, look it over and write a half-page about how successfully the author predicted and dealt with your responses—was he hearing you?

Superman has taken the morning off. Although appearing among us in mufti, he is immediately identifiable by his square jaw and the comma of dark hair upon his forehead. He greets with an affable hello the other Hollywood Boulevard regulars who have gathered, along with a small crowd of tourists, outside the classical facade of the former Masonic Temple, now the TV studio where Jimmy Kimmel does his evening talk show. The USC Trojan Marching Band, or at least a skeleton crew thereof, goes through its paces, a casually synchronized, loose-limbed routine in which its members instrumentally exhort us to do a little dance, make a little love, and above all, get down tonight. Superman bops his head, enjoying his moments of freedom. In a while he will have to put on his blue tights and red Speedo and go to work, posing for pictures with the tourists in front of Grauman's Chinese Theatre. Maybe he'll stop on the way at the Coffee Bean & Tea Leaf, at the corner of Hollywood and Orange. Batman and the Cat in the Hat go there sometimes. ❖

(David Rakoff, "Streets of Sorrow,"
Conde Nast Traveller, November 2006)

EXERCISES

1. Do The Reader's Dialogue with the title and first six or seven sentences of a piece of your own. Don't forget the half-page discussion at the end.

2. Do Exercise 1 using a classmate as audience. Reveal your essay opening one sentence at a time and have him write his reactions down after each. Then look at the dialogue and write a half-page essay that assesses how successfully you predicted his responses.

3. Take one of the following essay first sentences and discuss what kinds of reactions the author should expect and why he might want those reactions and use them to his advantage.

   a. Once upon a time, a little boy loved a stuffed animal whose name was Old Rabbit.

   (Tom Junod, writing about Mr. Rogers,
   Esquire, November 1998)

b. A thought-provoking dispute has emerged in the homosexual-rights community in the wake of the controversial "Jenny Jones Show" verdict.

(Clarence Page)

c. I recently read the opinion column in the campus newspaper.

d. This country has a rich tradition of producing fads that make a great portion of the populace look ridiculous.

(San Francisco Chronicle, August 16, 2006, p. E1)

4. Write a thesis statement for one of your essays. Write three different likely responses readers might have to it.

5. Write three different likely responses readers might have to the opening sentence of one of your essays.

6. Write an essay you'd love to read out loud to the class. Then read it out loud to them with as much drama and "performance" as you can manage.

7. Find an essay, in a newspaper or magazine, that "breaks the rules" in a way you like. Write a short (a page or so) essay discussing what rules are being broken and why, and explain why the rule breaking works. Bring it to class, and share it with your classmates. Find out what they think about the rule breaking and what they think of the essay. Did they respond like you did?

Part Two

PLANNING AND DRAFTING

Chapter 3

FINDING SOMETHING TO WRITE ABOUT

The next eight chapters imagine that you'll be going through a series of steps called the writing process: prewriting, drafting, organizing, polishing, editing, and submitting. The step-by-step approach can be helpful because it reminds you that you don't have to do everything at once. But there's a danger to steps: They suggest that the writing process is a lot neater and more regimented than it really is.

Most writers don't do one step, then the other; instead, they do them all, all the time. The mind's a messy place, and it's happiest when multitasking: It will leap from note taking to paragraph writing to outlining to rewriting. While you're writing page 7, it will be rewriting page 5 and thinking up great lines for page 10 or another essay. You must let your brain go about its messy business. *Take what comes, whenever it comes.* When I write, I constantly insert into parentheses stuff that I don't have time to think about right then. It might be a note to find a better word, later; it might be a reminder to keep that part of the essay in mind when I write the conclusion. It might be a note to myself to remember to return someone's phone call, or to prune the hedge out back. Naturally, all that parenthetical stuff comes out later.

Where Do Good Essays Come From?

Some people have no trouble finding things to write about. For others, it's the hardest part of writing. Sometimes, we don't have as much choice as we'd like to because of the assignment and the parameters we're forced to work within. I'll talk a lot more about this latter problem in Chapter 16.

In a sense, we know we all have lots to say because we all talk effortlessly and endlessly with our friends. So "having nothing to write about" can only mean *that we define writing in some unhealthy way* that gives us writer's block. And we'll solve the problem by *redefining writing to be more like talking to our friends.*

Let's explore that. First, we know that writing isn't about having a rare moment of inspiration or a unique experience, because we know we don't talk to our friends only when we've had a stroke of genius or have just gotten back from Nepal. We talk all the time, about everything. And writers write about everything. Writing essays is like being funny. A comic isn't a person who happens to have funny things happen to him; he's a person who sees humor in whatever happens. Similarly, an essayist lives a life like yours; he just sees the potential essay in what he experiences. Here's the essayist John Gregory Dunne explaining how it works:

> My house was burgled twice and the two resulting pieces netted me a lot more than the burglars got. I can recall one columnist who eked three columns out of his house burning down: one on the fire, a second on the unsung dignity of fire fighting, and a third on his insurance adjuster and a long view on the charred artifacts of a lifetime. So avid for material is your average columnist that once, when my daughter caught my wife and me *flagrante delicto*, I seriously wondered if there was a column in it. (As it turned out, only a column mention.)

Once you catch on to the trick, you'll have more essay topics than time to explore them.

Second, the difference between talking to friends and writing is not one of *content* but of *audience*. It's not that you have nothing to say; it's that you have nothing to say that *you think your imaginary essay audience wants to hear.* You're trying to write to instructors, bosses, or other authority figures, and you're telling yourself they only want to read something that's never been said before and is brilliant. But most writers don't write to those audiences. Granted, sometimes circumstances force you to write only to your instructor, and you will probably someday find yourself writing a memo to an employer. On the other hand, most writing is for the author's peers or novices (people like themselves or people who know less than they do) and they only ask themselves to say something their peers will find touching or interesting, or something the novices can learn from. Once you think this way, you realize that everything you know or have experienced is of use to someone, because people who haven't experienced it can profit from your knowledge and people who have will appreciate knowing they're not alone:

> If you've ever been anywhere, you can tell people who haven't been there what it's like.

If you've ever done anything, you can show how to do it to people who don't know.

If you've ever read a book, seen a movie, or eaten in a restaurant, you can review it and tell potential customers whether
it's worth the money.

If you've ever suffered, you can assume others are suffering the
same way, and you can assure them what they're going through
is normal.

If anything ever happened to you that was funny, touching, or
infuriating, you can describe it, ideally getting at what was
universally human about the experience.

You don't even have to be smart, because humans are happy to hear
you talk about your ignorance, confusion, and doubt. In fact, not only
do you not need to be exceptionally smart, but look at it this way: how
do you respond to someone who talks as though he has all the answers, that he's got everything, or at least the topic at hand, all figured
out? Personally, I immediately get skeptical, turned off by arrogance.
I much prefer to be around people who have questions, who are puz-
zled, and who are self-effacing. Writing's like that too. You're much
more likely to win over your reader if you demonstrate a sense that
you're trying to figure it out. Obviously, your reader will feel ripped
off if she gets to the end of your essay and isn't rewarded in some way;
your thesis can't be "I don't have a clue." However, if you ask some
interesting questions, or even suggest looking at something in a new
way, you're way more likely to be successful than if you "preach." For
example, wonderful essay topics—for the appropriate audiences—
would be how bewildering it is to be a freshman on campus, how hi-
lariously confusing it was the time you tried to program your VCR
guided only by the instructions in Japanese English, or how you're of
two minds about getting married.

To convince yourself that most good writing springs from minds
and lives like yours, consider these topics of student essays:

I went home for vacation and had to listen to my father tell me
one more time how he disapproves of my life.

Mornings with my two-year-old are a joyous, comical circus.

I wonder if this semester I'll finally get organized and actually
get something out of school.

Why are men genetically unable to clean bathrooms?

The last time I got panhandled I said no. I felt guilty, but I'm
not sure I should have.

My mother never listens.

I may have finally found a car mechanic I can trust.

There's nothing new or dazzling there, but they all made good
essays. And for a final bit of evidence, here's a splendid essay about
the most trivial of subjects:

THE EGG AND I REVISITED

KRIS TACHMIER

Kids can be finicky eaters. My own three-year-old son will put up determined resistance if he sees one Brussels sprout on his plate. One hour after dinner that singular Brussels sprout will still be on his plate, undisturbed. Similarly, my seventeen-month-old daughter cringes at the sight of a carrot and immediately clamps her jaws shut, making passage into her mouth by a fork laden with the vegetable impossible. But I really have no right to single out my children when their own mother is the classic persnicketist: I cannot and will not eat eggs.

Ever since I can remember, I have hated eggs. I'm not really certain why—maybe it's their texture, or maybe it's the notion that they're really hen ova, or maybe it's the idea that eggs can assume so many disguises. A Brussels sprout will always remain a Brussels sprout; a carrot remains a carrot; but an egg will scramble, fry, poach, coddle, benedict, and devil in the twinkling of an eye. I simply cannot trust eggs.

For a while, my childhood breakfasts included some sort of egg concoction, but the minute my mother stepped out of the kitchen I would sneak over to the sink, tilt my plate upside down, and watch the shimmering yellow creation slip down into the darkened cavity of the drain. This bit of cunning was a great success until one fateful morning. I must have left a few damning fragments of eggy evidence. I was interrogated by my mother: how long, how often, how come? The next morning a glorious bowl of Cheerios was awaiting me. The egg and I were finally separated.

In the years following, my mother learned to keep eggs out of my path, but all her efforts were not enough. During lunch at high school I would invariably sit next to someone who would pull a hardboiled egg out of his sack (together with one of those miniature salt shakers) and sit there happily sprinkling and munching on it. Too bad he never stopped long enough to notice me turning green on his left . . . I might have spoiled his appetite. And there was always some inconsiderate friend who ordered egg salad sandwiches at restaurants. The mixture would always be thick and runny, and globs of it were forever dripping out of all sides of the sandwich.

With marriage, I realized that my attitude toward eggs was a little ridiculous. I decided to give the egg a second chance. I can remember the event clearly: the morning sun was shining, the smell of fresh-perked coffee filled the kitchen, and there, flattened out in submission on my plate, was one fried egg, barely distinguishable for all the salt and pepper I had poured over it. I resolutely picked up my fork, stabbed a section of the egg, thrust it into my mouth, gulped it down, felt it rumbling its way toward my stomach, and blanched as I realized it was rocketing out of my mouth. So much for a second crack at the egg.

Today I still keep my mouth empty of eggs, but my refrigerator is full of them. For the last year or so I've been raising chickens. Every day I march out to the coop and gather a half-dozen freshly laid eggs. As soon as I have several dozen I call up friends to check if they want any eggs free of cost. I think the operation a stroke of genius: I have cleverly combined charity with penitence. ❖

Assuming you hate at least one kind of food, I'll rest my case. Now let's look at some practical ways to encourage those potential essays to make themselves known to us.

Five Principles for Getting Good Ideas

Here are some things to keep in mind that will greatly increase the chances of your finding good ideas to explore in essays:

Don't begin with a topic.
Think all the time.
To get something out, put something in.
Go from little, concrete things to big, abstract ones.
Connect.

Since getting ideas and learning are similar processes, many of these are revisitings of principles in the Guide to Studying. We'll talk about each in turn.

Don't begin with a topic. A topic is the thing you're writing about, the subject: abortion, recent advances in weight training, your first date, how to apply a tourniquet. Anything that fits in the following blank is a topic: "This essay is about _____." If a topic could start an essay, we could open the dictionary and point.

Good seeds for essays come in many forms:

Questions: "Is there any real difference between the Republicans and the Democrats anymore?" "Why is Ralph so mad at me?"

Problems: "I'm always behind in my work." "Violent crimes against women are on the increase."

Intentions: "I want to tell people about what's really going on in this class." "I want to let people know about alternatives to the corporate coffee chains."

Theses: "You should patronize locally owned coffee shops instead of corporate-owned ones." "Old people are the victims of silent injustice in our culture."

Feelings: "I was furious when the instructor suddenly announced there would be a term paper no one knew about due in three weeks." "I was surprised to see my father crying."

Think all the time. We talked about this earlier. If you have a sense of humor, you know that the surest way to prevent yourself from being funny is to have someone demand that you be funny *now*. Instead, mull on the essay with a part of your brain all the time as you go through your days. Honestly, I've come up with some of my best ideas for essays while riding my bicycle through the park, trout fishing, and reading my favorite magazines.

To get something out, put something in. One popular, poisonous metaphor for thinking is the light bulb clicking on over our head—the notion that ideas spring from within us, caused by nothing. To become good thinkers, we have to replace that metaphor with another: think of thoughts as billiard balls on a pool table, idle until other balls—external stimuli—slam into them and set them in motion. Seeds for essays are *re*-actions—we have them in response to prompts. Many of us have learned to separate input and output modes: we are either putting information into our brains or asking our brains to put out thoughts, but we don't do the two jobs at the same time. But when things are going in is the best time to try to get things out. Children do this naturally; try reading a book to a three-year-old, and listen to her react to everything she hears or sees, or take her to a movie and watch her struggle not to talk back to the screen.

Are you a reactor? Answer the following questions:

Do you find yourself silently talking back to the newspaper when you read it?
Do you write in the margins of books you read?
Are at least 25 percent of the notes you take during course lectures your own thoughts, questions, doubts, and reactions?
As you meet up with life's outrages, do you find yourself complaining to imaginary audiences in your head?
After you see a movie that you really like, are you eager to tell people about it and encourage them to see it?
When you listen to a speaker or a teacher, do you find yourself itching to get to the question-and-answer period?

If you said no to these questions, you're going to have to practice your reacting skills.

Any external stimulus can be a prompt, but the best writer's prompt is another piece of writing. So if you're looking for something to write, *go read something.* You can do this in two different ways:

Content prompts: Reading can move you to write if it makes you want to say something back. *Harper's* magazine published an essay by Jerry Jesness called "Why Johnny Can't Fail" (Sept. 1999), in which Jesness, a career teacher, slammed the public school system for what he called "the floating standard," by which all students are allowed to pass and standards are simply lowered when students can't meet them. Writing student Nancy Guinta was bothered by the piece and was moved to respond:

LONG LIVE THE FLOATING STANDARD

He's a beautiful child, kind-hearted, personable. He loves people and they love him. Last winter he worked at a ski resort in the mountains, and they loved him for his enthusiasm and his energy. He even won the Employee of the Month award. His dream was to be allowed to run the snow plow. He's now working his way through the local community college while toying with several dreams: being a professional snowboarder and being a brewmaster are just two.

High school was difficult for him. Science and chemistry lured him, math tormented him, English often baffled him. He was triumphant at high school graduation, and it never would have happened if a host of sympathetic teachers hadn't given him the extra credit assignments and art projects that allowed him to pass. I thank them—those teachers with the floating standards. Without them, my son would be without a diploma, unable to go on to college, branded a failure . . . and who would have gained?

Kids the schools fail—what happens to them? Homeless people, criminals, welfare recipients, drunks—people who have been rejected by society, and who take it out on themselves and us for the rest of their lives. If we let them pass, we just prolong the time they have to find themselves and choose to become productive and not live off you and me. And how much does it really matter if they don't do the science experiment very well or their insight into *To Kill a Mockingbird* isn't sufficiently deep? Failing them just makes sure they're cut off from the real lessons of school: how to be a member of the team, how to work with other people, how to communicate, how to love learning. My son is a perfect example. The essays may have had a lot of spelling errors, but he came through the system looking at life and saying, "I can do this."

Anyway, floating standards don't end at the high school's parking lot. They're in every college, every company, on every job site. In any university you can find classes where the assignments are few and the grading is easy. Yet every study shows that going to college benefits those who go. The system is always set up to let those who can't perform slide by. By letting them slide, we let them learn.

Eventually, each individual decides what standards to set for himself in this life. I hope my son sets high ones for himself. He seems to be doing that. And I believe he is doing that largely because the System kept telling him "You're still one of us" until the maturity had time to kick in. ❖

Models: You can use your reading to inspire you to explore new techniques. You read the piece and say, "Wow! I like the way she did that. I'd never have thought to do it that way. Maybe I could do something sort of like it." That's called *modeling*. People who are learning to do things do it all the time. You watch a good dancer, tennis player, or guitarist, and then you try to do it like that. Naturally, in time, you'll develop your own moves, serve, or licks, but when you're learning, it's a good idea to try to do it like people who do it well. You can use any technical feature as a model: the structure, the opener, the tone, the use of dialogue or narrative, the use of the ellipsis or the dash—anything you never tried before. Here's an inspiring model, a description by the poet e. e. cummings of his father:

> My father . . . was a New Hampshire man, 6 foot 2, a crack shot & a famous flyfisherman & a firstrate sailor (his sloop was named The Actress) & a woodsman who could find his way through forests primeval without a compass & a canoeist who'd still-paddle you up to a deer without ruffling the surface of a pond & an ornithologist & taxidermist & (when he gave up hunting) an expert photographer (the best I've ever seen) & an actor who portrayed Julius Caesar in Sanders Theatre & a painter (both in oils & watercolors) & a better carpenter than any professional & an architect who designed his own houses before building them & (when he liked) a plumber who just for the fun of it installed all his own waterworks & (while at Harvard) a teacher with small use for professors . . . & my father had the first telephone in Cambridge & (long before any Model T Ford) he piloted an Orient Buckboard with Friction Drive produced by the Waltham watch company & . . . my father's voice was so

magnificent that he was called on to impersonate God speaking from Beacon Hill (he was heard all over the common) & my father gave me Plato's metaphor of the cave with my mother's milk.

Here are two essays that students were inspired by e. e. cummings's model to write:

Dave's porch has everything you ever wanted in a porch and more & it is located right next to the freshman dorms & you sit there in the sunshine & you can meet tons of people and most of those people are girls & they like to drink beer & we are always drinking beer on the porch & that way we can meet girls & we like the porch because it has a big chair on it and it's comfortable and the porch is made of redwood and Dave and Phil built it (with Dave's dad's wood) & it's sturdy & it's small but it's fine & you get to see all the people drive by & I can't think of where I'd rather be than on Dave's porch.

(Jeff Ochs)

My ex-boyfriend was a baby-faced, wavy-haired blonde with blue eyes that could be warm as a smile while his thoughts would be as cold as ice scraping against raw metal and he could charm anyone like an alligator and you couldn't get away because he would find you and follow you silently and he would watch and find out every move you made and he would just wait and wait until you made a wrong move and then he would pounce with words like claws and he was a better liar than anyone I ever knew and he would look at you with those alligator eyes and you would freeze like a deer caught in headlights because he knew you were scared and he wanted you to be scared because he let you know that he would hurt you if you ever crossed him because he collected guns and throwing stars that he would throw, embedding them deep into wood, and he would always carry two knives on his belt, one visible and one hidden, and you knew they were there and he knew that you knew and that's what he wanted and he would manipulate anyone like a chess piece (not that he ever learned to play chess, it was a sissy game) and he would do whatever he could to whoever he could to get what he wanted with that alligator smile that was like someone walking over your grave and he wants to be a politician.

(Kathleen Siemont)

Responding to visuals: Many writers get inspiration from what they see. In fact, while a picture may indeed be worth a thousand words, sometimes a picture can *inspire* millions. Consider how much has been written in response to the horrific images from Abu Ghraib prison, for example, or how many pundits, columnists, and letters-to-the-editor writers weighed in after the infamous Super Bowl "Wardrobe Malfunction."

Similarly, a poet might respond to a sunset or a rainstorm—or like William Wordsworth to a field of daffodils and Walt Whitman to a battlefield. Woody Guthrie, John Lennon, Bruce Springsteen, and Bono—among countless others—have written songs in response to visual images. And in fact, it's some writers' jobs: the art critic, for example, has to look at a photograph, painting, or sculpture and respond with written words—and indeed, it's common in art history classes for students to be assigned to write papers in response to artwork.

Technical writers, too, frequently must look at graphs and charts and drawings and put those data into words. And then sometimes it works the other way around: they convert text into visual images. Either way, in technical writing, and often in long research projects in school, images and text complement each other to make the material more accessible to the reader. (I'll talk about this more in Chapter 18.)

As a student writer, you can use what you see to inspire you to write. Certainly you've been moved by images: Why did you choose the screen saver you're currently using? Why put that particular picture on the wall in your dorm room? Obviously, those images mean something to you. Can you convey that in a meaningful way to a reader? Can you use the image as a jumping-off point into an essay? Perhaps the photo on your parents' wall of you and the first fish you ever caught could inspire an essay about your decision to go into the field of wildlife management. Perhaps the photo of the cows crowded into the corral and awaiting slaughter could jump-start an essay about the value of being a vegan.

Go from little, concrete things to big, abstract ones. The best thinking follows a predictable course: from little, concrete bits of experience to large, abstract implications. You see an ad on TV, start thinking about it, and it leads you to speculations on American consumerism, media manipulation, and the marketing of women's bodies. Or you see a parent disciplining a child in a grocery-store aisle just for being alive, and it makes you think, "Why are people without training or talent allowed to do this all-important job called child raising?" or "Parents need time off too."

Many of the essays in this book model this progress from a minor personal experience to a big issue. In "Why I Never Cared for the Civil War" (A Collection of Good Writing), Shawni Allred studied a muddy pool of water in the fifth grade and used the experience to discuss what's wrong with traditional classroom teaching styles. In "Given the Chance" (Chapter 14) Melissa Schatz met Stacey, and her

experience with Stacey led her to question the entire state drug rehabilitation program.

Connect. We talked about connecting before ("Prologue"). A lot
of thinking begins by noticing that two things are related. Here's an example. One day when I was a freshman at a community college in
California, I was driving to an afternoon class. It was pouring rain, and
I was on the freeway in an old Volkswagen Beetle, the windshield wipers
working feebly to try to keep the windshield clear of sheets of water.

It so happened that I hated the class I was going to; in fact, I
didn't like most of my classes and wasn't even very happy about being in college. I didn't have a major, didn't have direction. Everything
seemed too complicated, too difficult. I wished I were back in high
school, where little mattered except my friends and just showing up
for class. Life was so much simpler then.

As I drove through the rain, I found myself glancing into the
rearview mirror, out of which I could see perfectly clearly. When I
looked ahead into the storm, I could hardly see. I looked through the
mirror again and out the back window. Perfectly clear. So clear, in
fact, that I was drawn to keep looking out the back window instead
of out the front.

Suddenly, I felt the bump, bump, bump of the lane dividers.
I had accidentally almost swerved into the next lane! I quickly
corrected, and vowed to keep looking ahead.

That's when it hit me: "keep looking ahead." Of course, it was
easier to look behind me, but that's not what I needed to see. I needed
to look in front of me, even if that were more difficult, not as clear.
If I kept looking behind me—wishing I were still in high school—I
would surely drive right off the road.

I didn't go to class that afternoon. Instead, I went to see an academic adviser to talk about my future, and I ended up filling out
the paperwork to a four-year college. It would be difficult, I knew,
and sometimes not as clear, but at least now I was looking forward,
not behind me.

It's hard to say how those kinds of connections are made, and
sometimes you make them when you try to, when you think about
making them. But, strangely, sometimes you just make them. They
seem to come out of nowhere. All the more reason to be thinking
about—or at least be open to—new ideas and ways of seeing your
world.

Naturally, the more *un*-like two things are and the less obvious
the connection, the more fresh and stimulating is the connection
when you make it. This is the Head Principle. Mr. Head was an avi-
ation engineer who got interested in downhill skiing. Apparently no
one had ever connected aircraft technology and skiing before; Mr.
Head took a few runs down the hill and realized that he could make

a better ski if he simply made it with the principles and materials used in making airplane wings. He invented the Head ski, the first metal ski, and made millions of dollars. He then did the same thing to tennis, inventing the Prince racket. Apparently aircraft engineers didn't play tennis either.

The Head Principle says you can't predict what will connect with what. So you can't tell yourself what information to seek. You can only amass experience and information voraciously and stir it all up together. If I'd been trying to think about how driving through the rain was symbolic, or trying to think of something that reflected where my life was heading, I might never have made the connection, but because I was open to the possibility of connection—to the fact that unexpected things can relate to one another—it happened. If you're writing about Charles Dickens and you read only about Charles Dickens, you're just making sure you won't make any connections except those other Dickens critics have already made. Instead, go read *Psychology Today*, read Hillary Clinton's memoirs, see a movie, watch a documentary on insect societies, or visit a mortuary.

Most of us do the exact opposite of these five idea-getting principles. We set aside a block of time for thinking, cut ourselves off from the outside world by locking ourselves in a stimulus-free study room and look within ourselves for a large, abstract topic to write on. If you're doing any of that, you're less likely to be successful.

Writing from Rage

If your due date is near and you're still having trouble finding a topic, there might be a way out: write from rage. I've had students write uninspired, boring essays all semester long until something finally makes them angry enough to respond in writing, and suddenly their text springs to life. In fact, one of my favorite pieces of my own writing came about when, after being awakened early one Sunday morning by the neighbor's leaf blower, I went to the computer and wrote a guest editorial for our local newspaper. Titled "The Monsters of Fall," the piece took to task those hideous machines and those who I felt were shattering the peace and quiet of early mornings.

A word of caution: writing from rage can get you in big trouble too. Surely you've been made angry by a friend's e-mail—or behavior—and fired off a response before waiting to cool down and think clearly and rationally. That can happen just as easily in essay writing. While the rage can fuel your writing, you need to able to step back enough from your subject so that you can see it clearly—and realize the effect you'll have on your reader. Once when Ernest Hemingway was living in Florida, his editor, visiting from New York, commented on the beauty of the area and asked the famous writer why he hadn't written about it. Hemingway responded, "Because I haven't been away from it for ten years." So let your emotions fire you up, but be cool and rational—and try to get some distance from your topic—when you write.

Also, as I've said before, sometimes your assignment or prompt doesn't provide you the luxury of choosing a topic out of thin air. I'll talk more about this in Chapters 14, 15, and 16.

I recently overheard an odd conversation in the hallway outside my office. A young woman of eighteen or nineteen was talking on her cell phone—not at all unusual—and I was hardly paying attention. But then I heard her say, in a bit more urgent voice than she had been using, "Really, you've got to stop smoking crack." I was astonished. College students talking about smoking crack, with first-hand experience? I was suddenly forced to reconsider what I thought were the life experiences my students were bringing to college. I had thought these "kids" led pretty sheltered lives, but here was evidence to the contrary. And a perfect essay topic: not all college students are as naïve as they might seem to be.

And there are lots of ways to explore such an essay. It could be written as the personal story of a college instructor's epiphany, learning his world was not what he thought it was. It could be written as an argument, with either students or instructors as its audience: get to know your classmates/students; they might need more help navigating their social lives than you think. Or it could be written as an informative piece about the prevalence of drugs on campus, in which case it would require a significant amount of research.

WRITER'S WORKSHOP

Finding Essays in Your Life

Professor Rawlins once asked his class for a volunteer who "had nothing to say," someone whose life had been "nothing special." He and the volunteer (Sally) talked for twenty minutes and then looked back over their conversation for possible essay topics. Here's their conversation, with the ideas for essays in parentheses.

JR: Tell me about yourself. What do you do?

S: I'm a student. I work in a restaurant, and I enjoy sports.

JR: What kind of sports do you do?

S: I used to compete in track, but now it's for my own enjoyment. (*Compare being athletic in formal competition with being athletic just for fun, arguing that athletics outside of organized competition is healthier, more fun, less stressful.*) I run, play basketball, do cross-country skiing, downhill. I play a little bit of volleyball, swim, play softball. I've only just started cross-country skiing. I really like it because of the solitude; there's more physical exercise. Downhill I like because of the speed and getting accuracy down. (*Write to downhillers, arguing that cross-country skiing is less crowded, cheaper, better for your body, and better for your spirit.*)

JR: What did you do in track?

S: Shot put and half mile. I had a lot of strength from weight lifting.

JR: Did you ever take any flak for doing something that was as "unfeminine" as putting the shot?

S: Sure. We were considered jocks. There was a lot of stereotyping. . . . (*Write to large, strong girls, sharing your experience pursuing a "manly" sport and encouraging them not to be intimidated; or defend the thesis: Even after the women's movement, female athletes still face prejudice.*) I was used as a guinea pig for a program. Since I was a good athlete, they wanted to see how strong they could really make me. But I ended up getting injured. They didn't provide the equipment I needed—belts and stuff like that. I strained my back. From trying to squat too much. (*Write to beginning women weight trainers, offering training tips and cautioning them about the dangers.*)

JR: Tell me about your past. What was your childhood like?

S: We grew up fairly poor. My mom divorced when I was seven, so it was just the girls in the house: my two sisters, Mom, and me.

JR: What was it like when your parents divorced?

S: I was happy about it. I was scared to death of my father. He hit us a lot. The way I look on it now, that was the only way he had to communicate. That's the way he was raised. I was scared to death of him and anyone who was ever going to raise a hand to me. It caused many problems with our relationship. To the point where I didn't know him—though he doesn't live very far from my hometown. (*Write to children of divorce, sharing your feelings and the insights you've gained from the experience; or write to children physically abused by their parents, sharing your experiences and your feelings; or defend the thesis: Sometimes divorce is good for the children of the marriage.*)

JR: How did your father's treatment of you affect you?

S: It made it hard to be affectionate with people—I'm beginning to outgrow that. Also I felt like I was a bad person, but that's also because he would tell me bad things about myself. I wanted to be a lawyer all my life, but he always told me, "Nope, you'll never be good at that, you'll never be good at that." And he told me that so many times, I tell myself that. He wanted a boy. (*Write about what it's like growing up with parents who tell you you're bound to fail; or write about what it's like being a girl in a family where a parent wanted a boy.*)

JR: Did you always live in the same place when you were growing up?

S: No, in high school we moved and I had to change schools. My mom thought I was a little too radical and the neighborhood was a bad influence on me.

JR: Do you agree?

S: No. There was definitely a better grade of education in the new place, but the new high school was in a richer neighborhood and was really into cocaine. The girls were all daddy's little girls, they got everything they wanted, they didn't have to work for anything; the guys all thought they were cowboys, which I thought was funny, since they probably never had been near a horse. (*Write a satire laughing at the foolishness of parents who move to upper-middle-class neighborhoods in the mistaken belief that they're escaping the problems of poverty or the city; or defend the thesis: "Better neighborhoods" aren't always better.*)

JR: Were you doing drugs?

S: I drank a lot, but never when I was playing any sport, because it would screw me up. (*Defend the thesis: We*

*should fight drug abuse by helping kids find some-
thing they love so much they won't risk losing it.)*

JR: How did you ever survive long enough to make it to
college?

S: I had the influence of my mother, which was very positive, very striving. She works in a field where very
few women do, general contracting: multimillion-dol-
lar buildings. She doesn't have a college degree, so she
doesn't have a title, but she travels all over the country, part engineer work, part administration; she heads
a marketing team. . . . She's a super-intelligent
lady, and the kind of person who, when something
isn't supposed to be possible, can get it done. *(Write
about your mother and your relationship with her,
showing the ways she helped you survive your youth.)*

JR: It sounds like your mom was a very good influence.

S: Almost too much so. I'm in awe. And I have a stepfather who's a doctor and very successful, who's also
very intelligent. *(Write about the pluses and minuses
of having a stepparent; or write about the pluses and
minuses of having parents who are superheroes.)*

JR: What are your plans?

S: I intend to go overseas and teach. That's what I'd like.
Teach English for a while. *(Write to English majors,
defending the thesis: You should consider teaching
English overseas for a year or two.)*

That's sixteen essays in twenty minutes from what Sally
was convinced was a "nothing" life. Of course, Sally's life turned
out to be anything but ordinary, but the funny thing is that the
same thing happens with every life, including yours, when you
start looking at it this way.

Now it's your turn. With a classmate, do Sally-type interviews of each other. Have her interview you for fifteen minutes;
then you interview her. Together, find as many essay seeds in
each interview as you can. Try to find personal essays, informative essays, and arguments. Make sure that none of the seeds
is a topic (a noun or a noun phrase).

EXERCISES

1. For two days, record (in a notebook or journal) all the striking prompts you encounter: fragments of conversation overheard in the grocery store, startling ads on TV, unusual moments in class. Take two and recast them as ideas for essays, a sentence to a short paragraph each.

2. Make a list of things that have made you mad recently. Take one and explore its possibilities as an essay.

3. On pp. 40–41 is a list of five ways to find essay ideas. Find one in your life via each item in the list. For example, for the first item, pick some place you've been and describe it to someone in a couple of sentences.

4. Go back to the Five Principles for Getting Good Ideas. Try to come up with one of each of the five.

5. Find an essay, in *The Writer's Way* or elsewhere, that sparks a thoughtful response in you. Turn that response into an essay.

6. Find an essay, in *The Writer's Way* or elsewhere, that has a technical feature you like but have never tried. Using the essay as a model, write a short essay mimicking that feature. At the bottom of the page, identify the feature you're mimicking: e.g., "I'm mimicking the use of dialogue."

Chapter 4

FROM FIRST THOUGHTS TO DRAFTS

In this chapter we'll take that set of good intentions we fleshed out in Chapter 3 and turn it into a bunch of pages of text (called a draft) that's crying out for rethinking, reshaping, and resaying (called revision). This stage should be playful, messy, and meandering. Writing teachers call it "prewriting" or "brainstorming," but you can call it scribbling or noodling if you want.

Many people, without saying so, have decided that this kicking-around stage shouldn't have to happen and that if it does, something's wrong. My students are always surprised when I tell them how different my own first drafts are from their final and often published versions. Honestly, you might not recognize that a first and "final" draft were written by the same person, and in fact, you might think that the topics weren't even the same. In that case, you'd often be right. I frequently use drafts to figure out what I want to say, and along the way change my topic altogether. I once (thought I) was working on an essay about how easily and inexpensively one can keep a car in good running condition, but as I worked my way through the first few drafts, the essay sort of took on a mind of its own—like it wanted to be about something else. For a couple of drafts, then, it was about my father teaching me to drive, and from there it became a very personal piece about how painful it was the first time I lost a friend in an automobile accident.

Similarly, I once read in a local newspaper an opinion piece by a friend, and when I saw him several days later told him how perfect I thought the last sentence was, how it tied the whole essay together. "Thanks," he said. "I thought of that line when I was thinking the piece was almost but done, so I had to rewrite the *whole thing* so that I could make that one line work."

Drafting should be as easy as talking, and most of us talk without effort. But it isn't, and the only difference is fear. When we write, we feel there's a lot on the line, and it ties us up. That feeling of constriction is called writer's block. *Our only goal in drafting is to make writer's block go away so the words keep coming.* If we keep the words coming, we'll write our way to good stuff.

Writer's Block: Myth or Reality?

I was once at a journalism conference where there were roughly equal numbers of students, professors, and professional journalists. After one particularly stimulating session—about writing editorials—there was question-and-answer time for the panel. A member of the audience stood up and asked a newspaper editor if he ever got writer's block. His answer was honest and simple: "I don't have time for writer's block."

That is, he works on deadline and simply has to get the job done. Can you imagine a plumber stopping suddenly and saying, "Sorry, I can't go on. I have plumber's block"? Or a dairy farmer: "Sorry, I have milker's block." The editor simply sat at his desk and did the work he had to do.

Obviously, writing is different in many ways, but a big part of writing is simply sitting down in front of your computer and writing—it will get done. If you have to wait for the muses, you're likely to wait a very long time. Besides, the muses are much more likely to "speak" to you when you're sitting there writing than when you're in the kitchen making cookies because you're telling yourself—and perhaps others—that you have writer's block.

Conversely, writer's block can be a very real problem, which people get largely because they define writing and their relationship to it in terms opposite to the ones we practiced in Chapter 1. They don't feel like writers. So they try to be someone they're not when they write; they try to fake it. They write to people they aren't comfortable talking to. They equate their writing with their self-worth: "If I write a bad essay, I'm a bad person." So they ask too much of themselves, try too hard, and write to avoid failure. We have to replace those attitudes with healthy alternatives. Here are eleven ways to cultivate them.

Defeating Writer's Block

1. Call yourself a writer. We talked in the Guide to Studying about how important this is (Prologue). If you've been putting it off, now's the time. You can't play good tennis telling yourself over and over, "I'm not really a tennis player; I'm not really a tennis player."

2. Give yourself a lot of time. How obvious. Yet no rule of writing is broken more often. We wait until the last minute before a paper is due, conning ourselves into believing that we write better under pressure. But we don't. Time pressure always heightens fear. So instead of trying to force out a draft the night before it's due, set a part of your mind nibbling at the project from the moment the assignment is made, and keep nibbling off and on throughout the day, every day, catching your thoughts as they fall in a pocket notebook.

3. Write as yourself. The less you have to disavow yourself when you write, the less writer's block will touch you. Writer's block comes from fear of being found out. If you write to convince the reader you're someone you're not, the risk of being found out increases. Mark Twain said the great advantage of telling the truth is that you don't need a good memory. Similarly, if you're your true self, no one can expose you. The draft you produce this way may not be ready to hand in, but you'll have the draft, and that's what matters.

4. Write to your favorite audience. People get tense when they try to talk to strangers. You'll make it easier on yourself if you write to someone you can talk freely to.

Most people choose to write to one of the three toughest audiences in the world: no one, the instructor, or the whole world. No one is hard because you know the writing is pointless. The instructor is hard because she knows more than you, and she's judging (grading) you instead of reading you. (I know that in reality you *are* writing to the instructor and writing for a grade, but there are some realities it's wise to forget, and this is one of them.) Writing to the whole world is hard because there is little you can say that the whole world wants to hear.

The audience that's easiest to write to is small and homogeneous: It's made of people with the same interests, values, level of sophistication, and education. It knows less than you on the subject. It wants what you have to offer. It doesn't threaten you; it's not made up of people who are richer than you, a higher class than you, academically more advanced than you, or whatever makes you feel at a disadvantage. This audience is pulling for you: friends, family, pen pals, classmates. As always, the draft you produce this way may not be ready to hand in, but you'll have the draft, and that's the important thing.

5. Don't write; talk. Since most of us are used to being ourselves when we talk, if we talk on the page we'll feel that it's the real us writing. We're also better at talking because we've done so much more of it, so we'll be more successful writing talk. Again, a first draft you've *spoken* may not be ready to hand in, but you can fix that later.

The basic way to write like you talk is to imagine yourself talking and write down what you hear. But if that isn't enough, you can make the talk real. You can talk to yourself, out loud—when you get stuck, stop typing and speak aloud to the air what you're trying to say. Or find a listener: Rush out of the room, grab the nearest victim, and dump what you're trying to write into her astonished ear.

Or you can go all the way and literally dictate your text into a tape recorder and then type a transcript. Once I was asked to edit the narrative for a film on conservation. The author of the text said it didn't sound like a person talking, and he asked me to fix it. Instead of rewriting the text, I turned on my tape recorder, read the first paragraph of the text to see what it said, and tried to *speak* the content—without looking at the written text—into the recorder. I worked my way through the text in this way, and the product was the same text, now in the language of a human speaker, not a stiff and artificial writer.

Remind yourself to use your talking language by using contractions: *can't, it's, I'm.* Every time you write *cannot* or *it is,* you remind yourself that you're not allowed to be you when you write; every time you write *can't* or *it's,* you'll remind yourself that's not so.

6. Take your ego out of the loop. We get stage fright because we feel our ego is on the line: if we fail, we've proved we're bad, inept people. The essay *is us,* and we crash if it crashes. To escape that fate, we have to unlearn the ego identification. *You are not the essay.* If it crashes, you can still be a worthy person who occasionally writes essays that don't work.

The first step in this unlearning is to realize that we choose to equate our egos with things, and can choose not to. I can go out and play soccer badly and not grieve, because I am not my soccer game, but if I write badly I must hate myself, because I am my writing. But there is nothing inherent in soccer or writing that makes me assign those values to them—I choose it. I have the power to move writing over to the "It's not a big deal" category any time I want.

Second, realize that the result of assigning such import to an action is destructive. I may tell myself that I'm helping myself write well by caring so much, but in fact the only result is that I can play soccer without fear (and therefore boldly, joyfully, and well), but I dare not write—there's too much to lose.

Third, understand how audiences read. *You* think the essay is you, but *they* don't. Imagine a guitar student with extreme stage fright. But the teacher was smart. The teacher said, "You fear because you think the audience listens to *you.* They do not. They listen to Bach, or Villa-Lobos. You are merely a messenger. You are nothing. They don't hear you. Remember this, and you'll disappear. Then there is no reason to be afraid."

7. Don't demand that you know where you're going. Geniuses have something in common: a talent for working without rigidly defined goals. They're willing to let the investigation work itself out and discover where they'll end up when they've gotten there. Less creative minds want to know exactly where they're going before they start. The genius wisely says, "How can I know I'm going to invent the laser or discover the theory of relativity when no one knows such a thing exists yet?"

Sometimes school teaches you the reverse, by telling you that you need discipline and structure and requiring you to use outlines, thesis statements, and other tools that force those skills. If someone tells you that, learn to say, "Those tools are nice when I'm revising, but NOT NOW!"

8. Lower your standards. We're talking about the damage done by *feeling obligated*. A football player who chokes because he's anticipating getting clobbered is said to "hear footsteps." Most people write hearing footsteps: the footsteps of their own critical selves, coming to clobber them for not measuring up.

Most writers are burdened with obligations: obligations to the English language, to the spelling system, to the rules of grammar, to the noble art of composition, or to their parents, who are paying for their college education, to instructors, to the demands of the five-paragraph format. All those obligations instill fear and make it harder to write. To silence them, *lower your standards*, fool around, and indulge yourself at every turn. Ask as little of yourself as possible.

It works. Here's how Lewis Thomas, a modern master of the essay, discovered the benefits of not trying hard when he turned from writing medical research and tried his hand at essay writing for the first time:

> The chance to . . . try the essay form raised my spirits, but at the same time worried me. I tried outlining some ideas for essays, making lists of items I'd like to cover in each piece, organizing my thoughts in orderly sequences, and wrote several dreadful essays which I could not bring myself to reread, and decided to give up being orderly. I changed the method to no method at all, picked out some suitable times late at night, usually on the weekend two days after I'd already passed the deadline, and wrote without outline or planning in advance, as fast as I could. This worked better, or at least was more fun, and I was able to get started.
>
> *(Lewis Thomas, The Youngest Science)*

Three years after that beginning, those essays won the National Book Award.

If your guilt reflex tries to tell you that excellence lies in sweating the details, assure it there will be ample time for that during the polishing stages. Write the last draft to suit others, and write everything else to suit yourself. After all, when in the writing process do you owe other people (audiences, bosses, teachers, grammarians) anything? Not till the moment you hand the essay in. Writing's one great advantage is that none of it "counts" until you say it does. Don't throw this advantage away by insisting you write well from the first page of the first draft. What do you care how good the first draft of *Harry Potter and the Sorcerer's Stone* was?

Once you know your internal voice of self-criticism is active, you can set up a writing regimen that denies it an opportunity to speak. Forbid yourself to reread what you write until you are at the end of the draft. Or use the voice's input to your advantage. Make a rule that you never cross out anything. When the voice says that something you wrote isn't good enough, leave it and write onward, saying it all over again better or discussing what you didn't like about it. That way the voice of criticism becomes a force for *more* writing, not less.

Sheer speed helps, because it prevents you from thinking too much about what you're doing. Good early-stage writers write fast. Your normal composing pace should be as fast as your fingers will move.

9. Quit when you're hot, persist when you're not. Ernest Hemingway is said to have always quit writing when he knew exactly what was going to happen next, not when he ran out of things to say. That way, he was always excited about going to work the next day instead of dreading it. Hemingway understood that every time you stop writing, whether it's for five minutes or five months, you run the risk of finding out you're blocked when you come back. Get around the problem by quitting when you're hot. Take a break on a winning note, not a losing one. Stop writing when things are going well, when you feel strong and know where you're going next. When you're at a loss, don't let yourself quit; stick with it until the block dissolves, words come, and you've triumphed momentarily.

The principle behind this is basic behavior modification. If you quit when you're stuck, you're in fact rewarding your failure: you're learning that if you get stuck you get the reward of getting to eat, to stretch, to escape. If you stick it out, wait until the words come, and then quit, you reward success. At first it seems contrary to logic: why stop when the words are flowing? The answer is only apparent when you try it: if you quit when you feel good about the writing, you feel good all during the break and come back to the computer feeling strong. If you quit when you're stuck, your break is filled with dread and worry, and the return to the computer feels like the climb to the scaffold.

The longer the break, the more important it is to quit knowing what you'll do next. When I break for five minutes, I want to know what sentence I'm going to write when I come back; when I break for the day, I typically finish with a sketchy paragraph summary of where the discussion is going in the next few passages—a map of tomorrow's journey.

10. Sidestep the thing that blocks you. Identify the thing that stops you from writing, and figure out a way to go around it.

Do you ever refuse to begin the essay until you sweat out a title? Do you ever refuse to write the body of an essay until you've ground out an opening paragraph that refuses to come? Do you ever write and rewrite a sticky passage, refusing to go on until it's just right? Do you ever interrupt the steady flow of words to check a spelling in the dictionary? All these behaviors may be excuses to stop writing.

There are an infinite number of ways to stop yourself, but three are so common we'll name them.

Fear of page one. Renowned literary scholar Dwight Culler said he used to roll the paper into the typewriter and stare at page 1 in blank terror. Then he got an idea: He rolled the paper into the typewriter, typed "page 10" at the top . . . and found he could write with relative ease.

Fear of the page limit. This is where you are assigned a ten-page paper and are terrified you'll never find enough to say to fill ten pages. Attack this in two ways. First, fill pages quickly: double-space, use large margins, and ramble—be as wordy and redundant as you please. Pile up text until you're well past the page limit. Now the problem is no longer how to stretch to fill the assigned space, but how to cut down to fit into it. It may all be an illusion, but you'll feel better nonetheless. Second, don't let yourself know how many pages you've written.

Fear of the essay. This is perhaps the most common source of writer's block. Most of us write lots of things more easily than we write essays—so don't write essays, until the last draft. Instead . . . .

11. Write un-essays. Here are seven ways to get writing out of yourself that have friendlier names:

Reactive reading. This is an old friend—we talked about it in Chapter 2 and Chapter 3. You read something stimulating on your chosen issue and jot down all the stuff pouring from you in response. Follow three rules. (1) *Write your reactions down as you read*—don't read, then write down your thoughts, because by then they'll be gone. (2) *Don't write on the prompt,* like in the margins; write on a notepad. Don't tell yourself you'll transcribe the notes later—you won't. (3) *Don't take notes on what the text says;* record the reactions you're having to it. If this is hard for you, force yourself by drawing a vertical line down the middle of the note page and writing text content on the left side of the page and your reactions on the right. Force yourself to fill the right side as well as the left.

Brainstorming. Brainstorming is messy chatting with colleagues accompanied by note taking. Brainstorming differs from the conversations we hold with friends every day in four ways: (1) Brainstorming is done as fast as possible. (2) Brainstorming is unstructured—you try to spit out single words and phrases as well as sentences or whole thoughts, and you take whatever comes, however fragmented, however ill-phrased, however apparently irrelevant. (3) You have no standards. And (4) you record everything people say.

Mapping. Mapping is my students' favorite prewriting tool. You can use it to find a seed (Chapter 3), but it's usually used when you've found one. Write the seed in the center of a piece of paper and circle it. You don't need a thesis or a great idea—you can start with a word, a suggestive phrase, a visual image, a picture. Now begin brainstorming or free-associating connections between the seed and other thoughts. Let the other bits be whatever they are—words, sensations, questions. As each bit comes, write it down on the paper somewhere, circle it, and draw a line from it to the bit on the page it seems somehow connected to. Work out from the seed in all directions, letting bits cluster as they will. Try to connect everything in the map to something else in the map, so you're making a spider web, or highway system, or whatever you want to think of it as. On page 61 is a map of the essay about the sinister boyfriend from Chapter 3.

If a bit doesn't seem related to any other bit, don't worry about it; just write it anywhere and circle it. Don't demand that you know what the bits or connections mean. If you momentarily run dry, keep doodling or retrace the spider web, so your hand keeps moving and invites your brain to contribute.

If, as you're mapping, you catch glimpses of essay structure, record them somewhere. If you notice, for instance, that many of your bits concerning industrial pollution are about the history of the problem, many are about public opinion on the issue, and many are about the federal government's role in the problem and its solution, you can try to cluster the bits around three main arteries in the map, respectively labeled "history," "John Q. Public," and "Feds." But you needn't do any of that now. You're *generating;* you can sort, label, sequence, and analyze later.

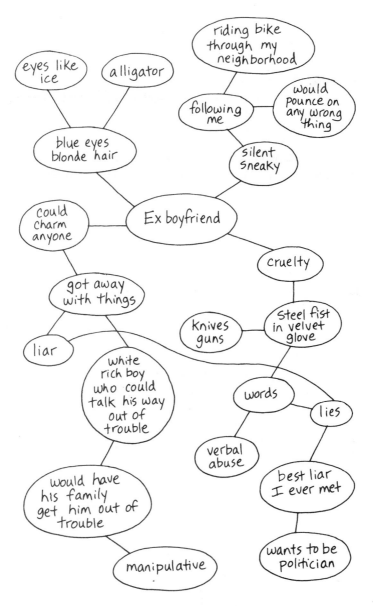

As you map, keep reminding yourself:

Don't map only nouns. Map everything—nouns, verbs, adjectives, adverbs, phrases, sentences, pictures, questions. . . .
Circle everything. Connect every circle to something via a line.
Use circles, not boxes—boxes are prisons.
Don't be linear—use all 360 degrees of the circle. Wander.

Don't think you're now committed to writing an essay that follows the map. You don't owe a map, or any other prewriting tool, anything. If you have to prove this to yourself, take a part of the map that you like, move it to the center of a new piece of paper, and map around it.

Journals. A journal is a notebook or binder where you dump everything you think, feel, or observe. It's written to and for you, and you write in it every day or nearly every day—not just when a good idea strikes. It's the only one of the prewriting tools that you use on schedule, so it gives you a lot of writing practice. But there's more to it than that: it teaches you to monitor your mind and heart constantly, as a part of life, and to value what's pouring out of them. We're always moving, breathing, thinking, and feeling; if we're writers, we observe and record what we think and feel. Most good writers keep journals, at least for a year or so until the monitoring habit is firmly established.

People who don't keep journals can't figure out what people who do keep journals find to put in them, so here are some entries from the journal of Susan Wooldridge. Susan kept her journal for more than twenty years, just writing down things she was noticing and recording her reactions to them. Eventually, Susan published her journal as *Poemcrazy*, a wonderful book that is at once insightful, whimsical, and useful—and a great resource for writers.

> Happy morning.
> Tiniest sprouts in our herb garden. Sunlight on our plants.
>
> Aristophanes—
> "Who's there?"
> "An ill-starred man."
> "Then keep it to yourself."
>
> Perhaps the heaviness will leave soon. Perhaps I can will it away, perhaps it will just lift. All right, why is it here. Heavy dreams. Kent interested in someone else, though not truly, I knew that in the dream. Heavy weather. Anger at myself for having a job so basically useless to the world and to me. Every day. Morning energy lost on it.
>
> André Malraux said of Goya:
> "He discovered his genius the day he dared to give up pleasing others."
>
> I urge Smokey into the large field, recently plowed, we trot, canter, turn, figure 8, etc. I watch our shadow galloping across the field and try to convince myself that this, truly, is my childhood dream come true. Me galloping through a green field with my own beautiful horse. Sometimes it feels right. Sometimes I feel guilt. Self-indulgence! Bad Sue. You should be out in the ghettoes carrying bundles of food to the starving and poor.

Doing office work. Typing like an automaton. Breathing stale smoke smells guardedly through my nose, occasionally flailing a broken fly swatter at a spiraling bumpy fly that refuses to land except on fragile typewriter parts.

Cows in the fog, dumb and heavy. Vague clumps of cows, a hog and sows in pale rows in a bog of weeds and grass and cows vacant as glass in the fog.

Words. Reasons, worries, flight.
Birds. Nested birds.

Think, when I have worked on a poem for a certain time, if it isn't getting better, if it doesn't intrigue me, it's not going to be any good.

Opened the dictionary to "fipple flute" while looking up "apposite," and found a lovely reproduction of fingerprints on this post-Halloween morning.

We went, with the rent, for another chat with Clarence and Grace. Good folk in their way. Clarence like a big cumbersome child, devilish. Grace somewhat shy, somewhat sly. Real country folk. She had pet pigs once. Cows. Clarence delivered milk during the depression. Real Illinois farmers. Clarence has been to 4 funerals this week, friends.

There will be snow tonight. And perhaps tomorrow I shall speed, skate, spin on thick ice.

Our tree is lying frozen outside. I just got the strange idea that at some level, the tree had consciousness, awareness of dying, even an ability, at an unheard level, to call to us, to appeal. But I am making this up.

And oh, this curse of words, endless rumination, introspection and self exposure. Here it is: I am a writer I am a writer I write I write I am a person who writes I am a woman I am a woman who likes to write, who chooses to write. I am a writer. No more fudging on this one, Susan, this drive will not be submerged, this is a need, a want. So follow it. Do it. Hell. Hello. Hell, Hello.

There are two things worth noting here. First, in conventional terms *nothing has happened* in Susan's life. She sees cows. She looks a word up in the dictionary. Nothing more. As always, it's the watchful eye and heart of the writer that makes things worth saying, not the experiences themselves. Second, these entries aren't mini-essays or proto-essays. They're written for the journal-keeper—an audience of one. Writing to others is different.

Letter writing. Most of us write well when we write letters, because we're writing as ourselves to a real audience we feel we can talk to. Write about the events of the day if that's all you feel up to; if you want to ask more of yourself, write, "I've been mulling over this thing for this essay I'm writing for a class. It's about...," and block out the essay for your reader.

Discovery drafts. A discovery draft is a first draft that's purely exploratory; you just keep saying things and see where they lead you. You ask nothing, but you hope that by the time you're done, you will have written yourself to a sense of what you're going to do. It's sort of like a football team doing calisthenics before a game—just loosening up. No one really cares to watch. It's not for the benefit of the audience/crowd anway; it's for the benefit of the players, who wouldn't be ready to play without warming up first.

Writers often call this kind of loosening up "free writing." In its most extreme form, you write for a predetermined period of time and keep writing sentences no matter what happens. If you have nothing to say, write, "I have nothing to say" over and over until you find something else to say. Write song lyrics, gibberish, "The quick brown fox jumps over the lazy dog," or whatever, but keep writing.

Abstracts. Abstracts can be intimidating, but they can also be liberating if you have been mulling the essay over, your head is full of what you want to say, and you just try to dash the abstract off, like a cartoon before the detailed drawing. In Chapter 6, I'll talk more about how to write abstracts.

Don't outline. Outlining isn't an un-essay because it's an organizing discipline, not a prewriting tool. It's rigid, mechanical, structured—the opposite of everything we want at this stage. It closes you down instead of opening you up. Map or write an abstract instead.

EXERCISES

---

1. Identify an idea for an essay (see Chapter 3). Then do the following things with it:
   a. Make a map from it.
   b. Brainstorm it with a classmate for ten minutes.
   c. Write a real letter to a real friend of yours in which you say something like, "I've been thinking about this essay I'm writing for my comp class. It's about..." Then tell your reader the essay, keeping him interested.

    d. Talk the essay into a tape recorder; then transcribe the tape. Rewrite it into an essay. Write a paragraph discussing what changes the spoken text needed.

    e. Via the Internet or elsewhere, find a piece of writing that addresses your essay's issues. React to the piece, and rewrite your essay to include the new thoughts generated by the reading.

2. Write a half-page essay in which you identify precisely what you're afraid of having happen when you write. Then go do a discovery draft in which you try to make those frightening things happen.

3. Write a half-page essay in which you identify precisely what gives you writer's block. Then write another essay in which you plot ways to sidestep the blocker—ways you can write so it comes up never or later.

4. Keep a journal for a week. Write in it at least once a day. Then take two entries and rewrite them as essay seeds.

5. Start a letter to a friend, in which you plan to give her some good news or to tell her something important. But don't get that far. Stop when you know exactly what you will say next, and then don't write again until the next day. See how you *look forward* to writing when you know exactly what you're going to say?

Part Three

REVISING AND EDITING

Chapter 5

THESIS, PURPOSE, AUDIENCE, TONE, AND STYLE

The Spirit of Revising

Now that you've produced a draft, it's time to rewrite it. No other step in the writing process is so badly done by so many writers as rewriting. Shake a tree and a dozen good first-draft writers will fall out, but you're lucky if you get one good rewriter.

Most of us give ourselves rewriter's block by buying into one or more of several bad arguments. Many writers argue that since they rewrite badly, rewriting must be useless: "My rewrites are always worse than my first drafts," they boast. Other writers define rewriting in least helpful terms and equate it with mechanics: rewriting is proofreading, checking grammar and spelling, and replacing words with better words. Others define rewriting in negative terms: rewriting is looking for errors and blemishes and eliminating them.

As long as you hold any of these beliefs, rewriting will be an unproductive pain. Instead, adopt a new mindset:

Rewriting is rethinking, experimentation, adventure, boldly going where no first draft has gone before.

Rewriting is positive, not negative: You're enriching and expanding, not correcting; instead of deleting, you add.

Rewriting, like writing, fries the biggest fish first. You give first priority to the big deals—Do I really believe this? What else does my reader need from me?—and last priority to cosmetics like spelling and grammar rules.

Rewriting is *liberating*. Feel free to toss out stuff from the first draft; in fact, feel free to toss out most of the first draft and start anew. Feel free to add material that you hadn't even encountered when you wrote the first draft. I recently had a student bring to class a first draft in which she was arguing that despite claims that America's a "melting pot," in reality, people hang with people much like themselves. It just so happened that the day before, the producers of the TV reality show *Survivor* had announced that in the new season the "tribes" would be organized by *ethnicity*, and one of her classmates described an article she read about it. This led to a lively class discussion, and afterward the student writer rushed home to begin revising so that she could include the *Survivor* example as part of her argument.

How to Feel About Rules

Before we start revising, let's clear something up. This book offers you a few thousand rules of revision. How much allegiance do you owe them? Do you *have to* follow them? Is a rule ever wrong?

There are two extreme attitudes that don't help. The first says, "I am a student; I must obey." The second says, "Hey, writing is creative—I'm above rules." The first reduces you to marionette status, the second suggests that you're not thinking about your reader.

What works is something in between. First, writing consists of two large stages: the creative stage (composing) and the corrective stage (editing and polishing). Your attitude toward rules differs for each. In the creative stage (from first thoughts through brainstorming, free writing, drafting, and revising), follow these principles:

> Do what works.
> Something "works" if it gets you the results you want.
> Break a rule when breaking a rule gets you the results you want.
> Break a rule when you have a good reason for breaking a rule.
> When you break a rule, know you're breaking it.
> Follow rules unless there's a good reason not to.
> If you're not sure what to do, try following the rule—it might help.

In other words, a rule is a tool. Use it the way you use a crowbar—when it helps you out of a jam. But that means you must know what your *purpose* is. If you find yourself saying, "Hmmm—should I use a hammer or a sewing machine here?" you've lost sight of what you're trying to accomplish.

In the corrective/editing stage (spelling, grammar, formatting, following the boss's instructions), think another way. Here, follow rules slavishly. It makes no sense to say, "I am an *artiste*—I am above indenting paragraphs or spelling 'accommodate' correctly." If you don't see why, the next time you play baseball, try telling the umpire you'd like four strikes, please, instead of three. See where that gets you. On the other hand, during batting practice (the creative stage), you should have been taking lots of swings and trying new stuff.

Revision Tools

Revision is hard because we don't know how to reduce it to concrete steps. We need a recipe ("First, combine all dry ingredients in a large bowl . . ."), and we need tools—concrete gizmos like measuring cups and sifters we can hold in our hand and do the steps with. Part Three of this book is a loose sort of recipe, and it will offer you a series of such tools. All craftspeople know you can never have enough tools, so I'm going to give you the whole hardware store. When we're done, our toolbox will consist of thesis, purpose, audience, tone, and style (all in Chapter 5); mapping, outlining, and abstracting (Chapter 6); tools for making drafts longer or shorter (Chapter 7); beginnings, conclusions, and titles (Chapter 8); peer feedback (Chapter 9); and editing (Chapter 10).

What do we know about tools?

1. Tools are for you, not the customer. When you sell the chair you made, you don't sell the saw and drill along with it. So don't write the outline for the reader or attach the thesis statement to the essay.

2. The purpose in using a tool is never simply to use the tool. Nobody ever said, "I think I'll go run my sewing machine for an hour." You run the sewing machine to make a dress. So if you outline just to make an outline or peer edit just to have a peer-editing experience, you've lost sight of your real purpose. With revision tools, your purpose is always *to produce a better draft*, and if you don't end up with that you wasted your tool time.

Rule 2 may sound obvious, but in fact writers make this mistake all the time. They'll take a draft, outline it, maybe even learn some interesting things from the outline, leave the draft largely unchanged, and say, "See, Teacher, I outlined," as if the act itself should be admired.

3. Using a tool takes skill, which comes with practice. Even a hammer takes years to learn to handle well, as anyone who has watched a master carpenter can tell you. So we have to expect to put in some time learning to use a thesis statement or peer-editing session.

4. Tools don't make the project good by themselves. Even if I'm the world's greatest user of a sewing machine, the machine by itself can't make the dress beautiful. Tools just make the work easier—it's hard to sew cloth or shape wood with your bare hands. So a thesis statement will help you make a great essay, but it won't make the essay great. You still need talent, inspiration, passion, and the like.

Diagnostic Tools

Some of the tools we're going to master belong to a special category of tools called diagnostics: tools that provide you with data you use to draw conclusions—the way tape measures, thermometers, CAT scans, and blood tests do. A thermometer tells you if you have a fever. An abstract tells you if a draft has any transition problems.

We know lots of interesting things about diagnostic tools:

1. Diagnostic tools see things we can't see. CAT scans see inside your brain. Outlines see inside your essay.

2. The diagnostic tool makes the problem concrete, so we can figure out what to do about it. It changes "I don't feel well" into "I have mononucleosis." It changes "This draft seems choppy" into "The sentences are too short."

3. Diagnostic tools always must be *read*, and the reading requires training. First our dad has to show us how to read the thermometer; then we have to know that 98.6 equals normal. Reading writers' tools means answering questions like, What can I learn from this outline? What is the thesis statement telling me about the draft? And that takes practice.

4. Diagnostic tools don't tell you what to do. A tape measure tells you how long the board is; it can't tell you how long the board should be. A thesis statement or an outline will let you see what's going on in the draft. That's its only job. It's your job to take that insight and decide what, if anything, you should do about it. Stylistic analysis will tell you your sentences are short. Only you can decide if you should make them longer. But you need to know the sentences are short before you can make that decision.

Making Your Own Tools

Writers' tools differ from shop tools in one important way: Shop tools are made by Black and Decker and other manufacturers; writers' tools you make yourself. You build the thesis statement or the outline. Then you use it, by learning from it and applying what you learned when you revise. This two-step model contains three vital implications:

1. We have to build the tool correctly, or all the information the tool gives us will be unreliable.

2. We have to do *both* steps. Making the saw is merely a preamble to the real work of making the chair. It's easy to do just Step 1 and quit—"See, Teacher, I made the outline! Am I done now?"

3. A problem can crop up in Step 1, in Step 2, or in the draft. You need to know in which one of the three the problem lies. If the problem lies in Step 1, you fix it by repairing the tool (rewriting the thesis statement, for instance). If the problem lies in Step 2, you fix it by learning to interpret the data better. And if the problem lies in the draft, you fix it by revising.

Rule 3 is usually obvious in life. If you take your temperature and the thermometer reads 103 degrees, you don't blame the thermometer for reading so high, since the tool is just doing its job and the problem lies in your body. But in writing, we love to blame our tools for revealing problems in our drafts. For instance, when students are asked to outline their essays and then to critique the outline, they'll often say, "This outline is terrible, because it's choppy and confusing and boring." But probably the outline is doing its job, which is to reveal things about the draft, and it's the draft that is choppy, confusing, and boring.

Revision in Four Steps

Revision is a messy process, so we're going to reduce it to four steps. Step 1: Trouble-shoot thesis, purpose, audience, tone, and style (this chapter). Step 2: Trouble-shoot organization (Chapter 6). Step 3: Get peer feedback (Chapter 9). Step 4: Edit for grammar and mechanics (Chapter 10). The first step is discussed in the rest of this chapter.

Thesis, Purpose, Audience, Tone, and Style

The five most powerful diagnostic tools at a reviser's disposal are the thesis statement ("What am I saying?"), the purpose statement ("Why am I saying it?"), the definition of audience ("Who am I talking to?"), the definition of tone ("What mood is this essay in?"), and the definition of style ("How do I want to dress this essay to present it to the world?"). These are what the hammer and saw are to the carpenter. You'll use them every day of your writing life.

Of course, you've been working with your thesis, purpose, audience, tone, and style, at least unconsciously, since the essay project quickened in your brain. Now it's time to *re*-consider them. Most writers have a sense of these things when they begin writing, but they never lock them in, and when better ones come along they welcome them. Staying committed to your first thesis is like marrying the first person you go out with—it would be a miracle if you ended up with the best one for you. And demanding that you have a big important message before you start writing is a great way to give yourself writer's block.

How soon you arrive at firm answers to the five questions depends a lot on what kind of writing you're doing. Technical or scientific writing often is sure of purpose, audience, tone, and style long before the writing begins, when the experiment or project is first being designed. Argumentative writing or writing in the humanities may not discover the final version of the answers until a very late draft. If you write down your thesis when you start and promise to stick to it through thick and thin, you're just promising to *not learn anything* during the drafting and revising. "How can I know what I think until I see what I've written?" writing teacher James Britten says.

Topic: A Brief Review

Making the tool. We talked about topics earlier. Of course your essay will have a topic—it's impossible to write without writing about *something*—but topic is next to worthless as a revision tool. The only slight value in topic making comes from *narrowing the topic* by adding detail. Here, more is better. Begin with a topic label for your essay: "Education." Now add detail: "Problems in education." Keep adding detail, making the topic statement longer, until you can add no more: "How to make public education interesting to a generation of children raised on adrenaline movies and video games."

Using the tool. Since the topic statement is next to useless, make it useful by turning it into a *thesis sentence:* Just add a verb:

Noun/Topic	→	Thesis Sentence
Affirmative Action	→	Affirmative Action is a cancer on American society.
Rudeness of young people	→	Young people are no ruder today than they were in the past.

Thesis

The revision tool with the biggest bang for your buck is the thesis statement. Always begin your revision work with it. Your thesis is the statement at the heart of the essay—the topic sentence, the core, the point, the lesson, the moral, the content in a flash, the *one* thing you have to say. Here are theses for three of the essays in this book:

> "Given the Chance" (p. 269); The State of California's commitment to drug rehabilitation programs is so minimal that it's impossible for social service people to help those who need it.

> "Why?" (p. 270); Getting sickeningly drunk to celebrate your twenty-first birthday makes no sense, but we keep doing it.

> "Why I Never Cared for the Civil War" (p. 367); Traditional ways of teaching school are boring and don't work, but there are powerful, exciting alternatives.

Making the tool. Since the thesis statement has a great gift for pointing out when we aren't really saying anything, there is a temptation to build it wrong so we can escape its frightening revelations. Obey the following tool-making rules strictly:

1. *A thesis is one complete sentence and only one.* Not a noun phrase, however large, and not two sentences, because writing a thesis is the moment when you demand to know what's at the *center*, and there can be only one center.

2. *A thesis is a declarative sentence*—not a question, since theses are *answers*.

3. *A thesis must fit well into the following template:* "In this essay I say, '_____.'" Thus the sentence "This essay explains how to change the oil in your car" isn't a thesis.

4. *A thesis should contain or imply the word "because"*—to force you to have at least one reason.

5. *A thesis should contain or imply the word "should"*—to force you to think about what you're trying to *do*, not just *say*, with the essay.

6. *A thesis must summarize the* entire *essay*—all parts of the essay must serve to support it.

7. *The thesis is almost never present as a sentence in the essay.* Don't pick whichever sentence in the draft is closest to your thesis and call it your thesis, and don't feel obligated to declare your thesis somewhere in the essay. Compose the thesis in your head, and then use it in the essay in whatever way works.

Occasionally, a writer will write out the thesis in a sentence or two and hand it to the reader. In George Orwell's "Shooting an Elephant," he tells how he, as a minor British official in India, was forced by the pressure of an expectant mob to shoot an elephant that had gotten loose from its owner. He tells you exactly what the lesson of the story is:

> And it was at this moment, as I stood there with the rifle in my hands, that I first grasped the hollowness, the futility of the white man's dominion in the East. Here was I, the white man with his gun, standing in front of the unarmed native crowd—seemingly the leading actor of the piece; but in reality I was only an absurd puppet pushed to and fro by the will of those yellow faces behind. I perceived in this moment that *when the white man turns tyrant it is his own freedom that he destroys.* [the thesis is italicized].

But you can spread the thesis throughout a couple of paragraphs, imply it indirectly, or keep it to yourself—see "Why?" (p. 270) and "Dad" (p. 207) for examples. Similarly, you can put the thesis in the first sentence of the essay, the last, or nowhere. You're the boss. The only place you're obliged to have the thesis is *in your head.*

Some audiences and purposes demand an explicit statement of thesis, and others don't. Scientific and technical writing always states its thesis up front; fiction rarely states it at all.

8. *Every essay has a thesis, including informative essays.* In an informative essay, the thesis may not be the heart and soul of the piece, but it's there, however quietly. Here are theses for two of the informative essays in this book:

> "The Last Stop for America's Buses" (p. 363): If you understand how Mexico's bus system works, your vacation will be less expensive, more exciting, and a lot more educational.

> "Why Falling in Love Feels So Good" (p. 365): With a little knowledge about your own body chemistry, you can pick a mate wisely and avoid a lifetime of unhappiness or a messy divorce.

Using the tool. Once your thesis is well made, you employ it by asking it questions and answering the questions. The place to begin is at the beginning: *"Did I say anything?"* If the answer is yes, go on to questions like

> Did I say anything interesting?
> Anything useful?
> Anything risky?
> Anything new?
> Anything important to the reader?
> Anything important to me?

But don't limit yourself to a set list of specific questions; instead, as with all diagnostic tools, try to look at the thesis and learn from it whatever it can teach you. Ask, What's going on? What can I see here? What is this telling me about the draft? What seems to be going well and what's going badly?

Remember, a diagnostic tool can't tell you what to do (p. 71), so don't assume there are universally right answers to your questions. Not all great essays have earth-shaking theses (the "I hate eggs" essay on p. 39 doesn't). Not all great essays have "shoulds" in their theses (the ones mentioned on p. 74 don't). Not all great essays have theses that can be stated simply in words ("Dad" on p. 207). Not all great essays have theses ("how to" essays often don't).

Purpose

Our second diagnostic tool, the purpose statement, answers questions like

> Why am I writing this?
> What do I hope to accomplish?
> What do I want?
> What do I want the reader to do?

Like the thesis statement, it's small but mighty, and since it is terrifically revealing, writers will often go to great lengths to escape its lessons.

When we start thinking about why we write, most of our purposes are unhelpful ones:

> To complete the assignment
> To get a good grade
> To write a good essay
> To learn about the topic
> To practice researching, thinking, and writing
> To tell the reader something

The problem with all these purposes is *they don't tell you what to do.* A writer is constantly faced with decisions: How should I say this? Should I put this piece of information in or not? Should I do X, then Y, or the other way around? *The clearer a purpose is, the more it answers such writer's questions.* If I say, "My purpose is to write a great essay," that purpose answers no questions at all. If I say, "I want to make the reader sad," that purpose helps a little. If I say, "I want to capture the essence of my neighbor's daughter, Dee," I can start answering some specific questions about what I want to do. And if I say, "I want to capture Dee's ambivalence. She's absolutely brilliant but is reluctant to let people see that side of her, and I want to use that example to show how conflicted young girls often are in a culture that's afraid of smart females," I've got a purpose that will tell me exactly what to do.

Making the tool. Here are four rules to follow to ensure you're making the purpose statement right.

1. *Make the purpose statement an infinitive verb:* "My purpose is *to expose* the contemptible cowardice of the campus newspaper staff." You can start the sentence many ways: "I wrote in order to . . . ," "My goal was to . . . ,": "I want to . . . ," "I intend to . . . ," "I'm going to . . .". Any of these phrases will lead you to end with a verb, which is what you want.

2. *Ask "Why?" and keep asking "Why?"* Purposes come in series. The result you hope to cause by writing will cause something else, which in turn will cause something else: My purpose is to convince the reader to vote Republican in the next presidential election, *so that* the Republican candidate will win, *so that* he will increase defense spending, *so that* America will have a strong defense, *so that* we will remain safe from the threat of military attack, *so that* I don't end up in some concentration camp.

3. *Have at least two purposes*: to get something for yourself and to give the reader something he wants or should want. Humans are selfish; if there isn't something in it for you, you won't write, and if there isn't something in it for the reader, he won't read. Ask yourself how each of you is going to profit.

4. *Make sure your purpose is a version of the universal writer's purpose: to do something to the reader.*

Using the tool. Once you've written a well-formed purpose statement, the hard work is behind you. First, ask the central question: "Am I clear on what I'm trying to accomplish?" Then move on to questions like

Is my purpose constant throughout the essay?
Does it account for everything in the draft?
Is it important to me?
Will it be important to the reader?

Audience

A purpose is always an intent to do something to *someone.* The clearer you are about who it is, the better you'll write. Chapter 2 talked about this. Let's take it further.

Making the tool. Write a paragraph or so detailing everything you know about whom you're writing to. It sounds simple-minded, but don't sell it short. The audience definition is more powerful than it at first appears. And it's harder to produce than you'd think. The first time you try it, you usually end up saying something useless like "I'm writing to anyone who would like to read this essay."

We're audience-unconscious because a sense of audience in our *reading* is like air: it's always there, so we take it for granted. But the instant a writer fails to take us into consideration or assumes we're someone we're not, the significance of audience becomes deafeningly clear. Here is the opening of an essay that doesn't know who we are:

> Dance forms are characterized by the use of particular movements. The various forms of dance require differing degrees of body mathematics usage, strength, endurance, practiced ability, innate ability, and mental concentration.
>
> Butoh dance movement requires all of the above. The precision of body placement, the strength needed for sustained positions, the endurance necessary to sustain positions, the repetitive exercises to build strength and endurance, the natural ability to execute movement, and the high level of concentration are the components of the body and mind for the Butoh dancer. The development of these enable the dancer to tap inner and outer spheres of energy movement. The physical body is the initiator, receptor, and giver of these energy realms.

Our first question may be, what does this mean? But another question must be answered first: who is this for, and how is she supposed to use it? Once the essay declares an audience and purpose, meaning becomes a handleable problem:

> **Your First Butoh Concert**
> If you're a long-time lover of dance, you probably think you've seen it all. But the first time you attend a concert of Butoh, the new, exciting blend of Eastern philosophy and Western modern-dance technique, your immediate response may be, "But they're not *dancing* at all!" Well, they really are, but they aren't doing anything you're used to calling dance. Butoh looks odd, because it thinks a different way about movement than other schools of dance do, but once I walk you through it you may find it's something you want to see again and again—and perhaps try yourself.

Here's the first paragraph of another essay, titled "Make Them Pay," that forgot to think about audience:

> There are many people in this world that are against the death penalty. They think it is wrong, inhumane, cruel, and unusual, etc. They feel that no one has the right to take someone else's life. But what about the life that was taken by the criminal in question? What gave them the right to take an innocent life? I feel that the death penalty is sufficient punishment for violent crimes such as

murder and rape. Crimes like these are repulsive and should be considered crimes against humanity. Those who commit them should pay with their lives, not only as punishment for their sick mistakes, but also as a lesson to others that such offenses will not be tolerated in this society.

Naturally, this writer has aimed her argument at people who oppose the death penalty, but she hasn't really thought that through. The writer thinks, for instance, that if she can convince her readers that these crimes are heinous they will agree with her position. But most people who oppose the death penalty would already acknowledge that the crimes for which it is a sentence are "repulsive" and "against humanity." What this writer needs to do is learn about her audience: *what are the reasons* her audience is against the death penalty? Then she can begin to address those arguments.

So the first challenge is to convince ourselves that every piece of writing—from naval histories to menus to rental agreements—has an audience that is real and specific and that good communicators filter everything they say through a sense of who's listening.

If you doubt this, just take a look at the magazines on the racks at your school bookstore. There are publications for people who show golden retrievers, who restore Volkswagens, who collect baseball cards. Or think of it this way: imagine you've just flunked your first college midterm, and you decide to write three different e-mails explaining what happened—one to your parents, one to your best friend, and one to the instructor, asking if you can take the test again. Would you write just one letter and send it to all three? I didn't think so.

Using the tool. Now that you're a believer, follow these guidelines as you write your audience definition:

1. *The audience is never you.* However much you may feel that you're writing to educate yourself or writing to figure out what you think or writing to get something off your chest, as soon as you give it to someone else to read, you're saying, "I think this will profit *you.*" And then you need to know who that someone is.

2. *Audience must always be chosen.* There is no such thing as the only or the right or the inevitable audience for a piece of writing. You choose audience the way you choose thesis.

Let's assume that the trustees of your state university have just decided to raise the tuition . . . again. As one of the students, you decide to write an essay decrying this. Your purpose is clear: to stop the fee hike. Now, whom should you write to? There are many groups who have a say in the matter: students, parents, college administrators, state legislators (since they control the state university's purse strings), teachers, and citizens (since they elect the legislators). Within these groups are smaller groups. Within the student body, for instance, there's a group of students who think it's OK for rising costs to be borne in part by the students; there's a group that's vehemently opposed; there's a group that doesn't care; there's a group that hasn't heard about the issue; and there's a group that's on the fence.

Each audience has to be talked to in a different way. The students who are vehemently opposed to fee hikes need to be preached to like brothers; those who think the hike's a good idea need to be persuaded they're wrong; administrators need to be shown alternative ways to pay the university's bills; citizens need to be convinced that it's ultimately to the benefit of society that bright kids can afford to go to college. Writing to all these audiences at once is nearly impossible. So choose. And be especially careful to avoid those circular audience definitions that appear to define audience but really say nothing, like "I'm writing to anyone interested in what I'm writing about."

3. *Smaller means easier.* The narrower your audience, the easier it is to write to, because writing is about controlling the reader—and the smaller the group, the easier it is to predict how they will react. Your easiest audience is the smallest: your best friend. As the audience enlarges, the diversity of experience, tastes, values, and beliefs grows, the reactions become more unpredictable, and the challenge of controlling the audience grows. The hardest audience is "everyone," since "everyone" is almost totally unpredictable; but oddly, that's the one students are drawn to. Would "everyone" be interested in a review of the new Spearhead CD? Would "everyone" know what you meant if you wrote, "Sometimes you can improve performance by replacing your exhaust manifolds"?

There is a kind of writing whose audience is defined no more clearly than "every American citizen interested in social issues." It's what we see in *Newsweek* and *Time.* And since we see such writing all the time, we're in danger of concluding that most writing is to such audiences. But most writing isn't. For every *Newsweek,* there are a hundred specialized magazines that are just for Mac owners, or dirt bike aficionados, or scuba divers. For every national magazine, there are a thousand local club newsletters. For every newsletter, there are a thousand letters to friends. So the vast bulk of writing in our world is to narrowly specified audiences. And the essayists in *Time* and *Newsweek* are the best writers in the country. They have to be, because writing to "everyone" is that tough.

4. *Make the writing easy by choosing an audience like yourself, or make it useful by choosing an audience unlike yourself.* The more like you the audience is, the easier it is to write, because the easier it is to guess how they'll respond. That's why it's so easy to write e-mails to friends. Most writers know this and instinctively write as if all read-

ers are exactly like them—thus the number of essays I get about how much fun it was to get bombed last weekend. The problem is that people just like us can't profit much from our writing, because it has nowhere new to take them—they're already where we are (also see Chapter 14). If we're writing against tuition hikes, the administrators are the hardest to write to because they're least like you, but that means there's more to be gained by winning them over.

5. *Go beyond the simple label.* Most writers, when they first start trying to describe audiences, stop at noun labels: "My audience is college students"; "My audience is working mothers." That's not enough. Think again about magazines. Here's how the editors of *Redbook* magazine describe their readers: "*Redbook* addresses young married women, ages 28–44. Most of our readers are married with children 10 and under; over 60 percent work outside the home." So, ask questions about your readers:

> What gender are they?
> How old are they?
> How much money do they have?
> How much formal education do they have?
> Do they have a sense of humor?
> How sophisticated are their English language skills?
> How do they feel about seeing the word *asshole* in print?
> How conservative or liberal are they?
> What is their value system?
> How close- or open-minded are they about the issue in question?
> How interested are they in this issue?
> How well informed about it are they?
> What do they need to know from me?
> What do they want from me?
> How are they going to perceive me?
> How will they react to what I'm saying?

We always know much more about our audiences than we at first can say. John Mercer's audience in "The Last Stop for America's Buses" (A Collection of Good Writing) isn't just "people traveling to Mexico." They're people who haven't been to Mexico but would like to go, who know nothing about Mexican public transportation, who are shy about going because they're worried about being out of their depth, but who like adventure and aren't looking for luxury and security. They're probably young or middle-aged, and they travel to encounter the culture. They know very little about the Mexican national character. They have a sense of humor about the little disasters of traveling. And so on.

There's one question you can't avoid answering: how much does your audience already know? Because every time you tell the reader something, you're assuming she doesn't already know it, and every time you *don't* tell her something, you're assuming she does. If I say, "Next, remove the tire's lug nuts with a tire iron," I must either explain or not explain what lug nuts and tire irons are, and either choice requires a decision about my audience's prior knowledge.

6. *More is better.* Since we want to know as much about our audience as we can, the longer a definition of audience gets, the better it must be. So keep adding detail to your definition as long as you can.

Using the tool. Reread the draft, keeping what you now know about your audience in mind—imagine *saying* everything to them as you read, and imagine their reaction: "How will they react when I say *this*?" You can judge the quality of the draft by the clarity of your answers: If you have a pretty good idea what the reader would say in response to every line, how he would feel, the draft is sound.

Tone

Tone is the emotional mood of the writing and is described by the same *adjectives* we use to describe people's moods or personalities: angry, sweet, frustrated, formal, snide, silly, cold, melancholy, professorial, stuffy, hip, and so on.

In school we tend to be deaf to tone. Odd, since in life mood is the first thing we notice. Yet often students tend to notice tone last, if at all, when they read. They'll talk about on an essay's content for hours, but not notice it's funny. And of the five big issues—thesis, purpose, audience, tone, and style—tone is the one students have typically not thought much about. So train yourself to be tone-sensitive when you read and when you write. You already know how to "do" tone—you know how to sound angry or sad. It's just a matter of giving yourself permission.

How important is tone? It's more than garnish—often it's more important than content. People often care more about how others "feel" to them than about what they say. Every time there's a presidential debate, we see that Americans care more about how a candidate's personality comes across (does he seem warm? does he seem trustworthy?) than about his political platform.

Mastering tone begins with the realization that *you can't not have one*, any more than a person can be in *no* mood. If you ask someone how he feels and he says, "I feel nothing," you know he's in denial—and so are you if you say your writing has no tone. Any set of words will create a tone, just as any set of clothes will make some impression, so your only choices are to control tone or be out of control. Don't strive for blandness unless the boss orders you to. Few people seek to feel nothing, few people say beige is their favorite color, few love Pablum above all other foods, and few people read to feel nothing. So don't strive for tonal neutrality unless you're sure your purposes call for it—as in legal depositions and medical research. For most of us, emotion is good. The most common problem with writing is that it's too flat, *so push toward the brighter colors*—outrage, impishness, absurdity, fright, joy.

Once we grant that tone exists, we like to escape responsibility for choosing the tone of our writing, saying, "My tone is forced on me by my subject matter (or my thesis)." Never. *Tone is chosen,* just like audience. Any subject matter and any message can be presented in any tone. Dramatist Craig Wright has written a comedy about the day after September 11 (*Recent Tragic Events*), and he was also the head writer for HBO's *Six Feet Under*, a television show about undertakers!

Cultivate a large vocabulary of tones. Tones are tools, and the more tools we have, the more powerful we are. Writing everything in the same tone is as impractical as hitting every golf shot with the same club and as boring as always wearing khakis. Anyway, tone is where the fun is. Imagine writing a letter to your bank telling them they've once again fouled up your checking account. Try several different tones:

> **Sarcastic:** I have to hand it to you guys—I never thought you'd find a new way to foul things up, but you have.

> **Sympathetic:** We all make mistakes—I know, I make them myself all day long. I appreciate the load of work you guys are under. I realize how it can happen, but you seem to have gotten my account confused with someone else's.

> **Indignant:** I have never in my twenty-five years as a businessman witnessed anything like the level of administrative incompetence that is the daily norm in your bank . . .

> **Suppliant:** I don't want to make a nuisance of myself, but might I ask that you re-examine your records for my account? There seems to be a mistake somewhere, and I know it's probably mine, but . . .

Choose the tone that works—which always means the tone that gets the reaction you want from your reader. In other words, tone is dictated by purpose. Sometimes anger works for you; sometimes it works against you. Only a clear sense of purpose (and of audience) will tell you which situation applies in a particular essay. If you're trying to jolt the audience out of its complacency, you may want to be obnoxious, offensive, and profane, like Sinead O'Connor tearing up a picture of the Pope on television. If you're trying to soothe a patient just before his open-heart surgery, clinical objectivity is probably called for, since you want the patient as numb as possible.

Making the tool. A statement of tone often starts with a single adjective: "This essay feels _____"—informal, formal, informative, educational, personal, funny, comic, angry. But a tone is the mirror of a personality talking, and personalities can be very complex. So push beyond the single generic word. As with topic and audience, more is better. If your tone is "funny," ask, "What kind of funny?" Perhaps it's "slightly sarcastic, gently teasing, a little grumpy but basically good-humored and ultimately sympathetic."

Using the tool. Using a definition of tone comes down to asking two questions. First, "Is this tone intriguing/touching/powerful?" If it isn't, you may need to rewrite the essay in some color other than beige. Second, "How does this tone serve my purpose?" Your answer must be in terms of audience response: "This tone will make my reader react *thus*, and that's the reaction I want." If you struggle in answering, the problem may be in your purpose—if you aren't sure what you're trying to do, you can't tell if the tone will help or not.

Style

Writing style is like clothing—the decorative covering we put over the content. This tells us everything we need to know about it:

Style is independent of content. You can say any message in any style, just as you can put any sort of clothing on any body. Anyone can wear a tutu or a wetsuit or a belly-dancing costume. You may get laughed at or run from, but that's a different issue.

This is the most important lesson about style to learn, because writers defend bad writing by insisting that what they say determines how they say it. "I have to be stuffy and pretentious, because I'm talking about this very serious issue," they say. Never.

Style is chosen. You decide what style to use, the way you decide what clothes to wear. Even if you got dressed this morning without thinking about it, you decided. You could have worn something else. You're responsible for the choice.

You can't *not* choose. You can't write without style, any more than you can dress in no way at all. Whatever language you use will have a certain sentence length, be passive or active, use Latinate words or avoid them. Doing what's "in" or what everyone else is doing is still a choice. Since you can't not choose, you want to control your choosing.

Style sends a message. Some believe it shouldn't be that way, but it's true: the way you use language, like the way you dress, is heard as a message by everyone who sees it. Style, someone famously once said, is the subtlest level of meaning. If you wear your baseball cap backward, people will assume you're telling them something. If you wear a business suit, people will assume you're telling them something.

Choose your style for the effect it has on the reader. There is no good or right style, only styles that produce the response you want in the reader and those that don't.

Remember, controlling effect never equals doing what the reader wants. You *may* want to please, but you don't *have to*. You can wear a clown suit, or nothing, to class if you're willing to take the predictable reaction.

Alternatives equal power. The more ways you can dress, the more places you can go and the more things you can do. If you can only wear a T-shirt and jeans, you can't go to the ball. If you don't own a wetsuit, you can't go scuba diving. Similarly, the more ways you can write, the more responses you can provoke and the more things you can do with your writing.

Most of us choose by habit. We write the way we dress—the way we always do, without thinking about it much. This is giving up our power to choose and thus control our audience.

Style is fun. Trying out different words and sentence structures should feel just like playing dress up or trying on clothes at the mall: it's a game. Try on the clown suit, sample a few wigs, slip into the slinky cocktail dress. . . .

How to master a style. Style is a series of *choices:* Do you make the sentences long or short? Do you write in first person or third person? To control a stylistic choice, you have to do two things:

Believe you have the choice. English offers you the options. Everyone knows that English will let you write long sentences or short ones, for instance. Sometimes it isn't so obvious. Not all of us realize that English will let you write passive sentences or active sentences, and almost no one outside the academy realizes that in English you write Latinate words, Romance words, and Germanic words.

Many writers say, "Sure, I know that English makes it possible to write in concrete language and short sentences, but I can't do it here—I'm writing about serious, sophisticated stuff, so I *need* big words and long, complex sentence structure." Any time you tell yourself that your topic or your message dictates your style choice, you're wrong. You can say anything about anything in any style.

Understand the effect of your choices. You must know what happens if you do it a certain way. If you make your sentences short, how will readers react? If you make them long, how will they react?

As with all predicting of human behavior, this is an inexact science. If you wear your baseball cap backward, some people will react with "Oooh, he's cool" and some with "What a doofus." If your teacher wears a tie to work, some students will react with "He's a competent professional" and some with "He's stuffy and boring." As always, expect readers' responses to be a lot like your own: how do *you* feel when you read a lot of short sentences?

Let's practice these steps, using three elements of style: sentence length, Latinate diction, and concretion.

Sentence length. First we must believe that sentence length is something we can control independent of content. We can prove this to ourselves either by taking a passage of very long sentences and dividing them up (that's easy) or by taking a passage of very short sentences and combining them (that's harder). Here's a passage from a student essay about Buddy Bolden, the legendary blues man, in various sentence lengths from short to very long:

> *Short*   There are some things historians agree on. Bolden played cornet. No one could play like him. His fellow band members said so. Even Jelly Roll Morton said so. Morton was egocentric. Bolden worked as a barber. He had his own business. By noon, he was working on his second bottle of whiskey. You had to go to him before noon if you wanted a decent hair cut. He gradually went insane. He was committed to a state mental hospital. That was in Louisiana. He was committed in 1907. He died there twenty-four years later. (15 sentences)

> *Medium*   There are some things historians agree on. Bolden played cornet like no one before or after him could do, for one thing. His fellow band members said so. Even Jelly Roll Morton said so, and he was egocentric. Bolden worked as a barber and had his own business. By noon, he was working on his second bottle of whiskey, so you had to go to him before noon if you wanted a decent hair cut. He gradually went insane and was committed to the East Louisiana State Hospital. He was

committed in 1907 and died there twenty-four years later. (8 sentences)

One sentence (which is how the student wrote it) Historians agree that Bolden played the cornet as no one before or after him was able to do (accounts of everyone from fellow band members to the egocentric Jelly Roll Morton confirm this), that he was self-employed as a barber (one to whom—if a decent haircut was important—you went before noon, by which time he was usually working on his second bottle of whiskey), and that he gradually went insane and was committed in 1907 to East Louisiana State Hospital, where he died twenty-four years later.

Listen to how sentences sound. Short sentences "feel" lots of different ways: earthy, plain, solid, masculine, childlike, simple-minded, choppy, wise, primitive, honest, blunt. Long sentences "feel" the opposite of all those: sophisticated, intelligent, intellectual, scholarly, clinical, educated, fluid, suave, subtle, deceptive, pretentious. Mid-length sentences feel in the middle. Armed with this knowledge, you can decide how you want to be "felt" and choose a length to produce that feeling. We can all break long sentences into shorter ones, but how do you combine short sentences to make longer ones? Consider a simple pair of sentences:

I went jogging yesterday. I saw a dead deer.

How many tools does English give us for combining these into one? The best-known is the *conjunction*:

I went jogging yesterday, *and* I saw a dead deer.

But conjunctions are just the beginning. Consider these possibilities:

When I went jogging yesterday, I saw a dead deer. (dependent clause)

Jogging yesterday, I saw a dead deer. (participial phrase)

During my run yesterday, I saw a dead deer. (prepositional phrase)

I went jogging yesterday; I saw a dead deer. (semicolon)

I went jogging yesterday, saw a dead deer, and . . . (compound verb)

The dead deer *that I saw* while jogging . . . (relative clause)

Any of these can be combined with any others:

When I saw a dead deer *during* my run yesterday . . . (dependent clause and prepositional phrase)

Now it's just a matter of forcing yourself to use the tools. Think like a skater in training: spend some time practicing axels, then some time practicing figure-eights. Work on turning sentences into participial phrases, then into dependent clauses, and so on.

Latinate diction. Few people have ever heard of Latinate diction, but it's perhaps the stylistic choice that packs the biggest wallop for readers. A brief history lesson: English is a Germanic language, which means it is descended from an ancient parent language spoken in Germany perhaps six thousand years ago. As a result, the ancient root of the vocabulary—words like *good, foot, dirt, water, mother,* and *eat*—are all Germanic and have been in the language from the beginning. These are the words that you learned first when you were growing up, the words you use most often and know the best. Centuries after that Germanic beginning, mostly between 1150 and 1800, English borrowed a lot of words from French and Latin. The French words were brought into English largely by contact with French high culture, so the French vocabulary in English tends to feel arty or genteel: *banquet, dine, fashion, genteel, cuisine, honor, virtue,* and *chef.* Our Latin vocabulary was brought into English by scholars and scientists, who were all reading books in Latin and trying to reform the English vocabulary so it would be as much like what they saw there as possible, so it feels scholarly, scientific, and clinical: *condition, instinctual, relativity, procedure, effective, factor, element, consideration, criterion,* and *process.*

You can say anything in any one of these three vocabularies, Germanic, French, or Latinate. Again, the way to prove this to yourself is to take passages using one of them and rewrite them in another:

> *Germanic:* I saw the guy who I think did it leave the place with two other white guys—I don't know who they were.
> *Latinate:* The alleged perpetrator was observed to exit the premises in the company of two unidentified male Caucasian individuals.

> *Latinate:* Violation of any of these statutes will result in immediate and permanent expulsion.
> *Germanic:* If you break any of these rules, we'll kick you out.

The effect of using French vocabulary turns out to be so minimal that we'll ignore it. But the effect of Latinate and Germanic vocabulary hits readers like a sledge hammer. Since we all learn Germanic vocabulary before we're seven years old, it remains associated with "the basics." Germanic writing feels earthy, strong, honest, childlike, male, "real"—all the things we said about short sentences, in fact. Since we learn our Latinate vocabulary primarily in school, and especially in college, it always feels professorial, intellectual, professionally competent, and fake. In addition, Latinate words are simply *harder* for us to understand, since we learn them later in life, so the more of them you use the harder a reader will have to work to understand you. If we use enough Latinate words, the style is distracting. It's like a stained-glass window, keeping your reader from seeing what's on the other side.

This is a very dangerous thing and an omnipresent cancer in our society. The disease goes by many names: BS, bureaucratic English, bureaucratese, political English, Pentagonese. Not surprisingly, the people with the most to hide and the greatest need to impress—the government, the military, advertising, the police, politicians, and all bureaucracies, including your college—use it the most.

And we all fall for it. Here's a highly Latinate passage. See how impressed you are by it, and how unimpressive its Germanic revision is?

> ***Latinate:*** Studies of a significant number of choice situations in the main conclude that when faced with an alternative between an object (either material or abstract) of lesser value and a high degree of certainty of attainment and an object of greater value and a low degree of certainty of attainment, the certainty of the former object renders the object a greater value than the potentially obtainable object. In fact, it has been shown that in cases where the value of the potentially obtainable object exceeded the value of the certainly obtainable object by a factor of two, the uncertainty of attainment still rendered the less valuable object the more profitable choice.

> ***Germanic:*** A bird in the hand is worth two in the bush.

So in the case of this stylistic feature, we can talk about how much is too much. The typical Latinate level of U.S. newspapers is 20 percent, which means one of every five words on the page is from Latin. Significantly less—10 percent or lower—will feel earthy or simple when we read it. Significantly more—30 percent or higher—will feel intellectually impressive and begin to impair our ability to understand. Forty percent Latinity (four of every ten words) is incomprehensible to most of us. So unless you're engaged in an intentional snow job, keep your Latinate level below 30 percent. But don't strive for a percentile below 10 percent either, unless you want to sound like a child.

Concretion. *Concretions* are things you can perceive with the five senses—tastes, smells, sights, sounds, touches. The opposite of concretions are *abstractions:* thoughts, opinions, feelings, ideas, concepts. By extension, in language concretions are words or passages that *evoke* sensation—they make you feel like you're smelling, seeing, and so on, when you read them; abstractions don't. Concretions and abstractions can be nouns, verbs, adjectives, or adverbs.

Concretions: swim, jump, door, shoe, nose, crash, prickly, wet, slowly, saunter, trumpet, Hollandaise sauce, CD

Abstractions: idea, think, love, wonder, consideration, problem, anger, threaten, perversely, extreme, honest

As with all style features, we begin by convincing ourselves that any message can be said either in concretions or in abstractions. Most writers think that certain writing tasks are inherently concrete, like describing a car crash or showing how to bake a cake, and certain tasks are inherently abstract, like discussing philosophy or religion. To break down that prejudice, take "inherently" concrete or abstract statements and translate them into the opposite style:

Abstract: Modern society suffers from alienation.
Concrete: All of us walk through this world rubbing shoulders but never really touching.

Concrete: The car skidded off the slick macadam, rolled twice, and folded itself around a three-foot-thick oak.
Abstract: A terrible accident occurred.

Abstract: Gun ownership can lead to the possibility of serious injury.
Concrete: If you buy a gun, there's a good chance you'll shoot your foot off.

Concrete: His eyes were twitching, his hands were trembling, his brow was coated with sweat, and he kept pacing back and forth mumbling to himself.
Abstract: He was nervous.

Concrete language, because it involves the senses, is *emotionally intense*—it makes us feel. It's *easier to understand*, because humans are primarily feelers, secondarily thinkers. It's *compelling*—we believe it—because we feel like we're getting the facts, the actual evidence, instead of just the opinion. And finally, concretions are *fun*, because feeling is fun.

So where would you ever want to write abstractly? In school, where teachers are trying to get you to master abstract thought. In places where you want to remain rational and concretions would reduce the conversation to an emotional brawl, as in discussions of volatile issues like race or abortion. In places where clinical objectivity is a must, as in medical writing or reporting on scientific experiments. When you're applying for government grants, and you want to appear as professorial as possible. So as always you need both styles.

To control our concretion level, we first must be sure we can distinguish between concrete and abstract on the page. Begin by asking if you can perceive it with your senses. Be careful: we tend to say things like "I could *see* she was angry," but in fact you can't—you can hear that someone is shouting, see she's red in the face, and feel she's beating you with her fists, so those are all concretions, but anger is a *conclusion* you draw from the concrete data, so anger is an abstraction. And don't assume that if the word makes you feel, then it's concrete—lots of abstract ideas, like *racism* or *Christianity*, evoke strong feelings.

There are other measuring sticks:

> Most concretions are visual, so ask yourself if you can *draw* the word—if so, it's concrete.
>
> Ask yourself, "How do I know?" If you say, "The door is red" and ask yourself how you know, the only possible answers are "Because I looked" or "Because I have eyes." When you find the "How do I know?" questions producing only obvious or silly answers like this, you're dealing with a concretion. But if I say, "America is becoming more uncivil" and ask myself how I know, I realize I need *evidence* to back that up, and that's a sign that I've got an abstraction.
>
> Imagine you're serving on a jury and a witness makes a statement under oath. If the attorney can ask the witness to back up the statement with evidence or proof, it's an abstraction; if not, it's a concretion.

Once you know for sure whether a passage is concrete or not, how do you make it concrete if it isn't? Here are eleven ways.

1. Ask, "What's my evidence? How do I know?" and write down the answers. You write, "He loves me," ask how you know, and write down, "He leaves little love notes on Post-its in secret places, like in my physics class notebook, so I discover them when I'm in class."

2. Ask, "Who's doing what to whom?" Talk in terms of *people*. Almost everything you write is about humans doing things—express it in those terms. "Practice charity" becomes "Hand the next homeless person you see ten dollars." "The usage of a dictionary is encouraged" becomes "I encourage teachers to use a dictionary."

J. M. Barrie, who wrote *Peter Pan*, knew the power of people, so *Peter Pan* begins with this note:

> Do you know that this book is part of the J. M. Barrie "Peter Pan Request"? This means that J. M. Barrie's royalty on this book goes to help the doctors and nurses to cure the children who are lying ill in the Great Ormond Street Hospital for Sick Children in London.

People appear in those two sentences eight times: you, J. M. Barrie, Peter Pan, J. M. Barrie, doctors, nurses, children, and sick children. Take the people out, and the loss hits you like a chill wind:

> All royalties from the sale of this book are donated to further medical research in pediatrics and to help defer the cost of indigent pediatric medical care.

3. Use "I" and "you." You and the reader are the two concretions you've always got.

4. Let people talk. All quotations are concrete, because they're *heard*. Quote the speech of the people you mention, even if you have to invent it.

5. Concretize your verbs. Verbs are the parts of speech most likely to go abstract, so we want to focus on them and force them to concretize. Abstract verbs are like *is, are, continue, accomplish, effect, involve, proceed, utilize, initiate, remain,* and *constitute*. Concrete verbs run, jump, smell, fall, shrink, and fly.

6. Particularize your concretions. Some concretions are better than others—more emotive, more colorful. *Move* is colorless, *slither* is colorful. The difference is one of *particularity*. To particularize a word, ask yourself, "In what way did it happen?" or "What kind of thing was it?"

Less lively	More lively
move	slither, slink, sashay, saunter, crawl, skip
car	ragtop, four-door, SUV, lowrider
horse	pinto, Clydesdale, swayback plow horse
hairdo	mullet, cornrows

Particulars are more persuasive, as every good salesperson knows: the more particulars, the more we're *sold* on what we read. When you read an ad for a powerboat that says,

> Kurtis Kraft 10-inch runner bottom, blown injected, 1/4-inch Velasco crank, Childs and Albert rods, Lenco clutch, Casale 871 Little Field blower, Enderle injection,

even if you don't know what any of that means, you're probably thinking, "It must be a great boat!"

7. Tell stories. Narratives encourage concretion, because they're usually about things *people did*.

8. Use the active voice. Passive constructions make the people disappear. In an *active* sentence, the doer is the subject: "George broke the chair." A *passive* construction—a form of *to be* plus a past participle—doesn't need to mention the doer at all: "The chair was broken."

There is one large exception to this rule. In scientific and technical writing, if you are describing a process—a step-by-step series of events—then *what was done* is all that matters and *who did it* is a distraction, so use the passive voice. Write, "The surface liquid was drained off and the residue transferred to a sterile Petri dish"; don't write, "One of my lab assistants, Pippi Carboy, drained off the surface liquid and Lance Credance, a post-doctoral fellow who shares the lab, transferred the residue to a sterile Petri dish."

9. Use metaphors. A metaphor is an implied comparison. Instead of stating an abstraction, you state a concretion that the abstraction is *like*. That sounds intimidating, but in fact you use metaphors ten thousand times a day. Instead of saying to your roommate, "Your living habits are filthy and revolting," you say, "You're a pig." You can't articulate clearly on a sleepy Monday morning, and instead of saying, "My mental processes are impaired," you say, "I can't jump-start my brain." Instead of saying, "That rock band is out of date," you say, "They're dinosaurs."

Everyday English is stiff with metaphors. In the world of sports, for instance, teams lock horns, fold, choke, run out of gas, get snakebit, and look over their shoulder. Players press too hard, go flat, carry teams, get swelled heads, rest on their laurels, and coast. Quarterbacks pick defenses apart and have to eat the ball, and pitchers throw smoke, pull the string, and nibble at the corners. But the best metaphors are the ones you make up yourself. An interviewer once asked Charlton Heston what Cecil B. DeMille, the legendary Hollywood director, was like, and Heston replied, "He cut a very large hole in the air."

To make up a metaphor, you just take the abstraction and ask yourself, "What physical process is this like? What do I see when I try to visualize it? How does it feel in the body? How would I draw it?" Having your boyfriend terminate your relationship feels like getting your heart ripped out and handed to you; you imagine him booting you out the door and you landing on your butt on the pavement; and so on.

10. Use similes. A simile (pronounced "SIMMalee") is a metaphor with the comparison spelled out with the word *like* or *as*:

Writing unrhymed poetry is *like playing tennis without a net.*
(Robert Frost)

Like a bridge over troubled waters/I will lay me down.
(Paul Simon)

Students are more comfortable with similes than with metaphors because they're easier to spot.

11. Substitute examples. When you find an abstraction, ask yourself, "What's a concrete example of that?", and replace the abstraction with the example. On a TV show Stanley Kramer, the movie director, was talking about how he financed his first movie. Straight out of the army, knowing no one and nothing about getting financial backing, he walked into a bank and asked for the money. Kramer wanted to say, "I'd never been in a bank before except to conduct minor personal financial transactions." But being an entertainer, he knew how dull that would sound, so he said, "I'd never been in a bank before except to *take out twenty dollars.*" He was really saying something like, "I'd never been in a bank before except to (do things like, for example,) take out twenty dollars."

When Robin Lee Graham, who sailed around the world when he was sixteen and wrote a book about it, explains why he loved sailing, he might have said, "Sailing was a chance to escape from all the meaningless busywork of my life." Instead he says,

> It was the chance to escape from blackboards and the smell of disinfectant in the school toilet, from addition and subtraction sums that were never the same as the teacher's answers, from spelling words like "seize" and "fulfill" and from little league baseball.

The Bible loves to illustrate abstract lessons with concrete example. It won't say, "Be generous with others"; it will say, "Take your bread and divide it in half and give half to a stranger."

We've mastered three stylistic features—sentence length, Latinate diction, and concretion—but we're just getting started. We can use the same three steps to master dozens or hundreds of others that remain. For instance:

> Do you use adjectives rarely or often?
> Do you ever use dashes? Semicolons? Parentheses?
> Do you use the active voice or the passive voice?
> Which carry the weight, your nouns or your verbs?
> Do you use the first person, "I," or the third person?
> Do you use contractions (*can't*) or full forms (*cannot*)?
> Do you use slang or Standard English?

The world of style is all before you. Have fun exploring.

Purpose and Audience Tell You How to Write

Thesis, purpose, audience, tone, and style are not created equal. Nor is thesis most important, though we tend to think so. In fact, *purpose and audience are most important*, because they determine what we say and the tone we say it in. They tell us how to structure, how to begin, how to end, how long the sentences should be, whether to use slang or not . . . in short, everything. Writing is a constant series of "What should I do now?" questions: Should I state my thesis? Should I begin a sentence with "but"? Should I explain what I just said? Should I summarize in my conclusion? *Purpose and audience answer all such questions, and only purpose and audience can answer them.*

Example 1: Should you use slang, like "homie" for "buddy" or "whack" for "bad"?

It depends on to whom you're writing and why. Slang is fleeting. A few years ago my students were saying "hella cool" and "hella bad." Now no one says "hella." So if you want what you write to have a long shelf life, avoid slang because it will soon be out of date. Slang also marks you as a member of a certain group. If you're talking to members of that group, using slang may earn you instant acceptance. If you're talking to outsiders, using insider slang may advertise the fact that you're not one of them. You may or may not want to do that. In the sixties many black activists methodically used black slang when talking to white audiences, in effect saying, "I don't have to speak your dialect to be worth listening to."

Example 2: How should you structure the essay?

It depends on to whom you're writing and why. How-to essays usually go through a process step by step, because the reader is trying to go through the process herself with the essay as a guide. Technical reports usually begin with summary, conclusion, or recommendations, because they're read by bosses who don't have time to read the whole thing and want *an answer* where they can see it at a glance. Newspaper articles always put their most important information first and their least important information last, because newspaper readers skim the openings of articles, pick the ones worth reading, read until their interest flags, and quit. Arguments often start by declaring that there's something that needs fixing in the world but hold off telling the reader what the thesis is. The idea is to win the reader's attention but to give the writer time to talk him into agreeing with her. In each of these cases, organization is dictated by what you're trying to do to the reader and what he's reading you for.

Example 3: How much information should you give, and what style should you write in?

It depends on to whom you're writing and why. I was recently writing a review of the Bruce Springsteen CD *We Shall Overcome: The Seeger Sessions* for a northern California arts-and-entertainment weekly, whose average reader is probably about twenty-three years old. On the CD, Springsteen covers several songs made famous by Pete Seeger, the hugely important folk singer of the 1950s and '60s, as well as a handful of other songs from the civil rights era. I assumed that most of my readers knew Springsteen's music, but I figured they didn't know much, if anything, about Seeger. So I had to provide some background about Seeger and his time and music as well as talk about what Springsteen did with the songs. At the same time, I had to write it in a style appropriate for a young reader. And here's the catch: I was limited to 150 words. This is what I ended up with:

It's a natural: Bruce Springsteen, the working-man's rock star, meets Pete Seeger, American folk-music icon. Recorded unrehearsed at Springsteen's New Jersey farm, *The Seeger Sessions* captures the Boss and friends—on guitar, fiddle, piano, upright bass, accordion, washboard, tuba, trombone, banjo, and mandolin—playing with joy, passion, and apparently plenty of lubrication. At one point, Springsteen asks, "Anyone else need another beer? Let's loosen up on these vocals." While the party atmosphere makes it impossible not to get caught up in the music, it also risks undermining the political intensity of the original songs. On the other hand, the gospelly "O Mary, Don't You Weep" becomes a rousing call to arms, the entire cast belting out the vocals, painfully punctuated by the high hat that sounds eerily like a cracking bull whip, and the title tune is solemn and stirring, as is the gorgeous "Shenandoah." A "dual-disk," the *Seeger Sessions* includes a remarkable DVD of the recording, with bandleader Springsteen not only calling out solos and key changes but thoughtfully discussing in quiet interviews the songs and the importance of "recontextualizing" the music. ❖

WRITER'S WORKSHOP

Revising for Thesis, Audience, Purpose, Tone, and Style

Here's a first draft that's full of interesting stuff but that hasn't yet tried to answer the four big questions.

NO TITLE WORTHY
ALBERT PIERCE

I think I got the date right. There isn't much else worth remembering. Oh, my thesis! A little advice for all you folks out there who still fall into the category defined by that all too oft-quoted song which I believe says something about those who have not yet accumulated enough scar tissue and believe that they still fit the category label "young at heart" (an interesting little concept when one stops to ponder its complexities): Boys and girls, marriage is for the birds. I could easily use stronger language, but, believe it or not, I'm turning this in as a representation of my consummate skill at argumentative articulation.

And you wonder what revelatory message I could possibly relate that would have any significance to your life? Frankly, I'm not sure that I give a damn if you read this or not.

Perhaps I should explain that it is quickly approaching two in the morning and that I didn't get any sleep last night either. I am perusing the bottom of a bottle of Jack Daniel's (I should have bought two) and my grammar, as well as my sense of good taste, are at a state so low as to not have been experienced before in my lifetime. No doubt, having read this far, you concur.

As to the matter at hand, my wife left me twenty-nine days ago, upon the date of my 37th birthday. So why, I hear you cry, are you still so damn depressed? Because marriages spanning twelve years just don't end that easily. First you have to go through two years of hell while you're still living together but don't know you're going through hell. Then your lady informs you that it's over. Naturally you don't believe it, and in your vain attempt to sway the opinion of your soon-to-be-estranged mate, discover all kinds of things which she never told you about. Excuse me a minute while I pour myself another drink.

At any rate, during the week that it takes you to find an apartment, she discovers that she has made a terrible mistake. And so begins the reconciliation. Now you are totally enamored of each other. You talk incessantly. You have sex in the kitchen. This lasts about two weeks.

After this period begins the stage in which she doubts that the two of you can really make it after all. Wednesday after the Sunday upon which she professed undying love, she tells you she "needs some space" and she hopes you will "always be her friend." This is followed by the Thursday when she won't talk to you except to say that she doesn't want to talk to you. You buy a bottle.

Excuse me, I need more ice.

This last event is quite predictable. It happens within three days prior to the due date of at least three large school projects. No problem!

And now for the first time in your life you discover real pain. I just wrote another poem and put it under her windshield wiper. I will probably never know if she reads it. I will never see her laugh, cry, complain. Twelve years. It wasn't worth it. Don't get married. It's three a.m. I'm going to bed now. ❖

The horsepower is great, but Albert knows he hasn't a clue about who it's talking to or what it hopes to do to the reader. So far it's just personal therapy.

After thinking about it, Albert realized he hadn't really considered an audience for the piece, but he also knew that there was one, out there somewhere. So instead of just writing to get this stuff off his chest, he decided to write to his brother, John, who had just gotten married, and by implication to all other newlyweds. His purpose would be to prepare them for the inevitable agony of divorce. Choosing an audience and purpose led to choosing a structure: the essay would be a letter and a list of tips. Here's how the next draft came out:

BEST-LAID PLANS

Dear John:

I loved your wedding. The flowers were lovely, and the bride looked radiant.

I'm writing to offer you the benefit of my experience as you start out on this new phase of your life. Marriage is a big step. It requires planning and foresight. You should be receiving this about two weeks after the ceremony, so the first flush of love is past and it's time to start planning for your divorce.

You may think I'm being a little hasty, but consider. More than half the people who get married these days get divorced. That means the odds are against you. Wouldn't it be wise to take some precautions? Having some practical experience in this area of the human experience, I will be your mentor.

First off, accept the coming divorce as an inevitability. Begin thinking of your spouse as "your future ex-wife." The agony of divorce is largely in the surprise.

Second, accept the fact that the person you're living with isn't the person you'll have to deal with during the divorce. Your loving spouse will overnight become a ruthless enemy bent on domination. You will be amazed at the similarities between dealing with an ex-wife and a gigantic corporation planning a hostile takeover of your company.

In fact, accept the fact that your spouse isn't the person you think she is *right now*. During the divorce proceedings, she will cheerfully tell you that everything you thought you knew about her was a lie: she never liked you, she always thought your jokes were lame, she really hated sex with you and just did it out of a sense of duty, etc., etc.

Now that you have the right attitude, what practical steps can you take? Prepare for the divorce in a businesslike manner. Do exactly what you would do in a business relationship with a shifty partner. Trust no one. Make sure you have at least seven bank accounts, so when her lawyers find three or four of them you'll be left with something. Make sure everything you own of value is heavily mortgaged. Have no significant liquid assets, except whiskey, which will be tax deductible after the divorce as a medical expense. Don't count on your premarital agreement saving you—all legal contracts can be broken. Most important of all, fight for your own interests. Let the other guy look out for the other guy; she will, I assure you.

Lay plans to handle the sense of worthlessness. Start seeing a therapist *now*, to get a head start. And don't make the novice spouse's mistake of severing all ties with members of the opposite sex. I'm not advising having affairs, but when the break comes you'll need women friends to pat you on the head, say you've still got what it takes, and listen as you say loathsome things about your ex.

Know the traditional behavior of the divorcing spouse and expect it. For instance, there is the False Reconciliation. She discovers that she has made a terrible mistake. Now you are totally enamored of each other. You talk incessantly. You have sex in the kitchen. This lasts about a week. Wednesday after the Monday when she professed undying love, she tells you she "needs some space" and she hopes you will "always be her friend." This is followed by the Friday when she won't talk to you except to say that she doesn't want to talk to you. You go into shock. This will always happen three days prior to the due date of at least three large school projects. Plan ahead!

If you take this advice, divorce, like thermonuclear war, can become an unpleasant but survivable disaster. And incidentally, since these realities have nothing to do with the personalities involved, I'm sending a copy of this letter to your wife, with suitable pronoun changes, to be fair. After all, after the divorce I'm hoping to stay friends with both of you. ❖

Now it's your turn. Here's the first draft of an essay that hasn't yet committed itself to a thesis, audience, or purpose. Read it closely, and then brainstorm a list of three potential audiences for it and possible corresponding theses and purposes.

UNTOUCHABLES

DUNCAN THOMSON

Women! Can't live with them, can't get near them, drink another beer. Sweet dreams. Is it in the eyes of the beholder? I think not. You see them every day on campus, do they acknowledge you? Maybe, maybe not. They say that love comes from the heart, for a guy, I think it comes from his zipper most of the time. For a gorgeous girl, I think it comes from her attitude. Maybe you truly just have to know someone until you can truly judge them.

She was my *Cosmo* woman, my runway girl, I still think about her and miss what we once had. I feel so stupid for letting her get away to pursue her modeling career. It's over now but for the longest time I couldn't even think about another woman. Life really didn't seem worth living. Will I ever meet her again? I'm looking and she's out there, I just don't know who she is. Is this her?

It's Friday night and you're ready to hit the town. If you're under twenty-one it's a piece of cake, but if you're over twenty-one that means a night at the bars. Why we go, man, I'll never know. You're getting ready. You pick what you think will make you the most attractive person on the face of this earth. Now I feel like a million bucks. There is so much confidence in this bathroom as I stare into the mirror. You see, Mike's is to many of us guys the ultimate place to meet women. From 9 p.m. till 1, the place is completely packed with both sexes.

This is it, the time to find my Christy Brinkley, Elle McPherson. Anything is possible. This is the place where confidence becomes reality: dance, rate the pairs in the room, buy her a drink, throw some one-liners, anything to strike up a conversation. "Those are the most beautiful eyes I've ever seen." It may be corny but it does lead to an interesting conversation.

I'm all fired up as I wait in line to get in. We're going out to get drunk and meet women. Is this paradise or am I just stupid? The fellas and I head for the bar. "Two pitchers and three shots please." No, why oh why did I order shots? Oh well, here we go again.

There she is, oh god, just look at her. Blonde hair, blue eyes, but that's not where my eyes are wandering. What curves! The complete package. I can feel my body start to shake. "Hey bartender, one more shot please." I feel sick, I start talking to myself: Relax, jerkface, you haven't even talked to her yet. I still have this really nervous feeling inside but on the outside I still have that confident 90210 look.

I'm really starting to feel good from the alcohol. That other girl who didn't look so hot earlier is all of a sudden looking good. So many women! Blondes, brunettes, tall, short, skinny, voluptuous, and of course the total packages. Most other women call them sluts but I think they got it so they flaunt it. Why are they so hard to meet? I'm a nice, attractive person with a lot going for me. I stumble over to talk to one. "Do you want to dance?" I say.

"Maybe next song," she replies. I turn to say hello to a friend and the snooty little bitch is gone. She was just another untouchable.

Some of these girls are so incredible, most men don't even have a chance with them. You have got to have either money, some kind of title, or something that makes you desirable. Everything you try is wrong. I know I'm probably not going to meet this woman in a bar but it's a good place to start.

Let me tell you, when you get to date one of these women just once, your whole world is great. Each day is bright, the sun is shining. Everyone looks at you with this girl, the other guys are thinking, "What? That little dork with such a hot woman?" The world is your oyster. Your dreams become reality. I know, no woman has enough power to do that. Wrong! An untouchable woman is the best thing in the world.

Then that day will come, she's gone. No heart, no soul, worthless. It crushes you for at least six months. Eventually you get over it. Is that why I'm still in this bar?

I'm heading home, with nothing but a piece of pizza in my hand. I get home and grab that little black book and dial for a girl until I pass out. Women! Can't live with them, can't get near them, drink another beer.

God life is great. ❖

EXERCISES

1. Write an essay describing your typical revision process and your personal definition of revision. Compare it with the ideal in the chapter. Write a list of changes you need to make.

2. Write down five topics. Then translate the five into thesis statements.

3. Convert the following topics into thesis statements:

   a. Organic food
   b. SUVs
   c. The image of African-American athletes in the United States
   d. The rising cost of a university education
   e. The effect of TV on children

4. Narrow the following topics. Example: Shakespeare → Shakespeare's mixed feelings about civil disorder.

   a. SUVs
   b. TV
   c. Education

  d. Child raising

  e. Race in America

 5. How well does each of the following obey the eight tool-making rules we've looked at in this chapter? Are there one or more rules it fails to obey? If necessary, rewrite it as a perfect thesis.

  a. You can't legislate morality.

  b. This culture is so racist!

  c. My thesis is that boxing is brutal. It's incredible to me that in a society that bans cock fighting and bear baiting, we permit the same sort of thing with human beings.

  d. But I need at least a B—my parents will kill me if you give me a C.

  e. What do you mean, you won't lend me your car? I loaned you ten dollars last week.

  f. Why do we let TV corrupt our children?

  g. Why World War II was unnecessary.

  h. I love the new Ben and Jerry's flavor, Purple Haze.

  i. Three reasons why everyone should exercise regularly.

 6. For each of the theses you revised in Exercise 5, think about at least two potential audiences for each. Write them down, and then describe in a brief paragraph how you would approach each thesis for each specific audience.

 7. For each of the broad audiences following, write half a page detailing everything you know about them. When you don't know something, narrow the audience by choosing an audience within the audience. Example: I'm writing to readers of restaurant reviews → I'm writing to readers of restaurant reviews, who live in the Boston area, and who are fighting high cholesterol.

  a. Registered nurses

  b. Working mothers

  c. College professors

  d. Republican voters

  e. Readers of movie reviews

 8. For each of the following tones, describe a more precise tone by adding detail.

  a. Sad

  b. Formal

  c. Informative

  d. Angry

 9. Pick any essay in A Collection of Good Writing and answer the following questions about it:

a. What's the topic?
b. What's the thesis?
c. Where, if anywhere, in the essay is the thesis?
d. What's the purpose?
e. What's the audience?
f. What's the tone?
g. How does the tone suit the purpose?

10. Do Exercise 9 using an essay of your own.

11. For each of the following opening paragraphs, write descriptions of the work's thesis, purpose, audience, tone, and style. How do tone and style suit the purpose?

a. The Brookfield Unified School District maintains an educational program that provides special learning opportunities for pupils who, after consideration of all pertinent data, evidence exceptional intellectual capacity. Recently your child was identified as having demonstrated a significant number of characteristics of intellectual giftedness. Therefore, he/she was nominated to participate in the identification process for possible inclusion in the program.

b. I GIVE UP. I have finally decided that Miss/Ms. Right isn't going to walk through the door. Never would I have thought that I would end up resorting to a public appeal such as this. I've been to bars, churches, the YWCA, the YMCA (was that a mistake), NOW, and every possible spot this wonderful mystery woman might be, all to no avail. This is my last resort. If you desire to help a frustrated and very nice guy, read on.

c. After hunting for a parking space, wading through a crowded registration line, and forking out $375, I expect to be entertained. That's why I decided to sign up for a film class. Besides, I needed three General Ed. units, and English 37, seriously titled "American Film as Literature," seemed to fit the bill (no pun intended).

   At the first class meeting, I watched twenty graduating seniors from Signa Phi Nothing attempting to add and wondered why. Was the course an easy A, as the Greek connection implied? Or was there more to it?

12. Take a familiar expression, either an old saw, such as "Don't count your chickens before they've hatched," or perhaps an advertising slogan, such as "Just Do It," and write it in a wordy, passive, Latinate style, like we did with "A bird in the hand is worth two in the bush." Share them with your classmates. Extra credit if they have absolutely no idea what you're talking about (but they must familiar with the one with which you're working).

Chapter 6

ORGANIZATION: MAPPING, OUTLINING, AND ABSTRACTING

Once you have a general sense of what you're saying, why you're saying it, and to whom, you need to ask the next large question: "What shape should all this stuff be in?" In this chapter we're going to practice making and using three tools that will help answer that question—mapping, outlining, and abstracting. But first let's walk through the process to see what reorganizing looks like and to see in action some of the tools we'll be working with. Here's a brainstormed first draft describing a student's friend:

Tony can fill a room with excitement. He's very handsome. He used to have a mustache, but he shaved it off. He tells marvelous lies. He wants to be a professional actor. His eyes mist over when he talks about emotional things. He can talk well on almost any subject. Women melt before him. Tony has worked very hard at karate. He's as graceful as a panther. When he fights, his eyes burn with a passionate wildness. Onstage, he acts with unpolished, startling energy. He sweats when he acts. Last week he told me that he wasn't happy. He said he was burned out. An old back injury had suddenly recurred. He said he feared he was going insane. Today I saw him walking down the street, wearing the latest fashions and beautifully tanned. He smiled a hard plastic smile. He talked excitedly about a potential job and hurried off without a backward glance. He's twenty years old. He lives at home with both his parents. He has no job and doesn't want to go to college. He stays out and parties heavily until two or three o'clock in the morning. His mother always waits up for him.

That's twenty-five items—too many to see at a glance. Let's reduce by summarizing the twenty-five to five:

> Tony is energetic and attractive.
> He's an eager conversationalist.
> He's an expert at karate.
> Last week, he said he was miserable and acted rushed and insecure.
> He's twenty and has no prospects.

Now we can see that these five items are really two: (1) Tony has a lot of gifts and (2) his life is a mess. We can now express this as a thesis sentence: *Tony is wasting his great talents.* Now we can see how all the twenty-five original parts have jobs in that large design. Tony has power (social, sexual, physical) but can't find anything to do with it. Karate gave him a bit of an outlet, and acting a bit, but acting is only professional faking, and Tony does too much of that already. With all his gifts, he's burned out and directionless—he's wasting his time in pointless partying, and he can't get it together enough to leave his parents. Now we can *outline* the draft:

I. Tony has power and talent to burn.

   A. Sexual: Women swoon over him.

   B. Social: He can walk into a room and every eye will turn to him.

   C. Physical: He's a panther at karate.

   D. Psychic: He's a dominating force on the stage.

II. But he can't seem to do anything with his power.

   A. He's burned out.

   B. He wears slick duds but looks dead inside.

   C. His body's failing him.

III. He's twenty years old but still living like a child.

   A. He just goes partying every night.

   B. His mother still waits up for him.

And we can *abstract* the outline:

> Tony is so attractive he can walk into any party and fascinate everyone there in five minutes. He has so much natural energy that he's an expert at karate and a stirring actor. Yet he tells me he's burned out and miserable, and he seems empty, in a hurry but with nowhere to go. He's twenty years old, but without a future; he spends his time going from one meaningless party to another, with his mom always waiting up for him.

The Organizing Attitude

Before we pick up a tool, let's make sure we have the right attitude:

1. Organizing begins with making a model. To organize anything, you have to see the entire design at a glance, and that means making a miniature version of it—just like the models of buildings or golf courses architects make before the bulldozers go to work. Maps, outlines, and abstracts are just three different kinds of models.

Reorganizing a draft is like rearranging the furniture in a room. You can do it one of two ways: you can move the furniture itself around, stopping from time to time to see how it looks, or you can make a model, by drawing a diagram of the room and cutting out paper representations of the furniture. Making a map or outlining or abstracting is like using a model—obviously a lot easier, and offering an excellent sense of how the room will ultimately look.

On the other hand, sometimes you just need to push the furniture around to actually experience what the room will ultimately look like. So, as you work on your model, remember that you are still not committed and that it is meant only to help you see the bigger picture. Remember, too, that the beauty of models is that you can do several simultaneously and look at them side by side.

We know how big the model should be initially, thanks to the Magic Number Seven (Prologue): seven or fewer standard sentences. You usually don't need seven; here's an essay in condensed form, shrunk to just three:

> I "did well" in school but was bored and learned little, because school was boring and irrelevant. But it doesn't have to be that way—there are ways to make classrooms exciting and useful. And they work: I still remember about paramecia because of the time my class took a field trip to the pond. ("Why I Never Cared for the Civil War," A Collection of Good Writing)

As soon as you understand your structure on this basic level, you can start adding details, making the model more complex. When we're completely lost we want a map of extreme simplicity, but the better we know the territory, the more map detail we can handle.

2. Organize after you draft. It's hard to arrange the furniture in a room when you don't have any furniture. You need to produce stuff before you can ask, "What shape should this stuff be in?" In the sciences, you're often required to use an organizational template, so you break this rule there, but in essay writing the structure is something you *discover*.

3. Experiment freely. The beauty, and the fun, of this stage of writing is that you can't be wrong, because you haven't committed yourself yet. You really have nothing to lose by moving the couch over by the window to see how it looks there; if it doesn't work, move it somewhere else. Note: use whatever format will allow you the most freedom. If working on a computer is liberating, then work on a computer. If you feel more free to experiment by scribbling in longhand on a sheet of paper, then scribble in longhand on a sheet of paper.

4. Take time to reflect. Don't just move the couch over by the window and then immediately decide it looks horrible there. Make another model and look at them side by side. Take a break and fix yourself a cup of coffee or a snack, and then come back for another look. Reflect on your model until that reflection leads to concrete revision strategies: "I think I'll start the essay with the old paragraph 3 and see where that goes."

5. Learn to organize by reading for the craft. Essay organization is hard in part because we never get much practice in it. A lifetime of talking leaves us unprepared to organize essays, because talk is just one thing tacked onto another. So practice observing structure when you read: ask yourself, How is this put together? How did the author get it started? How did she end? And remember, only essays can model for you how to structure essays.

We'll practice three diagnostic tools for organizing: mapping, outlining, and abstracting. Each gives us different data.

Mapping

Making the Tool

Mapping is looser and messier than outlining and abstracting, so you can do it at many different stages in the writing process, though it's most useful when you're *prewriting*, that is, before you've written a single word of your draft, or later, once you've got the rough words of a draft on paper (or screen). Mapping is like taking the pieces of the essay and tossing them into the air. It's freer in four ways. First, you can map in all 360 degrees of the circle, and you can connect anything on the page to anything else on the page via a line, as opposed to outlining and abstracting, which limit you to linear thinking. Second, a map has no starting and ending points and no sequence—there's no order to the spokes on a wheel—so mapping forces you to rethink sequence. Third, you can map anything—fragments, words, pictures—whereas outlines and abstracts work with whole sentences. Fourth, maps have *centers*, but outlines and abstracts don't, so use mapping when you're still tinkering with the essay core.

Using the Tool

With all three of our organizing tools, the art is in the interpretation of the data. After you make the map, what does it tell you about the draft? Only practice will teach you how to answer that question. On the facing page is the author's map for "Legalize Hemp" (Chapter 9). What does it suggest Todd should think about in the revision? First, Bubble A logically should be an offshoot of Bubble B. Second, Bubble B promises solutions to "political" problems, but the map never shows us any. Third, items in the map are mentioned more than once in the draft—Bubble D, for instance. Fourth, Bubble E hangs alone and unexplained, and it shows up in the draft in the last paragraph without explanation. Fifth, Bubble F seems to be from a different essay. Sixth, Bubbles F, G, and H are all together in the map but spread throughout the draft. So Todd has six decisions to make. Is there a problem here? What should he do about it?

Outlining

Of our three organizational tools, the most popular is outlining. We see outlines everywhere: instructors outline their lectures on the chalkboard, books are outlined in their tables of contents, religious services often hand out programs that outline events in chronological order, and so on. To outline, you reduce the draft to a series of sentences and list them in a vertical column.

Making the Tool

Outlines are wonderfully revealing diagnostic tools, but can go wrong in lots of ways, so here are several guidelines. To begin, since outlines are rigid, intimidating things that have a tendency to freeze a writer's blood, stay loose by following these four rules:

1. Outline in three to five parts only. According to the Magic Number Seven, we could have a few more, but outlining is so rigid that we want to keep things very simple.

2. Outline in a flash. Write the entire outline in a minute or less. Don't labor over it—try to grasp how the whole essay works in three or four steps and write them down.

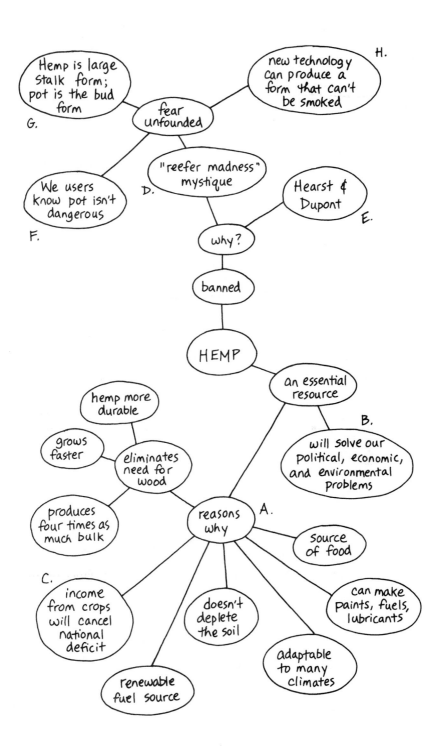

3. Don't use Roman numerals, or any numbers or letters at all. Don't use indentations and subsections and sub-subsections. All that stuff stiffens you up.

4. Stay loose. Feel free to scribble your outline on a sheet of paper. If you do all your prewriting on a computer, keep it loose. Remember, you're still just playing at this point.

Some people flatly refuse to do those four things. They like to labor over an outline and make it gleam with Roman numerals and lots of subsections. The finished outline looks very impressive, but the writer has turned into a slab of ice.

Now that we're loose, follow these additional rules:

5. Don't describe; summarize. Don't tell the reader what you did or are going to do; instead, speak the essay, in reduced form. Don't say, "I list the causes of the Civil War"; say, "The causes of the Civil War weren't racial; they were economic." You know you're doing it right when a reader can read the outline and feel he has the essay itself in short form—not a promise of an essay.

6. Preserve the sequencing of the draft. Don't rearrange the essay content, because then the outline can't diagnose structural problems. Make sure the first item in the outline is the first large thing the draft says, and the last item is the last large thing the essay says.

7. Don't quote sentences from the draft. As with thesis sentence writing, it's rare that the best sentences for the outline can be plucked as is from the draft. Don't *select* sentences for the outline; *compose* them.

8. Outline whole sentences only. If you don't outline sentences, you'll outline nouns and fragments only. Here's a nice-*looking* outline:

    I.   Weapons of mass destruction: the present crisis

   II.   Historical causes

        A.   The fall of the Soviet Union

        B.   The Mideast conflict

        C.   Cold War mentality

  III.   Proposed solutions

        A.   American proposals

        B.   Israeli proposals

    C.   Proposals of other nations

    D.   Why they don't work

IV.   My solution

Looks great, doesn't it? And it's a complete smokescreen. You could do the same thing with virtually any topic, whether you know something about it or not.

    Outlining what the draft says turns out to show only half of what we want to know, and the less important half. Remember, we're not in the business of *saying things*; we're in the business of saying things *to do things to readers*. So we need to make two outlines simultaneously, a *content* outline and a *function* outline. The content outline is the kind we just made. We'll write it on the left side of the page. The function outline will run down the right side of the page. For each item in the content outline, there will be a matching item in the function outline, explaining what *job* the sentence in the content outline is doing. Here's a dual outline for the essay called "Given the Chance" (Chapter 14).

Content	**Function**
1. I met Stacey, a likable drug addict, when I was working at our Group Home.	1. Win reader's sympathy for Stacey.
2. She needs a rehab program, but she can't get into one.	2. State the problem.
3. The State refuses to pay for it.	3. State the source of the problem.
4. The State isn't giving Stacey and me a chance.	4. State thesis.

Function outlining is a continuation of our work with purpose in Chapter 5—now we're just asking ourselves what the purpose of each essay *section* is. Follow these rules while making function outlines:

    9. Use your favorite synonym. If the word "function" isn't to your taste, you can call those things "purposes," "intentions," "jobs," or "chores."

    10. Make the function statements verb phrases. All purpose statements are inherently verbal. You can use imperatives ("Hook the reader"), infinitives ("To hook the reader"), or participles ("Hooking the reader")—it doesn't matter.

11. Keep function statements short and familiar. Most of the time the function of a passage is something short, simple, and well known, because when you get right down to it there are only a few functions writing can have. You can state a thesis, you can defend it, you can hook the reader with personal narrative, you can marshal facts in support of your argument, you can refute counterarguments, you can consider the consequences of taking action, and so on. Look back at the sample function outline: the four functions are all short, all ordinary. And that's good. If your function statements get complicated and strange, suspect that your intentions are really simpler than you realize.

12. Don't reproduce content. This is a version of the point we made about purpose statements (Chapter 5). If you write function statements like "Say what's wrong with affirmative action," "Tell the story about the car accident," or "Describe her parents," you're really just reproducing the stuff from the content side of the outline in altered form. If you do that, the function statements can't teach you anything new. To avoid the trap, *ask yourself, why?* Why are you saying what's wrong? Why are you telling the story? Why are you describing the parents?

13. Avoid universal function labels like "introduction" and "conclusion." Such labels don't lie, but they're so broad they won't teach you anything. Since they'll work for any essay, they can't be insightful about what *this* essay is doing. To avoid the trap, *ask yourself "How?"* How does this essay introduce? How does this essay conclude?

14. Troubleshoot by asking questions. If you have trouble grasping the function of a sentence in the outline, ask yourself, "Why is it there?" You can rephrase the question in several helpful ways: What job would go undone if you didn't include that sentence? What were you trying to accomplish by including it? What are you trying to do to the reader by including it?

Using the Tool

The first and largest question to ask of an outline is "Does this structure work?" It's a huge and slippery question, but you will probably know the answer. Beyond that, an outline can teach you a host of interesting things about a draft, so many that I can't list them for you. Each outline will teach its own lessons. So let's practice listening to outlines and seeing what they reveal. Here are three outlines, all of film reviews, to practice on. The outlines aren't perfect, so sometimes the lessons offered are about tool making and sometimes they're about revising the draft:

Outline A

Content	Function
1. *Kids* is a dramatic film about adolescence.	1. State thesis.
2. A great script and young actors add to the reality of this film.	2. Support thesis.
3. There is a complex and dangerous relationship between youths and their social environments today.	3. State problem.
4. We must acknowledge the hell our kids are living in.	4. State solution.

What looks good? The outline is about something important—our kids are living in hell. And the essay moves from the small, particular thing (the movie) to larger issues—a good strategy. What needs work? Content 1 is safe and doesn't say very much, so the writer should probably look for a way to begin the essay with more energy, more risk. Nor does there seem to be much of a logical connection between Contents 2 and 3. If there is one, it needs to be made clearly. Finally, the function statements don't really let us know what the essay's thesis is. We've got a "thesis," a "problem," and a "solution"... which one is the real thesis?

Outline B

Content	Function
1. *Crash*	1. Introduce the reader to the topic
2. Although the movie seems to combine tactics from previous movies, it's a refreshing change from the average movie.	2. Catch the reader's attention.
3. All your feelings and emotions will be experienced during this film.	3. Convince the reader to see the movie.
4. Future movies have a new standard to live up to.	4. Conclude.

What looks good? The outline is willing to take a stand; it doesn't sit on the fence. Content 4 has a nice punch-line ring to it. And the outline language is straight and clear. What needs work? Content 1 is the weakest of the four, so the writer probably doesn't have to say it at all. Function 1 acknowledges this by admitting that not a lot is going on here. Content 2 seems to contain a contradiction— the movie is simultaneously innovative and familiar—so the writer would want to make clear in the draft how that could be true. Function 2 sounds like the job of an opening, so the writer should probably find a clearer sense of Content 2's job or move it to the front of the draft. When the outline ends, we've been told three times in four sentences that the movie is really good, but we don't have much in the way of a reason. In fact, we really have no idea what the movie is like or even what it's about. Content 3 is a step in that direction, but not enough—the writer should probably shore up her evidence by doing more describing. Function 4 says nothing, so the writer should probably ask, "How?" until she knows how the conclusion is working.

Outline C

Content	Function
1. *Jackass: Number Two* is a terrible movie.	1. Inform my readers of my opinion.
2. The movie failed in its efforts to be funny; it was just stupid.	2. Give reasons.
3. The first few minutes introduced the characters and what they were doing.	3. Tell audience about the characters.
4. The movie felt like it dragged on forever, wasn't funny, and never made any sense.	4. List faults of the movie.
5. Although the movie is terrible, I would still recommend it just so you can form your own opinion.	5. Recommend the movie even though it's bad.

What looks good? An opinion is stated clearly, without hedging (the movie's terrible), and three solid reasons are given (it's slow, not funny, and incomprehensible). What needs work? Content 1 has no sense of "hook." Content 3 seems to add nothing to the argument, and it also seems to float alone, out of sequence. Function 3 is repetition of content, so it obscures the function instead of revealing it. Content 4 repeats Content 2, and Function 4 is a rewording of Function 2, so he should check to see if he's repeated himself. Content 5 takes the wind out of my sails and makes me wonder why I read the outline at all. The author's just bailing out. I'd take the risk and stand by my judgment: the movie stinks. Function 5 repeats content, so I'd keep asking, "Why say that?" until I got an answer.

Abstracting

Once you've outlined and the outline says the draft looks good, you are *not* done, because writing isn't a list. There's something else, something *between* the items in your outline. Students usually say writing that has it "flows," and when it doesn't have it, they say the writing sounds "choppy." Choppy writing sounds like this:

> I think requiring deposits on soda bottles is unfair. I clean up my own litter. How much is a clean roadside worth to Americans? Glass is not something we're likely to run out of soon. Why should people be forced to do something they don't want to do?

Missing from that passage is what writing teachers call *transition* (or *transitions*). An outline encourages you not to think about the matter, by reducing the writing to a stack of parts. So we need an organizational tool that focuses on transition, and the *abstract* is it.

What exactly is transition? There are lots of ways to describe how it *feels*. In transitionless writing, the separate bits feel isolated, like shy strangers at a party. When you read it, you feel like you're constantly starting and stopping, like when you were first learning to drive a car with a manual transmission. You stopped and started abruptly, without graceful forward movement. Writing without transition is like that. It feels rough, jerky—yes, choppy. Writing that has transition feels smooth, easy—yes, it flows. It's like driving with a manual transmission after you've mastered it (or driving with an automatic transmission). And readers feel just like the passengers in your car: they'll move forward without even realizing you're changing gears.

Transition and Readers

Writing turns out to feel rich in transitions when both the writer and the reader agree that the next thing the text says follows gracefully and naturally what went before. We can describe this in two ways. One way is in terms of the reader's dialogue we tracked in Chapter 2. The writer writes something; the reader reacts with a question, a want, a feeling, a request for clarification; and the writer responds by addressing the want. That response prompts another reaction from the reader, and the back-and-forth continues to the end of the essay. If we try to carry on such an exchange with the author of the piece on recycling, we see the problem—she's not listening to us:

AUTHOR: I think requiring deposits on soda bottles is unfair.
READER: *Why?*

AUTHOR: I clean up my own litter.
READER: *So what?*

AUTHOR: How much is a clean roadside worth to Americans?
READER: *I don't know—what's the answer? Why does it matter?*

AUTHOR: Glass is not something we're likely to run out of soon.
READER: *So what?*

AUTHOR: Why should people be forced to do something they don't want to do?
READER: *Because people aren't naturally given to doing what's best for society? HELLO!!? ARE YOU LISTENING TO ME!!?*

Writing with transition is a back-and-forth between attentive equals. Here's Sheridan Baker discussing paragraph structure:

> Now, that paragraph turned out a little different from what I anticipated. I overshot my original thesis, discovering, as I wrote, a thesis one step farther—an underlying cause—about coming to friendly terms with oneself. But it illustrates the funnel, from the broad and general to the one particular point that will be your essay's main idea, your thesis.
>
> (*Sheridan Baker, The Practical Stylist*)

And here's the dialogue between Baker and the reader:

> Now, that paragraph turned out a little different from what I anticipated.
> *In what way was it different?*
>
> I overshot my original thesis.
> *Why did you do that?*
>
> Because I discovered, as I wrote, a thesis one step farther.
> *What kind of thesis?*
>
> An underlying cause.
> *What was it about?*

About coming to terms with oneself.
So your previous claim was wrong?

No, the paragraph still illustrates the funnel.
In what ways?

It still goes from the broad and general to the one particular
point that will be your essay's main idea.
What's that idea called?

Your thesis.

Obviously, this approach only works if you *do something to the
reader*, from the very first sentence; if you don't provoke a response,
the reader is mute, and you have no reason to keep writing.

Transition and Connectors

The second way to think about this notion of "the appropriate next
thing to say" is to focus on *connectors*. Connectors are devices that
link one clause to another. They look like this:

and	so	but
still	yet	first, second, etc.
because	thus	even though
since	for instance	therefore
furthermore	nevertheless	moreover
however	finally	instead
although	rather than	too
also	in fact	for example
consequently	in other words	on the other hand
while	that	as a result

Connectors express logical relationships between sentences—they say,
"I'm putting this sentence after that one for a reason, and here's what
the reason is." *But* means "I'm going to qualify what I just said or disagree
with it in some way." *So* means "I'm going to draw a conclusion from
what I just said." *Instead* means "I'm going to offer an alternative."
    The most familiar connectors are conjunctions (*and, but, so, if*),
but some adverbs connect (*therefore, however*), and some punctuation marks do. The punctuation marks that end sentences (question
marks, periods, exclamation points) *don't* connect, because they only
tell us about what just happened, not how it relates to what's coming.
Commas *don't* connect because they give us no specific relationship
information. But the semicolon and the colon are highly specific connectors. The semicolon means "The next sentence is the second half
of the idea started in the previous sentence." The colon means "Now
I'm going to explain or list examples of what I just said." The typical

connector is one word long, but connectors can be large blocks of text, like "Despite all that, . . ."

Now we have two ways to diagnose the quality of the transitions in any piece of writing in front of us. Writing has transitions (1) if we can write out the reader's half of the dialogue between the sentences, and the product sounds like a smooth conversation, or (2) if we can put connectors between all the clauses, the connectors make sense, and the text reads well. Armed with this knowledge, we're ready to abstract the draft.

Writing Abstracts

You can write an abstract simply by writing all the sentences in it one after the other across the page instead of in a column. Or you can look at the essay, say, "What does this say, briefly?", and spew it out. Here are abstracts for three of the essays in this book:

"Grateful" (p. 204):
Mai Thao had just moved to California from Thailand, and I was going to show her around our school. We were both eight. The first week was difficult; she was distant and seemed angry. Finally, she told me how wasteful Americans appeared to her, and she pointed out specific examples. Through Mai's eyes I learned to appreciate how fortunate I am to be an American and to appreciate what I have. We are still friends today, and I still try not to be wasteful.

"The Sprout Route" (p. 362):
If you're interested in your health, you should consider adding home-grown sprouts to your diet. Not only are they a living food supply—full of nutrients and enzymes—but they're very easy and inexpensive to grow, as well as easy to cook with. To start, all you need are some seeds, available in bulk at health-food stores, and some canning jars.

"The Good Mother" (p. 370):
If you're raising a child and it's going beautifully, you may be doing a great job, or there may be another explanation. When I raised my first child, he was an angel and I got rave reviews from myself and other parents. I assumed I was different from those other moms, who screamed and spanked. Then I had my second child, who was difficult. I tried all the right parenting responses, but they didn't work, and he turned me into the cranky, spanking mom of my nightmares. From this experience I learned that children aren't created by grown-ups, and that people (including me) aren't as simple as they think they are. This knowledge will come in handy when I'm a teacher and it comes in handy now in my relationships with my peers and family—I'm more tolerant, more willing to listen, less sure I'm right.

Abstracting asks more of you than mapping or outlining, but it also tells you more. It's the greatest diagnostic tool an essay organizer has. And since abstracting will do everything outlining can do and more, once you master abstracting you might be able to skip the outlining stage altogether.

Making the Tool

As you abstract, follow these rules, many of which are versions of our rules for outlining:

1. Summarize; don't describe. With abstracting even more than outlining, the temptation is to dodge all the hard work by telling the reader what you *did* instead of saying what you *said*. Such abstracts, called *descriptive abstracts* by technical writers, usually begin like this:

I'm going to . . .
This essay is a description of . . .
How to . . .
In this essay I said . . .
An introduction to . . .

Descriptive abstracts have their uses for *readers*, but they tell the *writer* nothing. Prove it to yourself by writing a descriptive abstract for an essay you can't write: "This essay solves the problem of world overpopulation, suggests a workable cure for cancer, and proves that Elvis is really alive." If you find yourself irresistibly sucked into describing, write, "Next in this essay I say . . . ," finish the sentence, and then delete those first six words.

2. Preserve the essay's sequencing.

3. Don't quote from the draft.

4. Use the voice, tone, and point of view the essay uses. If the essay is in first person, make the abstract in first person. If the essay is funny, the abstract should be funny.

5. Write it fairly quickly. Pondering too long might make you belabor details. We're looking at the bigger picture right now.

6. Write the abstract in one paragraph only. The abstract is primarily good for diagnosing flow. A paragraph break is a big interruption in the flow, so it will obscure any transition problems and taint the diagnosis.

7. Make the abstract about 100 words long. It's possible to abstract to any length, and each length will teach you something useful. But for most people the abstract is most productive if it's 70–150 words, ¼ to ⅓ of a single-spaced typed page, about seven normal-length sentences. Don't make the abstract longer just because the draft is longer—the Magic Number Seven never changes, and every map in your glove compartment probably is the same size whether it's for your town or your state.

Using the Tool

As with the thesis statement and outline, begin using the abstract by asking any and all large questions about what's going on: Did you say anything? Is it interesting? Did you take any risks? and so on. But since abstracts are primarily good at diagnosing transition, focus on transition issues: Does the abstract flow? Does it read well? Do you feel *pulled through* the abstract as you read?

Let's practice reading the following three abstracts critically:

> **Abstract A** Mark Twain is the best writer in American literature, because he could do things Cooper and Whitman couldn't do. Cooper's works were inconsistent and unrealistic. Whitman was also very influential, and liberated American literature from taboos about sex and free verse. Twain tackled taboos more successfully. In summation, American literature was shaped by Twain, Cooper, and Whitman. Twain was unique in his tact, the vividness of his descriptions, and his frank honesty. He died penniless and mad, cursing the human race. Hemingway said that all modern American literature comes from *Huckleberry Finn*. ❖

What's going well? The abstract has a lot to say and seems excited by it. The voice seems direct and forceful—not boring. The abstract starts right off with a meaty first sentence that wastes no time and gives itself a worthy task to perform. *What needs work?* The sequencing is shaky. We can get specific about where the problem manifests itself:

1. Sentence 3 seems to contradict sentence 1.
2. The *also* of sentence 3 implies this is the *second* of something, but we can't see the first.
3. *In summation* comes in the middle of things, and it doesn't summarize, since it tells us something new.
4. We can't see how "He died penniless and mad" is logically connected to anything.
5. The last sentence doesn't seem to end anything.

We can fix all these problems by resequencing:

> **The Rewrite** Hemingway said all of modern American literature sprang from *Huckleberry Finn*. Why would he say that? What's so special about Twain among the other great nineteenth-century American writers? Two things: he did what greats like

Cooper and Whitman did, only better—like break social and artistic taboos; and he had things they didn't have, like tact, descriptive accuracy, and, most of all, a willingness to look at the dark side of human nature. That willingness was so uncompromising that it drove him mad and left him penniless. ❖

Abstract B A favorite way to spend Friday night for many people is to watch hardball. My nephew plays and is talented and confident. I wonder if my five-year-old son will have the chance to build his confidence. Some kids make it through without getting hit by the ball. Many parents oppose the use of the standard hardball because it's dangerous. Cost and tradition are the biggest reasons for not changing over to the ragball. The Little League Association needs to adopt the use of the ragball in this beginning league; it works just as well. Why should a potentially dangerous ball be used when technology has produced a good and safe alternative? ❖

What's going well? The abstract has a strong thesis, a clear sense of purpose, and a passion. *What needs work?* We need to declare the problem earlier, telegraph the transitions, and make only one sequencing change: put the refutation of the opposition's argument ("cost and tradition are the biggest reasons . . .") *after* the declaration of thesis. You can't address the rebuttal before you've stated your case:

The Rewrite A favorite way for my family to spend Friday night is to watch hardball. My nephew plays with confidence, but sometimes I wonder if my five-year-old son will have the chance to build his confidence. Not all beginners get hit by the ball, but many do, and those who do often are injured and quit in fear. But there's a way to avoid that: switch from the conventional hardball to the ragball. It works just as well as the hardball without the danger. Why should a potentially dangerous ball be used when technology has produced a good and safe alternative? The only arguments against it are cost and tradition, but certainly the added expense is worth it and tradition isn't worth the cost in frightened children and injuries. ❖

Abstract C The search for a golden tan is an annual quest for many white students. Tan skin is risking skin cancer, premature aging, and wrinkles. A tan is a status symbol, but it doesn't necessarily make you a better person. I'm pale and have heard all the pale jokes, but I still don't think a tan is important. The stereotypes applied to pale people are just as bad as those applied to tan people. A tan may be nice now, but it can create wrinkles that will last a lifetime. I may never be tan, but I'll have smooth skin when I'm old. ❖

What's going well? The thesis is clear, the author knows what she wants, she's alive, and she has arguments to support her thesis. *What needs work?* Every sentence seems unconnected to the sentences before and after. A clue is the lack of connectors: only four, and all *but*'s. Let's up the number from four to ten (two are colons):

The Rewrite The search for a golden tan is an annual quest for many students, *but* tanners don't realize what danger they're in: tanning is risking skin cancer, premature aging, and wrinkles. A tan may make you look great now, *but* it can create wrinkles that will last a lifetime. *Of course,* a tan is a status symbol, *so* not having one means you have to put up with a certain amount of guff. *I know*—I'm pale and have heard all the pale jokes and the stereotypes. *But* you can learn to live with it. *And* there are payoffs later: I may never be tan, *but* I'll have smooth skin when I'm old. ❖

Diagnosing Transition by the Numbers

Often you can just *feel* transition or sense that it's missing—and that's all you need to know to fix the problem. But if you want to quantify transition, here's a by-the-numbers diagnostic program:

1. Insert all the connectors between the ideas and points in your abstract.
2. Identify places where connectors are missing between ideas and points. Try to add connectors in these places.
3. Identify all *false connectors*—connectors that promise logical relationships that aren't there. When you start trying to add connectors to your abstracts, there's a huge temptation to make all transition problems seem to disappear by filling your abstract with snappy-looking but dishonest connectors. They sound like this:

   You have to have respect and then you'll be OK; *for example,* when you're a veteran nobody messes with you.

   I was struck by a careless driver who ran a stop sign. I was able to survive; *consequently* the accident resulted in complete damage to my car.

   Wherever possible, replace all false connectors with honest ones:

   I was unhurt, *but* my car was totaled.

4. (This is the key step.) Any place where good connectors wouldn't go easily is a structural trouble spot. What can you

do to solve the problem? How can you resequence the abstract to make the transitions smoother?

5. Check to see if the sentences are combining and thus becoming fewer and longer. If they are, transition is getting better. That's what connectors do—they combine short sentences into longer ones. If you do your transition work perfectly, you'll end up with an abstract that is one huge, complex, but clear sentence. But remember, ungrammatical sentences, empty connectors, and false connectors don't count.

Structural Templates

We've talked about organization as if a writer always starts with a draft and, through tools like abstracting, seeks the essay's own unique, ideal structure. And it often works like that. But there are other ways to organize thought, so essays usually turn out to be versions of conventional essay *templates*, archetypal structures writers have been recycling for centuries. You could approach organization by picking a template and fitting your draft to it:

For a restaurant review: Follow the customer through the stages of the meal. First discuss the ambiance, then the service, then the menu, then the salad, the soup, the main course, the dessert, and the bill.

For an investigative essay: Pose a fascinating question. Gather data toward an answer. Answer the question, and discuss the implications of your answer.

For an argumentative essay: Declare a thesis. Marshal arguments, supportive evidence, and examples to prove it. Finally, discuss the implications of the thesis.

For a lab report: Summarize the experiment and its findings in the introduction, describe what was done in the experiment in the methods section, reproduce the data gathered in the results section, and discuss your findings in a discussion.

This approach works, and it's a lot simpler than what we've been doing, but it isn't much fun and may doom you to a certain mediocrity.

On the other hand (note the transition/connector), some templates do allow you to have some fun, as well as offer an opportunity to rise above mediocrity. I often use a template when I write profiles: I start with a physical description of my subject, in present tense, and then throw in a snipped of dialogue: "Stan Hopkins rolls his swivel chair away from his desk, loosens his tie, and swaps his shiny brown wingtips for a pair of red high-top Chuck Taylors. 'Come on,' he says, draining the last sip of coffee from a Styrofoam cup and dropping it into the trash can. 'Let's get out of this friggin' office.' "

Paragraphing

Now that we know about transitions, we can answer a favorite writer's question: How do you know where to put the paragraph breaks? If paragraphing just happens for you, let it. Don't think about it unless you know it's a problem for you.

If it is a problem, deal with it with what we've learned. Good writing isn't a list—it's a logical or emotional process. Thus there are no real "stops" along the way—one thing always leads to another. So if your paragraphs are all short, it can only mean that you haven't found the strong sequencing that allows the reader to keep moving down the road. Use outlining and abstracting to get it. If your paragraphs are too long, it probably means that you just don't like to take breaks. That's a healthy sign, but you need to learn to take pity on the reader, who needs them. Keep in mind that there's more than one reason to break your text into paragraphs. While what you learned in junior high school is true, that a paragraph is usually the development of a single part of a larger idea or argument, if you think about it that simplistically, you're asking for trouble. I've had students justify writing page-and-a-half-long paragraphs by saying, "But it's all about the same idea." Right, but just *look* at it. Surely you've opened a textbook to a page on which the entire text is flush left. It's daunting. "I'll never get through that," you tell yourself.

So look at your page-long paragraph and ask yourself not only, "Where's a good place to break this up *logically*?" but also "Where should I let my reader come up for air?" And put your paragraph break, or breaks, there, roughly one every quarter or third of a single-spaced page, unless you want a special effect: short paragraphs for jerky, explosive effects, long paragraphs for tension building. Here's George Orwell doing the first in his essay "Marrakech," where the first paragraph is one sentence long:

> As the corpse went past, the flies left the restaurant table in a cloud and rushed after it, but they came back a few minutes later.

Tom Wolfe does the latter in Chapter 2.

EXERCISES

1. Critique the following map: Which of the map-making rules laid down in Chapters 4 and 6 does it follow, and which does it break?

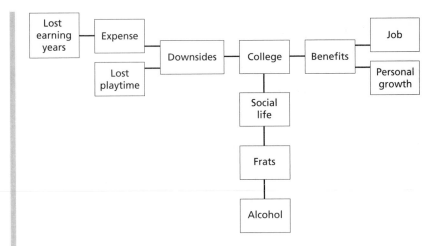

2. Pick an essay from A Collection of Good Writing and map it. Write a critique of your map: Does it obey the tool-making rules in Chapter 4 and Chapter 6? If not, revise the map.

3. Pick an essay from A Collection of Good Writing and outline it. Write a critique of your outline: Does it obey the tool-making rules in Chapter 6? If not, revise the outline.

4. Do Exercise 2 using one of your own drafts.

5. Do Exercise 3 using one of your own drafts.

6. Write a critique of each of the following outlines, in two stages: First, describe how well it follows the fourteen outline-making rules of Chapter 6. Second, rewrite the outline to eliminate any problems. Third, make a list of everything the outline tells you about the draft. Fourth, make a list of concrete suggestions for revision.

Outline A

Content	Function
1. Small-breed dogs aren't real canines; big dogs are.	1. To put different dogs in different categories and explain why some dogs aren't considered dogs.
2. Rocket dogs are Weimaraners, and the author used to have one.	2. To explain what a rocket dog is and her own experience with owning one.
3. Some friends own a black Lab the author hangs out with now.	3. To contrast a Lab owned by her friends with her old dog.

Outline B

Content	Function
1. The institution of marriage has been tarnished in my eyes because of my roommate.	1. Make the reader laugh.
2. Since my roommate got married, he has dropped out of school and become haggard.	2. Win the reader's support for my stance on marriage.
3. Marriage has lost all importance in America.	3. Suggest to reader that marriage is a sham.

Outline C

Content	Function
1. Darwin changed his mind about his own theories.	1. Evolution is not sound science.
2. Scientists hang on to Darwin's original theories.	2. State the problem.
3. Science only knows what it knows.	3. State the source of the problem.
4. It takes just as much faith to believe in evolution as creation.	4. State thesis.

7. Write a critique of the following abstract: Which rules for abstract making does it follow, and which does it break?

I describe the parking problem at the university. How the problem came into existence. The administration is responsible for the problem.

Possible solutions. Riding bikes. So we could build a parking garage for students.

Read the following three abstracts. Then follow the instructions in Exercises 8–10.

A. Because information learned in conjunction with music is retained accurately and for a long time, music can be considered an effective learning tool. Rating a child's musical abilities can cause egotism, self-doubt, or total rejection of music. While providing educational benefits, music also promotes creativity and reveals the beauty surrounding knowledge—an essential in the learning process. Music when incorporated into the school curriculum must not be performance oriented or stressful in any way.

B. Most articles on surviving in the back country tell how to live off the land, but I think they ignore prevention. Real survival is knowing how to avoid the dangerous situation in the first place. One survival article showed how a guy snowed in on a deer hunt couldn't start a fire, couldn't retrace his steps, etc. With a little forethought, none of this would have happened. An important factor in survival is keeping your head. Once I went goose hunting without my pack, got lost, panicked, and spent a cold night out. I learned my lesson. To survive, you don't need to know how to live off the land—just take the right equipment and keep your head.

C. Advertising is making all of us hate the way we look. Every company offers products to improve our bodies. We're sicker and fatter now as a result. Bulimia and anorexia nervosa are two diseases commonly suffered by young women and sometimes men. Last summer I got to know my sister's friends. Iris admitted she was bulimic. Iris's problem wouldn't go away. Advertising has made fat one of our ultimate taboos. At an interview I was told to lose fifteen pounds. I wasn't fat then. Have we gone too far? Maybe we should reduce advertising until we become accustomed to imperfect people again.

8. Write a critique of each abstract asking if it obeyed the seven rules for abstract making. Rewrite the abstract so that it does.

9. For each abstract, go through the five-step diagnostic program beginning on page 122.

10. For each abstract, write a paragraph critiquing it. Make a list of concrete suggestions for revising the draft, such as "Move the anecdote about the wedding to the front." Rewrite the abstract so that it follows your suggestions.

11. Write an abstract for an essay in A Collection of Good Writing. Do Exercise 8 with it.

12. Write an essay using a structural template you like, whether in *The Writer's Way* or not. Add to the essay a brief description of the template.

Chapter 7

MAKING THE DRAFT LONGER OR SHORTER

It's time to practice the writer's art of writing to the assigned length.

Beginning writers usually think an essay should be as long as it takes to do the task at hand—you write till you've said it all. That almost never works, because in life there's almost always a length limit. I recently wrote a story for a newspaper's Sunday travel supplement about a bicycle tour I took of western Ireland. The piece was about 1,100 words long. A couple of months later, I had the opportunity to publish it again, although the editor of the second publication told me I'd need to cut it down to 850 words. So I had to go back through the piece, cutting and tightening, making decisions regarding what was absolutely necessary and what wasn't. Then I sent him the shorter version.

Imagine my surprise when he e-mailed me back and said that the paper had recently changed its format and that they had room for only 500 words. I almost wrote back and told him to forget it, that I couldn't reduce it to that length. But I worked some more, cutting and tightening, painfully deleting stuff I really liked. That version ran in the paper the following Sunday. (All three versions are reprinted below.)

In the beginning of your career, the problem is usually that the draft is too short. But after you've been writing for a few years, the problem reverses itself and the draft is almost always too long. So we'll talk about making drafts longer and shorter, and if you don't need both skills now, you might later.

Begin by drafting everything you have in you—don't think about length at all. Then compare what you've got to the length you're shooting for and cut or expand accordingly.

Making It Shorter

You make a text shorter in one of two ways: say it all, faster, or say less.

To say it faster, we need only notice that Chapter 5 reduced essays to single sentences (thesis statements) and that Chapter 6 reduced them to three to five sentences each (outlines) and paragraphs (abstracts), so any coherent text can be reduced to any size. Just to prove it, here are successively shrunk versions of "A Moral Victory?" (see its 500-word form in A Collection of Good Writing):

The half-size version:

> In 1984, some white male police officers sued San Francisco, claiming they were the victims of reverse discrimination because they had been passed over for promotion in favor of less qualified minority officers. The U.S. Supreme Court has refused to hear their case. This may seem to be a victory for minorities, but isn't it really a loss for us all?
>
> I'm married to a white male, and I've seen a lot through his eyes. He's an engineering professor who has worked in industry for thirteen years. Unfortunately, reverse discrimination is for him a fact of life. Employers are forced by federal quotas to give preference to Hispanics, blacks, and women.
>
> My sister is also an engineering professor in the same system, but basically what she wants she gets, because the quota system makes her a sought-after commodity. It took my sister a long time to appreciate the injustice of this.
>
> Right now her department is interviewing for a new instructor. The department doesn't actually have an open position, but the university has funding for a certain number of faculty who meet "specific criteria." The candidate is black, so of course she's irresistible!
>
> We feel an awful sense of collective guilt in this country for what we've done to women and minorities, and we should. But can we really right past wrongs by creating new ones? I don't propose that we forget our past, but I think it's time to forgive ourselves and move on. ❖

The quarter-size version:

The U.S. Supreme Court has refused to hear a reverse discrimination case concerning San Francisco policemen. Is this a victory for minorities or a loss for us all? My husband is an engineering professor. Unfortunately, reverse discrimination is for him a fact of life. Employers are forced by federal quotas to give preference to Hispanics, blacks, and women.

My sister is also an engineering professor, but basically what she wants she gets, because the quota system makes her a sought-after commodity. Right now her department has a job that's open only to people who meet "specific criteria"—being black, for instance.

Americans feel guilty for past racism and sexism, and we should. But it's time to forgive ourselves, and move on. ❖

The eighth-size version:

Reverse discrimination isn't a victory for minorities, it's a loss for us all. For my husband, reverse discrimination is a fact of life. But my sister gets anything she wants, since she's female, and her department has a job that's open only to minorities. We should feel guilty about our past, but it's time to forgive ourselves and move on. ❖

The sixteenth-size version:

Reverse discrimination is a loss for us all. My husband suffers from reverse discrimination daily, but my sister gets anything she wants, since she's female. Guilt is good, but let's forgive ourselves and move on. ❖

On the head of a pin:

Reverse discrimination is a loss for us all; let's forgive ourselves and move on. ❖

To say less, you think differently. You reduce the essay to a short list, and you pick from the list. You think, "I'd like to talk about the San Francisco discrimination case and my husband's experiences with reverse discrimination and my sister's change of heart and the hiring her department is doing, but I just don't have the time, so instead I'll focus on my sister's change of heart and leave everything else for another day."

Sometimes, shortening a draft and cutting stuff forces you to let go of material that once held the piece together. Take a look at the three versions of my bicycling-in-Ireland story below. In the longer one, I had the luxury to explore the way riding my bike through a land where people had been passing before me for thousands of years made me think about the concept of time differently, and I got to play with the meaning of the word *cycle*. I tried to use that idea to give the story shape. In the shorter versions, I was pretty much restricted to describing the trip itself. See what you think. Here's the longer one first:

CYCLING THROUGH WESTERN IRELAND

It's a Monday afternoon in late May in western Ireland. A gentle breeze drifts through the Lough Inagh valley and teases to tiny whitecaps the cold cobalt surface of the narrow lake. I brake to a stop beside the road, straddle my bicycle, and take a long pull from my water bottle. Brilliant green fields—dotted with shaggy sheep and wild red rhododendrons—roll away from the shore, rise up out of the valley, lift to hillsides of shifting light, then disappear in the shadowy forests of the Twelve Bens (mountains) of Connemara, over a century ago one of Oscar Wilde's favorite parts of his native country.

A century ago. It seems that long since a car has passed me, in either direction, although it's probably only been a half hour. But right now, time seems somehow irrelevant—the pre-Celtic ruins, the endless, centuries-old stone walls, the abandoned Famine-era cottages all linked into a timeless continuum by the people who have passed through this rugged, unspoiled part of the world—"a savage beauty," according to Wilde.

As a guest of Tourism Ireland, I am four days into a five-day bicycle tour of counties Clare and Galway, including the stark Aran Islands. I have wanted to visit Ireland for as long as I can remember and it is all I had hoped it would be and more. Already I feel an odd, nearly palpable connection to the land and the people, perhaps a result of family bloodlines: my father's Irish Catholic mother, Alice Rooney, and other family, such as the Hugheses and McConnells, who left Ireland for America in the nineteenth century.

I arrived at Shannon Airport in Limerick on Friday morning at 8 A.M., exhausted, having left Sacramento some twenty hours earlier and having slept little more than a couple of hours in flight. At Shannon, I was met by John Heagney, owner/operator of Cycle Holidays Ireland, who whisked me by van to my hotel with instructions to meet back in the lobby at 11:00 ready to ride. A power nap later, I was back downstairs, where I met the other seven with whom I would be traveling. All seemed as exhausted, but excited, as I was.

Heagney, an affable 30-something dairy farmer and former competitive cyclist and rugby player, has been offering cycling tours of western Ireland since 1998. We would learn later in the week that long before he met us at our hotels some mornings, he had raced home on his motorcycle to help his wife milk the cows.

Our introduction to western Ireland was a visit (Heagney delivered us by van) to the 26-acre Bunratty Folk Park, alongside the well-preserved Bunratty Castle, which dates from the twelfth century but was built on the site of a much older Viking settlement. The park is a reconstructed pre-Famine village (though some of the buildings are original and were moved to the site), where visitors can watch women in period costume making bread and pies over peatfires and squeeze into tiny, one-room thatched-roof homes where families of up to 20 once lived—and, during the Famine, often starved.

Then it was time to meet the bicycles, which Heagney had set up for us based on inseam measurements we had sent him. He gave us all laminated maps—map on one side, intersection-by-intersection directions on the other—which we attached to our handlebars, and we were off.

By now a heavy mist had begun to settle on the little backroads, softening the landscape—the empty roadways, lined to their shoulders with blackberry vines, and the simple cottages we passed from time to time, many of which had been converted to bed and breakfasts.

Later that afternoon, after having been awake for some thirty hours and ridden as many miles, my first Irish pub called. Actually, did more than call. It reached out for my trusty steed, grabbed it by the top bar, and yanked it to the roadside. I could do nothing but ride along. That was the best Guinness this Guinness fan has ever tasted.

Dinner that night was a "medieval feast" in Bunratty Castle, where we drank mead, ate pork ribs and capon with our fingers, and were entertained by a lively group of actors and musicians. I ran into the young fiddler at a nearby pub later and complimented him on his work. "Well, I did study at one of your schools," he said. "The Juilliard. Perhaps you know it. . . ."

Day Two, after a hearty Irish breakfast of eggs and bacon and tomatoes, we were off again, this time for the little town of Doolin, the unofficial traditional-music capital of western Ireland. Along the way we passed through the hauntingly beautiful Burren, 160 square miles of gray, mostly treeless limestone that drops down to cliffs, pounded ceaselessly by breaking Atlantic swells. The most stunning are the world-famous Cliffs of Moher, five miles long and nearly 700 feet high. We also passed through tiny Lisdoonvarna, long famous for its matchmakers and today for the annual Lisdoonvarna Matchmaking Festival each September. High on a rocky windswept ridge, we saw the Poulnobrone dolmen, the ruins of a 5,000-year-old tomb whose capstone weighs five tons. That night we dined on fresh Atlantic salmon before a brief visit to a pub for some live reels and jigs.

Day Three we loaded our bikes onto a ferry for Inishmor, the largest of the Aran Islands and home of Dun Aengus, the remains of a huge, cliffside stone fort at least 2,000 years old—about a half-hour ride from the ferry landing. The Aran Islands, to which electricity was not brought until 1974, are also famous for their wool fisherman's sweaters, whose individual weaves were originally family-specific—in order to identify the decomposed bodies of drowned fishermen. You can buy sweaters today at the homes of weavers themselves or at the Aran Islands Sweater Market.

Later, in Spiddle, County Galway, I listened long into the night to a crooked little chap playing guitar and singing traditional Irish folk songs. I was brought nearly to tears by the haunting "Grace," about Grace Gifford, who wed Joseph Plunkett, one of the rebels of the 1916 Easter Rising, two hours before he was executed by English soldiers.

A highlight of Day Four was lunch in the tiny seaside town of Leenaun—fresh oysters, mussels, salmon—where even in this remote village, cranes and concrete trucks signal Ireland's economic boom. (The European Union, identifying Ireland as a developing country, is pumping millions into the economy. Unemployment is almost zero. Many locals told me that those who long for the "good old days" are crazy.)

That afternoon, we stopped at Kylemore Abbey, near Letterfrack, a daunting lakeside neo-Gothic mansion built in the nineteenth century. Today it serves as a convent for Benedictine nuns, who run the visitors center and the restaurant, where they serve fresh local salmon and their homemade jams and scones. Later, we passed through the "savage beauty" of the Lough Inagh Valley, where, exhausted after some 40 miles, we stopped for drinks (Guinness is good for you!), before piling the bikes onto the top of Heagney's van, for a short ride to Clifden.

Day Five was a potpourri of scenery, tiny fishing villages, green pastures sloping down to the sea, stone walls sprawling in every direction, sheep in the narrow roadways, tiny cemeteries beside the ruins of centuries-old stone churches, and peat bogs, where men, their cattle dogs resting nearby, dug peat bricks by hand and stacked them to dry by the roadside. On distant hillsides, "Famine Ridges," where blighted potato crops were left unharvested a century and a half ago, still crease the land.

Soon, we met up again with Heagney, who transferred us to Galway City, a lively university town, where music and youthful energy seem to pour from every doorway. I could have easily spent a week here, exploring the narrow little streets and historical sites, including the Spanish Arch, through which Portuguese and Spanish ships entered the city in the sixteenth century carrying wine and spices. Galway is also where Nora Barnacle, James Joyce's wife, grew up, and today the family home is a museum dedicated to the couple.

It's a Wednesday morning in late May in western Ireland. Heagney's van pulls to a stop at Shannon Airport under a sign that says "Departures." Unexplainably, or maybe not, I'm completely choked up and have to look away from Heagney and my mates.

Could that have really been five days?

Heagney gives me a hearty, rugby-player's handshake, and I head into the terminal to double check my flight time: 11:15. Correct. Damn!

Five days?

Five short days when time did indeed seem irrelevant.

In a land to which I'll someday, somehow, cycle back. ❖

Now here's the 850-word version:

CYCLING THROUGH WESTERN IRELAND

Late afternoon, County Galway, Ireland. A gentle breeze drifts through the Lough Inagh valley and teases to tiny whitecaps the narrow lake's gunmetal-blue surface. I brake to a stop beside the road, straddle my bicycle's top bar, and take a long pull from my water bottle. Brilliant green fields—dotted with shaggy sheep and wild red rhododendrons—roll away from the shore, lift to hillsides of shifting light, then disappear in the shadowy forests of the Twelve Bens (mountains) of Connemara, a century ago one of Oscar Wilde's favorite parts of his native country.

I had arrived just after daybreak on a late May morning at Limerick's Shannon Airport, where I was met by John Heagney, an affable 30-something former competitive cyclist and rugby player who has been offering cycling tours of western Ireland since 1998. Heagney helped me load my luggage into his waiting van, then whisked me to my hotel with instructions to meet back in the lobby at 11:00 with the group. A dairy farmer by family trade, Heagney races home on his motorcycle most mornings long before dawn to help his wife milk the cows.

Our introduction to western Ireland was a visit to the 26-acre Bunratty Folk Park, where women in period costume made bread and pies over peat fires and where we squeezed into tiny, one-room thatched-roof homes where families of up to 20 once lived—and, during the Famine, often died of starvation. After the tour, we got on our bikes and headed out into the countryside.

By now a gentle rain had begun to fall, softening the empty roadways, lined to their shoulders with blackberry vines. Later, after having been awake for some thirty hours and ridden as many miles, I heard my first Irish pub call. No Guinness ever tasted better. Dinner that night was a "medieval feast" in the well-preserved twelfth-century Bunratty Castle, where we drank mead, ate capon with our fingers, and were entertained by a lively group of actors and musicians. Afterward, I ran into the young fiddler at a nearby pub and complimented him on his work. "Well, I did study at one of your schools," he said. "The Juilliard. Perhaps you know it. . . ."

After a breakfast of eggs and bacon and tomatoes, we were off again, this time for the little town of Doolin, the unofficial traditional-music capital of western Ireland. Along the way we passed through the hauntingly beautiful Burren, 160 square miles of gray, mostly treeless limestone that drops down to cliffs, pounded ceaselessly by breaking Atlantic swells. High on a rocky windswept ridge stood the Poulnobrone dolmen, the ruins of a 5,000-year-old tomb whose capstone weighs five tons.

The third day, we loaded our bikes onto a ferry for Inishmor, the largest of the stark Aran Islands and home of Dun Aengus, a Cliffside stone fort more than 2,000 years old—about a half-hour ride from the ferry landing. The Aran Islands, to which electricity was not brought until 1974, are also famous for their wool fisherman's sweaters, whose individual weaves were originally family-specific—in order to identify the decomposed bodies of drowned fishermen. You can buy sweaters today at the homes of weavers themselves or at the Aran Islands Sweater Market.

Later, in a pub in Spiddle, County Galway, I listened long into the night to a crooked little chap playing guitar and singing traditional Irish folk songs. The haunting "Grace"—about Grace

Gifford, who wed Joseph Plunkett, one of the rebels of the 1916 Easter Rising, two hours before he was executed by English soldiers—nearly brought me to tears. Deep into several Guinnesses, I thought about my own family bloodlines: my father's Irish-Catholic mother, Alice Rooney, and other family, Hugheses and McConnells, who left Ireland for America during the late nineteenth century.

A highlight of the fourth day—in addition to the scenic Lough Inagh Valley—was lunch in the tiny seaside town of Leenaun—fresh oysters, mussels, salmon—where even in this remote village, cranes and concrete trucks signal Ireland's economic boom. (The European Union, identifying Ireland as a developing country, is pumping big money into the economy. Unemployment is almost zero. Many locals told me that those who long for the "good old days" are crazy.)

The last day was a potpourri of scenery, tiny fishing villages, green pastures sloping down to the sea, stone walls sprawling in every direction, sheep in the narrow roadways, small cemeteries beside crumbling, centuries-old stone churches, and peat bogs, where men, their herding dogs resting nearby, dug peat bricks by hand and stacked them to dry by the roadside. On distant hillsides, "Famine Ridges," where blighted potato crops were left unharvested a century and a half ago, still crease the land.

Too soon, Heagney's van pulls to a stop at Shannon Airport under a sign that says "Departures."

"See you again," he says, giving me a hearty, rugby-player's handshake.

That, he will. ❖

And finally, the 500-word version.

CYCLING THROUGH WESTERN IRELAND

County Galway, Ireland. A gentle breeze drifts through the Lough Inagh valley and across the narrow lake's gunmetal-blue surface. I brake to a stop, straddle my bicycle's top bar, and take a long pull from my water bottle. Brilliant green fields—dotted with shaggy sheep and wild red rhododendrons—roll away from the shore, lift to hillsides of shifting light, disappear into shadowy forests.

Three days earlier, I had arrived at Limerick's Shannon Airport, where John Heagney, an affable 30-something former competitive cyclist and rugby player, loaded my luggage into his waiting van. A dairy farmer by family trade, Heagney races home on his motorcycle most mornings long before dawn to help his wife milk the cows.

By early afternoon, we were strolling through 26-acre Bunratty Folk Park, where women in period costume cooked pies over peat fires and we squeezed into one-room thatched-roof homes in which families of up to 20 once lived—and, during the Famine, often died. Afterward, we cycled down quiet, narrow roads into the misty green countryside.

Dinner that night was a "medieval feast" in the twelfth-century Bunratty Castle. Afterward, at a nearby pub, I complimented the young fiddler. "Well, I did study at one of your schools," he said. "The Juilliard. Perhaps you know it. . . ."

The next day, on the way to tiny Doolin, the unofficial traditional-music capital of western Ireland, we passed through the Burren, 160 square miles of gray, mostly treeless limestone that drops down to dramatic cliffs, pounded ceaselessly by crashing Atlantic swells. On a rocky windswept ridge stood the Poulnobrone dolmen, the ruins of a 5,000-year-old tomb.

The next morning, we loaded our bikes onto a ferry for Inishmor, the largest of the stark Aran Islands and home of Dun Aengus, a cliffside stone fort more than 2,000 years old. The Aran Islands are also famous for their wool fisherman's sweaters, their individual patterns originally family-specific—to identify the decomposed bodies of drowned fishermen.

That night, in a pub in Spiddle, a little man played guitar and sang traditional Irish folk songs, including the haunting "Grace"—about Grace Gifford, who wed one of the rebels of the 1916 Easter Rising two hours before he was executed by English soldiers. Deep into several Guinnesses, I thought about my own family: my father's Irish-Catholic mother, Alice Rooney, and others, Hugheses and McConnells, who came to America in the late nineteenth century.

In the remote seaside town of Leenaun, where we ate fresh oysters and salmon, cranes and concrete trucks signal Ireland's economic boom. (The European Union, identifying Ireland as a developing country, is pumping big money into the economy. Many locals told me that those who long for the "good old days" are crazy.)

The last day, we rode through sloping green pastures, past crumbling cemeteries, and raced sheep in the narrow roadways. In far-off fields, men dug peat bricks by hand, and on rolling hillsides, "Famine Ridges," from blighted, unharvested potato crops, still creased the land.

Too soon, Heagney pulls his van to a stop at Shannon, helps me unload, and gives me a hearty, rugby-player's handshake. "See you again," he says.

Indeed. ❖

Seeing the Mode

Here's a photo I took that accompanied the 500- and 850-word versions of the story, and in fact I think the same photo could illustrate
a much longer and a much shorter piece. If I were writing a longer
piece, I'd take the time to explain running into this guy out in the
middle of County Clare, how he seemed kind of surprised to see us
on our fancy bikes and with our helmets on but still waved us a good
day. I might also discuss how his smile, his leisurely pace, and his
modest bicycle seemed to capture so much of the feel of the people
and the Irish countryside. On the other hand, the photo could also
work to illustrate a shorter piece, in which I'd hope that the image
itself would do the actual work of words, suggesting to readers those
same ideas.

Making It Longer

Making a text shorter is pretty easy compared to the harder problem
you face when the teacher says "Give me five pages" and you've run
dry after two paragraphs.

We work on this throughout this book. In Chapter 4 we brainstormed and free wrote to expand a seed into a draft. In Chapter 9
we'll use peer editing to show how the draft could become something bigger and better. In Chapter 13 we'll use a thesis statement
as a springboard to an endless conversation. All of these activities
are based on the idea that a draft is just a starting place.

You can expand in three ways: filling in, expanding the canvas, and asking the next question.

Making It Longer by Filling In

Saying it in more detail does *not* mean saying exactly the same thing in twice as many words. It means filling in blanks and providing background detail. An essay is like a painted portrait. The one-paragraph version is like a happy face—nothing but a circle for the head, a curved line for the mouth, two circles for eyes. Now we're going to go in and start adding details—lips, ears, irises, pupils. Then we can add details to the details—chapped skin on the lips, ear hair, bloodshot eyes. We can keep adding details forever, like sharpening the resolution on a TV screen by increasing the number of pixels. Imagine a passage from an essay on changing a flat tire, in various degrees of detail:

> *Short version:* Remove the hubcap.

> *Longer version:* Remove the hubcap with the tire iron.

> *Still longer:* Find the tire iron. It's a long iron bar. Stick one end under the lip of the hubcap and pry until the hubcap comes off.

> *Even longer:* Find the tire iron. It's a long iron bar and is probably alongside your jack, either in the trunk or under the hood. Stick one end under the lip of the hubcap anywhere along the circumference and pry until the hubcap comes off.

> *Longest so far:* Check to see if you have a hubcap—a Frisbee of shiny metal covering your lug nuts. If you do, you have to remove it. Find the tire iron. It's a long iron bar and is probably alongside your jack, either in the trunk or under the hood. If you want to stay clean, be careful—it, like the jack, is likely to be pretty yucky if it's been used before. Grasping the iron in your left hand (if you're right-handed), stick the end that is flattened and slightly canted under the lip of the hubcap anywhere along the circumference and push hard on the other end with the flat of your right hand. The hubcap should pop off. If it doesn't work, push harder. Don't worry—you can't hurt the iron or the hubcap. Keep prying until the hubcap comes off, whatever it takes. If it's stuck, try different spots around the lip. Above all, DON'T wrap your right hand around the bar when you're prying—if you do, when the hubcap comes loose, your fingers will be crushed between the iron and the tire or fender.

Former Chico State student Mark Wilpolt experimented with this idea by starting with the short sentence "I arrived at the gym" and then turning it into the following paragraph:

Yesterday the rain stopped and the sun came out. I had been doing homework all day, so I jumped on my bike to experience the
drying streets. Along the way I decided to turn the bike ride into
a trip to the gym. I arrived at the gym and worked out on the
Nordic Track for fifteen minutes. On the way home, I took the
scenic route along the creek, enjoying the fall colors, the clear
sky, and the foothills, with their new patches of snow, in the
background. Who says exercise isn't fun? ❖

Then he turned that short paragraph into this playful little narrative
essay:

The entrance to the Sports Club is its own little world. As I
walk through the lobby, the day care is on the right. A dozen
kids are running around the plastic playground as perfect smiling employees in their twenties look on—a Norman Rockwell
scene for the '90s. The beauty salon is next: women with big
hairdos and long, fluorescent fingernails giving their customers
that extra little something they can't get from the workout
floor. Then the big-screen TV, surrounded by comfy sofas, and
the snack bar, tempting you to just skip the exercise and veg.
  I hand my card to the girl at the front counter. Whoever
is on duty, it's always the same: a bubbly smile and a musical
"Hello, how are you today?, have a nice workout" as she zips
my card through the computer, like she's been waiting all day
for me to show up and make her shift. They must major in
Smiling, the people who get hired for that position. Tough job.
  Next I must negotiate my way past the aerobics room. Why
they make that whole wall one giant window of glass I'll never
know. Is it so women can see the class going on inside and feel
guilty because THEY don't look like that, or so men can watch
the proceedings and get their heart rate up in anticipation of
their workout? Whichever the case, there's a bench right there
in the hall inviting everyone to sit and stare. As I pass, I want
to sit and ogle the women of all shapes and sizes who are jumping and twisting and sweating in their Spandex. Of course they'd
probably revoke my membership.
  In the Big Room, a dozen machines, none of which I know
the name of, for shoulders, thighs, chest, back, quads, biceps,
even a machine to exercise your NECK for heaven's sake. A ten-
thousand-dollar machine to exercise your NECK? Also there's
a fleet of Stairmasters, a bank of treadmills, a rank of stationary

bicycles, a squadron of rowing machines—and the Nordic Track. None of them going anywhere, but some of them being driven pretty hard. The humorless faces of the exercisers say, "This is serious business."

All the machines call to me, "Me, do me first. No, work on your arms first," but it's hard to hear them because a dozen TV sets suspended in rows where the wall meets the ceiling are blaring, "Watch ME instead!" No way to avoid it—you work out and you watch TV. "Wheel of Fortune" is on. I'm trapped. I get on the Nordic Track and stare. The clue is "Person," five words. The champ has the wheel.

"I'd like an S, please."

"Yes, two of them!" DING, DING. "Spin again!"

"I'd like an R, please?"

"Yes, there are FIVE R's!" DING, DING, DING, DING, DING.

The champ buys a couple of vowels. ❖

The tricky part is realizing that arguments or thought processes can be expanded just like information can. Shawni, the author of "Why I Never Cared for the Civil War" (A Collection of Good Writing) could easily expand it to book length by researching the degree to which American schools use the lecture-and-test approach to teaching, citing successful classroom alternatives to it, and detailing how they work and why they succeed.

Expanding the Canvas

Another way to lengthen is to ask, "What's the larger issue?" If the first way of lengthening was like adding details to a painting, this way of lengthening is like pasting the original work in the middle of a much larger canvas and painting the surroundings.

Seeing the larger issue depends on realizing that all issues are specific versions of larger issues:

Specific Issue	Larger Issues
Why I deserve an A in English 1	How grades are determined; what grades mean; how are students evaluated?
My father was a brute, and I couldn't do anything about it.	Psychological effects of bad parenting on children; why do people have children? children's rights

Why I don't vote anymore   What's wrong with American
                                  politics? America's apathy
                                  crisis

Asking the Next Question

Asking the next question means exactly what it says: When you finish the draft, you ask yourself, "What's the next question to be asked and answered? What's the next task that needs to be done?" No argument ends the debate; no task completed means the work is over. In writing as in science, answers only generate more questions, and there's always a next thing to learn or do. For instance, if you write an essay arguing that the United States shouldn't explore for oil in the Alaskan tundra, the next question might be, "OK, what *should* we do to solve our growing energy problem, then?"

WRITER'S WORKSHOP

Expanding Essays

Let's practice expansion on some student essays.

SEX AND TV
MARJORIE CROW

Do you hate turning on the TV and all you see are people touching each other sexually and some taking off their clothes? Well, I'm tired of it. There is much more to human relationships than sex. Yes, some people would agree that sex has a lot to do with a relationship, but sex on TV is what I'm most annoyed with. Sex is enticing and sex does make products sell, but the question is, should sex be thrown around like it's yesterday's lunch? I feel that something has to be done. It would be great if the media would monitor the shows that we see, but in reality they want to broadcast what will sell, and sex sells. ❖

Questions for Marjorie

1. *Filling in:*

What are some examples of how sex is portrayed on TV?
How does TV use sex to sell things?
What exactly are the messages we're being sent about sex by TV?

2. *The larger canvas:*

How our culture treats sex
How TV influences our values and beliefs
Our culture's portrayal of women

3. *The next question:*

How can we stop the marketing of sex?
Who is ultimately responsible?
What other ways are there that TV cheapens our lives?

TYRANT!

TRICIA IRELAND

Christopher Columbus should not be regarded as a national hero. He was a terrible man who worked only for selfishness and greed. He was not the first on his expedition to spot land; a man named Roderigo was. But according to his own journal, Columbus took credit because the first to spot land was to receive a yearly pension for life.

When Columbus landed in the Bahamas, he took the natives by force and made them his slaves. Hundreds he sent back to Spain; others were held captive in their own country. He made them bring him a monthly quota of gold, and when they did they received a copper coin necklace. If they were found without a necklace, their hands were cut off and they were left to bleed to death.

I don't know why we teach our children to admire and respect Columbus. There exists a terrible amount of ignorance regarding the truth around him. It's time to teach the truth. Columbus Day shouldn't be celebrated, and Columbus himself shouldn't be seen as anything but the cruel tyrant he was. ❖

Questions for Tricia

1. *Filling in:*

What else did Columbus do, good and bad? —tote up his virtues and vices.
What's the rest of his story? How did he get the idea to go exploring? How did he die? And so on.
How did the Columbus myth get started?

2. *The larger canvas:*

What's a hero?
Tradition vs. truth in history
The European bias in our view of history

3. *The next question:*

What about other heroes like George Washington—are they fables too? Should we also expose them?
Why does this matter, since it's ancient history?
How can we change the way we teach history so it isn't so biased?

   Now it's your turn. For each of the following essays, write out ways to expand the draft by (a) filling in, (b) writing on the larger canvas, and (c) asking the next question.

OPEN THE DOOR
PAULA BONKOFSKY

College-level students shouldn't be punished, or worse, locked out of classes if they arrive late. Certainly if it becomes habit the teacher should speak with the student and affect their grade accordingly. But on occasion, students who are never regularly late are late because of circumstances that were out of their control. These students should be allowed to come in and participate with their class. Yes, it really is their class because they paid for it. ❖

SEX, LIES, AND POLITICAL BASHING
KERI BOYLES

Lately, it seems as if you can't turn on the TV without seeing some political campaign commercial blasting the opposition. Instead of telling us what they stand for and what they plan to do in office if they get elected, they spend the majority of their time smearing their opponent. These commercials are exactly the reason why a lot of people are presently disgusted with politicians. Not only are they insulting to the voter, but they skirt the issues as well, focusing on their opponent's flaws instead of informing the voter on what their actual policies are and how they plan to "clean up" the messes that politicians (unlike themselves, of course!) have gotten this country into.

It's time to say enough is enough. These distasteful commercials shouldn't be allowed. Candidates should only be able to state what their beliefs and policies are, without smearing their opponent. Voters would then be able to make logical, rational decisions without being bombarded with all the other pointless garbage they are all subjected to when watching their favorite TV shows. Personally, I don't care if Clinton inhaled or not! ❖

EXERCISES

1. Pick an essay from A Collection of Good Writing and rewrite it to half its length in two ways:

   a. Say it all, but twice as fast.
   b. Cut the essay's scope in half.

2. Do Exercise 1 using an essay of your own.

3. Describe in one paragraph a recent personal experience; then retell it in two pages, adding as much detail as you can but without changing the scope.

4. Write a one-paragraph argument. Then write answers to the three questions from this chapter: How can this be filled out? What is the larger canvas? What is the next task? Be sure to deal with each of the three. Then rewrite the argument to 1–2 pages, using the material generated by the questions.

5. Write a one-paragraph argument. Read it to the class and ask them to respond to it, not to the writing style but to the logic. Rewrite the argument to 1–2 pages, using the material generated by the conversation.

Chapter 8

BEGINNING, ENDING, AND TITLING

Beginnings, endings, and titles are worth special attention. They're key moments of contact with your reader, and they're superb diagnostic tools. Essays that begin well, end well, and are titled well are usually good through and through.

Conversely, papers that have trouble in one of those areas usually suggest larger problems elsewhere. In fact, a writing teacher once told me that if I couldn't come up with a good title for a piece I was working on the piece probably wasn't done yet.

Beginnings

Making the Tool

The draft's first sentence is a popular place for writer's block. We've all had the experience of staring at the blank page, knowing pretty much what we want to say once that hurdle has been overcome, but not being able to budge. For help with that problem, follow these four rules:

1. Write the title last. Or rather, be on the lookout for a good title from the moment you start the project. Expect it to come late, and grab it and hold on to it when it comes.

2. If you can't find a good opener, have none. No introduction at all is better than an empty, formulaic one like this:

> After reading Frank Smith's book *Reading Without Nonsense* you could tell that the author has very definite views on how to teach

people to read. He lets the reader know exactly how he feels about different techniques of teaching children to read.

That's just ghastly.

3. Cut everything that precedes the first good thing you write. Instead of trying to write a great opener right off the bat, just freewrite. Then read your draft until you find a sentence that really starts something, and throw away everything above it. Assume that your first few paragraphs will be a warm-up and should be trashed. Essays don't need to gather momentum—just plunge in. Here's an opener that gets on with it:

> Frank Smith feels that reading via food labels, street signs, and board games is a good way to learn to read, because to learn to read, children need to relate the words to something that makes sense.

4. Use a stock opener. If you're still stuck, fall back on one of four basic strategies writers have been using for centuries:

The thesis statement. You declare up front (usually at the end of the first paragraph) the heart of what you have to say. Beginning writers and teachers like this one because it's easy, and bosses and other people in a hurry often like it because they can grasp the gist of a piece of writing in a minute. But it's unexciting unless the thesis is startling and provocative, like the newspaper article a while back that began, "Americans apparently like reading the newspaper more than sex," and it gives away the punch line up front, so the rest of the essay loses energy. However, scientific and technical writing usually demands thesis openers; there, you should use them.

The question. A question opener has three virtues. It forces you to be clear about your purpose, it's dramatic (it turns the essay into a detective story), and it shows you what to do with the rest of the essay: answer the question. Examples: Where's the best place for a student to spend Spring Break? What can you do with a major in history? Is joining a sorority really such a great idea? Is global warming real?

The hook. Also known as the grabber or the angle, the hook is the eye-catcher that sucks a reader into the essay like a vacuum cleaner: "When I was 6 years old, living in Vietnam, I saw Mrs. Lau, wife of our family servant, drag herself out of bed only a few hours after giving birth, to bury her newborn's umbilical cord in our garden" (*Andrew Lam*).

There are countless ways to hook a reader. You can start with a paradox, an idea that seems self-contradictory and therefore demands explanation—like "Americans are getting more liberal and more conservative all the time." You can tease the reader with a promise of excitement to come: "No one noticed that the world changed on August 7, 1994." You can drop the reader into the middle of things so she'll read on to find out how she got there—what Latin poets called beginning *in medias res:* "The President looked unamused as he wiped the pie filling off his face." Newspaper sports sections love hooks:

> A World Series involving the New York Yankees would not be official without a controversy. The 75th Series was stamped as the real thing yesterday at Yankee Stadium.

> Westside High's Cougars did what they had to and nothing more to hand Central a 24–15 defeat Saturday night.

Don't promise what you can't deliver. Don't hook dishonestly: "Free beer!!! Now that I've gotten your attention, I'm going to talk about brands of tennis shoes."

The narrative. Narrative openers—stories—work because they concretize and humanize right off the bat: "In the middle of the worst depression in our nation's history, one woman decided to leave her comfortable home and head west looking for a better life." "Given the Chance" (Chapter 14) and "The Last Stop for America's Buses" (A Collection of Good Writing) have narrative openers.

One subtype of the narrative opener always works as a last resort: the "how I came to write this essay" opener. Explain what started you thinking about the subject: "I was reading the newspaper the other day and noticed an article about the federal government taking over the Coca-Cola Company. I couldn't help thinking . . ." But be careful. You really risk having your reader respond with a big, "So what! I don't care that you were reading the paper the other day." Remember what we talked about earlier: you might write this to get yourself started, but then when you go back and look at it realize that it can be cut. In fact, the one above could easily begin, "A recent news article announced that the federal government is planning to take over Coca-Cola. . . ."

Once you've got an opener, make sure it performs the following three tasks.

5. Reveal the topic. This is easy, so do it fast. A whole sentence is too much because it invariably sounds like "In this essay I'm going to talk about. . . ." Reveal the topic as you're doing more important things:

> If you're an average, somewhat chubby individual wanting to get some healthy, not overly strenuous exercise, you should consider bicycling.

> When you start working as a pizza delivery person, you're going to get a new view of life.
> Most of us, if we're honest with ourselves, will admit we've thought about committing suicide.

6. Reveal the purpose. Every reader begins with some basic questions: Why are you writing to me? How can I use this? Why does this matter? Begin answering these questions from the outset.

7. Say, "Read me, read me!" An opener is like a free sample of salsa at the grocery store—it says, "Here's a typical example of the way I write; once you sample it, you'll want to read more." Just write a first sentence you'd like to read:

> In late July 1982, presidential press secretary James Brady sued the gun company that made the pistol used by John Hinckley.
> Grandpa drank too much beer the day he jumped into the pool wearing his boxer shorts.
> Most Americans do not get to experience the excitement and discomfort of train travel very often.
> If you'd like to murder somebody but receive a penance of one year's probation and a small fine, try this: Get yourself blind, staggering, out-of-control drunk some night and just run over some guy as he walks across his own lawn to pick up his newspaper.
> Many gun control advocates believe in the commonsense argument that fewer guns should result in fewer killings. But it may not be that simple.

The following openers make you want to stop reading:

> Handguns are of major concern to many people in the United States.
> Driving under the influence of alcohol is a serious problem in the United States today.
> Bilingual ballots have been in the spotlight for many years.

You don't have to shout; you can say "Read me!" with dignity and class too. Here's a beauty, the famous beginning of George Orwell's "Shooting an Elephant":

> In Moulmein, in Lower Burma, I was hated by large numbers of people—the only time in my life that I have been important enough for this to happen to me.

You can't say "Read me" more quietly or more powerfully than that.
Different kinds of writing value the three tasks differently. Scientific and technical writing values "Read me" hardly at all. As a result, few people read scientific and technical writing for fun.

Academic writing values thesis highly but doesn't think about purpose very much—who knows *why* you write an essay about sickness metaphors in *Hamlet?* Entertainment journalism values "Read me" above all and often has no purpose beyond momentary titillation.

Using the Tool

Begin by asking the central question: "Does this beginning make me want to keep reading?" Next, ask if the other two tasks were accomplished: revealing topic and revealing purpose. If you can't find a sense of purpose, make sure the draft has one and that you know what it is.

Let's practice on two professional openers. How well do the following beginnings do their jobs? Here is the opening paragraph of C. S. Lewis's *A Preface to Paradise Lost:*

> The first qualification for judging a piece of workmanship, from a corkscrew to a cathedral, is to know *what* it is—what it was intended to do and how it is meant to be used. After that has been discovered, the temperance reformer may decide that the corkscrew was made for a bad purpose, and the communist may think the same about the cathedral. But such questions come later. The first thing is to understand the object before you: as long as you think the corkscrew was meant for opening tins or the cathedral for entertaining tourists, you can say nothing to the purpose about them. The first thing the reader needs to know about *Paradise Lost* is what Milton meant it to be.

We know Lewis's subject: how did Milton mean for *Paradise Lost* to be used? We know his purpose: to tell us how Milton intended his poem to be used so that we may judge it truly. We know that this should matter to us: until we have what Lewis offers us, he implies, we are doomed to misconstrue Milton's poem.

Does Lewis say "Read me"? That depends on who we are. You can't write to everyone, and Lewis doesn't try. He's writing to college literature students primarily, so he speaks in a voice that is learned—to win our respect—but also personal ("you") and mildly witty (corkscrews and cathedrals) and forceful ("know *what* it is"). I think he does well.

The second example is by Bill Donahue from an article called "Under the Sheltering Sky" from the *Washington Post Magazine* (and reprinted in *The Best American Travel Writing,* 2004). It might be my all-time favorite opening:

> The coolest people in the world do not wear their baseball caps backwards or pierce their navels with diamond studs. They are old and their cool is subtle, carrying hints of wisdom and poise. Johnny

Cash, Marlon Brando, Georgia O'Keeffe: we behold their weathered sang-froid and we are ineluctably intrigued.

Does Donahue's introduction say, "Read me"? That depends on who you are and what you want. What he's doing, though, is fascinating: taking a handful of very down-to-earth and familiar images and people and juxtaposing them against rather academic and unfamiliar language. I don't know about you, but I want to read an essay whose introduction links the words *cool, backwards baseball caps,* and *Johnny Cash* to words that I'll admit to having to look up. In fact, the introduction was so compelling that I was hooked and kept reading despite not knowing precisely what two of the words meant. (I looked them up later: *sang-froid* means composure; *ineluctably* means unavoidably or inevitably.)

It turns out the essay is about the author's search in Tangier for ghosts of the American expatriot writer Paul Bowles. And by the way, it's an absolutely wonderful piece, instructive in many ways and very worth tracking down.

Finally, perhaps the best "Read-me" introduction ever written: "In the beginning was the word."

Conclusions

Making the Tool

Conclusions are almost as good at breeding writer's block as beginnings. Anyone who's ever found himself stuck on the porch looking for the right last words after a first date knows that. That's why we've invented lots of get-me-out-of-this formulas for concluding: "Last but not least, I'd just like to thank . . ."; "And so, without further ado . . ."; "Thank you very much for your attention to this matter"; "I'll call ya."

Concluding is surrounded by lots of toxic myths, so let's begin by clearing them out. Here are some rules for what *not* to do:

1. Don't formally summarize the essay or repeat the thesis. This is a shock to lots of people, but the fact is that unless the piece is a manual, a summary conclusion is a waste of time, a deadly bore, and an insult to your reader. Only do it if your teacher tells you to or the situation otherwise calls for it.

2. Don't seek the last word. If you write a paper on the national economy, you're *not* going to end all discussion of the national economy. Yet the conclusion must say, "Here we can stop for now"— like a campsite on a walking tour, a home for the night. To ask more of yourself is to guarantee writer's block.

3. Remember that a "conclusion" takes lots of different forms.
Don't feel obligated to have a formal conclusion. In fact, whatever you end up with, that will be your conclusion, so you just have to make sure that it suggests to your reader that your essay's done. Frequently, I'll suggest to students that they lop off their last paragraph. "But then I won't have a conclusion," they invariably say. "Yes, you will," I tell them. "Your conclusion will be what used to be your second-to-last paragraph." "Dad" (in Chapter 11) is a good example of an essay that despite not having a formal conclusion ("Thus, it can be seen . . .") concludes perfectly anyway.

The list of things to *do* is very short:

4. Study concluding by reading for the craft. (See Chapter 1.) As you read essays throughout your life, read with an eye on how each one solves the dilemma of ending.

5. Be thinking about your conclusion all along. The conclusion is the place your structure has been taking you. If you ask a question, you're committed to giving the reader an answer. If you're writing a lab report, you're committed to discussing the significance of what you learned. If you begin with a human interest story, you're committed to returning to the people in it so the reader isn't left wondering what happened to them. If you begin by stating a problem, you're committed to offering a solution (or confessing you have none).

Here's how it looks. A student reviewed a local taco stand. His thesis was that it was all right, but that it couldn't compare to the Mexican food he was used to back home in L.A. Here's an abstract of his essay, with his concluding sentence intact:

> When I was young, I learned to love the great Mexican food in L.A., but now that I'm here in the sticks I keep seeking a restaurant that comes up to that high standard. In that search I tried Alfredo's. It was pretty good, but hardly spectacular, and the search continues. Now, if you want real Mexican food, I know a little place not far from Hollywood and Vine. . . .

And here's an abstract of a review of a local counterculture restaurant, titled "Lily's Restaurant . . . And More":

> Lily's has a wide range of sandwiches, all tasty and reasonably priced—and more. Lily's has a clientele ranging from student hippie to lumberjack—and more. It has soups, vegetarian meals, and friendly, casual service—and more. It's also got cockroaches, so, no thanks, I'm not going back.

6. Use a stock closer. Conclusions, like introductions, fall into types. If you can't find a conclusion, do one of the following standards, but remember: Each one commits you to an essay structure that sets it up, so you can't paste it on as an afterthought.

The answer. "Given the Chance" and "Exactly How We Want It" (both from Chapter 14) do this. If you begin by addressing a problem, you naturally end by deciding what's to be done about it. If you begin by asking a question, you end by answering it.

The full circle. A full-circle conclusion ends by returning to where it started, to the very first thing the essay said. A student began a paper on a quiche restaurant by referring to the author of the bestseller *Real Men Don't Eat Quiche,* saying "Bruce Feirstein has obviously not been to Quiche Heaven," and he returned to that in his concluding line: "I don't care what Bruce Feirstein thinks; he doesn't know what he's been missing." If you begin with a *person,* return to that person: "Perhaps, if these changes are enacted, no one will suffer the way Alice suffered again." The essay on the Mexican restaurant does this, beginning with the author's beloved L.A. haunts and returning to them, as does "Scratch that Itch" (A Collection of Good Writing). But notice that coming full circle is *not* summarizing or repeating a thesis. Keep in mind, too, that the "full circle" and the "answer" conclusions are often the same thing.

Taking the long view. After you've arrived at your destination, you explore the long-term implications of your discovery, consider the larger issues, or raise the next question (Chapter 7). If you've argued that women are getting more into weightlifting, talk about the long-term implications for women's self-image, standards of female attractiveness in our culture, and sexism. This can work with personal writing, too. The long-view conclusion is just about the only way to conclude a thesis-opener essay without summarizing or restating. "A Moral Victory?" and "Why I Never Cared for the Civil War" (both in A Collection of Good Writing) have brief long-view conclusions.

The punch line. If no better conclusion has come to you, you can usually end with your best line. "How to Audition for a Play" (in Chapter 12) has a punch-line ending.

Using the Tool

There is no fancy diagnostic program for conclusions. Just read the conclusion and ask yourself if it works. If you think it does, it probably does. If it doesn't, assume that the problem is a symptom of a problem in the draft's overall design, and go back to abstracting. If you're not sure, have someone read the essay, looking specifically at the conclusion. As we've discovered, sometimes you get so close to your own work that it's difficult to tell what's working and what isn't. Readers can be an immense help.

Titles

The title is the drive-thru of revision, the quickest diagnostic tool a writer has. In about two seconds you can tell if the essay is complete or not.

Making the Tool

Some people seem naturally gifted at coming up with good titles. Others find it next to impossible. And although it's difficult to talk about titling in general—it's much easier to look at a particular essay and talk about possible titles—here are some things to think about:

1. Have one. The biggest problem with titles in school is a lack of one. Nothing's surer to turn your reader/teacher off than an essay without a title, or, perhaps worse, something like "Essay #3" or "Assignment #2."

2. Do the same three jobs you did in your introduction: Declare the topic, imply a thesis, a purpose, or a task to accomplish, and say "Read me, read me!" Any title does at least one of these three; the trick is to do all three.
Some titles just state topic:

Prayer in School
Friendship

Some titles do topic and purpose without much "Read me!":

The Joys of Racquetball
Mark Twain: America's Finest Author
Fad Diets Don't Work

Some do a lot of "Read me!" and no topic:

Give Me *Massive* Doses!
Killing Bambi

What we're striving for is the title that does all three:

Tube Addiction
Yes, Virginia, Leisure Is a Good Thing
Anatomy of the Myopic Introvert

3. Don't have your title state the thesis, because it's wordy and dull. It's enough to imply or suggest it:

Title	Implied thesis
A Gamble for Better Education	We should have a state lottery.
China Syndrome	The food at Ho Chin's is poison.
In the Long Run	Jogging is good for you.

4. Use a stock format. If you shy away from suggesting your thesis in your titles, you can force yourself to by using any of three title formats:

The question: "School Music: Fundamental or Thrill?"; "What Is Pornography?"
The "why" title: "Why I Hate Advertising"
The declarative sentence: "Breast Feeding Is Best"

Yes, that last one breaks Rule 3—see rule breaking, in Chapter 5.

5. Use a colon title. We've just said that a good title should declare a topic, imply a thesis, purpose, or task, and say "Read me!" But most titles are two or three words long, and doing all three tasks in such a small space is hard. One way around that is to stick two titles together with a colon. Write a title that does two of the three tasks, put in a colon, and then add a title that does the third. Colon titles are a bit stuffy, but they work. Sometimes you do the topic, put a colon, then do thesis and "Read me!": "Television: The Glamour Medium." Sometimes you do it the other way around: "Rotten in Denmark: Images of Disease in *Hamlet*."

6. Use language from your text. Sometimes you can find a snippet from the essay itself, often in the conclusion, and tweak it into a title. Look at the conclusion of "Scratch That Itch" (A Collection of Good Writing). Some possible titles taken from its language: "Fallen Barricades," "Minimizing the Damage," "Your Mother Was Right" (or, "The Truth Your Mother Told You"), "Goldenseal and Onions."

7. Play with a familiar expression. Another way to title your essay is by taking a familiar expression (cliché, film title, song lyric, etc.) and playing with its language. I wrote a travel story some years back about skiing in the French Alps—shortly after the film *The Unbearable Lightness of Being* had come out. I titled the piece "The Unbeatable Rightness of Skiing." Other examples: for an informative essay on horseshoeing: "Just Shoe It"; for a piece on etiquette at Fourth of July parties: "Star Spangled Manners"; for a story about an exceptional emergency-room nurse: "The Wizard of Gauze." A word of caution: don't let your cleverness get in the way. Obviously (just look at my examples), you at least risk saying "*Don't* read me" by going too far with this.

8. Consider how it sounds. Depending on your subject and tone, you might want to play with language. How about some alliteration? For an informative essay on cooking spaghetti: "Preparing Perfect Pasta." Or rhyme? For a personal essay about blowing it on a job and getting fired: "Lost, Bossed, and Tossed."

A final suggestion. Read newspaper headlines. Good headline writers know how to say "Read me" in interesting ways. Check out sports headlines especially: "Vikings Pillage Panthers in Easy Win"; "Bears Slumber in Loss to Wildcats"; "Forty-Niners Go for Gold in Overtime."

Oh, one more thing. Don't underline your titles or put them in quote marks. You might want to increase the font size a bit, but generally just center the title above your introduction.

Using the Tool

As with the introduction, ask of the title, "Does this work? Does it make the reader want to read the essay?" You'll know the answer. Next, ask, "Does it do the three tasks of a perfect title?" If the title is faulty, blame the draft. If you can't find a hint of thesis, it's probably because the draft doesn't have one; if you can't find signs of life, it's probably because the draft doesn't have any.

EXERCISES

1. Write a one-page essay describing how successfully each of the following openers reveals its topic, reveals its purpose, and says "Read me."

a. For at least the past 10,000 years, the Grand Canyon has been luring human beings into its depths. From the Desert Archaics, who left behind their split-twig figurines, to the Anasazi, who built villages of adobe; from John Wesley Powell's tumultuous 1869 river adventure to "Uncle Jimmy" Owens's turn-of-the-century mountain lion hunts; from the 40,000 annual visitors (out of four million total) who come to practice their survival skills below the rim to the handful every decade who choose the canyon as the place to end their lives: No one enters the Grand Canyon casually, and no one, I would wager, leaves it without being variously and sufficiently awed.
(Pam Houston, "The Vertigo Girls Do the East Tonto Trail")

b. On our frequent American road trips, my friend Guy de la Valdène has invariably said at lunch, "These French fries are filthy," but he always eats them anyway, and some of mine, too. Another friend, the painter Russell Chatham, likes to remind me that we pioneered the idea of ordering multiple entrées in restaurants back in the seventies—the theory being that if you order several entrées you can then avoid the terrible disappointment of having ordered the wrong thing while others at the table have inevitably ordered the right thing. The results can't have been all that bad, since both of us are still more or less alive, though neither of us owns any spandex.

(Jim Harrison, "A Really Big Lunch")

2. Do Exercise 1 using an essay from A Collection of Good Writing.

3. Do Exercise 1 using an essay of your own. Rewrite the opener to include any task you find missing.

4. Write four stock openers for one of your own essays.

5. Write critiques of the conclusions in three essays in A Collection of Good Writing: How do they work? Do they use any of the four stock conclusions? How does the essay design plan for the conclusion?

6. Do Exercise 5 using one of your own essays.

7. Here's a list of titles from essays on censorship. For each title, answer the question "Which of a title's three tasks does it do?" Rewrite any titles that don't do all three so that they do—make up content if you need to. Example: "Eating" → "Tomorrow We Diet: My Life as an Overeater."

a. Why Is Censorship Needed?
b. Who's to Judge?
c. From a Child's Point of View
d. You Want to Read *What*?
e. Censorship: The Deterioration of the First Amendment
f. Censorship

8. Write four titles for one of your essays, one in each of the four stock formats.

9. Write colon titles for three of the essays in A Collection of Good Writing.

10. Write a colon title for one of your essays.

11. Write a one-paragraph critique of the title of one of your essays: does it do the three tasks of a perfect title? If it doesn't, rewrite it so that it does.

Chapter 9

PEER FEEDBACK

Peer feedback goes by many different names: peer editing, peer evaluation, and workshopping, for example. These terms usually refer to sharing drafts of writing in the classroom. It's important to remember, though, that this process occurs outside the classroom as well. I don't know a single writer who doesn't have someone else read a draft of a piece she's working on before sending it out or otherwise presenting it to its real intended audience. I personally always have my wife—or sometimes one or more of my friends—read my work in draft stage. In fact, I often have her read it in several stages—usually fairly early on, which for me is about a fifth or sixth draft, and then again as I'm closer to being done. In fact, in our house it's become kind of a ritual: I give my wife a piece I'm working on, and she goes over to the couch to read it. Then I pretend to busy myself, while in reality I'm watching and listening closely—sometimes peeking around the corner from the kitchen—for her reactions.

Why do we need readers? Because writers know what they're *trying* to do, but there's absolutely no way to know whether they're succeeding without readers who can tell them if their words are having the effect they intended. I usually have some specific questions for my reader: Is the example in Paragraph 6 convincing? Is my tone effective? Is the language too slangy? Too formal? Is the pun in the title stupid? A former student of mine, Matt Kiser, recently e-mailed me a draft of a letter he was sending to *Spin* magazine to apply for an internship. While he wanted my general feedback, he had a very specific question: do I come across as arrogant? (He didn't—and got the position.)

Of course, as human beings we want our readers to say, "This is perfect (totally convincing, absolutely hilarious) exactly as it stands. Don't change a thing." But as writers we also have to keep in mind that it is in fact a draft and that our reader(s) will most likely make some suggestions for revisions—and those suggestions are at least worth considering.

Peer feedback in the classroom takes many forms. Some writing teachers have students make copies of their work to pass around to the entire class. Some teachers break the class into smaller groups. Some teachers have students make transparencies/overheads, and the whole class works on one essay together. Regardless, there are certain rules to follow and important things to keep in mind if the feedback session is to be worthwhile. And it's critical that readers have specific things in mind while they're reading—including, ideally, questions from the writer. Otherwise, peer feedback can be a complete waste of time. Writing "I liked it" on a draft is not helpful.

Rules for Readers

1. **Make sure you know who the writer's intended audience is.** If you don't know for whom the writer is writing, there's no way to know whether something's working or not. Is the language too formal? Depends. Should the term *conjunctive adverb* in the second paragraph be defined? Depends. How about the word *phat* in the third? Depends.

2. **Ask the writer if there's anything in particular that you should be looking for.** Usually, writers know that certain parts of their essays aren't working as well as others or that they're stuck in certain places. If you know where the writer is struggling, you'll more likely be of help.

3. **Fry the biggest fish first.** Address the thing(s) that will help the essay the most first and the thing(s) that will help it the least last. If someone asked you to help him restore a dilapidated 1957 Chevrolet, you wouldn't first suggest that he polish the chrome on the headlights; you'd probably suggest he reupholster the seats and rebuild the transmission, then wash and polish the car last.

4. **Don't focus on what's wrong or list mistakes.** Doing so is devastating for the writer, it's not how people learn, and there's no such thing as right and wrong in writing. Instead, do the following:

5. Tell the writer how the text reads to you. Say things like, "This paragraph confused me," or "I wanted to know more here," or "The title made me laugh." This is the one thing the writer can't do for himself. The writer hits the golf ball, but only you can tell him where it lands. You can't be "wrong," since you're just declaring what you experienced while reading. The writer can't argue with you, for the same reason.

If you do this one job, you'll have served your writer well, but there's much more help you can offer:

6. Identify the source of your reactions. Find what in the text is causing you to feel the way you do. You help a little if you say, "This essay feels cold," but you help a lot if you add, "I think it's because of all the academic jargon."

7. Suggest possible revision strategies. Show the writer possible ways to work with the essay features you're observing. You help a little if you say, "The opening paragraph seems lifeless," but you help a lot if you add, "Why not start the essay with the personal narrative in paragraph 4?"

Rule 7 runs a lot of risks. You must remember that it's not your job to tell the writer how to write, and the writer must remember that she doesn't have to follow your suggestions—she decides what to do, because she's the writer. But if you can both stay in your proper roles, "You could do this . . ." suggestions can be golden.

8. Generalize and note patterns. Make broad statements that apply to the essay as a whole. Note when the same sort of thing happens over and over. Every time you make an observation about a place in the text, ask yourself, "Are there other places where similar things occur?" If you don't do this, feedback tends to be an overwhelming flood of unrelated suggestions.

9. Give yeas as well as nays. Give as much energy to pointing out what pleased you as to what didn't. "Keep doing this, this, and this" teaches at least as well as "Dump that, that, and that." And it feels a lot better. Psychologists who study marriages say that in healthy ones affirmations outnumber criticisms by about five to one. You may not be able to maintain that ratio, but you can embrace the spirit of it.

10. Help the writer see alternatives and possibilities. Think about what the essay could be that it isn't yet. Ask, Where can this draft go from here? What else could it be doing? What related issues does this open up?

This is the most precious gift you can give the writer, because it's the one thing she's least likely to be able to do herself. To do it you have to stop staring at the draft and asking "What needs fixing?" step back, and think outside the box. Ironically, this is the easiest part of the feedback process for the reader, because all you have to do is *share your thoughts on what the draft says.* Since you didn't write it, you'll have things to say about it that the writer will never think of, and those thoughts will open doors and make new essays possible.

To do this last task well, both the writer and the reader must remember that the purpose behind peer editing is not to rid the draft of errors but to remake the draft into the best possible essay. That usually means replacing the essay with another. Looking for errors to fix creates a tunnel vision that prevents that large-scale growth.

11. End by prioritizing. Since a good peer-editing session touches on a dizzying range of issues, avoid overload by ending with a highlighting of the two or three suggestions that have the biggest potential for gain: "Of all the things we've talked about, I think those two ideas about opening with the story about you and your mother and dropping the tirade about rude telemarketers are the best."

Rules for Writers

While you can do several things to increase the chances of getting good feedback, you must first have the right attitude: you need to be open to feedback. If you're too defensive, you're not likely to listen. If you're too submissive, you're likely to assume that you should make every single change your readers suggest. So listen to what your readers say, but trust your own instincts and ideas as well—allow that your readers might be flat-out wrong sometimes.

Also, keep in mind that it's a good idea to let some time pass between getting the feedback and sitting down with it to consider what you want to heed and what you don't. You might want to wait a few hours; you might want to wait a few days. At any rate, you'll probably be more open to listening openly and honestly if you've let some time pass.

Then use the following guidelines:

1. Let your reader know, as specifically as possible, who your intended audience is. If she doesn't know that, she can't offer much in the way of feedback.

2. Let your reader know what you're trying to do with the piece of writing. While it might sometimes be good to let your reader come to the essay "cold," that is, without telling him what to look for—an ironic tone, for example—the more your reader knows about what you're intending, the more he'll be able to tell you whether you're being successful.

3. Provide specific things for your reader to keep in mind while reading. I always have my students write—at the very tops of the papers—at least one question they have about their work, or a problem they're having with it, for their readers to consider while they read. And, as I suggested with the rules for readers, fry the biggest fish first.

4. Ask for peer feedback before you're "done." If you wait until the project feels finished, you'll fight off advice as a parent fights off criticism of his children. The earlier you ask for feedback from readers, the better.

5. Memorize the following truism: some readers just won't get it, especially if you're trying something interesting or different. Some readers dislike the unexpected. Seek out readers who are interested in your work and who are smart enough to recognize and appreciate what you're up to. They might say that what you're doing doesn't work—but it won't be just *because* it's different from what they expected.

6. Have your work read by several readers. But keep in mind that different qualified readers will have different reactions to your work. When I was in graduate school, I showed a draft of my thesis to my two committee members. One of them bracketed a long passage and said, "Cut this, and the piece will work better." The other one bracketed the same passage and said, "Great! This really makes your argument effective."

Of course, you can get more readers, and that's a good idea—to try to find consensus—but you might continue to receive more varying reactions. Ultimately, it will come back to you. It's your work, after all.

7. When it's over, say "Thank you." Remind your editors and yourself that they were doing you a favor.

Peer Editing in Groups

Peer editing in groups can be an effective way for a writer to see what kind of effect her work is having on several readers at once. However, group peer-editing sessions risk becoming chaotic and nonproductive. To that end, here are some rules:

1. Raise one issue at a time. Good students violate this rule with the best of intentions. They come to class and want to get on with it, so they start the discussion with a list: "I've got four things I want to say about the draft: first, the thesis is unclear; second, . . ." When the lecture is finished, if you're lucky, someone will address one of the issues on the list and everything else will be forgotten.

2. Stick to an issue once it's been raised. If someone raises a question about structure, discuss structure until all comments on structure have been heard.

3. Stay with an issue until clarity is reached. This doesn't mean grind down all opposition until everyone in the room thinks the same thing. It means talk about it until the group figures out where it stands. If there are different opinions in the room, get clear on what they are, who's on what side, and why they feel that way.

4. Voice your opinion. Silence following a comment suggests consensus, but the writer wants to know how the piece is working on the group, not on one reader. So if someone says he thinks something is working particularly well, say, "I agree." Likewise, if you disagree, say so.

5. Use your organizing tools. Since group editing is much more fragmented and chaotic than editing one-on-one, you have to work even harder to organize the chaos by doing the things we've already talked about: look for patterns, connect, generalize, and prioritize. Keep saying things like

> I think what Will is saying ties in with what Eunice said a few minutes ago.
>
> In different ways, we keep coming back to structural issues.
>
> I'd like to get back to the question of purpose and audience—that seems crucial to me.
>
> So it sounds to me like some of us like the tone and some of us think it's too folksy.

The Writer's Role in Group Editing

A group needs a leader, and since the writer has the most at stake and knows what he wants, he may as well be it.

This role is fraught with peril. If you can't lead without being defensive, then ask a couple of questions to start things off and say nothing else. But if you have the necessary self-control, you can do yourself a lot of good by following one rule:

6. **Remind the group to follow the rules.** Keep saying things like

How many others agree with Nell?—a show of hands, please.
As long as we're talking about structure, what other structural
   comments do you have?
So what do you think I should do about it?
Are there other places where that sort of thing happens?
How big a problem is that?
So what does the essay need the most?

Peer Editing for Mechanics and Grammar

Mechanics and grammar—comma placement, sentence structure, spelling—are legitimate topics in peer editing, but most conversations on those topics turn into useless nitpicking and wrangling that helps the writer hardly at all. So before you bring those topics up, be sure you're practicing some of the chapter's now-familiar rules:

1. **Keep frying the biggest fish first.** Discuss mechanics only in those rare cases where mechanical problems are the overriding issue.

2. **Discuss grammar and mechanics only in general terms.** If the problem isn't habitual, ignore it.

3. **Prioritize all mechanical advice.** Tell the writer how serious the problem is. Are you saying, "Since we've taken care of everything that really matters, we'll tinker with spelling," or are you saying, "My God, we've got to do something about the spelling before we do anything else!"?

A Final Piece of Advice

I've found that students respond best when they have specific jobs to do, so I usually give them lists of things to do as they read their peers' papers. On page 165 is a template of a worksheet that I modify appropriately for various assignments. Sometimes I'll put it on a transparency on an overhead projector; sometimes I'll make copies and have students attach it to the fronts of their essays.

While number 3 might seem obvious, I've found it to be extremely useful. If the writer finds that his reader summarizes the essay in a different manner from the way he would have, then he has to find where the disconnect is.

English XX—Section 4
Fall 2008

Please attach this sheet to the front of your essay.

Writer: (1) identify, as narrowly as possible, your intended audience; (2) identify some questions or problems you have with the draft as it now stands. Be as specific as possible.

Readers:

1. Read the essay carefully, with the intended audience in mind; then, on one of the attached sheets of paper:

2. Address the writer's question(s)/problem(s).

3. Summarize the essay in one sentence.

4. Describe the degree to which the essay is appropriate to its intended audience, considering level of formality, definition of terms, etc.

5. Identify the most convincing piece of evidence.

6. Identify any counter ("yeah, but . . .") arguments that the reader hasn't considered.

7. Make one concrete suggestion for revision.

8. Sign your name.

Notes: (A) initial any in-text comments; (B) read as a writer—you can both provide feedback and learn from the writer's work; (C) feel free to talk about these and to consider aspects of the writing not specified above.

WRITER'S WORKSHOP

Peer Editing a Peer-Editing Session

Let's practice peer editing. Here's a draft that was submitted by Todd Burks, one of Professor Rawlins's composition students. Following it is the peer-editing conversation that took place after Burks had shared it with the class. The italics in the margins are Rawlins's notes about the degree to which the readers were following the rules.

LEGALIZE HEMP: AN ESSENTIAL RESOURCE FOR THE FUTURE

TODD BURKS

Hemp, falsely known to many as marijuana, is an essential resource for the future of the planet. In todays age of environmental awareness is seems silly that we are not taking advantage of such a valuable commodity. Not only would the legalization of hemp save our forests, but it would stimulate the presently ailing economy.

Although both marijuana and hemp are derived from cannabis sativa, you can't get "stoaned" from hemp. You see, hemp is the large stock form while marijuana is the small "budding" form. Unfortunately, negative stigmas have been placed on hemp since marijuana became a popular street drug back in the late thirties. "The flower was said to be the most violent inducing drug in the history of mankind." Those of us who have experimented with the marijuana form Know this to be false.

The legalization of hemp (marijuana) for personnal use does not concern me. However, the legalization of hemp as a valuable resource would alleviate many political, economic, and environmental ills that plague the world.

To begin, hemp legalization would virtually eliminate the need for wood in paper products. Four times the amount of hemp can be grown on an acre of land than wood. The hemp takes only four months until harvesting, compared to nearly ten years for trees. Furthrmore, hemp paper is more durable than wood paper, lasting four times as long, and it's cheaper to produce.

The adaptibility of hemp to many soils and climates would allow for extensive growth worldwide. Unlike many rotation crops that degrade the soil, hemp roots actually permeate the soil, allowing for more productivity.

Hemp seeds could also develop into daily diets around the world. "The hemp seed is the second most complete vegetable protein, second only to soybeans. However, hemp seeds are more easily synthesized by humans due to the high content of enzymes, endistins, and essential amino acids." The seeds can also be used to make margarine and a tofu-like substance.

Almost one-third of the hemp seed is oil. Hemp oil can be used in paints and varnishes, eliminating the need for petrochemical oils. The biodegradeable hemp seed can also be used for diesel fuel and lubricant, causing less environmental pollution.

Finally, the rapid growth rate of hemp makes it the number-one renewable biomass resource in the world. "Biomass is fuel, whether it be petroleum, coal, or hemp." Therefore, hemp can be used in place of fossil fuels. Rather than carbon monoxide hemp gives off carbon dioxide which is naturally synthesized by our atmosphere.

It is obvious that hemp has gotten a bad rap due to the popularity of marijuana as a street drug. Not to mention the false propaganda headed by Hearst and DuPont early in the twentieth cent. However, with todays technology in genetic engineering, we can produce a plant that is purely stalk and is not possible to smoke. Finally, with government regulation and taxation we could virtually wipe out the trillion-dollar deficit hanging over our heads. ❖

Here's the classroom conversation. "Remember to . . ." in the margin indicates the rule is being broken.

Remember to begin with the writer's questions.

It seemed like you jumped right into your argument, and you could hold off on that a little more—like in your introduction, explain what hemp is, what you're going to use it for, then start saying, "But this is the reason why it's not being used . . ."

Fry the biggest fish first.

There was one sentence I'd take out: "Those of us who have experimented with the marijuana form know this to be false." That could weaken your case, because we could say, "Oh, it's a pot smoker, he just wants it legal so he can smoke it."

Remember to stick with an issue once it's raised.

He says legalization for personal use doesn't concern him, but I think it does concern him, because I don't see how you can start reforesting the fields of hemp for commercial use without some people doing it for personal use too.

Remember to stick with an issue once it's raised.

He needs to make more of how he just wants to legalize the genetically engineered plants.

Remember to stick with an issue once it's raised.

A couple of things I thought when I read it: If we have all this hemp, what do we do with the pot? Do we legalize that as well? And this fossil fuel thing: I've heard there's about fifty or so alternatives to replace fossil fuel; the only problem is it's really expensive to do so.

Remember to raise one issue at a time.

Maybe you could argue, "The fossil fuels are limited, this is replaceable. . . ."

That gets around the cost issue.

It ends up you can still grow it in Mexico for a tenth the cost. There's no way we can compete with Third World countries where it grows wild along the road.

As far as throwing out the "those of us" sentence, I don't know. Because obviously in the back of the reader's mind they're saying, "Wait a minute—some people have experimented with it, and I'm sure they have something to say about it." But I think that could be a potentially strong argument.

Connect with previous comments. If you disagree, say so.

Everyone seems to agree that the essay should either drop that aside about personal use or develop it more. Let's get a show of hands: How many think it should be dropped? And how many want to develop it? *(Rawlins)* (The vote is to drop it.)

Stay till consensus is reached.

Todd, didn't you tell me that it's just the stalk that makes the paper and stuff, so there's no reason to even worry about it being misused as pot?

You can certainly breed out the THC content—they've been intensifying it for twenty years, so I'm sure you can reduce it by the same genetic engineering.

I'm sure if I'm a farmer I'm going to grow hemp when I can grow pot for twenty times the money.

I'm confused about whether hemp and marijuana are the same thing, because in the first sentence you say "hemp, falsely

Tell the writer how the text reads to you.

known as marijuana," and in the third paragraph you say "hemp (marijuana)."

Well, they're both *Cannabis sativa*, but one is the long stalk form and the other is the flower form. *(Author)*

Remember not to explain or defend yourself.

So they're from the same family but two separate plants?

Same plant, different breeding. *(Author)*

That issue seems to be an important one. Does the group agree that that issue needs to be clarified? *(Rawlins)* (Signs of agreement throughout the room)

Connect, generalize, prioritize.

I don't understand that bit about Hearst's false propaganda.

Tell the writer how the text reads to you.

Don't you remember the "killer weed" business in the fifties?

What's that got to do with Hearst and DuPont?

At the time hemp was the second biggest crop after cotton, and they were going to use it as an alternative to paper products. Hearst and DuPont rallied against it, because DuPont has the patent on sulfuric acid, which breaks down wood into pulp, and Hearst had huge tracts of forest land, so they didn't want hemp to hurt the wood paper market. That's when they started all this reefer madness thing. *(Author)*

That all sounds like great stuff—I'd put it right into the essay. *(Rawlins)*

Suggest revision strategies.

I'd just prefer "cent." to be turned into "century."

Remember to fry the biggest fish first.

Me, too.

How do you spell "stoned"? "S-t-o-n-e-d"?

Is spelling a problem in the essay? *(Rawlins)*

Prioritize mechanical issues.

Yes. *(Several voices)*

Like what? *(Rawlins)*

"Falsley." "Personnal." "Furthrmore." *(Several voices)*

Also there are two "finally"s. When I hear the word "finally" I think, you know, "finally," so when I hear it again I go "Whoa. . . ." I just deleted the last "finally."

You could say "sorta finally" and "really finally."

Before we turn to grammar and mechanics, are there any larger issues anyone wanted to talk about? *(Rawlins)*

Fry the biggest fish first.

In the last paragraph when you say "bad rap" I could tell it was your voice. The essay seemed so technical, when I got to "bad rap" I thought, "Gee, it's not so technical anymore."

Are you saying you *like* "bad rap" and want more of it, or that you *don't* and suggest Todd take it out? *(Rawlins)*

Turn comments into concrete revision suggestions.

It just seems like a contradiction—it sticks out.

So you'd like the tone to be more consistent. *(Rawlins)*

One question that I have: There are three large quotes in the paper and you don't say where they come from or who said them or anything. They're just kind of there, so . . .

On the first page you talk about "political, economic, and environmental" benefits of hemp. You talk mostly about environmental, and you mention economics at the end, but I really didn't see much about political.

Remember to stick with an issue once it's raised.

Is that the thesis of the essay there? Because I thought the end of paragraph 1 was the thesis.

You know, you talk about "negative stig-mas" twice, in paragraph 2 and the last paragraph. I wonder if you need to do that.

Remember to general-ize and connect. Sev-eral of the comments address structure.

Should this be two sentences: "Not to men-tion the false propaganda headed by Hearst and DuPont . . ." Maybe it should be a comma.

Remember to fry the biggest fish first.

Is punctuation a problem in the essay? *(Rawlins)*

Prioritize.

No. *(Several voices)*

You say it can be used for diesel fuel and lubricant . . . I'm sorry, I just don't get that. I don't work on cars.

Tell the writer how it reads for you.

I need to know more about hemp roots pen-etrating the soil. It's not that I don't agree— I'm just not going to buy it until I know what it all means.

I hear several of these comments address-ing the same issue: You'd like *more infor-mation*—what exactly the roots do to the soil, how exactly hemp and marijuana are different, how hemp can be used for diesel fuel. *(Rawlins)*

Generalize and connect.

I've been playing with this sentence in paragraph 2: "You see, hemp is the large stock form, while marijuana is the small 'budding' form." I tried, "While hemp is the large stock form of *Cannabis sativa*, marijuana is the small budding form."

Remember to fry the biggest fish first.

You could just cross out "you see," couldn't you?

The only sentence I had trouble with was "The flower was said to be the most violent inducing drug in the history of mankind." I'm not sure what a "violent inducing drug" is.

That's a quote from a book. *(Author)*   *Remember not to defend.*

I still don't understand it.

I think it should be "violence-inducing drug."

Okay, we're nearing the end. What are your biggest and most important suggestions to Todd? *(Rawlins)*   *Generalize and prioritize.*

Explain yourself more—like the roots and the soil.

Make it clearer what the difference between pot and hemp is, and how you can grow one without running the risk of growing the other.

Tell us more about Hearst and DuPont—that was interesting.

You know, many of your comments relate to structure. For instance, the way the essay talks about stigmas twice, and the two "finally"s, and the two thesis sentences, and the way it promises to discuss politics in paragraph 3 but never does. If we were going to restructure, I thought the very first comment of the day gave us a good design: First list the virtues of hemp, then explain why we're prohibited from using it, relate the history, and *then* argue that the ban should be lifted. That suckers the reader into agreeing before he knows what he's in for. (*Rawlins*)   *Connect, generalize.*

Now it's your turn. Have a classmate distribute copies of his draft to the class. Peer edit the draft as a group, in the manner of Chapter 9. Then individually write a one-page essay in which you critique the group's performance by answering the following two questions: Which of the chapter's rules did the group and the author follow? Which did they break? Then write down two resolutions: What two things are you personally going to do differently the next time you peer edit?

Chapter 10

EDITING

Now it's time to polish, to go over the text line by line—word by word, in fact—to make sure it's as clean and shiny as you can make it. This isn't just more of Chapter 5. There we worked on building sentences; here we're trying to make sure they're correct. It's like restoring that '57 Chevy: you've spent the last two years rebuilding the engine and redoing the interior. Now the day of the big car show is approaching. You want to clean the glass, polish the chrome, shampoo the carpeting. Of course, this is all superficial stuff, but it's what will impress the judges. That new engine might purr like a kitten, but the judges will still dock points for that coffee stain on the rear seat.

Getting the Editing Attitude

The trickiest part of editing is doing it for the right reasons. To do that, embrace the following five principles:

1. Editing is not writing. Many people believe that if you follow all the mechanical rules, you're writing well. That's like believing that if you're never offsides, you must be a great football player.

In fact, writing is the original multitasking activity, which is why it's challenging. To write, you must have thoughts, express them, organize them, polish your language, clarify your thesis, be aware of your audience, and follow mechanical rules. You must play well *and* never be offsides.

2. Editing is different from creating. A writer's tasks fall into two groups, creative tasks and obedience tasks. Everything we've done so far in Chapters 1–9 is creative, and rules have been something we've chosen to follow or not. Now we have to become obedient little rule followers. That means we literally have to shift into a different part of our brains.

If you don't make that shift, you can't edit. If you try to create and correct at the same time or try to edit out of your creative brain, all that will happen is that the creative brain will rule and you won't edit. That's why every publishing house employs line editors, people who do nothing but line edit and who aren't allowed to tinker with the creative side. So follow their lead, and create a step in the writing process when you redefine yourself as a line editor and then *edit, and only edit*. Obviously this line-editing step must come dead last, since if you do anything else afterward you'll have to line edit again.

3. Editing is like cleaning windows. Think of the printed page as a window. Your job as a writer is to show the reader what's on the other side of the glass. We talked earlier about how pretentious writing is like stained glass that the reader can't see through. Poorly edited writing is like a *dirty* window. You want the glass to *disappear* so that the viewer doesn't get distracted by streaks and fingerprints— that is, by run-on sentences, misspelled words, incorrect punctuation, even typos that call attention to themselves. You want 100 percent of the reader's attention on what you're saying. Trai reedign tHis, sentecne and yew'l see wut ii; meat. Every mechanical oddity is a tiny tug on the reader's sleeve pulling her focus away from your content.

4. Stripping to the skeleton makes mechanics easy(er). Most of us write problematic sentences, not because we don't know the rules, but because when the sentences get complex we can't see how the rules apply. Nobody would write *"It's a problem for I," but lots of people do write *"It's an ongoing problem for my husband, Andy, and I." The problem is simple busy-ness, and you fix it by simplifying the sentence until you can see what is basically going on. Strip the sentence down to its skeleton—its basic framework—and ask if the skeleton looks good by the rules you already know. If *"It's a problem for I" is incorrect, then *"It's an ongoing problem for my husband, Andy, and I" is incorrect, and we fix both sentences the same way, by changing *I* to *me*. (The asterisk in front of the sentence, which you'll see throughout this chapter, means the sentence is incorrect.)

To strip to the skeleton, toss out all the unnecessary parts of the sentence: prepositional phrases, all adjectives, all adverbs, all introductory phrases. Reduce compound verbs to simple verbs. Keep tossing until you see if the core is solid or not:

*I'm not so knowledgeable about computers that when problems are presented to me that I instantly find solutions.

Skeleton: *I'm not so knowledgeable that that I find solutions.

Rewrite: *I'm not so knowledgeable about computers that when problems are presented to me I instantly find solutions.*

*Spearguns come in two forms: the kind that you cock and fire by pulling the trigger (this kind has better range). The other kind is called a Hawaiian Sling, which doesn't fire by a trigger and is usually cheaper and more simple.

Skeleton: *Spearguns come in two forms: the kind you cock and fire.

Rewrite: *Spearguns come in two forms: the kind you cock and fire by pulling the trigger (this kind has better range) and the kind called a Hawaiian Sling, which has no trigger and is usually cheaper and simpler.*

Sentences that use *which* clauses often cause problems, and they frequently need extra help. Take the *which* clause by itself, replace the *which* with a personal pronoun, and reorder the words to make a sentence:

*The Board has set two ground rules which only one must be followed by manufacturers.

Skeleton of the *which* clause: *Only one they must be followed by manufacturers.

Rewrite: *The board has set two ground rules, only one of which must be followed by manufacturers.*

*Children aren't familiar with print and it becomes a challenge to them, a problem in which they can and must make sense of.

Skeleton of the *which* clause: *They can make sense of in it.

Rewrite: *Children aren't familiar with print and it becomes a challenge to them, a problem they can and must make sense of.*

5. Frequently, mechanics can't be explained. The rules are more complex than words can say. Consider the commas in these two pairs of examples:

A tall, handsome, unmarried stranger

A typical pushy American tourist

Why commas in the first sentence and none in the second? It's almost impossible to put into words, so *all handbook rules lie by oversimplification*, including the ones in this chapter. In the end, the only thing that will steer you right is a sense of how English "goes," and *that* you get from years of reading.

"Grammar"

The thing to remember about rules is that they didn't come first. It's sort of like driving. Long before U.S. vehicle codes mandated that people drive on the right side of the road, people were driving on the right side of the road. Later, it was codified, to decrease the chances of accidents.

Likewise, no one sat down and created a list of, say, comma rules and then invented writing. Instead, people wanted to write clearly and consistently; they wanted their readers to know what they meant. For example, if I write, "After eating my brother and I drove home," you're going to have to pause to make sense of what I meant. But if I write, "After eating, my brother and I drove home," you'll know exactly what I meant, and you won't pause to think, "What a bozo! If he knew how to punctuate his sentences he wouldn't be writing about eating his brother."

So, there's a comma "rule" at work there (use a comma after a prepositional phrase before the main clause), but that's not what's important. What's important is that the reader knows what you're saying or at least that she doesn't stop to question your credibility. And, naturally, you care far more about being clear—and credible—than you do about whether commas should follow prepositional phrases.

Nonetheless, it is helpful to know some grammar, basically a combination of at least three different types of rules: conventions, rules of logic, and rules of clarity.

Conventions

Conventions are rules that can't be figured out or explained or are sometimes used to make sense but don't any more—they're "just the way it's done." Language is conventional; so are lots of things. Think about driving, for example: Conventionally (and legally), we drive on the right side of the road here in the United States; conventionally (and legally), they drive on the left side of the road in England. That's "just the way it's done." Conventionally, we say, "She gets on my nerves," but that doesn't make much sense. In fact, perhaps, "She gets *in* my nerves," as a Japanese student of mine once wrote, makes *more* sense. But when I tried to explain to her why we say "on" instead of "in," all I could really say was, "That's just the way it's done."

Unless you're learning English for the first time, you already know at least one set of English conventions—the set used by your parents or peer group—and the only question is whether you need to learn additional ones. Any convention is as good as any other as long as everyone in the group agrees to abide by it, so there's nothing wrong with the ones you know or better about the ones you're trying to learn.

Most of us know the conventions of Colloquial English (CE), but the conventions of formal Essay English (EE) are occasionally different:

CE: Everybody has to bring *their* own pencil and paper.
EE: Everybody has to bring *his* own pencil and paper.

CE: Try *and* get some rest before the big game.
EE: Try *to* get some rest before the big game.

CE: *Can* I go now?
EE: *May* I go now?

CE: *Who* is this intended *for?*
EE: *For whom* is this intended?

Do we ever use colloquial English in writing? Sure. As usual, knowing your audience will help you make the call. For example, I'm in regular e-mail contact with a bunch of my high school buddies, none of whom are English teachers, writers, or particularly concerned with the correctness of language (actually, since "none" is a contraction of "not one," that should read, "*not one of whom* is an *English teacher, a writer, or particularly concerned . . .*"). So when one of them writes asking me if I'd like to meet them at a San Francisco Giants baseball game—as we do regularly—I write back using appropriately informal language. If I used "whom," even if context called for it, they probably wouldn't let me sit with them! On the other hand, when I'm writing letters of recommendation for students who are applying to graduate school, I use a very formal language. If context requires "whom" instead of "who," I use "whom."

In writing essays for college classes (as well as for some publications—note the difference in level of formality between the language in the *New Yorker* and in *Transworld Snowboarding*), you need to be as correct as possible—not only because your professors expect it but because even the tiniest of glitches can give your readers reasons to question your credibility.

How do you know whether "who" or "whom" is correct? Good question. And though writing handbooks try to explain this and other grammar rules, they unfortunately have to rely on readers already knowing a lot about how language works. So even detailed explanations aren't always all helpful. The bottom line, again, is exposure: you simply need to read lots of professional essays to get a feel for the language. Eventually, you'll soak it up and do it naturally.

Rules of Logic

Some people think that all grammar is logical. We now know better, because many conventions have no logic, but there is a small pocket of grammar that is logic-based.

All of the following examples are illogical.

*Q: Do you mind if I sit here? A: Sure.

*That's a very unique sweater.

*He won't do nothing about it.

*I could care less if he quits.

Here are the logic problems:

"Sure" must logically mean "I do mind!"

Unique means "unlike everything else," so it's logically impossible to be *very* unlike something—either it's unlike or it isn't.

If he won't do nothing, then logically he must do something.

If you could care less, then logically you must care some.

The heart of language logic is consistency, which grammar calls *parallelism*. Once you start doing it one way, you must keep doing it that way:

If you're making a list and the first item in the list is a verb, make all the items in the list verbs; if it's a participle, make all the items participles. The same goes for nouns, adjectives, full sentences—anything.

If you start telling a story in the past tense, stay in the past tense.

If you start talking about *parents* in the plural, stay in the plural.

If you start referring to a hypothetical person as *her/him*, continue calling her/him *her/him*.

The four most common parallelism problems are unparallel lists, tense changes, subject–verb agreement problems, and noun–pronoun agreement problems.

Unparallel Lists

*I gained organization and speaking skills, along with thinking quick.

The first item in the list is "skills," which are things you possess; the second item is "thinking," which is an action. Things you *have* aren't parallel with things you *do*. You could fix it in several ways:

> Rewrite: *I gained organization and speaking skills, along with the ability to think quickly,*

or

> *I gained the ability to organize, speak well, and think quickly,*

or

> *I got good at organizing, speaking, and thinking quickly.*

Tense changes. The law of parallelism says, Stay in the same verb tense unless your meaning has shifted tense too.

> *A spelling game *may* excite the children and make learning fun. The class *will be* split in half. The first half *will* continue reading and writing while the second half *plays* the game. The group playing the game *would* line up across the room. Each child *is* given a chance to roll a set of dice.

Here's a revision in present tense:

> Rewrite: *A spelling game can excite the children and make learning fun. Split the class in half. The first half continues reading and writing while the second half plays the game. The group playing the game lines up across the room. Each child is given a chance to roll a set of dice.*

Subject–verb agreement. Subjects and verbs are supposed to agree in number—they should both be singular or both be plural. Most agreement problems occur when the subject and verb get separated by distracting business in between:

> *If a child is made to write on a topic of little interest to him, the *chances* of his learning anything from the experience *is* slim.

> Rewrite: *If a child is made to write on a topic of little interest to him, the chances of his learning anything from the experience are slim.*

> *The price of letter-quality printers have fallen dramatically.

> Rewrite: *The price of letter-quality printers has fallen dramatically.*

Pronoun agreement. Pronouns *refer to* nouns: in "George said he could," *he* refers to "George." A pronoun has to follow four rules. The noun it refers to must be physically present on the page. The noun must *precede* the pronoun. The noun must be the *first* noun you reach, reading back from the pronoun, that can logically be the pronoun's referent. And the pronoun and noun must *agree in number:* they must both be singular or plural. Colloquial English violates the fourth rule in two cases:

1. Pronouns like *anyone, anybody, everybody, no one,* and *nobody* are logically singular, so possessive pronouns that refer to them must also be singular:

   *Everybody has to bring *their* own juice.

   Rewrite: *Everybody has to bring her own juice.*

2. Anonymous single people ("a student," "a parent") need singular pronouns:

   *The key to writing success is choosing subject matter *the child* is familiar with and a vocabulary level *they* are familiar with.

   Rewrite: *The key to writing success is choosing subject matter the child is familiar with and a vocabulary level he is familiar with.*

Note: some writers use "their" or "they" to refer to a preceding noun in order avoid sexist language, obviously a good idea. Purists (myself among them), however, shudder at the thought. Purists who want to avoid sexist language have several options. Consider the following sentence in which the pronoun doesn't work:

Everyone should bring their own camping gear.

1. Switch to plural: *All campers should bring their own camping gear.*
2. Use the feminine pronoun: *Everyone should bring her own camping gear.*
3. Use "his or her": *Everyone should bring his or her* (or *her or his) own camping gear.*

   Note: if you do it this way, you must keep the sentence parallel throughout, and this often leads to problems: *Everyone should bring his or her own camping gear, unless he or she doesn't own any, in which case he or she might be able to borrow some from one of his or her friends.*

4. Alternate use of feminine and masculine pronouns. Naturally, you don't want to alternate midsentence or in a way that would confuse your reader: *Everyone should bring his own camping gear unless she doesn't have any.* But you can do this in longer passages. Maybe you've noticed that I've been doing this throughout *The Writer's Way.* Sometimes I use "he," and sometimes I use "she."

   Interestingly, this can backfire on you. Consider this sentence: *A student who doesn't understand her homework might want to find a tutor.* Uh oh! I was writing an article for a skiing magazine several years ago and, trying to be sensitive, wrote something like, "The ramp at the top of this chairlift is steeper than most and a skier unloading from it needs to be careful that she doesn't fall." So much for Mr. Sensitive. What, only women fall? No, no! That's not what I meant! So I changed it to *Skiers unloading from this chair need to be careful that they don't fall.*

5. Finally, sometimes you can simply rewrite the sentence so that it avoids pronouns altogether: *Camping gear is the responsibility of individual campers;* or *Camping gear must be provided by individual campers.*

The limits of logic. The only problem with approaching language logically is that it often doesn't work—logic will talk you into error almost as often as it will help you out of it. Here are two examples.

1. Essay English disapproves of *"A crowd of people are outside," because *crowd* is a singular noun and requires a singular verb: We should write "A crowd of people *is* outside." But if that's so, then, since *lot* is also a singular noun, it too should take a singular verb, so we must write *"A lot of people *is* outside," which is nobody's English.
2. "It's raining" violates the first three rules of pronoun usage above, but everyone agrees it's good English.

So remember, *convention always trumps logic*—if the two are in conflict, be guided by convention.

Rules of Clarity

Pronoun reference. Some language rules try to prevent confusion and misreading. We've already mentioned one set: the rules governing pronoun use above, which are designed to prevent confusion like this:

*I placed my order at a counter *that* looks like a regular fast-food restaurant. (The counter looks like a restaurant?) *It* is partially blocked off so *it* didn't bother me while I was eating. (The restaurant is blocked off? What didn't bother you?) After I ordered and paid for *it*, I sat down. (What did you pay for?)

Rewrite: *I placed my order at a counter that looks like the counter in any fast-food restaurant. It's partially blocked off so I wasn't bothered by sights of food cooking while I was eating. After I ordered and paid for my food, I sat down.*

Misplaced modifiers. A *modifier* is any word, phrase, or clause that modifies (roughly, "tells you something about") a noun or verb.

When words modify other words, make sure the reader is in no doubt about which words modify what. Most of the time it's obvious and there's no problem: if I say "As the sun was sinking in the west, the tall Texan slowly lowered himself onto the stool," *tall* modifies *Texan*, and *slowly, onto the stool*, and *as the sun was sinking in the west* all modify the verb *lowered*. But modifiers get unclear in two positions.

First, when a modifier ends a sentence, it can be hard to tell which preceding noun or verb the modifier refers to:

> *County Sheriff Wayne Hamilton this morning discussed where to put prisoners arrested for drinking with the Jefferson County Commissioners.

"With the Jefferson County Commissioners" modifies some verb, but we can't tell which one, so the sentence ends up implying that people are getting drunk with the Commissioners. To solve the problem, *move the modifier*:

> Rewrite: *County Sheriff Wayne Hamilton this morning discussed with the Jefferson County Commissioners* where to put prisoners arrested for drinking.

Second, when a modifier begins a sentence, it's often unclear what part of the sentence it refers to, so Essay English lays down a rule that it must always refer to the subject of the sentence.

> *As a future teacher, censorship seems to me to be an overblown issue.

(Sounds like *censorship* is planning on becoming a teacher.)

Rewrite: *As a future teacher, I think censorship is an overblown issue.*

> *Despite having spent $1.3 billion since 1992 on county jails, the need for more jail cells is still strong.

(Sounds like *the need for more jail cells* spent the money.)

Rewrite: *Despite having spent $1.3 billion since 1992 on county jails, we still need more jail cells.*

> *Driving to work this morning, a cat ran out in front of my car.

(Sounds like *a cat* was driving to work.)

Rewrite: As I was driving to work this morning, a cat ran out in front of my car.

Or: Driving to work this morning, I almost ran over a stupid cat.

Or: Driving to work this morning, I had to avoid a cat that ran out in front of my car.

Punctuation

People often think of punctuation as a guide to reading *rhythm*—a set of instructions about where and how long to pause. There's some truth in that. Consider the following four sentences, all correct, all read a little differently:

> George the gardener was arrested yesterday.

> George, the gardener, was arrested yesterday.

> George—the gardener—was arrested yesterday.

> George (the gardener) was arrested yesterday.

But punctuation is a guide to pausing only about 10 percent of the time; otherwise it's a guide to *syntax*—a set of instructions about the grammatical structure. The capital letter beginning every sentence is saying, "New sentence begins here." The colon is saying, "We just finished an independent clause and are about to start a list or explain what that *independent clause* means." The dread consequence of this is that in order to see where the squiggles go, you must understand how your sentence is put together—you must know when you're ending one independent clause and beginning another, for instance. Sorry about that.

The Comma

The comma is the all-purpose mark that says, "An infinitesimal interruption or pause goes here." It's the most common punctuation mark, it does the most jobs, and it's the most loosely defined, so it's also the hardest to master. Ninety percent of all punctuation errors are comma placement errors. To confuse things further, commas are often optional (but note the difference between this example and the sentence on p. 176 that begins "After eating my brother," where we truly need the comma and it's not optional):

> After working all day we'd all pile into George's old pickup.

> After working all day, we'd all pile into George's old pickup.

Commas do four main chores:

The introductory comma. Commas mark when a long introduction is over and the main clause begins:

> After the town had been battered by high winds for seven straight days, the rains came.

If the introductory bit is short, the reader probably won't need the comma's guidance, and you can leave it out:

> After dinner I went to bed.

The conjunctive comma. Commas mark when one independent clause ends and a coordinating conjunction begins another:

> The rage swept through him like the angel of death, and he stooped and picked up the knife.

> The loss of Flanagan will certainly hurt our offense, but we've devised some trick plays to make up for that.

There's a trick to remembering all the coordinating conjunctions: the acronym FANBOYS spells them out: **f**or, **a**nd, **n**or, **b**ut, **o**r, **y**et, and **s**o.

As with the introductory comma, this comma can be dropped if the clauses are short and the reader is unlikely to get lost:

> The rage swept through him and he picked up the knife.

Parenthetical commas. Commas *surround* parentheticals—that is, clauses, phrases or even single words—that interrupt the flow of the sentence. They come *in pairs*, like parentheses:

> He stood over Ragnalf, sword drawn, and exulted.

> I backed the old Rolls, inch by inch, into the narrow parking space.

> My friend, my best friend, just lied to me.

Parentheticals have to be *felt*—there is no hard rule about what's parenthetical and what isn't:

> Sometime after 3:00 a.m. he staggered slowly across the lawn.

> Sometime after 3:00 a.m. he staggered, vomiting, across the lawn.

Lots of little things are conventionally treated as interruptions even though they don't feel very interruptive, and you should just memorize the fact that they're surrounded by commas: names in direct address, states or countries after cities, years after days, exclamations:

> Bill, will you tell Harry that, uh, that guy out in Cleveland, Ohio, needs that stuff by March 13, 2008, or we're in trouble. Oh, damn, I already told him.

Series commas. Commas punctuating a series of *three or more* go between each pair, including the last one:

> He turned slowly, sensually, and seductively.

Generations of students were taught to leave that last comma out, and newspapers may not include it, but formal essays put it in.

Believe it or not, you can actually have fun with comma rules, or at least punctuation geeks (such as I) can. At this point, feel free to skip directly ahead to "Things Commas *Don't* Do," but if you're interested in seeing where this goes, come along.

Question: how can both of the following sentences be both true and punctuated correctly?

My sister, Peggy, lives in California.

My brother Rick lives in Idaho.

I'll let you think about that for a little bit.
Now consider these two sentences:

Bruce Springsteen's CD *We Shall Overcome: The Seeger Sessions* is his best yet.

Bruce Springsteen's most recent CD, *We Shall Overcome: The Seeger Sessions*, is his best yet.

Both are correct.

See how it works? If your reader will still know what you mean when you take the information out, then you need to put commas on both sides. If your reader needs the information, you don't want the commas. So if I remove the title of the CD from the first sentence, my readers won't know which CD I'm referring to, but if I take it out of the second one, they would.

OK. How can the sentences about my brother and sister both be true and punctuated correctly? Anyone get it? A show of hands, please.

Answer: I have one sister but two brothers. So I can take "Peggy" out of the first one but I can't take "Rick" out of the second one.

Things Commas *Don't* Do

Beyond putting commas where they belong, you have to make sure you don't put them where they don't belong.

First, commas do not go between a subject and its verb, even if the subject is huge:

*The reason I didn't tell you about cracking up the car and having to spend the night in jail, is that I simply forgot.

Rewrite: *The reason I didn't tell you about cracking up the car and having to spend the night in jail is that I simply forgot.*

Second, commas do not go between conjunctions and their following clauses:

*I never showed up because, my parents wouldn't let me have the car.

Rewrite: *I never showed up because my parents wouldn't let me have the car.*

Third, commas do not go between two sentences with no conjunction:

> *The teacher cannot teach children to read or write, this can only be learned through doing it yourself.

> Rewrite: *The teacher cannot teach children to read or write; this can only be learned through doing it yourself.*

> *Paella is a traditional rice-and-seafood dish from Barcelona, it is also popular in other parts of Spain.

> Rewrite: *Paella is a traditional rice-and-seafood dish from Barcelona, and it is also popular in other parts of Spain.*

That no-no is called a *comma splice*—the splicing together of two sentences with only a comma. It gets a huge amount of attention in school and from some readers outside school, so it's worth learning to avoid. Say to yourself, "A comma isn't big enough to join sentences by itself; I need more." *Don't reword the sentence;* replace the comma with a semicolon, colon, or dash, or keep the comma and add a conjunction.

A popular comma splice is the *however* comma splice:

> *I'd really like to come, however my scheduling just won't allow it.

> Rewrite: *I'd really like to come; however, my scheduling just won't allow it.*

However (and words like it—*nevertheless, therefore*) is really an *adverb*. Since it's not a conjunction, it and a comma can't join independent clauses. You need a semicolon.

Fourth, commas do not go between *pairs* joined by conjunctions, except pairs of sentences:

> *He stooped with an air of graceful insouciance, and picked up something shiny from the gutter.

> Rewrite: *He stooped with an air of graceful insouciance and picked up something shiny from the gutter.*

Fifth, commas do not surround "anything that can be taken out of the sentence." Use your oral reading sense to tell you where there's a sense of interruption or turning aside:

> The Boston Red Sox, who are my favorite team, seem determined to break my heart.

> The Boston Red Sox who trashed that reporter's car should be heavily fined.

Finally, commas don't go "where you pause." Sometimes they do, but it's a rule that will lead you astray as often as it pays off.

The Semicolon

The semicolon does two things:

The antithetical semicolon. This semicolon joins sentences that are halves of a balanced pair—an *antithesis*. It says, "Don't think the thought is over just because the sentence is over. Keep reading; you're really only half done":

> Personal writing isn't trying to sell you anything; it's just trying to share a part of the writer's life.

> If it's above 70 degrees, he's too hot; if it's below 70 degrees, he's too cold.

The semicolon is correct if a comma *and* a coordinating conjunction (FANBOYS) would work but there's no coordinating conjunction.

The series semicolon. Consider this sentence:

> The panel included Celine O'Malley, a doctor, Georgia Nilsson, an attorney, and Hannah Rose, an art professor.

How many people are on that panel? Six? Three? Actually, according to the list (and our comma rule: commas between items in a series), there are six. If I meant that Celine's the doctor, though, that Georgia's the attorney, and that Hannah's the art professor, then I need to separate them, and I do that with semicolons:

> The panel included Celine O'Malley, a doctor; Georgia Nilsson, an attorney; and Hannah Rose, an art professor.

So the rule then is, use a semicolon to separate items in a series when the items themselves use commas.

As with these:

> We visited Prescott, Arizona; Salem, Oregon; and Tempe, Arizona.

and

> The professor suggested several classic works of literature, including *The Great Gatsby*, by F. Scott Fitzgerald; *Moby Dick*, by Herman Melville; *Don Quixote*, by Miguel de Cervantes; and *Frankenstein*, by Mary Shelley.

Things Semicolons *Don't* Do

Semicolons do not join sentences and following fragments—use a colon or dash instead:

> *There is only one reason the new sex education program will never succeed; parental objections.

> Rewrite: *There is only one reason the new sex education program will never succeed: parental objections.*

Semicolons do not come before a list. Use a colon or nothing, depending on how you set it up, instead.

> *The panel consisted of several experts including; a doctor, an attorney, and an art student.

> Rewrite: *The panel consisted of several experts: a doctor, an attorney, and an art student.*

> or

> *The panel consisted of several experts, including a doctor, an attorney, and an art student.*

The Colon

The colon comes *after a complete sentence* and announces that what follows will list or explain something the sentence *promised* but didn't specify:

> Every time we try to make the relationship work, we run up against the same two obstacles: my personality and her personality.

> There are three secrets to a successful business: location, location, and location.

Many people say a colon precedes a list, which is okay as long as you remember that it can be a list of one *and* that it must follow a complete sentence:

> She knew what she needed: chocolate.

> He suddenly had a wonderful idea: why not hold the show right here?

Things Colons *Don't* Do

Colons do not follow sentence fragments. When you feel the urge to do that, either use no punctuation or rewrite the opening so it's a sentence:

> *The three main problems facing the Middle East today are: poverty, Iraq, and religious fanaticism.

> Rewrite: *The three main problems facing the Middle East today are poverty, Iraq, and religious fanaticism.*

> or

> *The Middle East today faces three main problems: poverty, Iraq, and religious fanaticism.*

The Dash

The dash is not only the most loosely defined punctuation mark, but it is also characteristic of a relatively informal level of writing. It works in most essays—I've seen it in the *New Yorker* and the *Atlantic*

Monthly—but you probably would want to avoid it in a formal master's thesis, for example.

Most dashes come in two places. The first is between a sentence and a following fragment:

> He either had to say yes or tell her why not—a hopeless situation.

> It's already raining outside—pouring, in fact.

The second use of dashes is to surround a drastic interruption in the middle of a sentence:

> Suddenly there was a noise—it sounded more like a cannon than anything else—and the south wall disappeared.

> It was Shakespeare—or was it Madonna?—who once said, "All the world's a stage."

Most word-processing programs don't have dashes on them, so when you want to use one in your writing, type two hyphens—otherwise it will look like a compound word. It should look like this, "word—word," not like this, "word-word."

Parentheses

Everybody knows that parentheses indicate a whispered aside, but punctuating around them can get confusing. Punctuate the sentence without the parentheses; then put the parentheses in, leaving all other punctuation untouched:

> He was tall and mean-looking.

> He was tall (very tall, in fact) and mean-looking.

> He was tall, but his legs were short.

> He was tall (very tall, in fact), but his legs were short.

Question Marks

Put a question mark after any sentence that is syntactically a question, whether it "feels" like a question or not:

> Why don't you come over tonight and we'll order pizza?

> Will you be kind enough to reply as soon as possible?

The Hyphen

The hyphen is a word-making tool. It lets us combine words and affixes to make three kinds of words:

The compound adjective hyphen. The hyphen adds words together so they can be used as adjectives.

five ten-gallon hats
a nine-to-five job
a soon-to-be-fired-for-his-incompetence employee

In practice it's hard to tell if a familiar two-word adjective should be written as two words, a hyphenated word, or simply one word: is it *red hot, red-hot,* or *redhot*? Just look it up in a dictionary. If it isn't there, hyphenate.

Another way to check is to see if using it changes the meaning. Consider:

Used car salesman

Used-car salesman

In the first one, the car salesman is used; in the second one, his cars are.

Recently, the editors of our local newspaper apparently forgot how a hyphen can change meaning, in this case humorously, and ran a headline that read "Nude Bar Owner Arrested." See? According to the headline, the owner of the bar was nude, when they meant to say that he owned a nude bar.

Sometimes, on the other hand, convention tells us to ignore the rule. Technically, you'd hyphenate "high school students"; otherwise, it'd mean that the school students were "high." But I've never seen that phrase hyphenated, probably because we're so used to seeing, and saying, the words "high" and "school" together that there's not much chance of misunderstanding.

The verb-phrase noun hyphen. This hyphen adds a verb and its following adverb together so they can be *used as a noun*:

We were on a stake-out.

The car needed a little touch-up.

Both of these hyphens say, "Take this group of words and think of it as a single word." The key is that *the phrases have been moved from their natural position*. In their natural positions, they have no hyphens:

The hat held ten gallons.

I worked from nine to five.

The employee was soon to be fired for his incompetence.

We were going to stake out the house.

I asked him to touch up the paint on the car.

The prefix hyphen. Hyphens join prefixes to words if the joining is an awkward one:

ex-husband vs. extinction

pro-choice vs. productive

The Apostrophe

There are three kinds of apostrophes.

The contraction apostrophe. This apostrophe marks places where letters have been dropped out in contractions and reductions:

could not → couldn't

I will → I'll

I expect he is swimming about now. → I 'spect he's swimmin' 'bout now.

The apostrophe goes exactly where the letter dropped out, and you need one for each place where a letter or letters used to be:

Write *doesn't*, not **does'nt*.

Write *rock 'n' roll*, not **rock 'n roll*.

The same is true for numbers, such as decades. Write '60s, not 60's.

The possessive apostrophe. This apostrophe marks possession, which is a loose kind of ownership:

The pitcher's absence forced the cancellation of the game.

The men's room is locked.

The book's disappearance remained a mystery.

The rules for positioning the apostrophe are inflexible:

1. If the noun is singular, add *-'s*:

    one dog's collar

    Do this even if the noun ends in *-s* already:

    one dress's hemline

2. If the noun is plural and is pluralized with an *-s*, add the apostrophe after the *-s* that's already there:

    some dogs' collars

    some dresses' hemlines

3. If the noun is an irregular plural, add *-'s*:

    the men's department

    the octopi's mittens

4. If the word showing ownership is a *pronoun*, use no apostrophe at all: *his, hers, theirs, yours, ours,* and especially *its*. Memorize it: *Its* means "belonging to it"; *it's* means "it is" or "it has."

5. If the noun is singular and ends in *-s*, sometimes the possessive looks or sounds funny, in which case some people give you permission to drop the second *-s:*

Ted Williams's batting average

or

Ted Williams' batting average

The odd plural apostrophe. This apostrophe separates a plural noun from its pluralizing *-s only if* it would be confusing to the eye to use a normal plural form:

I love the Oakland A's.

Give me two 10's.

How many *e*'s are there in *separate?*

Quotation Marks

Quotation marks do four things.

They surround someone else's exact words when you quote them:

I can still hear Monique saying, "But I didn't *mean* it!"

Her exact words were that she didn't "have a clue" about his whereabouts.

Use quotation marks even if the speaker or speech is imaginary:

I can just imagine what my father would say: "How are you going to pay for that?"

Nobody ever said, "Have a lousy day."

They create ironic distance: the punctuational equivalent of a wink. They surround language you use but want to disown—language representative of the way *someone else* talks:

Doctors never like to talk about pain. When I'm sick, I don't "feel discomfort"—I *hurt!*

Unions are always talking about "parity."

I don't want to meet your "special friend."

They surround minor titles: titles of little things or parts of things, like chapters from books, songs, essays, short stories, or newspaper articles. The titles for the big, whole things (books, anthologies, newspapers) are *italicized* or <u>underlined</u>.

"The Telltale Heart" vs. <u>The Collected Works of Edgar Allan Poe</u>

"Man Bites Dog" vs. the *New York Times*

They surround words as words:

How do you spell "necessary"?

I hate the phrase "special education."

Sometimes italics do this job.

Things Quotation Marks *Don't* Do

Quotation marks don't surround your own title at the head of your essay. They don't give emphasis to words or suggest heightened drama:

　*Win a free trip to "Paris"!

　*"Special" today, broccoli 35 cents/lb.

This a common mistake and like so many others can lead to unintentional humor. Every August an apartment complex near the university where I teach erects a huge sign that says Welcome Back "Students."

Spacing and Positioning

Follow periods and all sentence-ending punctuation marks with one space. Follow all commas, semicolons, and colons with one space.

Parentheses surround words without internal spacing (like this) (*but not like this).

Dashes and hyphens have no spaces around them—like this—but not —oops!— like that.

Quotation marks always come outside commas and periods; they come inside colons and semicolons; and question marks and exclamation points go wherever the sense dictates: if the question or exclamation is a part of the quotation, put it inside (He said, "Why?"); if the question or exclamation is the whole sentence, put it outside (Why did he say "ragmop"?).

Incidentally, you can't really learn spacing by looking at books, because typers think differently than typesetters do.

Spelling

Bad news: First, the world has decided that spelling matters enormously. If you can't spell, most readers will conclude you're illiterate, stupid, or both. Second, the world's spelling standards are very high. Two misspellings per typed page is considered poor. Third, spelling English is fiendishly hard, and nothing can make it easy. Fourth, spell-checker computer programs won't save you, because a misspelled English word often looks just like another word (*their/there, planning/planing*). The only good news is that spelling is one of the world's most fascinating games.

The five most common ways people try to spell don't work. Let's rule them out now:

Don't try to spell by rule. There are a few rules that help you spell (see below), but each will solve only one problem in a hundred.

Don't try to spell phonetically, by sounding words out. Most of the words you use a lot don't follow the rules.

Don't spell by mnemonic devices. A mnemonic device is a trick, jingle, or story to help you remember something: "the princi*pal* is your *pal*"; "I shot *par* on two se*par*ate golf courses." Mnemonic devices work, but they're slow and cumbersome. I learned to spell *receive* via the famous mnemonic "*I* before *E* except after *C*," and thirty years later I still have to stop and recite the jingle every time I write the word.

Don't try to learn to spell by reading. Good readers are often terrible spellers, because reading well depends on *not* focusing on the letters.

Don't rely on your computer's spell checker. Spell checkers can't determine context, so all they can do is tell you that a word doesn't exist—in their own dictionaries, that is. A student of mine was working on a paper on Duke Ellington, and he simply did a global "search and fix" before he submitted it to me. Because his computer didn't recognize "Ellington," he ended up with a paper about "Duke Wellington." I handed it back without reading past the first paragraph.

My personal pet peeve, though—and, honestly, I see this a half dozen times a semester—is when a student submits a paper that he thinks uses the word *definitely* but that he has misspelled as *definately*, and the spell checker then "corrects" it as *defiantly*.

Note: spell-check programs can be useful. Just don't *rely* on them. Look closely at the word the program is suggesting as a replacement. Make sure it's what you want.

So much for what doesn't work; here are six techniques that do:

Spell for fun. Fall in love with language and words and become fascinated by how they work. Read books about words. Trace interesting etymologies in the dictionary. Play spelling games like Scrabble, Boggle, Password, and Perquacky; do crossword puzzles.

Spell by recognition. You can train yourself to recognize correctly spelled words the same way you remember faces or the names of movie actors. You look at *doesn't* and say "That looks right" and you look at **dosen't* and say "That looks funny." This method is effortless—you don't really work at remembering Brad Pitt's name—but it doesn't happen until you *care*.

Spell morphemes, not words. A morpheme is a piece of meaning. Words are made out of them. *Unlisted* has three: *un-* (which means "not"), *list*, and *-ed* (which means "past tense"). The vocabulary of English really isn't a million unrelated words; it's a million recombinations of a few morphemes. If you can spell the morphemes, you can spell the words. Once you learn the morpheme *syn-*, meaning "together," you've learned the tricky part of spelling *syndrome, syndicate, synchronize, syntax, synagogue,* and about 450 others. Once you learn the morpheme *par*, meaning "equal," you've learned the tricky part of spelling *parity, disparate, compare, disparage, reparation,* and dozens more.

If you're unsure of a word, break it into its morphemes and spell each morpheme:

> *familiar = family + ar* (so **fimiliar* must be wrong)
> *vicious = vice + ious* (so **viscious* must be wrong)
> *preposition = pre + pose + ition* (so **prepisition* must be wrong)
> *definitely = de + finite + ly* (so **definately* must be wrong)

Get hints from other forms of the same word. Often a letter we can't hear in one form of the word sounds distinctly in another:

> circUit: think of *circuitous*
> musCle: think of *muscular*
> mouNtain: think of *mount*
> condemN: think of *condemnation*
> critiCize: think of *critic*
> grammAr: think of *grammatical*
> utIlize: think of *utility*
> definItely: think of *definition*
> sentEnce: think of *sententious*
> relAtive: think of *relate*
> corpOration: think of *corporeal*

Make your own list of demons. Most of us only misspell forty or fifty words. It doesn't take long to make a list of them; then you can drill on them.

Memorize a few rules. A very few rules are worth learning:

1. *I* before *E* except after *C*, or when sounded like *A*, as in *neighbor* and *weigh*.

2. In stressed non-final syllables, double the consonants after short vowels; keep consonants single after long vowels. *Matting* needs two *t*'s, *mating* needs one.

3. Final *-e*'s disappear before suffixes starting with vowels; they don't disappear before suffixes starting with consonants: *manage → managing, management; consummate → consummation, consummately.*

4. Final *-y* becomes *-i* when followed by a suffix: *pity→pitiful, rely→relies, controversy→controversial, family→familiar.* Exception: *-y* before *-i* or after a vowel stays *y: pity, pitying; stay, stayed.*

The Worst That Can Happen to You

Many students deal with mechanical problems by avoiding any situation in which they might arise. If a word is hard to spell, they just don't use it. If they aren't sure how to use a semicolon, they don't use it at all. Once they realize that long sentences risk structure problems, they use only short, simple sentences. In a sick way, this approach works, but it's the worst thing that can happen to you, because once you start writing with the purpose of avoiding error, the logical end result is to not write at all. Writing is inherently risky, like skiing or driving a race car. That's why it's a rush. Embrace the risk, the way a race car driver looks forward eagerly to the twisting stretch of road.

Following Format

A format is a set of rules about how an essay is laid out on the page: how big to make the margins, whether to type the title in full capitals or not, where to put the page numbers. Some students consider such matters too trivial for their attention, but editors and publishers don't. In fact, editors and publishers consider them *very* important and often will not even bother with a piece—no matter how profound or compelling—if it doesn't follow their format. If you're thinking of submitting a piece for publication, take a look at the publication's writers' guidelines, usually available by calling and asking or by going to the publication's homepage and clicking on "writers' guidelines."

There are no universal format rules, so the only way to know what the format is is to ask the boss. Use this format for school papers if your instructor hasn't mandated one:

1. Use only one side of standard size (8½" × 11") paper of medium weight (20 lb.) or heavier.

2. Print—never hand-write—using a quality printer with a relatively new cartridge.

3. Proofread carefully, and make all handwritten corrections or additions neatly, in black ink.

4. Keep a margin of one inch on all four sides of the page. Approximate the right margin, breaking long words with hyphens to get close to the one-inch border.

5. Center each line of your title. Don't underline it or put quotation marks around it (unless it's a quote). Don't use full capitals; capitalize the first letter only of the first word and all important words: all nouns, verbs, adjectives, adverbs, and anything over four letters long. Put more space between your title and the text than there is between the lines of text themselves: If you're double spacing the text, triple space between title and text. Don't have a separate title page unless you're told to or the essay is more than thirty pages long.

6. Put in the upper right-hand corner of page 1 the following information: your name, the course *number* (e.g., Anthro. 210B), and the date.

7. Connect the pages with a staple in the upper left-hand corner. Don't fold the pages or dog-ear them.

8. Use 1½ spacing if your printer has it; if not, double space.

9. Indent the first line of each new paragraph one tab stop, which should be set to five spaces. Don't put extra space between paragraphs.

10. Number all pages after page 1. Put the page numbers in any one of three places: upper right corner, top center, or bottom center.

11. Use no eye-catching fonts or letter sizes. Be simple, conventional, and understated.

Proofreading

Proofreading is reading over the text to look for places where your fingers slipped and you typed *natino* instead of *nation*. It's the very last thing you do before printing the final copy. To get in the mood, begin by realizing four truths:

Realize why proofreading matters. You become a zealous proofreader the day you grasp how destructive a typo is to your reader's concentration. A single typo can undo all your hard work. How do *you* react when you read about "fist graders," "shot stories," or "censoring textbools"? Well, everybody else reacts that way too. And as a writer you'd rather be dragged naked through cactus than get that reaction.

Realize how proofreading problems are fixed. Spelling problems are problems of *knowledge,* and you fix them by *learning;* typos are just finger slips, and you fix them by learning to *look.*

Realize that your word-processing program's spell checker won't save you. Spell-checker programs make typo problems *worse,* because they lull you into thinking they've fixed the problem when they haven't. The program will catch all the "hte" typos, but it leaves all the ones that produce another word: "shot stories," "fist graders," and so on.

Realize why proofreading is hard. It's because all your life you've been practicing the art of *not looking at the letters.* Good readers read by skimming and guessing—experts estimate you're actually seeing perhaps 25 percent of a text.

To proofread well, you stop *reading* and start *staring.* Here are nine principles to guide you:

Proofread from hard copy. Most people simply do not see the mistakes on a screen that they will see on a piece of paper. So print out a copy, proofread, make the corrections, print out another copy, make the corrections, and keep doing that until you've got it.

Assume there's at least one typo. If you don't, you'll never find any.

Set aside a time for nothing but proofreading—you can't do it and anything else too, since it uses your eyes and brain in a unique way.

Ignore content. As soon as you start listening to what the text is *saying,* you'll start seeing what you expect and not what's there.

Read backward, to prevent yourself from predicting.

Go slow. Any attempt to hurry and you'll start guessing and skimming.

Don't just proofread individual words; proofread phrases and clauses. Otherwise you'll miss goofs like these:

*I would explain that in our society there correct and incorrect forms to use.

*The little cap just pulls off it you put enough effort into it.

*After two weeks, it is evident that the that the consistent and continual printing errors are the result of a defective printer.

Proofread the new text and everything surrounding it when you revise a proofread text to make sure you haven't introduced large-scale problems like lack of parallelism.

Get help. It's easy to get so close to your work that you just don't see it clearly anymore. I've proofread and proofread and proofread and, finally, thinking I've caught everything, shown it to my wife for one more go-over. Almost every time she catches something: *You don't need the second "the" in "the the best way to proofread,"* she'll say.

EXERCISES

1. List three mechanical *facts* (not principles or attitudes) you didn't know before you read Chapter 10. Begin each with "I didn't know that . . ."

2. Line edit a page of manuscript in class as a group. Have a volunteer distribute a double-spaced page of essay to the class. Divide the readers into teams of two. Have each team make a list of three mechanical problems in the text, each with a repair and a clear, concrete explanation for why it's a problem. Have each team identify one problem, repair it, and explain it in front of the class. Discuss each presentation to see if the group agrees.

3. Make a list of mechanical topics covered in this chapter: format, parallelism, semicolon usage, etc. Have each member of the class sign up as class expert on that topic. Line edit a classmate's essay page as in Exercise 2, with each expert reporting on any problems in her area of expertise that appear in the draft.

Part Four

MODES OF WRITING

Chapter 11

PERSONAL WRITING

When you're doing personal writing, the basic rule is the same as for all writing everywhere: you can't do it if you haven't read a lot of it. So the easiest way to write a good personal essay is also the most pleasant: read all the personal essays in A Collection of Good Writing and then *write one like them*.

What's Personal Writing?

Personal writing is both the easiest kind of writing to do and the most difficult. That is, it's easy to write about your experience, to recall details from your life, to jot them down on paper. Plus, you can't be wrong! Yet, you need to make that experience—those details from your life—*matter*, to a real reader.

That's why the what-I-did-last-summer essay has become a joke. Who cares? Not I—unless you somehow *make* it matter, or, as my students like to say, make it so readers can "relate to it."

Frequently, students will respond to a peer's essay by saying they can "relate to it" because they've had the same experience. Perhaps a student has written about his parents' divorce, so half the class (statistically) can relate because their parents, too, are divorced.

That's not what writing's about, though. Good writers can make readers who *haven't* had the experience "relate to it." If you've been to Maui and so has your reader, it's easy to write a piece that will make her "see" the island. But the writer's job, in this case, is to describe Maui in such a way that the reader who *hasn't* been there can "see" it. The same is true for the divorce essay. If the reader can "relate" because his parents are also divorced, that's the subject at work, not the writing.

So just how do you make personal writing matter?

That's what's difficult: it must somehow be bigger than its topic. That is, the divorce paper might become a paper about loss or disappointment or perhaps even about how odd it feels to become a statistic. I've talked off and on in this book—especially in Chapter 7—about the importance of the bigger picture. That's what personal writing must somehow consider. While the what-I-did-last-summer essay is indeed a joke, in reality, if handled properly—if it connects to a bigger picture—it can be quite powerful. In fact, it's a classic subject of literature, as well as of many excellent films. Consider *American Graffiti*, the story of one night in the life of several recent high school graduates in the summer of 1962. On one level, it's just a story about those kids—driving hot rods, drinking too much, and looking for sex. But it's about something bigger, too: the end of adolescence and how bittersweet a feeling that is. And that's something we all can "relate" to.

How do you connect to the bigger picture? There's no easy answer. The best thing you can do, of course, is to read lots of personal essays as models. Look at what's going on in them, at what the writers are doing to make the subjects more than just what would amount to diary entries. Sometimes the writer steps away from the subject and comments directly. Consider, for example, Yer Thao's essay on page 204. Good television often does the same thing. In the early 1990s there was a Steven Bochco–produced television show called *Doogie Howser, M.D.*, about a teenage genius who had already graduated from medical school. At the end of every episode, Doogie would sit down at his computer and type a sentence or two that generalized about what the episode we'd just seen meant.

Sometimes the writer achieves this distance through tone. A good example is another great old television show, *The Wonder Years*, in which the narrator describes, in voice-overs, events from his life from the perspective of an adult looking back on his formative years. That way, he's not so emotionally connected to them that he can't see what they "mean."

Personal writing doesn't teach the reader something utilitarian, like how to crochet or what to do with bored children on a rainy day. It doesn't argue the reader into buying a thesis, like "We should immediately offer economic aid to Russia." Instead, it's a sharing of the self, or a reaching out. When Kris Tachmier wrote the wonderful personal essay about how much she hated eggs (Chapter 3), she wasn't trying to teach us something new about eggs that we could put to practical use, and she wasn't trying to convince us that we should hate eggs too. She's just kind of poking fun at herself for having this irrational—but very real—hatred of eggs, and we can "relate" to it because irrational feelings are universally human. The fact that they're eggs doesn't even much matter. We also simply like the writer. Since she's self-deprecating instead of preaching, we feel a real connection to her, as though we've made a friend. And what could be more universal than the joy of new friendship?

Most personal writing is in one of three forms:

Narrative: "This happened to me . . ."

Character sketch: "I know this interesting person . . ."

Personal symbol: "This car/necklace/recipe means a lot to me . . ."

We can usually do good personal writing as soon as we know that anyone cares. Take a look at the following essay. It was written by my student Yer Thao after a class discussion, on the fifth anniversary of September 11, about what it means to be American. Yer was self-conscious about her language ability—her first language is Hmong—but she obviously had something to say. Note, too, that while the essay is about something very personal, she also connects that experience to the bigger picture.

GRATEFUL

YER THAO

They say that some friends come and go in your life without much of an impression, but others will leave footprints that will last forever. Mai Thao is one of those footprint leavers. She has not only taught me what it means to be a true friend, but she has also taught me what it means to be an American.

Plop, plop, plop . . . I awoke on that typical Monday morning to the sound of raindrops dripping from the bare branches outside my window to the puddles on the lawn. Yawning, I stretched my arms and looked at my clock. It was 6:45 a.m. Sitting up, I could already smell the aroma of mushroom and onion filled omelets wafting from the kitchen. Smiling, I jumped out of bed, grabbed my towel, and rushed to the bathroom for a quick morning shower.

After breakfast, Mom told me to hurry up and get ready because we also have to pick up Mai today. Mai and her family had just arrived from Thailand a week before so today was her first day of school in America. She was eight too, so we were going to be in the same class. I was supposed to show her around and help her adjust to her new life. Nodding, I washed my breakfast dishes and ran back to my room to get my backpack. In ten minutes, we had picked Mai up from her house and were on our way to Wyandotte Elementary School. During the ride to school, Mom tried to make little conversations, but Mai just answered whatever question that needed to be answered. Then she was silent again.

After we were dropped off, I led her to our third grade class. She was silent the entire way. At first, I tried to make conversations with her, but it was no use. She wasn't interested in talking. "Here's our classroom," I told her as we stood outside room 9. And then, with a comforting smile, I told her not to worry because Mrs. Bloomingcamp was a very nice teacher. She smiled bravely back at me, and then we opened the door and we both stepped through the threshold.

At lunch, I invited her to eat with my friends and me, and she sat down with us, but five minutes later, she got up and walked away. My friends looked at me questioningly, so I got up and followed her. I found her sitting alone outside on a bench eating a green apple. I walked over to her and sat down. The rain had stopped and the sky was just starting to clear. The November air felt so fresh and clean that I couldn't help but smile. At first, she didn't even notice me. She was staring at the other kids and, strangely, at the trash cans. "What are you looking at?" I asked her. "Nothing," she replied. Then she got up and gathered her books and walked away. I looked at her and with a shrug got up and walked back to my friends.

For the entire week, we carried on that same routine. She would arrive to class with me every morning, but since she was assigned a desk three rows ahead of me, we hardly got to talk. After the first day, she started disappearing at lunchtime, so it wasn't until Friday that I actually saw her at lunch again. I had just thrown away my half-eaten fries when I spotted Mai walking out the door. Curious, I followed her out into the playground but lost her in a crowd of students playing dodge-ball. It was five minutes later when I found her in the back of the playground sitting in a hidden corner with her knees pulled up and her face hidden behind them.

"Are you okay?" I ask her.

"Go away!" she snapped.

"What's wrong? Are you sick?" I asked.

"Go away, you stupid American." She yelled at me as she raised her head up and glared at me through angry, teary eyes. "You are the most spoiled people I've ever met! You wake up, go into a room, turn silver knobs and clean warm water squirts out to wash you! You have free education and you are encouraged to get it. You drive to school like kings and queens even though the weather is fine. You waste perfectly good food every day! And worst of all, you're still complaining all the time! You all don't even see what you have! Back in Thailand, we wake up before dawn every morning to walk twenty minutes to the nearest well to bring water back to boil for usage. We don't waste water the way you Americans do. Many children would love to have the opportunity to get an education, but most can't afford it and are needed in the fields. Even after a hard year of toiling in the fields, food is still scarce! You are the most ungrateful pigs I have ever seen!"

Astonished at her outburst, I stood in front of her, speechless, for what seems like hours. Finally, I was able to utter the words, "I had no idea."

All this time, she had been quiet because she was watching and listening to everything and everyone around her. It was true that kids all around her complained about their parents and homework and friends all the time. It was true that Americans are tossing out billions in food each year. It was true that we sometimes act as though electricity and indoor plumbing are a right and not a privilege. It was then that I realized how fortunate we Americans are. Most of us don't even know the true meaning of starvation, even though we always complain even before lunch time. We're spoiled and take everything for granted!

It's been ten years since we first met, and Mai and I are still best of friends. Even though her family moved to Sacramento in the middle of high school and we both have our own different schedules now, we still keep in touch as much as possible. Just this Thanksgiving, my family and I, as well as a few other relatives, were invited to have dinner with her family in Sacramento. The first thing I told her, after I gave her a hug, was about this paper. We both laughed remembering that day long ago when we first came to understand each other. Then we made a plan.

After everyone around the enormous rectangular wooden table had said what they were thankful for, the Thao family started to pass around the beans and ham and rice. But they didn't get far before Mai and I stood up, with our glasses full of Sunny Delight, to declare a toast.

"A toast," Mai began, "to our good health, our refrigerator full of bountiful food, and this society with numerous opportunities for a man to create his own fortune."

"A toast," I began, "to none of us wasting not even a single grain of rice." Then squinting my eyes at everyone around the table, I ended, "GOT IT?"

"Cheers," everyone agreed heartily and not a single grain of rice was wasted that night. Thank you, Mai, for opening my eyes. I will continue to try my best to never waste even a single grain of rice for as long as I live. ❖

Often, personal writing has little visible sign of structure, thesis, or purpose, but often that's the fun of it. Some writers can keep you reading—with their attention to detail or perhaps their idiosyncratic voice—and you don't realize until you get to the end that there was a whole lot going on. Read the following piece and note how the structure of the last three sentences—short, simple, even naïve—provides resonance to the rest of the essay.

DAD

MICHAEL CLARK

I remember he used to take forever in the bathroom. Some mornings I could get up, eat breakfast, get ready for school, and leave without ever seeing him. I'd hear him, though: coughing, spitting, and gagging himself. Anyone else hearing him in the morning would probably think he was going to die. But he had always done that, and I figured it was just the way all grown men got up in the morning.

When he came home in the evenings you could tell he was glad not to be at work any more. It was always best not to ask him questions about anything or make any kind of noise. Mom would ask him a couple of things while she was fixing dinner. He'd answer her. Otherwise he'd just sit at the dining room table with his martini, reading the newspaper.

At dinner, Mom would make most of the conversation. He generally reserved his participation for when we kids got too lighthearted or proud or disrespectful or something and needed trampling.

When I played in Little League, he'd drive me. The Conservation Club was next to the park. He'd hang out there until practice was over. Once he ambled over a little early. He interrupted the coach and insisted on explaining the infield fly rule—not just once but three times. He'd have gone on like a broken record if the coach hadn't stopped him and thanked him and quickly dismissed the team.

I always hated riding home with him after he'd been at the Club. Winter was the worst. We'd take our trash to the town dump. The dump was also right next to the park, so naturally we'd stop in at the Club. We'd always stay past dark. On the way home I always wanted to tell him you shouldn't drive so fast on a day's accumulation of ice and snow, but I never did. The couple of times we slid off the road didn't convince him. He'd just rock the car out, get back on the road, and drive on as if nothing had happened.

As time went on, he'd come home later and later in the evenings. Often he'd come through the door all red-faced and walk straight into the bedroom, where we'd hear him moan a little and talk to the dog. Then he'd pass out and we wouldn't see him again until he came home the same way the next evening.

With my brother in the Army and my sister at college, I was the only one around to see that Mom was spending her nights on the living room couch. Though it didn't surprise me, the divorce came as kind of a blow.

I've seen him a couple of times since then. He's remarried. I think I called him last Thanksgiving. ❖

Sometimes a little chaos just adds to the believability:

Well, the big news is I'm pregnant. Boy, do I hate that word—PREGNANT, sounds so harsh. "With child" sounds positively smarmy. "Expecting" always makes me want to say, "Expecting what?" It's not that I'm not pleased about this—I just don't think I'm comfortable with the jargon yet. And oh boy, is there jargon! La Leche League, Bradley, Lamaze, LaBoyer, transition period, episiotomy, and baby blues. In my naive way I assumed I'd have this baby, take a week off, and then jump into student teaching. Then I read the books, became acquainted with the terminology, decided to take the whole semester off. What I'm slowly realizing is that I'm not just PREGNANT, I'm having a BABY—that books about the next twenty years. This is going to CHANGE my lifestyle! AAAGGGHHH! ❖

Burn out. I've been doing this for too long, and it seems like everyone around me feels the same way. I want to go beyond bitching this semester, so like the last three semesters I've told myself I'm going to take it easy. This time I mean it. I really do.

I can already see I'm lying. I want to audit the modern poetry class. And I want to keep tutoring. And I need to keep a few hours on the job. The money will be nice, and if I stop I'll have to start at $3.35 an hour when I go back. Then there's the newspaper. That ought to take a couple hundred hours. And I want to save time for my own writing. I've told myself I need to keep Tuesday and Thursday afternoons free. I'll probably have to tutor at one of those times, but if I'm lucky I'll be able to keep the other one free.

Planning. That's the key. I've got to stop bitching and start planning. If I'm still bitching two weeks from now, I'll have to say it's hopeless. ❖

If personal writing doesn't need coherent organization or thesis, what *does* it need? First, dramatic intensity: The reader feels he's in the scene, living it along with the writer, feeling the wind in his hair and catching the tang of gunpowder in his nostrils. Second, a sought effect: The reader senses that everything in the essay adds up to one thing and takes us to the same endpoint. Let's look at ways to get each one.

Show, Don't Tell

There's a paradox about drama: the worst way to communicate to the reader how you're feeling is to tell him. Yer Thao wouldn't strengthen "Grateful" by saying "People should be careful not to take for granted the things they have"; she would weaken it. Michael wouldn't strengthen "Dad" by saying, "My father was a pathetic drunk, and I *feel* like I lost out on having a father as a result"; he would weaken it. Instead, Yer puts us at Wyandotte Elementary School and lets us *feel* Mai's anger. Michael lets us *watch* his father act out his life and witness his isolation.

Writing teachers traditionally express this insight by the ancient incantation, "Show, don't tell." These are just different words for the basic lesson of the concretion section of Chapter 5. To get life, concretize and particularize. Avoid generalized abstractions: "He was really weird"; "It was the most exciting class of my life"; "I was so scared." Replace them with concretions.

Imagine you're directing a movie, and you've just filmed an actor doing a scene conveying her sadness over the loss of her father. As a director, you don't get in front of the camera and say, "Look! Isn't she sad?" You let the particulars, the details, do the work, and you trust your audience to understand why you've chosen to use them.

Remember, too, how subjective those kinds of abstractions are. Surely you've had the experience of saying something like, "I met this totally hilarious guy at a party last week—he was in the dining room doing impressions of Saddam Hussein as a Catholic priest!" only to have your listener/audience say, "That's not hilarious; that's disgusting." So it's better just to describe the person *acting* and to leave the generalizing/interpreting to your reader. This passage from a first draft does it wrong:

> She was impulsive, funny, and highly irresponsible. I liked her because she did things I wouldn't do. I was reliable, down to earth, and boring. She was spontaneous. I looked up to her. In my eyes, she was a leader because she did things I was afraid to do. In many ways, she was immature. She had no concept of responsibility. I loved being with her, though, because she was fun. Being with her was like being on a vacation.

We understand perfectly, but we feel nothing. When the author rewrote to *show*, the new version began,

> "Hey, Cathy, I'm dying for an In-N-Out burger and fries and, you know me, I don't want to go alone. I'll pick you up in ten minutes." "But Nikki, it's . . . CLICK . . . ten o'clock at night," I respond to a dial tone.

Later in the new draft we get this:

> During the freshman initiation ceremony in high school, our friendship was born. We were dressed in costume (unwillingly) and instructed to do something totally silly and asinine in front of the entire student body. Nikki, dressed as Pinocchio, was told to tell a lie. "I love this school," she blurted out emphatically. Everybody booed.

Now we really *get it*.

More is better. "He didn't respect his students" doesn't say much. "He would always tell his students they'd never amount to anything" is better. Better still is "He scowled, dropped our math tests in the wastebasket, and said, 'See you losers Monday.'" Here's a nice more-is-better description of an eatery:

> I was living in Laguna Beach and working at Tip's Deli. Tip's served beer and wine, chopped chicken liver, lox and bagels, pastrami on Jewish rye, and imported cheeses to a colorful clientele. Wally Tip was a short, plump, balding Jew originally from Toronto who claimed to have been a pimp in Las Vegas and made one believe

in the possibilities of a Jewish Mafia. I liked him a lot. On Sunday morning he cooked breakfast himself, sweating and swearing over his tiny grill as he made his Tip's Special Omelet, which he served for a ridiculously low price to local businessmen and hippies and outsiders from Los Angeles who bitched about the fat on the pastrami, compared the place unfavorably to Ratner's, and left looking pleased. There was usually a long wait. Every time an order was turned in, Wally looked dismayed and muttered that the bastards would have to wait.

One of the best ways to "show" is to use dialogue. It's a great way to reveal character. Consider the following: He was a redneck who didn't care about school versus "I ain't got time for homework. Me and Dan are gonna change the oil in my pickup and then we're goin' squirrel huntin'."

In fact, just think how frequently you use dialogue in conversation. Most likely, you've recently described someone you've met by "quoting" him—or using dialogue: "This guy came up to me after class yesterday and said . . ."

Keep in mind, though, that there should be a reason for using dialogue. Apparently, some students have been told "Show, don't tell" and to use lots of dialogue but not to think about why. There's little that's more annoying than pointless dialogue. Well-chosen dialogue, however, can go a long way. In fact, it can even result in a "movie" (and plays are *all* dialogue, save for minor stage directions), which the writer doesn't need to interrupt at all:

FORGET HOMEWORK

JENNIFER WISSMATH

"Jen, please!"

"Jeez, Darron, relax—I'm coming."

"I called you three times; this food has been sitting here forever!"

"I was taking an order and it hasn't been here that long. Where's the ticket for this order? I don't know where it goes."

"Table three. Hurry up . . ."

Man, he gets on my nerves. This plate is really hot. Hurry up, lady, move your stupid salad plate. "Here you go. I'll run and get you some Parmesan cheese. Do you need anything else?"

"Is our bread coming?"

"Oh, yes, it should be right out."

Okay, Parmesan, water—whoa! I almost slipped. There's a puddle in here the size of Lake Michigan. This whole station is a mess! You could never guess that there were two other waitresses who were supposed to do sidework before they left. I'm going to be here until way after 10—shoot, it's 9:45 right now. I guess my homework will just have to wait. "Here you go. Enjoy your meal—I'll be right back with your bread. Darron, I need the bread for Table 3."

"I already sent that out!"

"Well, Table 3 didn't get it. Hurry, the man on that table has been waiting forever."

There's the door—oh shoot, more people. Why are they coming in so late? I'd love to tell those jerks to leave—we could all get the hell out of here a little sooner. Let's see: Table 3— bread; Table 2—eating; Table 11—almost finished, they'll leave first; Table 8—okay; Table 16—take order.

"Hello, how are you doing this evening? Are you ready to order?"

"Yes. Honey, you go first."

"Um, okay. I think I'll get the eggplant."

"Oh, I was going to get that. Hmmm, I guess I could get lasagna and we could pull the old switcheroo."

("Jen, please!")

"But, hmmm, I'm not sure I really feel like lasagna."

Oh, God, could you please hurry up?

"Okay, she'll have the eggplant and I'll have the raviolis."

"Honey, I don't like raviolis."

"How about . . . well, I'll just stick with the lasagna."

What a revelation. Don't waste my time or anything. I don't think I'll ask them if they want salads. "Would you like any garlic bread?"

"Oh, yes—Honey, let's get it with cheese?"

"I don't like it with cheese . . ."

("Jen, please!!!")

"Will that be all for you?"

"Honey, don't forget the wine."

"Oh, yes, we would like a liter of White Zinfandel."

Oh, please, make my night longer. I don't have anything else to do. I don't really need to read those three chapters for my history quiz, and I'm sure my teacher wouldn't mind my handing in a late paper. This job is too much. If I didn't need the money so badly, I would probably get straight A's.

"JEN PLEASE!!!"

Damn. Let's see—this goes to Table 8. Oh my gosh, they don't even have their drinks. I just love getting a late rush. "Here you go—I'll be right back with your drinks. Do you need some Parmesan cheese?"

Okay—drinks, drinks, Parmesan. Then deliver food, check water, pick up plates, pour coffee, add tickets, clear tables, be civil, do sidework, fill Parm holders, fill sugars, clean station, clean salad bar, mop floor, go home, *forget homework*, go to bed. ❖

Chapter 5 gives you a list of ways to concretize an essay. But they are revision strategies—they think in terms of *adding* concretions to something you've already written. Instead, build the essay up from concretions. Instead of brainstorming by asking abstract questions ("What sort of a person is he?" "How do I feel about her?"), begin by listing objects, gestures, or fragments of dialogue that capture the spirit of your subject. Ask yourself questions like this:

How does she dress? Birkenstocks? Red Converse high tops? Hemp necklaces?

What kind of car does he drive? Raised Ford F-350 with a Ducks Unlimited bumper sticker? Toyota Prius with a "Think Green" bumper sticker?

Does she have any verbal idiosyncrasies? Remember, using dialogue is a great way to "show" a person's character, so if he says "ain't," use it. If he, like, habitually uses, like, a certain word, use it.

What does he own that is meaningful and that defines him? A German Shepherd named Spike? An Elvis lunchbox? A $4,000 mountain bike?

Is there a specific story about her that people tell when describing her? Did she organize a car wash to raise money for Hurricane Katrina victims?

"Dad" might have begun with a list like this:

Coughing and spitting in the bathroom
Explaining the infield fly rule to coach
Talking to the dog
The Club
Sliding off the road in the car

Choosing an Effect

Once we have good concretions to work with, we need a rationale for putting them together in some way. Don't outline—it will just drive away the spontaneity. And don't begin with thesis, though thesis may emerge, because it forces you back into telling instead of showing.

Instead, think about effect: What are you trying to do to the reader? That effect may involve a thesis or a moral, but it doesn't have to. You can leave it pretty vague in the beginning: "I'm trying to capture what it feels like to play in a rec-league softball tournament"; "I want the reader to meet my father." The sought effect will become more specific as you work. Here are specific effects for some of the essays in this chapter:

> "Dad": to capture the miserable alcoholic isolation my father lived with, and my inability to get near him.

> "Forget Homework": to capture how hysterical, frustrating, and dehumanizing my night-time job is, and to show how infuriating it is to have it ruin my schoolwork.

Does Personal Writing Have a Thesis?

Personal writing is a sharing of the self, and teaching and sharing often don't mix. If we're chatting with a buddy and we suddenly sense that she's trying to teach us something, we'll probably feel condescended to. So personal writing usually doesn't have a sense of "The lesson to learn here is . . ." On the other hand, almost all writing has a central idea. Essays like "Forget Homework" and "Dad" don't really teach, but they do have theses. The thesis for "Dad" is "My father was cut off from the human race and his family by his alcoholism." The thesis in "Forget Homework" is something like "My wage-earning job often prevents me from being the best student I can be." And if we wanted to, we could turn any personal essay into an argument by drawing larger conclusions from the experience. We could use "Dad" to make the argument that our culture teaches males to deal with their emotional pain through silence and self-inflicted isolation. We could use "Forget Homework" to make the argument that it's to society's advantage to support student aid programs, so worthy students can concentrate on getting the most out of their education. Chapter 14 has two essays that use personal narrative in this way, "Given the Chance" and "Why?"

Seeing the Mode

Here's an image that's etched in the minds of hundreds of millions of people around the world—at least, those who were six or seven years old or older on September 11, 2001. What do you remember about that day? What memories does this photograph recall? Are there "bigger issues" that you could address by writing about that day in your life? The importance of family? A child's confusion? The power of the media? Or even the loss of innocence—of a child, of a nation?

© Sean Adair/Reuters/Corbis.

WRITER'S WORKSHOP

Concretizing Abstract Generalizations

Let's look at how a writer revises a very "tell-y" character sketch so that it "shows" instead.

MY MOTHER

LORI ANN PROUST

She is understanding and always there for me. She listens and is full of positive support. I am lucky to have someone who is both a close friend *and* a mother. Not everyone has this kind of a relationship.

I could find endless words in the thesaurus to describe my mother, but the one word that stands out above the rest is "incredible." She is my sole support system. Whenever something exciting happens or there is a crisis in my life, she is the first person I turn to. I have seen many friends come and go in my life, but my mother is different. For eighteen years of my life she has always been there for me. No matter the distance in miles between us, we are always close. She understands me and knows me better than anyone else I know. She doesn't make demands nor does she pressure me with school and my future. She has complete faith and trust in me that I am doing the right thing with my life. I make her happy by letting her know I am happy and like who I am and where my life is taking me.

Every day I count my blessings and think about how grateful I am to have a mother who loves me. Not once do I take this for granted. I cannot imagine my life any differently without her. One thing is for certain: it just wouldn't be the same. ❖

Lori Ann's classmates said they simply didn't *believe* the essay—it felt like a sales pitch. They encouraged Lori Ann to start from concretions. She said, "Well, I just had a phone conversation with her that was pretty typical—maybe I could use that." She did, and this is what she got:

MOTHERS . . . ?!!

"Hello?"

"Hi, Mom. How was your day?"

"What's wrong?"

"Nothing is wrong, Mom. I just called to tell you I found an incredible place to live next year! It's an apartment in an antique house. It has hardwood floors, high ceilings, it's close to school, has lots of potential, and the rent is *only* . . ."

"Does it have summer rent?"

"Yes."

"Forget it then."

"Fine, Mom."

"I already told you that neighborhood is dangerous and full of rapists."

"Mother, I've lived on this street for the past *three* years now."

"And what about the fraternity boys across the street? Do you know what you're in for?"

"Mother, these guys are my friends and I have also lived across the street from a fraternity house before . . ."

"Forget it."

"Fine, Mom. Would you rather pay $225 a month for me to live in a two-bedroom apartment instead of $150 a month? You'd also have to buy me a car because the only apartments available in September are five miles from campus."

"Does your friend Denice know what a slob you are? Does she know *you're* the reason why you had cockroaches in your apartment last year?"

"Mother, that's because I lived in a *dive!* I found cockroaches before I even moved in . . ."

"Oh, are you suddenly scrubbing floors now? I just don't see why you can't wait until September to find a place to live. I'm *not* paying summer rent."

"Fine, Mom. I just thought you might *appreciate* my consideration in letting you know what I am doing with my life before I sign the lease."

"Well, it sounds like you're going to do it anyway."

"Thank you for your support, Mom."

"Bye." Click.

"Good-bye, Mom; I love you too."

To think that mothers are understanding is the world's ultimate illusion. I had to sit in the bathroom as I was talking to my mom because there were thirty screaming girls in the hallway; stereos were blasting, and if this wasn't enough, the smoke alarm was going off because the cooks were burning dinner. I had to control myself from sticking the phone down the toilet and flushing it. That's how understanding she was being.

My mother can be full of positive support but not when you need to hear it the most. "I'm sure you can find something cleaner, can't you? You're such a slob—I guess it wouldn't matter anyway." Right, Mom. To my mother's dismay, I am an immaculate person—just ask any of my friends. She is practically married to the Pine Sol man. She thinks her house is as sterile as the hospital. Well, I have news for her . . .

Whenever something exciting happens in my life, my mother is usually the first person I turn to. I don't know why because she always shoots down my dreams. I sent her flowers and a poem I wrote myself for Mother's Day and what does she do? She acts irrational over the telephone. "Why can't you wait until September to find a place? I'm not paying summer rent." Right, Mom. I already told her twice I would pay summer rent myself. Anyone with common sense would realize that it's an advantage to find the best place *now*. That way you don't have to pay storage over the summer.

For eighteen years of my life she has raised me. She knows me better than anyone else I know. It just doesn't make sense why she can't be more sensitive and supportive of my dreams. All I wanted was to hear her say, "It sounds great!" But it was obviously too much to ask.

The phone rang as I was finishing this paper tonight.

"Hello?"

"Hi. I've been talking to your father about that apartment, and he said he would pay half your summer rent. That way we don't have to pay for storage." (What did I tell you, Mom . . .)

"So go ahead and sign the lease." (I didn't tell you before, but . . . I already did!)

"I'll see you soon, Mom. I love you."

My mom will never know this, but I went ahead and signed the lease yesterday, without her approval or support. I felt good about it, knowing I did the right thing. Today's phone call reassured me that I had done the right thing. Although my mother can be irrational sometimes, she is still my mother and I love her dearly. ❖

The phone conversation forced Lori Ann to come out from behind the safety of the first draft's clichés and face some complex, feisty realities. There's much more to say now, and the essay crackles with the energy of conflict.

Now it's your turn. Write a draft of a personal essay. Highlight every abstraction. Replace the abstractions with concretions. Then delete the abstractions.

EXERCISES

1. List the objects, verbal expressions, and behaviors that capture the essence of someone in your life. How does he usually dress? What are his verbal tics? What possessions matter to him? And so on. Write a paragraph showing how one item on the list reveals the heart and soul of the person.

2. Make a list of three abstract generalizations about someone in your life ("He's very generous"). Imagine how a director would film scenes to show that the person is what you say she is. Then write an essay showing those scenes without telling. Share it with your classmates. See if they can guess what abstraction you were trying to convey. Notes: (a) Don't set it up like a

riddle. You're trying to be clear, not trick your reader. (b) Don't use synonyms. (c) Remember that not everyone will guess the same abstraction, which is exactly the point: what's hilarious to one person is disgusting to another; what's proud to one person is self-centered to another.

3. Write a half-page to one-page monologue or dialogue that reveals the character of someone in your life.

4. Use one of the personal essays in A Collection of Good Writing as a model and write one like it.

5. Describe a setting from your life that matters to you, like the deli earlier in this chapter, in a paragraph or two. Then rewrite it to twice that length by doubling the specific concrete detail.

Chapter 12

WRITING TO INFORM

There are many different kinds of informative writing, and it might be the one you do the most of outside of school. Every time you give directions to your house, give someone a link to a website, write down the ingredients in your favorite smoothie or chocolate-chip cookies, you're doing informative writing.

That means you're probably already pretty good at it. I guarantee, assuming you do in fact *want* that person to find your house, that the writing's going to be pretty darn good: clear, concise, reader appropriate, with a built-in purpose. Of course, because there are different kinds of informative essays, you should read a lot of them if you want to learn to do them well. Start by taking a look at the ones in A Collection of Good Writing.

What's Informative Writing?

In informative writing, the reader is going to go out and *do* something practical with the information: plant a garden, learn to water-ski, get a good deal on a used car. Most of the writing that's earning money in the real world is informative: service manuals, cookbooks, technical and scientific reports, encyclopedias, textbooks, travel guides, and 90 percent of every newspaper or magazine.

Since purposes are independent of content, the same material can be turned into any kind of essay. Professor Rawlins's student Aaron Kenedi wanted to write about his memories of watching his grandmother slaughter chickens, but he couldn't decide if he wanted to focus on his relationship with his grandmother or teach the reader the practical ins and outs of chicken slaughtering. Rawlins suggested he write two essays, one personal and the other informative. So he did. Both are good. Here's the personal version:

INVITATION TO A BEHEADING

AARON KENEDI

When I was about nine, my grandmother came to visit us on our little farm in California. She was from Freeport, Long Island, and if you couldn't tell by her accent, the way she dressed would have given her away, in pleated polyester slacks and a loud plaid shirt, complete with long red nails and a sprayed coif like plaster of Paris. Thus attired, she turned to me one day and out of the blue said, "Ya neva know when ya might need to kill a chicken" and headed for the hen house. After a moment of reflection I decided she had a point, and so, partly horrified and mostly fascinated, I followed her. The chickens we raised were strictly for eggs, so it was all new to me.

She prepared herself like a Zen master—meditation, deep breathing exercises, and stretching. In her thick Hungarian/New York/Jewish accent, she told me, "Chickens aw de tastiest boid in de land when dey aw fresh. Yaw grandfathah loved de chicken in goulash, paprikash, you name it. Oy, dat he didn't have dose triple and double and God knows how many bypasses. It vas de cigars dat kilt him, lemme tell you . . ."

"Foist thing you do," she explained, "is get yourself a pair of gloves, an old shirt, a plastic bucket, a shawp ax, and some running shoes. Nikes are de best—dey got dat little swoosh on de side, makes you look fashionable. It's impawtant to always look good." When I asked her why running shoes, she looked at me blankly and said, "You ever tried to catch a chicken dat knows it's about to die?" I stepped aside and let Grandma limber up.

Next she stepped into the chicken coop, looking like some sort of lunatic surgeon—yellow gloves, black boots to her knees, and an apron reading "Party Animal." She propped a cardboard box up on a stick with a string tied to it, handed me the string, and gave chase. She was indefatigable, unyielding. It was a scene out of Monty Python, but it worked, I pulled the string, and finally the chicken clucked nervously under the box.

I brought the chicken over to the chopping block. Grandma felt the edge of the ax blade in her hands. I thought maybe I could see a slight grin on her lips when she declared it "not quite shawp enough" and proceeded to hone it with a stone until it glinted in the sunlight. She took some practice swings, saying,

"Ya don't vant to botch de first try. Ya vant clean, quick cut right through de old neck. Nothing woise than a howling chicken." She didn't need to convince me.

She set aside her thick glasses and I held the bird carefully. Summoning all her might, she perfectly separated the head from the body. Before I realized it was dead, the bird got up, flapped its wings as if merely startled, and took off in circles around the wood pile. The blood spurted from its neck in thick streams, and it would convulse with each spurt like some avant garde modern dance student. "Dat's nawmul," Grandma said as she leaned on her ax and wiped her brow. "Dey usually jog around a bit afterward."

After the chicken fell in a heap in front of her, Grandma wound its feet together and hung it on an oak branch to let the rest of the blood drip out. "It's a bit like drip-drying the wash," she told me. "Only you vant to make sure the dogs and cats— or the flies—don't get at it."

We moved the operation into the house, and Grandma changed out of her bloody shirt and into an apron. She dunked the bird in a pot of boiling water, sat down on a stool on the front porch with a big garbage bag next to her, and began pulling out clumps of feathers like she was petting a shedding cat. "De hot water loosens up de hold de quills have on the feathers, just like a chuck key does a drill," she explained. Pointing to the now-naked bird, she said, "Heah's de tricky pawt. You see doze little bristles where de feathehs used to be? Vell, ve don't vant to eat dem. So ve got to singe dem off." And she pulled out a Zippo lighter, flicked it on smoother than any movie gangster, and ran the flame lightly over the skin.

The next step was harder to take. Grandma set the bird on its back on the cutting board, took a cleaver, and hacked the neck off with such force that it flew across the room. Then she put on a rubber glove, gritted her teeth, and stuck her hand down the hole where the neck used to be. It sounded like mushing a banana around in your mouth, which was bad, but the smell was horrendous, like a rotten deer carcass in the woods. She pulled out the heart, giblets, and liver and showed them to me like a Mayan priest at a sacrifice. Next came the gizzard. "Chickens swallow all sawts of crap," Grandma explained excitedly. "You never know vat you'll find in a gizzard. Once yaw great grandmother found a gold ring." We tore it open and there before our eyes were some roofing nails my dad had used to build the chicken coop, one of my Matchbox cars, and a penny.

I wanted Grandma to cut off the feet, but she insisted they were delicious to "suck on." "Now ve boil the whole damn thing and make soup—make the best chicken soup you've ever had," she said. "And tomorrow I'll show you how to make a zip gun." ❖

Here's the informative version:

YOUR FIRST KILL

AARON KENEDI

Foster Farms no longer raises chickens. Instead, they raise large-breasted mutants so juiced on hormones they make Hulk Hogan seem normal. Armour raises its poultry in an environment so unspeakably inhumane that it makes you ashamed to be a human being when you hear about it.

You probably know all this—that's why you've decided to raise your own chickens. You're willing to do the work it takes to eat meat that's tastier, cheaper, healthier, and easier on your karma. But chickens don't come chopped up and packaged, so eventually (around the time of the summer's first barbecue) you're going to have to butcher a chicken yourself. Here's how. The method you're about to read is my grandma's, so you can rest assured it's quick and safe.

The first thing you need to know is that, unless you get emotionally attached easily, it will be easier to kill chickens than you think. Chickens aren't cuddly or adorable, and they aren't loyal—they'd do the same to you if the roles were reversed. And they can't cluck, poop, or peck when they're dead.

Roosters are okay to eat, but hens are better, because they're plumper and you'll have more of them in the coop. But before you grab your least favorite and start whacking, do some things first. Dress in old clothes you can throw away, because killing a chicken is about as dirty a job as it sounds. Wear comfortable shoes, preferably running shoes, because a chicken that senses doom is as difficult to catch as an Elvis concert. Consider laying a trap: Tie a string to a stick, use the stick to prop up a box, and chase the chicken until she chances to pass under—then pull the string.

Now comes the icky part. You can do it two ways: Either swiftly and violently twist the bird's neck until it snaps, or sharpen your trusty ax, have a friend hold the little bugger on a chopping block, and unleash a mighty whack on the bird's neck. Cut cleanly the first time, because a half-beheaded chicken makes a sound you've never heard before and will never want to hear again. Snapping is cleaner, but it takes some strength. Axing is easier, but the bird will run around for a few minutes. It's a shock at first to see a headless bird sit up and start jogging, blood spurting out of its neck causing it to shake and convulse, but you have to drain the blood anyway, so this method kills two birds with one stone (sorry).

After the chicken has exhausted itself, tie its feet together and hang it on a branch or clothesline over a bucket to let the remaining blood drip out—about two hours. Don't let dogs, cats, or flies get at it. Meanwhile, boil a large pot of water, prepare some table space, and sharpen your cleaver or largest knife. Put the carcass in the boiling water for about one minute *only*. This will loosen the quills and make picking the bird much easier. Pull out all the feathers, containing them immediately, while they're still wet, in a large trash bag or something similar.

Now you have a naked bird covered with little bristles where the feathers used to be. You can't eat them—it's like eating the rough side of those two-sided kitchen sponges—so you must burn them off. Light a gas burner or a cigarette lighter and, without cooking the chicken, carefully singe off each bristle. It's the most time-consuming step in the process, but it's essential for your gastronomic well-being.

Your chicken now looks a lot like the thing you buy in Safeway. Except on the inside. Now comes the other icky part. If you opted for the snapping method earlier, you first must chop off the head where the neck meets the body. You can also cut off the feet at this point, though Grandma swears they're the tastiest part. Now put on a rubber glove, take a cleansing breath, stick your hand down the hole where the neck used to be, and pull everything out. It's gross, it's messy, it smells like death, you'll feel like a brute, but it must be done. An alternative is to take your knife and split the carcass from the butt to the collar and pry the breast apart with your hands. This method is cleaner because you don't have to grab and squeeze any entrails, but the smell is just as bad. Once laid open, the inside of a chicken is practically designed for disemboweling—just remove everything. Throw the organs away like I do, or fry them up and eat them like Grandma does. The small thing that looks like a Hacky Sack footbag is the gizzard, where the chicken grinds to dust what she eats. If you're curious, cut it open and see what the chicken's been eating. Grandma insists her mother once found a gold ring in one.

Now rinse the bird under cold water and decide how to cook it. Chop it into pieces (that's another essay) and prepare a nice Kiev or marsala sauce, or plop it whole into a large pot, add vegetables, and make the tastiest, cheapest, healthiest chicken soup you've ever had. Grandma would be so proud. ❖

In informative writing most of what you say isn't a matter of opinion, and your relationship to the audience is different from what it is in writing an argument. For example, when you argue, you're trying to talk your reader into giving up her opinion and accepting yours, and she doesn't want to go along, but in informative writing the reader grants that she needs what you're offering—a new owner of a DVD player doesn't need much persuading to convince him that he needs help programming the thing. Aaron's chicken-slaughtering experience could easily have been turned into an argument—perhaps making the case that Americans have lost touch with the eternal verities like birth and death and need to get their hands bloody once in a while.

The Three Challenges

Informative writing offers the writer three challenges: (1) we don't feel knowledgeable enough, (2) it's boring, and (3) something called the COIK problem is ever-present. Let's find ways to deal with each.

You Don't Feel Knowledgeable Enough

It feels fraudulent to set yourself up as the expert. This is entirely a problem of audience definition. You are the teacher the moment you're talking to people who know less than you do. If you know how to play solitaire or Tomb Raider and the reader doesn't, you have knowledge she wants.

You've been learning all your life. And for everything you've learned, there's someone who doesn't know it and would profit from learning it. If you've been in Mrs. Mercer's twelfth-grade English class at Holy Name High School, there's someone coming into the class blind who doesn't know how the class works and who could benefit from your expertise. If you watch football on TV, there's someone who doesn't and who would benefit if you explain what he's seeing.

To make sure you and your reader know your respective roles, lay them out in paragraph 1. Tell the reader up front that you know something he doesn't know and that he will profit from knowing it:

> OK, so your boyfriend dumped you. If your relationship was anything like mine, you probably feel like the lowest, most good-for-nothing human being on earth. Well, I'm here to tell you that

you can and will survive your breakup. Here are some things you can do to speed your recovery.

Is there central heating and air? Does the place have a dishwasher? Is the rent reasonable? Of course they're important considerations. But when looking for a place to rent, in our obsession with the inanimate, we often overlook one of the most important questions: What's the landlord like? If you're looking to rent, you should be asking yourself some key questions about your potential landlord.

Warm up with a mock-informative essay. If the role of teacher feels awkward, warm up by doing a teacher *parody*. Write a *mock-informative essay*, a send-up of informative essays where you take something dead simple—chewing gum or putting toothpaste on a toothbrush—and pretend it's as complicated as building a space station. Here's a masterpiece of the genre:

THE SEMI-SWEET SCIENCE:
ONE, TWO, THREE, FOUR. I DECLARE . . .
OSCAR VILLALON

This happened to me some years ago.

I was in a deli in the East Village. Behind the counter was this plump, short guy with a little mustache, wearing a white butcher's coat. He calls out my number. I lean over the counter and hand him my paper ticket. As he takes it from me, he says, casually, "Nice hams."

I thought I misheard him, so I gave him an "excuse me?" look. He then holds up his mitts, his palms out toward me. He tilts back and moves his hands up and down for me, like a stumpy T-Rex. "Nice hams," he said. "You know?" No, I didn't know. He then pinched his fat palm. "Your thumbs, brother. They got thick hams." I had nothing to say to that.

Later, eating my hot pastrami sandwich, holding the greasy thing away from me between bites, I couldn't help but study what he called my "hams." He was right. That knotty bulb of muscle anchoring my thumbs looked . . . tough. Pronounced, even, like the calves of a bodybuilder. I guess you could call them nice, but so what?

But physical gifts account for only a fraction of my or anybody else's success in competitive sports. Dedication and technique must be part of the mix, too, for mastery of the semi-sweet science of thumb wrestling. The allusion to boxing isn't frivolous.

Many of the techniques that make boxing "sweet," that is, those things I'm guessing make it sweet, in an ironical way, are prominent in thumb wrestling, which, in truth, should be called thumb boxing. However, thumb boxing conjures the unfortunate image of fighters throwing very awkward punches, followed by the even more unfortunate image of a roundhouse connecting to an opponent's forehead and a thumb snapping off. So thumb wrestling it is.

The Approach: Cocked Like the Hammer of a Colt

There's a reason why people shake hands, and it's not merely because it's a cheap, if rather work-intensive, means of waging germ warfare. It's because you can size up a person in a way that the eye simply can't. Is this person confident? Equivocal? Sick? Granted, you should be able to tell all these things by sight. But what if your eyesight isn't so hot? Then you have a problem. But the truth can't ever hide when skin touches skin.

How you grip your opponent's fingers at the incipiency of the match can set the tone for the battle ahead. It's all about gaining a psychological edge.

First, be sure to grip your opponent's fingers firmly, but take care not to dig your nails into his joints. That signals nervousness on your part, or lack of feeling in your extremities. Either one is bad. Remember: The vibe you want to send is, "I'm no stranger to these parts." Not, "I think I'm having a heart attack."

Second, be sure to keep your thumb ramrod straight, but do make it sizzle a little, like a live wire waiting for a wet foot to step on it. By that I mean let it pulse side to side a couple of times so it gives your opponent something to think about, thus throwing him off his game.

The Haka

New Zealand is home to two great and proud peoples: Crowded House fans and the Maori. The Maori were fierce warriors, much more so than any of the lineage connected to the Finn brothers, and their martial traditions have been incorporated into that antipodean nation's general culture. The rite of facial tattooing didn't really take hold, unfortunately, but performing the war chant of the haka did.

Before rugby matches, soccer games, and possibly even bridge tournaments, teams will greet each other with ritualized dance and ancient song, expressing respect for an opponent along with an unreconciled need to terrorize them before a match.

Thumb wrestling, too, has its haka, and it's as necessary to the competition as, say, hands. Its beauty is its simplicity: "One, two, three, four. I declare a thumb war!" Remember, savor this ritual and use the time it takes to execute the chant to assess your opponent's thumb strength, mental focus and sense of rhythm.

The Attack: Establish the Jab

Passivity has never won the day in thumb wrestling. Only an onslaught of aggression has ever meant a damn to the sport, and the fuse that lights the touch hole that sets off that cannon of flying fingers is the jab. Remember, as soon the haka is over, you must keep your thumb busy, preferably by attacking your opponent's thumb. Don't try to go for the one-hitter-no-quitter. Instead, keep your opponent off guard by going to his thumb continuously. Keep at him and you'll find out if he's the kind who just curls up and dies or if he's got fight and jabs you right back.

The Volley

If your opponent has got heart, that means you'll have to keep jabbing. This is called the volley, just like in tennis, and this is good. Just like tennis, if there isn't a volley going on, then no-body's going to watch the game. This brings us to a dirty secret about thumb wrestling: It's not only a sport, but it's also en-tertainment, and you have got to put on a show for the crowd. Even if you know you can take out an opponent in the bat of an eyelash, toy with him. Do it for the children, if you must.

Don't Believe Your Eyes

When you're in a fight, do you spend the entire brawl looking at your fists, trailing them with your eyes to see where they will land? No, you do not, unless you're very drunk or are fight-ing with boxing gloves 10 times too big for your hands. The same applies to thumb wrestling. Don't be one of those people who look down at what I like to call "the arena of flesh," mes-merized by the speed of their opponent's thumb, trying to keep apace, all slack-jawed and drooling. Instead, look your opponent straight in the eye and jab away. You can do it. This is the clos-est mortals like us living in the Milky Way are ever going to come to using the Force. Don't be afraid. Turn off your brain. Be the Yoda. Remember, every victory worth attaining should be a no-looker.

The Take Down: Give 'em a Nail for Knuckle

So the fight has been going your way. Your opponent has no an-swer for your jab. Your reflexes are such that he's afraid to go for you lest he get pinned. Your eyes are watering from drilling your stare into him, and the children are nodding their approval at each other. It's time to put him away.

Here's one way: Trade him your nail for his pride.

A rank rookie mistake made in thumb wrestling is trying to pin an opponent by his thumbnail. That's never going to work unless you have a little bit of stickum on the pad of your thumb, which is illegal in North America but fine in Southeast Asia, where they like to mix things up a bit. Your thumbnail is nature's linoleum, which means it's slick most times, but after 15 seconds of sweaty tangling, it is positively margarine-like.

First, hesitate for just a second, and let your exhausted, deluded opponent think he's worn you down and triumphed. Second, in a wolverine's heartbeat, you slide your thumb right out from under him and thunk it on either the first or second knuckle of his thumb. I prefer landing on the second knuckle; that way if he's strong enough to resist, your thumb will slide down on the first knuckle. By then the ref will have counted to three, and that's that.

Playing Possum

But what if your opponent is smart, or crafty, even? What if he doesn't go for the nail? Then you go to Plan B. It is, however, risky. This strategy follows the boxing axiom of "taking leather to give leather." Willfully ignoring the S&M subtext, I take it to mean that you sometimes have to lay it on the line if you want to win. So if you can't beat the opponent outright, if his skills demand respect, then you're going to have to offer up your very flesh for bait. This works just like the nail trick, but the potential for backfire is high. You must have the speed and strength to pull out from under a solid pin and turn the tables on your opponent. It's a moment of truth for all thumb wrestlers. It's what separates the wannabes from the champions.

Gut It Out

So what happens if you try both of those and no pin?

What if, instead, you and your opponent are going back and forth, attacking and counterattacking, the tendons in your forearms swelling, the sweat coming down over your faces like a sacred scrim, the air slowly leaking out of the room, and a vision swirls into form in your mind's eye, and you see the girl you loved when you were in the second grade, waving to you from the top of the slide, the airy tinkle of the ice cream man's truck reverberating in your skull, the music coming from afar?

Then, my friend, you have stepped into the zone the an-cient Greeks thought could be occupied only by the gods. This is your chance at glory, and for you to seize it, you must will it toward you. Iffy officiating and a partial judge have been known to be factors. But still, you must have the will to win, because it's that cussedness, along with a reputation for awful impulse control, which may intimidate the judge into steering the stalemate your way. ❖

Mock-informative essays are great fun, but they're only good as ice-breakers, because they dodge the teaching challenge. The joke lies in making simple things difficult, which is the opposite of what good informative writing tries to do.

It's Boring

While informative writing might sometimes lack the emotional wal-lop of a personal essay or the intellectual drama of an argument, it has its own distinct advantage: ostensibly anyway, the reader *wants* the information. That is, she's not likely to put down the instruc-tions for setting her new atomic clock because the *writing* isn't riveting—she'd do so only if it's unclear.

That's not to say you should write lifeless prose, letting the subject itself do all the work—and forget that your reader is a living human being who wants to read the words of another living human being. On the contrary: you want your informative writing to be lively, specific, distinct, even humorous, if appropriate. With that in mind, even recipes can be brought to life. Here's an essay/recipe by the wonderful food writer Henri Bourride:

ALL RISE

HENRI BOURRIDE

While much of America spent the first Sunday in February watching television—men in tight trousers kicking and throw-ing a ball around and piling on top of each other and Madison Avenue ad agencies attempting to outdo and outspend each other—Henri spent the day in a much more civilized fashion. Not to be too disparaging. After all, Henri did grow up in the Midwest before fleeing for the Big *Pomme* and the world beyond, and he still has a soft spot in his heart for the unvarnished, including their obsession with sports—though he is genuinely flummoxed by *fromage*-head hats.

So, as true-blooded Americans everywhere drank beer and soda and ate all manner of dreadful approximations of food—Doritos and bean dip and little brown wieners on toothpicks—Henri was in the kitchen, in apron and chef's hat, glass of Bordeaux in hand, making bread and listening to Billie Holiday, Edith Piaf, and Barbra.

Bread. The staff of life. And also where we get our words "companion" and "company"—in ancient Rome, a *companio* was one with whom you broke bread, or *pan*. Henri can think of little better on a winter's day than homemade bread fresh from the oven, sliced and toasted to a golden brown and slathered with butter and honey. And bread is much easier to make than you might think.

Following is Henri's basic foolproof bread recipe, with virtually unlimited possibilities for improvisation and personal touches. Substitute whole-grain for white flour—or use half of each. Throw in some herbs—rosemary, oregano or thyme. Use molasses or honey instead of sugar. Cook it on a flat sheet (for French-style loaves) or in a muffin pan (for rolls) instead of in loaf pans. Sprinkle the top with poppy or sesame seeds. Flatten the dough before making the loaves, brush with melted butter, sprinkle with cinnamon and sugar and roll tightly to make cinnamon bread.

Henri's Easy-to-Make Bread—No-Frills Version

Note: Henri prefers to use a Kitchen Aid or similar mixer, though he understands purists would scoff at such contrivances, preferring to combine the ingredients in a bowl and knead by hand.

Warm mixing bowl by filling with hot water. Empty and add two and a half cups lukewarm water, into which dissolve yeast using beater attachment. (The yeast will go dormant if the water's too cold, die if it's too hot.) Add two tablespoons vegetable oil, two tablespoons sugar and one tablespoon salt. Add three cups flour and beat until smooth. Replace beater with dough hook, add four more cups flour, and knead until dough doesn't stick to your fingers. (If you're not using a dough hook, knead by hand on lightly floured flat surface or cookie sheet.)

Remove from mixing bowl and place in a large lightly buttered bowl, cover with clean dry dish towel, and allow to rise until doubled in size—one to three hours. Punch it down, and then let rise again to same size.

Remove from bowl, divide dough in half and shape each to fit into a loaf pan, rolling underside into itself and spanking the top (*bad bread!*) to remove air bubbles. Place upside down in lightly oiled loaf pans, then roll back right-side up (this is to lightly coat with oil what will be the crust).

Allow to double in size one more time, and then cook for about 20 minutes in pre-heated oven at 400 degrees, or until tops are golden brown. To see if it's done all the way through, thump the top with your knuckle. It should sound hollow.

Brush butter or margarine on crust and allow to cool. Slice and enjoy. ❖

COIK Is a Constant Problem

Surely you've noticed the Idiot's Guide series. Bookstores are packed with them: *The Idiot's Guide to Starting a Rock Band, The Idiot's Guide to Learning Italian, The Idiot's Guide to Creating a Web Page, The Idiot's Guide to Buying and Selling a Home.*

Of course, they're not for idiots at all, just for people who don't know much about that particular topic. What the books' writers do, generally, is take knowledge and language that are known to a specialized group and make them accessible to a broader audience.

And that's more difficult than it seems it would be, because of a little problem called COIK, which stands for "Clear Only If Known." COIK writing can only be understood if you already understand it before you read it. Almost all the informative writing you see is COIK writing. You can't understand the auto manual unless you already understand auto repair; you can't understand the book on home wiring unless you already know how to do home wiring; you can't understand the chemistry text unless you're a chemist.

COIK problems are inherent in the way informative writing is made. You, the writer, know the information already—otherwise, you can't teach it. But because you know it, you can't remember what it's like to not know it. So you talk to the reader as if she already knows what you have to teach. Here's an extreme example of COIK, part of some instructions for adjusting a carburetor, from a GMC-truck repair manual (published by Chilton Book Company):

Intermediate Choke Rod

1. Remove the thermostatic cover coil, gasket, and inside baffle plate.
2. Place the idle screw on the high step of the fast idle cam.
3. Close the choke valve by pushing up on the intermediate choke lever.
4. The edge of the choke lever inside the choke housing must align with the edge of the plug gauge.

5. Bend the intermediate choke lever to adjust.
6. Replace the cover and set as in the following adjustment.

What? Was that English? To a mechanic, or someone who's worked on cars a lot, absolutely. But to most of us, these instructions are, well, baffling. They're "clear only if (the terms) are known." And for that reason, they work. The book is intended for mechanics, not you and me.

So how do you avoid COIK problems? Here are four suggestions:

Realize that COIK problems are inevitable, so you must maintain constant vigilance against them.

Define your audience's level of expertise precisely, and keep it ever in mind. Constantly ask yourself, "Will my audience understand this?" "What have I assumed they know, and am I right to assume it?" Hear them asking you questions like "What does that mean?" and "How exactly do I do that?"

Get yourself some real readers. Spotting COIK problems is hard for you but easy for them. Ask them to tell you where they're confused or what they were left wanting to know.

Finally, remember that it's usually better to explain too much than too little. At the risk of talking down to your reader, if you're unsure about his level of expertise, give him more information than he might need instead of taking the chance that he won't understand something. If he already knows that a specific step should be taken next, for example, or knows the definition of a term, he can skip ahead, but if he doesn't, he's in trouble.

Eight Teaching Tips

Now that you feel like a teacher, here are nine teaching techniques that help people learn.

Give an overview. An overview is a summary, a simple map of the territory you're about to traverse. If I'm going to take you through the thirty steps of a tricky recipe, you'll appreciate knowing that overall you're going to (1) make the stuffing, (2) stuff the meat, (3) make the sauce, and (4) bake the meat in the sauce. Overviews often use lists: "First, . . . second, . . . third . . ."; "There are three things you must do . . ." The typical overview is one sentence long, so it's in essence a thesis sentence. Here's an overview of "How to Audition for a Play" below:

Scoring at the audition comes down to four things: knowing what you're getting into, doing a little homework beforehand, dressing the part, and acting confident when you're on.

Overviews are most helpful when they come early in the essay. Overviews as conclusions usually make readers feel stupid.

Give examples. No generalization or abstraction ever existed that isn't easier to understand with a following "for instance." Here's an abstract definition:

> A thesaurus, like a dictionary, is arranged alphabetically, but instead of definitions it lists words that are synonyms or antonyms of your source word. It offers alternatives to words you feel are used too often, are too bland, are not descriptive enough, or contain connotations that do not apply.

That would have been COIK writing if the writer hadn't gone on to give an example:

> For instance, let's say you're writing about the desert and you realize you've used the word "hot" nine hundred and thirty-two times. Look up "hot" in the thesaurus and it will give you a list of similar adjectives: parching, toasting, simmering, scalding, scorching, and blazing.

If you need a crutch, force yourself to write *for example* and *for instance* a lot, but keep in mind that readers don't need these links and they can usually be cut out in the rewrite.

Use analogies. An analogy says that X is like Y: Writing is like playing tennis in the dark, style is like the clothing your essay is wearing, cannelloni are like Italian enchiladas. Analogies are great teachers because they make what the reader is trying to learn familiar by translating it into terms she already understands. Here's an analogy for how to breathe while singing:

> To use the diaphragm correctly, you must imagine your midsection is being pumped up like a tire.

Most analogies use the words *like, as,* or *as if,* but not always: "Imagine that your diaphragm is a tire being pumped up." "Cannelloni are Italian enchiladas."

Tell the reader what not to do as well as what to do. Warn the reader away from common errors she's likely to make. List the five most popular ways to screw up, and tell the reader not to do them. Among the best examples of this are the recipes in *Cook's Illustrated* magazine. While some recipes include only what *to do,*

Cook's Illustrated goes to great lengths to tell its readers what can possibly go wrong. In fact, the recipes are often parts of narratives in which the writers themselves admit to botching dishes by not pre-heating the oven or by using the wrong kind of beans.

Tell the reader why. For several years, I lived and worked at Lake Tahoe, where it gets very cold in the winter. When people would come to visit me, I'd always tell them not to set their cars' parking brakes at night, and they'd look at me like I was crazy, but when I added "because you're likely to get moisture on the cable, which will freeze, and then you won't be able to release the brake in the morning," they always followed my instructions.

To force yourself to say why, write "because" after every instruction, and go on to explain.

Use illustrations. Informative writing frequently calls for illustrations—charts, tables, graphs, drawings, and photos. If you're describing things you can see—how to tie a clove hitch, how rainfall is annually distributed over certain areas—your writing will be much more effective if you include an appropriate graphic. Food writers, travel writers, technical writers, and other professionals all know the value of illustrations and use them freely, but for some reason, students think using them is cheating. It's not. It's smart.

It's also easy. Not only is there almost an infinite number of illustrations that you can download to use in your own writing (as always, be sure to document your sources), but most computers come with programs that will help you convert your data into tables. A good example is Microsoft Excel Chart, which you can open directly from a Word document. In fact, with the click of a mouse you can view material that you have gathered in different forms—as a line graph, bar graph, table, pie chart, and so forth.

Use imperatives. Imperatives are commands: "Do this!" "Don't do that!" Shy writers find imperatives pushy, so they avoid them with passives and other circumlocutions. Don't:

The plugs should be tightened.→ *Tighten the plugs.*

A deep mixing bowl and a pair of chopsticks are needed for mixing.→ *Get a deep mixing bowl and a pair of chopsticks for mixing.*

Seek to persuade. Informative writing is almost defined by its lack of persuasive purpose—what's persuasive about how to change your spark plugs?—but we always write better if we're trying to sell something; it gives us oomph. It only takes a slight twist to recast a purely informative intent into a persuasive one:

Subject	Thesis
gardening	A backyard garden will provide you with cheap, healthy food, good exercise, and a tan.
choosing a landlord	Picking a landlord may be the most important part of renting an apartment.

Seeing the Mode

A bar graph is an excellent way to present to readers material you want them to compare. This is a single-bar graph—for West Side Unified School District. While the writer conveyed this same information in the text of a grant (where the writers provided the actual numbers), she wanted readers to be able to see the percentages at a glance.

Note: She could have also easily shown other comparisons—gender, ethnicity, income, geographical location of family homes—in a multiple-bar graph. If, for example, there were a difference in the numbers of boys and girls qualifying for free or reduced lunches, she could have indicated that with a second bar, colored or shaded differently, at each school year.

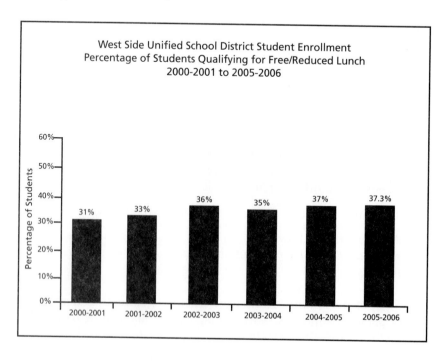

WRITER'S WORKSHOP

Informative Strategies—Action

Let's read through an informative essay and note when and where many of the teaching tips are used. I've marked such places with numbers and labeled each in the right margin.

HOW TO AUDITION FOR A PLAY

STEVE WIECKING

You're standing in the center of a room. Dozens of people surround you, watching intently your every move. You are told what to do and you do it. Sound like the Inquisition? It isn't, but some might call it a close relative: the audition.

Every few months of every year your college's drama department offers every student the chance to audition for a part in a stage production. (1) As a theater arts minor who was cast with no acting experience in a one-act play last October, I can tell you that auditioning for a play is a truly horrifying, but ultimately rewarding experience. Who wouldn't want to show their stuff up there behind the footlights? Auditioning is open to anyone, and the best way to go about it is to prepare thoroughly and go into it with a feeling of confidence.

(2) Just as if you were going to a job interview at your local Burger King, (3) you have to know some practical information before an audition. First, what kind of an audition are you going to? If the audition announcement calls for a "cold reading," you're in for performing any given scene from the play unprepared. Well, almost unprepared—there is some accepted cheating. (4) Go to your main library or the Drama Department's script library and

1. Persuasive purpose

2. Analogy
3. Overview

4. Imperative

check out the play. (5) Find out what that Macbeth guy is up to or what's bugging Hamlet. (6) Don't try to memorize; just be happy with the head start you'll have on the material because you know what's going on.

Instead of a cold reading try-out, you could be going to one that calls for a monologue. (7) In that case, prepare, *memorize*, a two- to three-minute scene of a single character speaking from any play of your choice (unless instructed otherwise). This requires some hopefully obvious rules. (8) Choose a character that suits you. Be as realistic as possible concerning age, sex, and situation. (9) Freshman girls not yet over the trials of acne should not attempt the death throes of Shakespeare's King Lear. (10) Avoid overdone roles like Romeo or Juliet—(11) to the directors, these have become (12) like hearing "Hello, Dolly" sung without cease. (13) And above all avoid Hamlet. (14) Each director has his own idea of what he wants Hamlet "to be or not to be," and it usually comes in the form of Sir Laurence Olivier—stiff competition at its worst.

Once you know where you're going and what to expect, the proper clothing is necessary. Dress subtly and comfortably in something adaptable (15) like jeans and tennis shoes. (16) You have to be able to move well, and (17) you don't want to be so flashy and singular that the casting director sees only a paisley tie or psychedelic tights instead of a possible character. (18) I recently watched a girl audition in a red, white, and blue sailor suit with spiked heels. If the directors had been casting "Barnacle Bill Does Bloomingdale's" she would have been a shoo-in, but otherwise it was man overboard time on the Titanic.

(19) Once prepared, at the audition nothing is more important than confidence. Present yourself well. (20) Eye the surroundings as if to say you know where you are and have control of the room, and greet the directors pleasantly to show them you want to be

5. *Example*

6. *What not to do*

7. *Imperative*

8. *Imperative*

9. *Example*

10. *What not to do*
11. *Why*
12. *Analogy*
13. *What not to do*
14. *Why*

15. *Example*
16. *Why*
17. *What not to do*

18. *Example*

19. *Overview*

20. *Imperative*

there. Handed an unfamiliar script? Make a
quick choice as to what you're going to do and
stick with it. (21) *Don't glue your eyes to the*   21. *What not to do*
script. (22) I guarantee no one has ever been   22. *Why*
cast for having a wonderful relationship with
a Xerox copy. When your turn is over, exit graciously with a smile and a "thank you" that
let people know the chance was appreciated.

Of course, this all sounds easier than it
really is, and you may say that I've left out one
key requirement: talent. But talent you either
have or you don't, and if you've seen many college drama productions you'll know that it
isn't exactly a huge prerequisite after all. ❖

Now it's your turn. Do to an informative draft of your own
what we did to Steve's essay: identify in the margins any places
that do any of the eight teaching tips we've looked at. If there
are any of the nine the draft hasn't done (and you should do most
of them more than once), rewrite, adding passages that do them.

EXERCISES

1. Do the first half of the exercise in the Writer's Workshop
(previous page) with any essay in A Collection of Good Writing.
Photocopy the essay and note in the margins where it uses the
tools. Then list all the tools the essay doesn't use. Don't rewrite
the essay.

2. Write a one- to two-page mock-informative essay.

3. Prewrite an informative essay by writing a list of every
possible question your reader might want answered.

4. Tell the class your informative essay topic and ask them
to generate every possible question they would like answered
or other readers might like answered.

5. Using the information from Exercises 3 and 4, write the
essay.

6. List all possible questions a reader might have after
reading the following restaurant review:

> Carmelita's is a pretty good Mexican restaurant. I recommend it
> if you like Mexican food. I especially like the carne asada, though
> it may be a little picante for your taste. The prices are low and
> the portions are ample. My one complaint is they don't have flan,
> which is something I really go to Mexican restaurants hoping for.

Chapter 13

WRITING AN ARGUMENT, PART 1: THINKING IT THROUGH

With argumentative writing, the basic rule is the same as for all writing everywhere: You can't do it if you haven't read a lot of it. So the easiest way to write a good argumentative essay is also the pleasantest: Read all the argumentative essays in A Collection of Good Writing and write one like them.

What's an Argument?

In an argumentative essay you try to move people to agree with you. That's different from personal writing, because personal writing doesn't seek agreement; we can love eggs and still connect with Kris Tachmier's loathing of them in "The Egg and I Revisited." And it's different from informative writing, because informative writing allows little ground for *dis*agreement. Bennett Lindsey's essay, "Scratch That Itch" (p. 360 in A Collection of Good Writing), suggests natural methods for avoiding mosquito bites but spends very little time discussing toxic sprays—assuming that not many readers will disagree with her that they're bad. Instead, Lindsey devotes the essay to *informing* readers about alternatives to toxins.

An argument isn't just a belief or an opinion, like "I like the Beatles," because an opinion gives the reader no grounds to agree or disagree, and it doesn't urge the reader to join you. An argument is an opinion with reasons to back it up and intentions to sell itself to others. As soon as you say, "Hip-hop culture is destroying modern society, and I'm going to try to get you to agree with me," you've got an argument on your hands.

240

An argument isn't a sermon, because a sermon preaches to the converted. Its listeners don't need persuading; instead, it *celebrates* a message the audience has already accepted, allowing them to renew their faith by agreeing all over again. Most so-called "arguments" are sermons in disguise, because they assume the reader grants exactly what they purport to be arguing for. Most arguments against gun control, for instance, assume that gun control equals gun prohibition, that the Constitution guarantees U.S. citizens the right to own handguns, and that citizens' ownership of handguns is a deterrent to crime—exactly those things your reader *doesn't* grant and will have to be convinced of.

If you're in doubt about whether you're writing an argument, reduce it to a thesis statement (Chapter 5) and apply two tests. To avoid merely stating an opinion, use the *Should Test*: does the thesis have the word *should* in it or at least imply it?

> You should buy your groceries at a local market, not at a chain store, because the owner cares about you and your money stays in town.

> You should go see Steven Spielberg's latest movie—it's marvelous.

To avoid the sermon trap, use the second test, the *Stand-Up Test*: how likely is it that a substantial number of the people in the audience will stand up after you state your thesis and say, "I disagree"? If you can't imagine more than a scattered few doing it, you're preaching. Go find something that will make more people want to stand up and confront you.

Finding an Argumentative Prompt

That's easy—arguments seek you out every minute of every day. You're being handed an argument every time

> you eat in a restaurant and like it (in which case you can argue that other people should eat there) or don't (in which case you can argue that other people shouldn't);

> a teacher or the university frustrates you or betrays you or treats you shabbily (in which case you can argue that something should be done so you and other students don't have to suffer like that anymore);

> you notice as you walk around campus that students seem to hang out in ethnic groups (in which case you could argue that even though we like to think of the United States as a melting pot, where diversity is celebrated, in reality Americans are not comfortable with people unlike themselves).

In short, the world is constantly presenting us with evidence that Things Aren't the Way They Should Be, and we should feel moved to try to Fix the Problem by arguing those who Don't See It into doing what we think they should do about it.

Thinking It Through versus Selling the Case

Let's assume you've found your argument. The work that remains can be divided into two stages. Stage 1 (this chapter) is thinking it through—what teachers call critical thinking, where you try to reason your way to a position you really believe and that really holds water. Stage 2 (Chapter 14) is selling the case, where you take the thought-through position and find ways to sell it to your audience.

The main problem people have making arguments is trying to argue and think at the same time. You must think before you argue, because if you try to do the two together, the second poisons the first. Seeking the truth is a process of exploration, risk taking, and discovery. It requires openness and a willingness to look stupid and fail a lot. Convincing others is about selling and winning. People trying to sell and win stop their ears to everything that doesn't strengthen their position. If you're selling a car, any sense of the car's weaknesses makes you a weaker salesperson, so you convince yourself that the car is a treasure. Most people, however much they tell themselves they're thinking, are in fact selling an idea to themselves, shouting down all thoughts that threaten to complicate the initial close-minded position. Here's an example: You've decided you need a new computer, and you're going to do some research, and read and listen to all the arguments for and against different models and brands. Of course, you've already pretty much decided on that MacDell x-2000, although you might not actually admit it to yourself. So you do all your researching and thinking and then—incredibly!—it seems like the MacDell is the logical choice.

Why Thinking Is Hard

We can't think well until we understand the obstacles in our way. Thinking seems to be an extremely difficult act, judging by the small number of people you and I know who do it well. How many friends do you have who impress you by how well they reason? I rest my case.

But thinking isn't hard the way juggling is hard. It's really just that we don't *want* to think, for a number of reasons, which we might as well face:

1. Thinking is unemotional: emotions blind us to reason. Since we are at the core emotional creatures, forsaking our emotions feels like forsaking our very selves. In science fiction, humans are defined by their emotionality, and the alien races are always scientific, sterile, and unfeeling. *Star Trek*'s Mr. Spock is lovable only because despite all his talk about hating feelings and being glad he doesn't have any, we always know he has them and that's what makes him human. Most of us are devoting our lives to learning to honor our feelings better and getting others to respect them, so telling our emotions to take a hike feels like a step backward.

2. Thinking is impersonal and objective: objectivity means that what's true for me is true for you. Though it's easy to give lip service to that idea, we all know it isn't so. You and I are fundamentally different—I'm me and you're not. If you're late, you should apologize; if I'm late, you should learn to be less rigid. Critical thinking says we don't get to be the center of the universe anymore.

3. Thinking is consistent: what's right and true now is right and true tomorrow and the day after, and what's right and true in one situation is right and true in another. Thus if Country X can invade Country Y because Country Y has the potential to make weapons of mass destruction, then any country can invade any other country that has that potential, at any time. If one president should be impeached for lying, any president who lies should be impeached. We hate having to embrace consistency. We want to use whatever "rules" prove the case we want to prove at a particular moment, but we don't want to have to live by those rules when they don't get us our way. Thus a political party out of power uses underhanded tactics to block the political appointments of the party in power, then complains when the tables are turned and the other party, now out of power, does exactly the same thing. Not fair! What's sauce for the goose is sauce for the gander, as the old folks used to say.

4. Thinking is debilitating: it makes us weaker in a fight. Anyone who tells you that critical thinking will make you a winner is mistaken. Just look at U.S. politics—does the better thinker win the election? No, the election is won by the person with the warmest speaking style or the best haircut or the catchiest slogan. Reagan was one of the most popular presidents in history, and not even his staunchest fans claim he was a thinker. Any politician who makes the mistake of actually *reasoning* in a public debate watches her ratings plummet. And no scientist or academician ever won an election without disguising her background. That's because people are persuaded by emotions and affect. Critical thinking (CT) strikes them as cold and clinical—inhuman, in short. Persuading is selling, and the best sellers, used-car salespeople, don't use logic.

So if you want power over others, the ability to manipulate them or control them, critical thinking isn't your friend. As you are about to crush your opponent with the killer argument, CT will rear its ugly head to remind you that you're being inconsistent and subjective.

So why put effort into thinking? Because life isn't always a battle for power or control. Because you want to know who you are and what's going on in your head. Life is about gaining self-knowledge. Your thinking is a huge part of who you are. Thinking badly is like shooting baskets badly in your driveway by yourself—there's no worldly penalty, but it's a crime against a universal rule: do things well.

These four principles come down to one fact: thinking demands a subjugation of the ego. If your ego is weak, you won't want to do this chapter's work. The ego is a good thing, but it isn't the only voice running your life. Do what you must to strengthen your ego; then, when it's strong enough to step aside, give it a rest and experience the pleasures of ego-free living. Now you're ready to think. And once you really *want* to think, I promise you that if you'll follow the steps of this chapter you'll think well. (And no doubt end forever your chances of getting elected president.)

How to Think: A Template

Thinking needs something to think *about*, so we'll begin by free writing a draft and reducing the draft to a thesis statement, à la Chapter 5. Now we can reduce the amorphous thinking process to three operations to perform on the thesis, in this order:

1. Eliminate language problems in the thesis.
2. Examine the principles and the consequences of the thesis.
3. Perform seven cleanup tasks (I'll explain later).

Eliminating Language Problems

Language problems in the thesis statement are anything in its wording that gets in the way of our thinking. If I say something and mean something else, or say something that can mean lots of different things, or say something that is so negatively worded that it judges the issue before I get a chance to think it through, my reasoning will be fatally corrupted before I begin. Language problems must be corrected before going on to Steps 2 and 3; otherwise, they'll keep reinfecting you, like poison ivy–infected clothing you keep putting on every morning.

We'll break the job of troubleshooting language into two steps:

a. Make a well-formed assertion.
b. Eliminate clouding language.

Making a Well-Formed Assertion

Before we start doing hard thinking, we must make sure we've got a thesis we can work with. When we make arguments, it's dangerous to be too bold or too definite, so we make *ill-formed assertions* that take little or no risk. Behind such remarks lie hinted-at arguments, and we must bring those arguments into the light of day:

> The police in England didn't even carry guns.
> (*What are you implying? That not carrying guns will prevent crime? Or that the English police were fools?*)

> Almost all of the world's great chefs are men.
> (*What are you implying? That women are inferior to men? Or that women are discriminated against in the restaurant business?*)

> Skateboarding is not a crime.
> (*What are you implying? That skateboarders should be allowed to do anything they want? Or that skateboarding should be a crime?*)

The two most popular ill-formed assertions are *rhetorical questions* and *reasons*.

The *rhetorical question* asks a question and hopes the reader will take the risky step of translating it into an assertion for you:

> Who are you to decide when someone should die?
> (*Implied assertion:* Capital punishment should be stopped, because no one has the right to decide when someone should die.)

> Why shouldn't young people be allowed to have a good time and blow off steam once in a while?
> (*Implied assertion:* The police should stop trying to break up parties, because young people should be allowed to have a good time and blow off steam once in a while.)

To translate a question into an assertion, do one of two things: *answer the question,* or *turn it into a declarative sentence:*

> Don't skateboarders have a right to be heard?
> (*Answer:* Skateboarders have a right to be heard.)

> If people are so concerned with the environment, why do they live in wooden houses?
> (*Declarative sentence*: People who profess to be concerned with the environment yet live in wooden houses are hypocrites.)

The *reason* is harder to spot, because it *is* an assertion—it's just not the final assertion. It's an assertion that states a *reason* and lets the reader do the risky work of arriving at the conclusion. It's the "because" clause that follows the unstated thesis. It's a popular ploy in conversation: "Sure, you're a man" means "You don't have any understanding of what women's lives are like and aren't qualified to speak on the subject, *because* you're a man."

Verbal fights are often nothing but a series of reasons without conclusions: "But you said you'd pick me up at 3 p.m.!"; "Well, you forgot to pick me up yesterday!"; "Yeah, well, I got called to a meeting I didn't know about"; "Well, you never even tried to call me." Entire political campaigns have been waged through them: "A woman has a right to choose" is a *because* in defense of the real thesis "Abortion should be legal"; "Skateboarding isn't a crime" is a *because* in defense of the real thesis "Skateboarders should be allowed to skateboard on the sidewalks." And some people use them to avoid making decisions: "Do you want to go to the movies tonight?" gets the response "Well, we haven't been out of the house for a while . . ."

To expose a reason posing as a thesis, put the word *because* in front of it and try constructing a "should" clause that can precede it and feels more like *the thing you're really trying to get:*

Step 1: Smokers have rights too.
Step 2: _____ because smokers have rights too.
Step 3: Smoking in bars should be allowed because smokers have rights too.

Eliminating Clouding Language

Now that you have a well-formed assertion, ask yourself what it really says. Language is *ambiguous*—most words can have a dozen meanings or more, and when we combine words in sentences the possible meanings multiply. We're wonderfully blind to this; we're always pretty sure we know exactly what we mean—but we're wrong. A student writes:

American children are really spoiled, and the schools are encouraging it.

That seems clear until we think about it for a minute. What does "spoiled" really mean? I could say that a spoiled child is one who has been treated too nicely and thus has come to ask for things he doesn't deserve. But if I think about it I have to ask: How can you be too nice to someone? How does being nice to someone harm him? Some people think it spoils a child to let him cry, listen to his complaints, or give him a voice in how a family or classroom operates. Others consider such things basic human rights and think it's unjust to deny them to children. If "spoiled" means "selfish," well, isn't everyone selfish—aren't you always doing exactly what you want to do, and isn't that a good thing? And if "spoiled" means "thinking you're something special," well, isn't it good to think you're special, and aren't you? And how much does a person deserve, and who decided that? If "spoiled" means "never learned you can't have it your own way all the time," well, some people do seem to have it their own way all the time, so are they spoiled?

The more familiar and accepted the assertion, the more likely that your meaning will go unexamined. "TV is mostly garbage" is a statement all of my students grant, but the more you think about it the harder it becomes to say what it really means. How can art or entertainment be "garbage"? Is TV supposed to be doing something and failing? What is "good" art? Is TV garbage because it's stupid (in which case, what's the intellectual level of an hour spent playing basketball or gardening?), or because it's full of ads (in which case, is all selling garbage, or just the highly manipulative selling, or what?), or because it's bad for you (in which case, how can art be good for you?)?

None of this is your fault. Language is inherently cloudy, for at least two reasons. First, *no one teaches you what words mean*—you just figure it out, by hearing others use them. Thus your sense of what a word means is quite literally your own invention, and not surprisingly, other people, who think differently and have different experiences with the word, come to different conclusions. Second, *words' meanings drift through use*. As people use words, they use them in slightly new ways, and those slight meaning shifts, multiplied through millions of uses, mean a word may mean something today it didn't mean last week or last year. There is no way to fix or stop either of these processes, no way to make language unambiguous; you can only work hard at damage control. And there is no step-by-step way to do that, beyond looking hard at language and asking "What does that really mean?" repeatedly. But there are two kinds of cloudy language we can be on the lookout for, loaded language and clichés:

Loaded language. Loaded language is language that contains judgment within it—it says "That's good" or "That's bad":

Neutral language	Loaded language
women	broads
homosexuals	fags
cops	pigs
Southerners	rednecks
sexually active	promiscuous
sexually explicit	smut

Like loaded dice, loaded language predetermines the outcome of the thinking process by assigning positive or negative value up front. If I say about a politician, "He conferred with his advisers," I've remained neutral; if I say, "He conferred with his *cronies*," I've damned him as a crook, and if I say, "He conferred with his *henchmen*," I've damned him as a thug.

Fixing loaded language is in theory easy: look for any words that evoke strong "yea" or "nay" responses and replace them with neutral substitutes.

Clichés. A cliché is a phrase you've heard so many times you don't stop to think what it means anymore: *dead as a doornail, until hell freezes over, the bottom line, dumb as a post, you can't fight city hall, tip of the iceberg, last but not least, how are you doing?, and so in conclusion, in the fast-paced modern world of today, farm-fresh eggs.* Politicians don't want you to think too hard, so political positions tend to get reduced to clichés: *law and order, pro-choice, save the whales, show the politicians who's boss, new world order, compassionate conservatism, stay the course.*

Clichés put your brain to sleep and prevent clear thinking by inviting a reflex response, like waving the flag at a political convention:

> College students have a *right* to *have a good time* and kick back once in a while.

> We must support the soldiers *fighting for our freedom* in the Near East.

> The university should do everything it can to encourage *diversity.*

Ambiguity increases with use—the more a word is used, the less sure its meaning becomes. So clichés, which are used constantly and everywhere, come to mean everything and nothing.

Clichés are easy to spot: if it's a word or phrase you hear everywhere, it's a cliché, and you've learned to stop thinking about it. With that in mind, sometimes it's fun to turn a cliché on its ear so that your reader/listener *has* to think about it. If it's an analogy, try tweaking it: *Life is like a box of chocolate-covered crickets.* Or play with the language: *The darkest hour is just before Sean.*

Since all words are ambiguous, the task of eliminating ambiguity in an argument would be never-ending. Instead, look at your assertion and ask, "Do any of these words pose *serious* ambiguity problems?" There is a set of hugely vague, heavily loaded American buzzwords that are guaranteed to bring any argument to a standstill: words like *sexist, racist, American, equality, freedom, liberty, rights, fascist, liberal, natural, environment, diversity, feminist,* and *conservative.* If you use any of them, it is pointless to continue until you break through the fog and figure out what you're really saying.

Examining Your Assumptions

Now that we have a well-formed assertion relatively free of cloudy language, we've got something we can think about.

Thinking about a thesis comes down to two tasks: understanding where the thesis comes from and understanding where it leads. Imagine the thesis as a step in a process or timeline: the thesis *emerges from* or *rests on* principles or assumptions, and it *leads to* consequences:

Principles→thesis→consequences

If we accept the principles on which a thesis is based and accept the consequences of supporting it, we truly support the thesis; if we don't, we don't.

Every thesis rests on basic principles or assumptions:

Thesis: Americans should never accept public nudity, because it would rob making love of all its intimacy.
Principles: *Making love depends on intimacy; intimacy in love-making is good.*

Thesis: The government has no right to tell me to wear seat belts, because it's up to me if I want to kill myself.
Principles: *The government does not have the right or obligation to protect citizens from themselves; suicide is a right; my death would affect only myself.*

Thesis: Meat is good for you—that's why Nature made us carnivorous.
Principles: *Whatever is "natural" is "right." We cannot or should not alter our primitive makeup.*

Thesis: Americans have the right to own and use automatic weapons because the Constitution says so.
Principles: *The Constitution is always eternally right; the language of the Constitution is unambiguous; "arms" means "any kind of arms."*

Principles are merely larger theses, the big beliefs that justify your smaller belief: "*Since* I believe that the Bible is the literal word of God (large belief), I *therefore* believe that the universe was created in seven days (smaller belief)." All thinking goes like this, from larger beliefs to smaller ones, so until we articulate those larger beliefs and see if we really buy them, we don't know if we believe the smaller theses or not.

Principles are beliefs or values, and there is no such thing as a true or false belief. So you'll never find yourself simply agreeing or disagreeing with the principle, unless you're a zealot. Every principle begins a slippery and fascinating conversation about *when, in what situations, and to what extent* you accept it. Let's begin that conversation with each of the four theses above and their underlying principles. If clothing promotes intimacy, does a member of a nudist colony feel less intimate with other members than clothed people do? If your own death is really just your business, why buy life insurance? If we should eat meat because we ate meat a hundred thousand years ago, should we also live in caves and kill our neighbors? If the Constitution is always right, why did it condone owning slaves and prevent women from voting? All principles produce such interesting conversations. To get started critiquing a principle, ask two questions:

"Where do I draw the line?" Since principles are never a matter of true or false, the real question is how far will you go in supporting them, and when do you bail? Everybody is for free speech . . . up to a point. Everybody thinks protecting the environment is good . . . up to a point. Everyone thinks the Constitution is a good document . . . up to a point. Everyone thinks we should be natural . . . up to a point. The question isn't whether you believe, but where you draw the line. Take the underlying principle, make up more and more extreme applications of it, and discover when you say "Enough's enough."

> Thesis: We need special university admissions standards for minority students. After all, they didn't ask to be born into disadvantaged environments.
> Principle: *Standards should be proportional to a candidate's advantages.*

Where do you draw the line? Should graduate schools have higher admission requirements for graduates of "good" colleges, since they've had the advantage of a good undergraduate education? Should personnel officers have hiring criteria that rise as a job applicant's family income rises? Should disadvantaged students in your class be graded on a grading scale less rigorous than the one used on you?

"What's the philosophical antithesis?" Another way of discovering where you draw the line is to imagine your principle as one half of a pair of opposites—an *antithesis*—and ask yourself to what extent you believe the *other principle* as well.

All principles come in opposite pairs: "Nature knows best" versus "We should evolve and rise above the level of beasts"; "The Constitution is a perfect document" versus "Governments should grow and evolve as we become wiser"; "I have a right to run my own life" versus "Society has a right to curb individual behavior for the good of all." Only zealots can pick one side of the antithesis and call it the right one; the rest of us find a working compromise, a spot on the spectrum connecting the two. We say, "I'm all for freedom of speech, but there are limits . . ." or "Sure, you have the right to live the way you want, but you have to consider your neighbors too."

Like two magnets, the two ideals pull at us, and we move between them until the forces are balanced. If you don't see the merit of both sides of the antithesis, you're missing something.

Imagine concrete scenarios where the principles come into play. For instance, we all believe that customers should be responsible for their own purchasing decisions—and that companies who make and sell things should be responsible for their products. So where do you stand between those two conflicting beliefs? Who's responsible when a boater ignores storm warnings, takes a dinghy out into the ocean, and drowns? Who's responsible when a tire manufacturer makes a flawed tire, knows it, covers up the fact and continues to sell the tire anyway, and drivers are killed? Who's responsible when a customer buys a cup of very hot coffee at a drive-through and spills it on herself? Who's responsible when tobacco companies tell customers that cigarettes cause cancer, then spend millions in advertising to persuade customers to smoke, and a smoker dies of cancer?

As you work with antitheses, guard against two popular mistakes. Don't work with the antithesis of your *thesis*; instead, work with the antithesis of the *principle*. And don't equate the antithesis with the simple negative of the principle—the principle with a "not" added. Notice that in every thesis/antithesis pair in our examples, the antithesis is more than the principle with a "not."

Examining the Consequences of the Thesis

Every time you argue for something, you have to think about what will happen if you get what you're asking for. All actions have consequences. If you can't accept the consequences of your thesis, you can't accept your thesis. If you see no consequences to your argument, you aren't arguing.

All actions have *an infinite number of* consequences, so some of those consequences must be good and some bad: AIDS reduces population pressure; recycling increases pollution from paper and plastic processing plants. If you see only one consequence to your argument, you're missing the others. If you see only good consequences to your argument, you're missing the bad ones. The question you must answer is, do the good consequences outweigh the bad or vice versa?

Weighing pros and cons is laborious, so we like to reduce our workload by pretending that actions have one and only one consequence: "Vote for A—he'll give us a strong military defense"; "Vote for C—he's a newcomer and we'll show the incumbents we're fed up." Single-issue voting is just another name for not seeing the *other* consequences of an action.

There are two kinds of consequences, logical and practical. Logical consequences are *the conclusions you are logically forced to accept if you accept your original thesis*. If an idea is true, then a host of other ideas that follow from it must also be true. For instance:

> **If** you argue that the cops shouldn't have arrested your friend Bill when he got drunk and began shooting off his shotgun at midnight because he wasn't trying to hurt anyone, **then** you are logically committed to arguing that no one should be held accountable for her actions if she doesn't intend to do harm, and **thus** the person who gets drunk and wipes out your family with his car can't be held accountable either, since he didn't mean to do it.

> **If** you argue that you should get a good grade in a class because you worked really hard, **then** you are logically committed to arguing that one's grade in a course should be determined by effort, and **thus** you must agree that you should get a lousy grade in any course where you get A's on the tests without trying hard.

> **If** you argue that the death penalty in the United States is racist because most people on death row are black, **then** you're logically committed to arguing that any system in which a group is represented beyond its demographic percentage is biased, and **thus** the NBA is racist and the death penalty is sexist against men.

Practical consequences are easier to grasp. They are the other events that take place if the action you're arguing for takes place:

> Thesis: Sex education is a bad idea because it undermines the authority of the nuclear family.
> *(It may have that one bad consequence, but it may also have good ones: it may help stop teen pregnancies and save people from AIDS. Are more people suffering from unwanted pregnancy or a non-authoritative family?)*

> Thesis: We desperately need a standardized national competency test for high school graduation, because high schools are graduating students who can't even read or spell.
> *(Such a test might mean that graduates spell better, but the other consequences might create a cure worse than the disease. More students would drop out, student fear would increase tenfold, and vast sums of money would be diverted from teaching to testing, just for starters. Overall, would we be better off or worse off?)*

Seven Cleanup Tasks

If you crafted a well-formed assertion and thought through its underlying principles and its consequences, you've done an honest day's work. But if you have energy left, there are seven cleanup tasks you can perform.

Ask, "How do I know?" A belief has to come from somewhere. Ask yourself where you got yours:

You lived through it.
You heard it on TV.
Your parents taught you.
Logic led you to that conclusion.

A belief is only as sound as the soundness of its place of origin. Arguments about morality that are defended by "The Bible says so" have only as much authority as readers give the Bible, which varies from total to none.

Ask, "What are the facts?" For almost all arguments, facts matter, and if you don't have any, then you're guessing:

Thesis: Most welfare recipients would jump at the chance to get off the dole and support themselves.
(Research question: *What percentage of welfare recipients say they would jump at the chance if they were offered a job?*)

Thesis: I don't want to wear seat belts, because I don't want to be trapped in the car if there's an accident.
(Research question: *How many people die in car accidents because they are trapped in the car by their belts, and how many die because they aren't belted in?*)

Ask, "Like what?" Force yourself to concretize all abstractions and generalizations with at least one "for instance":

Thesis: Schools should censor books that are clearly harmful to children.
(*Make a list of those "clearly harmful" books, and ask yourself how you know they're harmful.*)

Thesis: Punishment in schools is never necessary.
(*Make a list of specific imaginary disciplinary situations in the classroom and invent nonpunishing ways of handling them.*)

Ask, "What should be done?" Most arguments contain a call to action: "Somebody should *do* something about this." If your thesis doesn't have one, ask yourself what you want done and who you want to do it:

Thesis: TV is a waste of time.
(*What do you want me to do, shoot my TV? Limit my children's TV time? Organize boycotts of advertisers who sponsor violent programs? Do you want Congress to legislate guidelines for children's TV?*)

If you are arguing *against* a course of action—"We *shouldn't* do X"— ask yourself, "OK, if we don't do X, what are we going to do *instead*?":

Thesis: It's a crime to hand out condoms in elementary school class-rooms. It just encourages the kids to have sex at that age.
(*What are we going to do instead? Kids are having babies at age fifteen. Do you know something that will work better than hand-ing out condoms?*)

Ask, "How will it work?" If you're asking that something be done, ask yourself exactly *how* it will be done:

Thesis: College professors should be hired and promoted on the ba-sis of their teaching, not publication, because teaching is their pri-mary job.
(*Nice idea, but in fact no one knows how to measure good teaching. Should we test students to determine how much they learn during the term? Should we ask them how much they like the instructor?*)

Thesis: Salaries should be determined by the principle of compa-rable worth. Jobs that demand equal skills and training should pay equal wages.
(*How do we determine the worth of a job? How does the worth of an English professor with ten years of college who writes critical articles about unknown dead poets compare with the worth of an unschooled baseball player who swings a piece of wood at a ball? And which is harder to do, write a great essay on Keats or hit a curve ball?*)

Avoid black-or-white thinking. When we think, we like to make things easier on ourselves by pretending there are only two possibilities, black or white, and our job is to choose one. *This is never true;* there are *always* other alternatives, shades of gray. Black-or-white thinking is also called "playing either/or" or thinking in ab-solutes. When you find yourself doing it, ask yourself, "What are the options I'm *not* considering?"
Sometimes the words *either* and *or* are actually used:

Thesis: We can *either* spend some money and live in a healthier environment, *or* we can let the ecosystem get worse and worse.
(*What are the other alternatives? There may be ways to help the environment that don't cost money, and there may be better ways to spend our money than this proposal.*)

Thesis: The National Parks have to charge user fees *or* they'll have to close.
(*What are the other alternatives? There are other ways for the state government to fund the parks—taxes, for instance.*)

But often the either/or is disguised and we have to learn to see the implied dichotomy:

Thesis: I had to spank her—I can't let her think it's OK to smear peanut butter on the carpet.
(The implied either/or: *You have two choices, either to spank your kids or to let them run amok. What about other forms of reacting to negative behavior, like discussing it, modeling, or rewarding good behavior?*)

Avoid *post hoc* reasoning. Any time you argue "X caused Y," you have to watch out for the logical fallacy called in Latin *post hoc ergo propter hoc,* meaning "after this therefore because of this." It means you're assuming that because event X *preceded* event Y, X necessarily *caused* Y. That's not always so. The attacks of 9/11 may have happened shortly after you visited New York, but your visiting there didn't make the attacks happen. And if there is a connection, it's never easy to say what it is, because this world is a complicated place and outcomes usually have hundreds and thousands of inter-related causes. Pick any cultural event and ask "What made it happen?" and the answer will be "Lots of things." What caused the rising teenage pregnancy rate from 1950 to 1995? Teen movies, MTV, sex education or the lack of it, the lack of a social consensus on moral behavior, the automobile, working parents the decline of the church as mentor, peer pressure, alcohol abuse, laws limiting teens' access to birth control, male machismo, anti-abortion campaigns, the social stigma attached to buying condoms, and on and on. What caused the Hippie revolution in the sixties? The Beatles, the space program, John Kennedy, increased wealth among young people, a growing distrust of Eisenhower conventionality, Elvis Presley, LSD, Leo Fender, Andy Warhol, increased percentage of young people in college, the invention of polyester, the Viet Nam war, the civil rights movement, and on and on.

Sometimes *post hoc* thinking announces itself:

Thesis: Legalizing gambling leads to crime. In the sixteen years since they legalized gambling, New Jersey's crime rate has increased 26 percent.

But sometimes it's buried deep beneath the language, and you have to dig it out:

Thesis: Trial marriage doesn't work because statistics prove that people who live together before marriage are more likely to get divorced than people who don't.
(The *post hoc* assumption: *Since the divorces followed the trial marriages, the trial marriages caused the divorces. The logical weakness: It's also likely that the sort of person who is willing to flout society's customs by cohabiting also gives herself permission to leave a bad marriage.*)

When you spot *post hoc* thinking, just ask yourself, "Is there a provable causal relationship?" and "What are all the *other* factors affecting the outcome?" Keep reminding yourself how hard it is to prove causation. Americans have been trying for decades to figure out if the death penalty reduces crime rates or if violence on TV causes violent behavior in children, and after thousands of studies, we can't get definitive answers to either question.

Seeing the Mode

Graphic illustrations have been used widely in the discussions on climate change. Former Vice President Al Gore used graphs and tables to great effect in *An Inconvenient Truth*, the 2006 documentary that argued that humans have been largely responsible for global warming.

And here's a very effective photograph, taken to illustrate a story about the effect of human-caused climate change on the environment, particularly the dwindling polar bear population as a result of diminished habitat. Interestingly, similar photos have been used to make the case that annual spring thaws occur naturally and that global warming is historically cyclical, not caused by humans at all.

© Hans Strand/Corbis.

WRITER'S WORKSHOP

Using the Tools

Here's a thesis followed by the kind of conversation you might have with yourself about it, armed with the tools we've used in this chapter. Whenever I've used one of the tools, I've italicized it.

> Thesis: Capital punishment is wrong because we say murder is wrong and then we murder people for murdering. If we execute a criminal, we're as guilty as he is.

The first thing we need to do is reformulate the thesis to follow the principles of Chapter 5. Doing that gives us

> Capital punishment should be abolished, because murdering a murderer makes us as guilty as he is.

Now we're ready to get to work.

There's a question about *clouding language* here: what does "murder" mean? It usually means "killing I don't approve of," which only postpones the question of whether I should approve of state executions or not. If "murder" means "illegal killing," executions aren't murder because they're legal—but should they be? The language is also *loaded*, since murder is inherently bad. "Execute" isn't much better, since it's a euphemism that obscures the graphic ugliness of the act and is therefore loaded positively. Maybe "killing" is the only neutral word. The thesis is also a *cliché*, since the opinion has been expressed in these exact words a million times, so I might try to say it in fresher language or at least realize that it will be hard for me to be openminded about language so familiar.

There are several *underlying assumptions*: that all killing is wrong, that all killing is murder, that killing by state decree is the same as killing in passion and for individual profit, that performing an act to punish a guilty party is morally identical to doing it to an innocent victim for personal gain. I'd better *see where I draw the line*. Let's take the first one. Almost no one really believes that all killing is wrong, and neither do I. Killing is acceptable in some circumstances and under some kinds of provocation. Some people tolerate killing in battle; some don't. Most people grant police officers the right to kill, but only under the most strictly defined circumstances—what are they? Euthanasia is often favored precisely by the people least willing to grant the state the right to kill. Few people would call killing someone who was trying to murder you murder. So where do I draw the line? What are the features of acceptable killing that separate it from unacceptable killing?

It's not easy to say. Even if I decide that individuals can take life to protect themselves from danger, how immediate and lifethreatening does the danger have to be? Can I shoot someone who has just shot me and is reloading? Someone who is aiming a gun at me? Someone who is carrying a gun? Someone who has threatened to kill me? Someone who has tried to kill me, is now running away, but will probably try again?

I'm struggling here with a *philosophical antithesis* between two abstract principles: the belief that human life is sacred versus the belief that individuals and society have the right to protect themselves from grave threat. When does the threat become grave enough to justify killing the threatener? A few people say "Never" and will die without raising a hand against their killers. I'm not one of them. Some people say that individuals never have the right to take life, and that when the state takes life in war or law, that act represents the collective will and is therefore okay. That may be a moral cop-out—maybe every soldier should take personal responsibility for every death he causes. At the other extreme are totalitarian states that execute people who might someday cause the state inconvenience.

If I claim that killing is justified when innocent parties are under immediate threat, there are *other consequences* to that logic that aren't pleasant. For one thing, a state execution that takes place two years after the crime is unjustified, since no one is directly threatened. For another, it puts victims in the same quandary women face when they're told, "If you're being raped, be sure you get severely beaten up so you can show the bruises to the police." So if he's waving a knife at me I have to make him cut me?

Another *underlying principle* working here is that executing a convicted murderer is like murdering an innocent person. Do I believe that? If the criminal has committed a heinous crime, does that terminate his rights as a human being? And if he has been judged by a supposedly impartial legal system, and there is no passion or personal gain influencing the decision, doesn't that make it unlike murder? In fact, if killing a murderer is wrong, then a *logical consequence* of believing that is that we must question the entire morality of punishment: Why is it wrong to execute a murderer but okay to fine a traffic speeder or deprive a child of his dinner for mouthing off? All these principles and consequences are as open to questioning as the original thesis, of course.

If I abolish capital punishment, *what's the alternative*? I could lock murderers up for life, but is that really more humane? If killing criminals makes me no better than criminals who kill, doesn't imprisoning criminals make me no better than criminals who imprison? Lifelong imprisonment is certainly punishment, so if I convinced myself I didn't have the right to punish, I wouldn't like this any better than execution. If I resolve not to punish, what methods are left to me to deter violent crime? People talk about "rehabilitation," but that's a loaded cliché and *how will it work*? ❖

Notice how the discussion doesn't lead to final answers, but rather to more questions. That's always how it goes.

Now it's your turn. Pick one of the following statements and write a page of critical thinking about it, using all the tools of the chapter.

a. Prohibition proved that you can't legislate morality—if people want to do something, they'll do it.

b. Intelligence tests are racist. Blacks consistently score lower on them than whites.

c. Boxing is brutal. It's incredible to me that in a society that bans cock fighting and bear baiting, we permit the same sort of thing with human beings.

d. I didn't want to hurt him, but I had to say it or I wouldn't have been honest.

e. Twenty-five years ago the public schools abandoned sound-it-out reading approaches, and the nation's reading scores on standard tests like the SAT have been dropping ever since.

f. But I need at least a B—my parents will kill me if you give me a C.

g. What do you mean, you won't loan me your car?—I loaned you ten dollars last week.

h. Marijuana isn't so bad in itself, but it leads to heavier drugs. Most cocaine and heroin addicts started out on pot.

i. If my neighbors want peace and quiet, why do they live in a student neighborhood?

j. Female reporters have to enter male athletes' locker rooms. If they don't, they can't do their jobs.

k. Don't get mad at me—I didn't mean to do it.

l. Of course she deals drugs—how else can you make a living if you live in the projects?

m. He started it!

n. Vote for Jimenez—he's for the family!

o. You never bring me flowers anymore.

EXERCISES

1. Using the three generic prompts for arguments (see Finding an Argumentative Prompt on p. 241) as models, form two seeds for argumentative essays you might write.

2. Write a one-page essay exploring the ambiguities in one of the following italicized words. Don't grab at a quick, simplistic answer; explore the complexities.

a. When he never called me again, I felt *used*.

b. School libraries shouldn't include *pornography*.

c. I have the *right* to not breathe other people's smoke.

d. It's not *fair* to be graded down for being late when your car won't start.

e. I only use *natural* cosmetics.

f. The American legal system is *racist*.

3. Do the exercise in "Now it's your turn" using a thesis from an essay of your own.

4. Use a thesis from one of your own essays to answer the following question. What is the one step in the critical thinking process, from avoiding questions as assertions to avoiding *post hoc* reasoning that poses the greatest challenge to your thesis and promises to generate the most insight into it? Write a one-page essay applying the question to the thesis and reaping the benefits.

5. Do the following tasks with a thesis from an essay of your own:

a. List two principles it's based on.

b. Write out the antithesis of each principle. Make sure it isn't the negative of the principle.

c. Pick one principle; describe one hypothetical situation where you support that principle and one hypothetical situation where you don't.

d. In a half-page essay, discuss where you draw the line.

e. List two good practical consequences of accepting the thesis and two bad ones.

f. Write down one logical consequence of accepting the thesis.

Chapter 14

WRITING AN ARGUMENT, PART 2: SELLING THE CASE

Now that you've thought through your position, it's time to think about ways of selling it to your audience. You have to do four things:

Define your objectives realistically.
Identify your audience as specifically as possible.
Establish a positive relationship with your audience.
Find a dramatic structure.

Define Your Objectives Realistically

Many writers, when they undertake an argument, set out to do impossible things. They try to have the last word, to say the pure truth that no one else has ever said and that ends debate forever. That only gives you writer's block.

Instead, think of arguing as making your small contribution to the ongoing debate. The contribution isn't "truth"; it's your personal view of things. It doesn't end debate; it generates it by stimulating thought in other people. It needn't even be the only opinion you have—it can be just one of the many thoughts you have on the matter.

Think of this as the Stew Theory of argumentation. Imagine a gigantic pot of Argument Stew always cooking on the Stove of Our Culture. Every citizen is responsible for contributing something to this stew. The more varied the contributions, the better the stew gets. No contribution—no individual potato or carrot—is the "true" one, the "right" one that makes all the other ingredients unnecessary.

So don't try to toss in the potato that ends the stew; toss in *your* potato to enrich the mix. And it doesn't help to go up to the stew and say, "I really agree with the potato that last guy threw in," so simply agreeing with someone else's argument doesn't count. Arguing isn't voting.

You can see the stew-making process on computer network conferences. You toss in a potato by posting a thought you've had, and it may provoke a hundred thoughtful reactions in a day—all of them of value, none of them the "right" or "final" one that shuts everyone else up. For example, I gave my students a prompt on our English department's classroom computer network and asked them to react via their keyboards and then react to each other's reactions. Here are the prompt and the first few minutes of response:

The prompt:

A California School Board member has suggested that schools ban homework. He has two reasons: (1) homework is interfering with the family by taking the child away from family life, and (2) homework is discriminatory, because students with PCs and other assists have an unfair advantage over students who don't. What do you think?

The conference:

Eric: If we can't have homework because some people have computers and some don't, how can we have anything? Lectures are obviously "unfair" because some people hear better than others.

Lindsay: I find it hard to believe that there are absolutely no resources for these children who lack computers or typewriters. If this is indeed the case, then the rules should be changed, so that assignments could be handwritten.

Jill: I baby-sit a seven-year-old whose parents are poor and don't have the money for a computer—but the kid has a Sega system and dozens and dozens of games. So is it a problem of resources or priorities?

Eric: Trying to "fix" America's family or social problems by banning homework is like trying to clean up our toxic dump problem with a toothbrush. We're always looking for the quick fix, the regulation that will make our world a healthy, happy one. No such thing.

Lindsay: I loathed homework just like any other kid. But the plain and simple fact is, homework teaches responsibility. Every child is going to have to learn this sooner or later.

Aaron:	The new family structure is part of the problem. My aunt is a single parent, and she cannot say no to her son. She tells him to do his homework, he begs to play Nintendo, and she gives in. It's emotional blackmail, and lots of single parents feel it.
Adam:	I can see how it is unfair if one kid turns in a paper with amazing graphics and a pretty cover page and gets an A where someone with the assignment done on a typewriter gets a B. I have seen this injustice, and it must stop!!
Joan:	Stop the discrimination, sure, but stop it by stopping grading, not homework.
Aaron:	If families are worried about homework interfering with their together time, why don't they help little Timmy do his homework?
Lori:	Why do we assume that homework is boring and unrewarding?

We continued in this way for one and a half hours, and at the end had more to talk about than we did when we started. Nobody "won."

Identify Your Audience as Specifically as Possible

While all writing requires you to identify your audience, it's probably most critical in writing arguments. That's because to convince your reader to consider your position, you need to know as much as possible about hers. If you're trying to convince your readers to shop at locally owned stores instead of big-box discount stores, you need to know all the reasons they will come up with for not shopping locally, thank you very much. (See What is the opposition's argument? on p. 266.)

Along the same lines, it's usually best to *narrow* your audience. There's no way you can write a convincing argument about the merits of shopping locally for everybody (or, as my students like to say, "anyone who shops at big-box stores"). But narrow your target audience to college students, say, and you're more likely to be convincing. Narrow your target to male college students, and it's even easier. Now narrow it to male college students in your community, and you can really get some work done.

Why? Because in addition to the generalized points you might make about the value of supporting small businesses and keeping money local, you can be very specific in addressing your counterarguments, one of which, in this case, would probably be that big-box stores have lower prices, which of course they do.

However, one recent Sunday morning, I was replacing the washers in the stems of my garage-sink faucets. It was early and our local hardware store wasn't open yet, so, reluctantly, I headed out to a chain home-improvement store. Of course, they had a huge selection of replacement parts, but guess what? They didn't have just the washers I needed, which should have cost about twelve cents each. Instead, I had to buy entire replacement stems. And guess what? They didn't have exactly the ones I needed, but they had ones that were close ($7.95 each) and would, the nice man assured me, work.

Guess what? They didn't.

But by the time I'd installed them, and water was squirting in every direction, my local hardware store was open. I took my original faucet stems downtown, showed them to the man behind the counter, and within about three minutes I had my twelve-cent washers, and half an hour later had my old stems reinstalled.

Of course, I could use that story in an argument that I was writing for a broad audience, but if I were writing for a local audience, I'd point out that the hardware store I was talking about was Collier Hardware, on Second and Main. While prices might be a bit higher there than at Home Depot or Lowe's, out by the freeway, you can *save* money at Collier's. Not only can you buy just the parts you need, but the workers—owner Sal and his two adult sons, Mark and Steve—are also far more knowledgeable than the employees at Home Depot or Lowe's.

Establish a Positive Relationship with Your Audience

The Chair Theory of arguing says imagine your reader sitting in a room full of chairs, each chair representing an argumentative position. She is sitting in the chair that represents her opinion. You're sitting in your own chair, some distance away. Your goal as arguer is to convince her to get out of her chair and move to the chair next to you. What makes a person willing to move toward someone? Does a person come toward you if you tell her, "You're an idiot for sitting in that chair. I can't comprehend how anyone with the intelligence God gave a dog could sit in that chair"? Does she come toward you if you tell her, "Only an evil or cruel person could sit in that chair"? Does she come toward you if you coldly and impersonally list several strictly logical reasons why she shouldn't be in that chair? No. Yet most arguers approach their reader in exactly this way, and they harden her heart against them by so doing.

Let's take another approach. Let's agree that when you argue, you want to be the kind of person people find it easy to agree with and be convinced by. To be that kind of person, you have to do three things: be human, be interesting, and empathize.

Be Human

People aren't convinced by facts and logic; they're convinced by *people*. Every politician who makes the mistake of reciting lots of facts and figures loses the election. But most people do everything they can to hide their humanity when they argue.

A typical experience: A student of mine turned in an essay that began like this:

> Attempts to correlate murder to punishment rates have been made for a long time. Most of these studies were full of errors because they were showing the correlation between murder rates and the presence or absence of the capital punishment status, not to the actual executions, which are what really matter. Others failed to properly isolate murder rates from variables other than punishment, even when these variables are known to influence murder rates.

So it went for three pages—conventional dehumanized argument style. I asked her, "Why are you writing about the effects of incarceration anyway? What's it to you?" When she told me, I said, "Wow! Put it in the essay!" and the next draft began:

> I was in prison for four years. True, I was an officer there, but at eight hours a day, sometimes more, for forty-eight weeks a year ... well, I put in more time than most criminals do for their serious crimes. My opinions certainly did change while I worked there.

Now we're ready to listen.

Be Interesting

There's a myth out there that says scientists are convincing. So when we argue, we put on our imaginary lab coats and get as boring as possible. It doesn't work. Go the other way. Perform. Give the audience a good time. Instead of beginning a movie review with a thesis plop like "*Problem Child* is a hackneyed film that offers the viewer little more than a rehash of previous films in the genre," one reviewer began like this:

> *Problem Child* is the story of a misunderstood and unwanted boy who finds love from a caring adult who discovers a side of himself he didn't know as he deals with the child's painful struggle to be accepted.
> Vomit.

Empathize

If you ask people what they most want from the people they argue with—their spouses, partners, boyfriends, parents—the usual answer is "I want them to understand my point of view." Instead, most of us go the other way and advertise our lack of empathy: "I can't imagine anyone thinking that way; how can you possibly believe that? You can't mean what you're saying,", and so on. A simple "I see where you're coming from" can bring down a host of defenses.

You can do this as a ploy, but it's better if you see the truth of it: The other guy really isn't a fool, and he really has valid reasons for thinking as he does—remember the Stew Theory. As long as you believe that only a moron could disagree with you, you need to do more critical thinking (Chapter 13) to break you out of your narrow-mindedness.

This is a hard truth to grasp in our culture, because our model for argument is the two-party political process, which thrives on demonizing the opposition. But that's not *arguing*; that's *fighting*. So ask yourself, Is the fact that Democrats are encouraged to think Republicans are idiots and monsters, and vice versa, really doing the country any good? If you think not, don't add to the problem by doing it yourself.

Four Diagnostic Questions

To push yourself toward our new healthy relationship with your reader, answer the following diagnostic questions and put some form of the answer in the essay:

What is the opposition's argument? Keep in mind that your reader has valid reasons for his position. Don't condemn or ridicule him for them. Rather, anticipate them. And, respectfully, counter them. That is, say, "You're right," or "Good point . . . However . . ."

In class, I like to call the counterarguments the "yeah-but" arguments. You suggest your roommate try a particular restaurant because the burritos are so good. "Yeah, but they're so expensive," he counters. Your counter to that? "You're right . . . ," or "Good point . . . However, the portions are *huge*. Ask the waitress to box up what you don't eat, and then have it for lunch the next day."

Frequently, you acknowledge the counter ("yeah-but") argument right in your text and in fact use it for a transition: "Granted, the burritos at Tres Hombres are expensive. However . . ."

What would my reader most like to hear me acknowledge about him? If you're writing an essay addressed to the university administration and defending the thesis that the threatened fee hike for university students is unfair and shouldn't be enacted, what would your reader (the university administrator) most like to hear you acknowledge about her? Probably that administrators aren't fiends who just like to rip off students. So you add a passage reassuring her: "I know that administering a university isn't easy, especially in these hard times. You aren't raising fees just for the fun of it. We both want the same thing: to see the university be as good as it can be. I think we can avoid student hardship *and* keep educational quality high."

What is my reader's most likely fear in response to my argument? You're writing an essay arguing that the Green Tortoise, a counterculture, low-rent bus line, is an attractive alternative to planes, trains, or conventional bus lines. What is your reader's most likely fear in response to your argument? Probably that the buses are full of winos and creeps and driven by drugged-out slackers who aren't safe on the road. So you add a passage reassuring her: "I know everyone's image of cheap bus travel: being sandwiched between a wino in the seat to your left and a pervert in the seat to your right. But the Green Tortoise isn't like that. The customers are people like you and me: relatively clean, sober, normal people just trying to get somewhere without spending a fortune. Nor are the drivers and other employees your stereotypical space-case flakes, though my driver did wear a tie-dyed T-shirt; every employee I dealt with was sober, professional, and competent."

How is the reader likely to dislike me for saying what I'm saying? When you try to talk people out of their beliefs, they often resist by defining you in ways that justify their not hearing you. Ask yourself what form that dislike will take; then reassure them: "I'm not who you fear I am." For instance, if you're defending a thesis that says, "Formality is a dying art; people don't know how to dress up and be formal anymore," the most likely negative image your reader will get of you is that you're a snob. So you add a disclaimer: "I'm not one of those people who think Levi's or pants on women is a crime against nature. I love being casual, and I live in jeans most of the time. I'm not saying formality is better than informality; I'm saying that every once in a while knocking out a really fancy recipe, getting dolled up, and inviting friends over for grown-up time is *fun.*"

Find a Dramatic Structure

Many arguers figure that since an argument is won by cold facts and logic, the structure should be as rigid as a scientific experimental write-up: thesis at the end of the first paragraph, supportive arguments in numbered series, and so on. That doesn't work, because arguments are won by people, so go the opposite way: Avoid stiff, logical structures at all costs, and look for dramatic alternatives. Consider the following four experiments: a parable, two kinds of narrative, and a letter. Want more inspiration? The Writer's Workshop that follows has arguments in the form of a list and a satire.

EXACTLY HOW WE WANT IT

SCOTT THOMPSON

Marvin was almost finished. He was on his way to his final department: Body Parts and Functions. He followed the shadows into the arena. There were different lines for each piece of the human body. His first stop was Facial Features. Marvin selected two squinty eyes, a big nose with a mole on the end, a mouth with large loose lips and extreme overbite. This was perfect because it exposed the crooked teeth he carefully selected. Marvin looked in the mirror: "Ah, yes, exactly how I want it."

Next stop: Torso Department. After studying the different choices he selected Number 1: fat. Marvin looked in the mirror: "Ah, yes, exactly how I want it."

Off Marvin went to the Limbs Department. Here he chose a couple of chubby weak arms and legs. The legs he made sure were short enough to make his height under five feet, four inches. Marvin looked in the mirror: "Ah, yes, exactly how I want it."

As Marvin walked to the Externals Department, all he could think about was how perfectly everything was working out. He chose pale, mottled skin and lank, greasy hair. Marvin looked in the mirror: "Ah, yes, exactly how I want it."

Marvin was now on his way to the final department, Afflictions and Diseases. Marvin was undecided between cerebral palsy and muscular dystrophy. He figured that since he already had almost everything he wanted, he would leave the good diseases for others. He just took acne and poor eyesight.

Marvin took a good long look in the mirror: it was all exactly how he wanted it. In a few days, the paperwork was completed and he returned to his school. As he walked on campus, he was greeted with "Hi, Shrimp! Here's Dumbo! Hey, Four-Eyes, how many fingers am I holding up?" The day continued with pretty much the same treatment. Marvin came straight home from school, went to his room, lay on his bed, and, with a tear in his eye, whispered, "Ah, yes, exactly how I want it."

Doesn't make sense, does it? So why do we act as if it was true? People don't come into this world with a choice of how they look or what physical problems they have. Why treat them as if they're responsible and it's their fault? Next time, think about it and refrain from the stares, the gestures, the funny comments. ❖

GIVEN THE CHANCE

MELISSA SCHATZ

I met Stacey three weeks ago, when she came to live at the Group Home where I work as a counselor. I liked her immediately. She's a bright, friendly, attractive sixteen-year-old. She's on probation for two years for petty thefts, and she has a two-year-old son. But her biggest problem is that she's a speed freak—she's addicted to shooting methamphetamine directly into her bloodstream.

After spending a month in Juvenile Hall, where she went through withdrawals, Stacey came to the Group Home in fairly clean condition. But she has run away from here twice since then, staying out several days each time. She admits that she was "using." She says she's been an addict for several years now. Her parents are drug addicts too. Stacey wants to quit, but she needs help. She says she needs to go through a drug rehabilitation program. I believe her.

Unfortunately, I can't get Stacey into one. I've tried, but everywhere I've turned I've run into a wall. You see, drug rehabilitation programs cost big money—two to three thousand dollars for a one-month stay. And absolutely no one will pay for Stacey to go into a program.

Of course Stacey herself doesn't have any money. Nor do her parents. And addicts don't have medical insurance. This doesn't surprise me. What does surprise me is that the State, which has taken custody of Stacey, placing her in a group home in the first place, refuses to pay for drug rehabilitation. It makes me angry. I feel as if the State has said, "Here, hold on to this," and then chopped my hands off.

Now, I know that drug rehabilitation programs aren't cure-alls. It takes more to kick a drug habit and keep it kicked, especially a mainline habit. It's a day-to-day struggle. Yes, I've known addicts who make their annual trip to the drug rehab. But I have also known addicts who *did* turn their lives around on such a program. Doesn't Stacey deserve the chance? While the State has her in custody, the opportunity is perfect. We're at least obligated to try. And isn't it money well spent, if it saves us from having to support Stacey in prison in the years to come?

Given time, the Group Home could help Stacey work through her behavior problems, get through high school, and learn some social and emancipation skills. But the fact is that unless she kicks her drug habit, she probably won't stay long. Her probation officer told me the next time she runs away he'll put her back in Juvenile Hall to clean out. We both know this doesn't work. Just taking the drugs away isn't the answer. But apparently the State has decided the real answer is too expensive. They tell us to fix these kids, but won't give us the tools. They're not giving Stacey or me a chance. ❖

WHY?

DANA MARIE VAZQUEZ

I looked forward to it for months. I began the countdown in March. Only thirty-five days, only twenty-three days, only fourteen days. As the days passed and it got closer, my excitement grew. Finally it was the night before. I counted down the hours, minutes, and even seconds. "The time is 11:59 and 50 seconds—beep—the time is 12:00 exactly," the recording said as my friends yelled, "Happy birthday" and I popped the cork on my bottle of champagne. It finally happened: I was now twenty-one years old. My friends insisted that I drink the entire bottle of champagne myself. Why? Because it was my twenty-first birthday.

As I was guzzling the champagne, my friends were encouraging me to hurry because it was already 12:15 and the bars would be closing at 2:00. Oh yeah, I just had to go to Safeway and contribute to the delinquency of minors by buying for my twenty-year-old roommate. Snapping pictures the entire time, my roommates cheered me on until I reached the finale at the check stand and the clerk ID'ed me and announced to the entire store that it was my twenty-first birthday.

After a round of applause and much cheering in Safeway, I was dragged out the door and shoved into a car. "We've got to go to Joe's," they exclaimed as we raced towards my downfall. Once inside, I was given a drink that contained every alcohol known to Man. As I sucked mine down, my roommate kept refilling it. Why? Because it was my twenty-first birthday.

"It's her twenty-first birthday," my roommate shouted to a guy across the room she knew. "Then come join our game," was his reply. This dice game was quite easy. The rolls of the dice were counted and whoever reached twenty-one drank a shot. Lucky me—I was chosen to drink a shot of vodka and a shot of a Russian apple. Did my dice roll equal twenty-one? No. Then why did I have to drink? Because it was my twenty-first birthday.

"Yeah" my roommates shouted as I barely downed the vodka. "Let's go to Riley's," they laughed as we ran down the street. "Just a beer, all I want is a beer," I pleaded as we entered. Why was I still drinking even though I didn't want anything, even a beer? Because it was my twenty-first birthday.

So we all chugged a beer and raced on to the Top Flight. "It's her twenty-first birthday," they shouted at the doorman as he checked my ID and I swayed to the pounding music.

"Go tell the bartender and you'll get whatever you want," he screamed at me. I followed his command and ordered a Long Island iced tea. This wasn't a very wise choice because it also had many different types of alcohol in it, but at that point I really wasn't thinking. They were getting ready to close the bar, so I pounded my drink and we left.

About a half hour later—BOOM—it hit me. I began removing everything I had put in my stomach in the last three days. I did this, I'm told, for close to two hours. I was so hung over the next day that all I wanted to do was crawl into a hole and die. But did I go out to the bars still? Yes. Why? Because it was my twenty-first birthday.

I've thought about my birthday a lot lately, and I don't understand the rationale I and everyone else used that night. I don't like it, but I don't think it will change. You'd think I would be the first to want to change it . . . but it was my roommate's twenty-first birthday three days ago. We took her out to the bars and made her drink and drink. She got sick at Riley's, puked at Top Flight, and vomited at Shell Cove. She could barely walk, but we still took her to the Bear's Lair. Why? Because it was her twenty-first birthday. ❖

SCHOOL IS COOL

LAURA KATE JAMES

So you've found the school. You've found *the* school. And surprise, surprise, you've been accepted. Congratulations—I should be so lucky. The headaches are behind you now. No more essays, applications, scholarships. Your fate has been decided. Take your foot off the gas, recline your seat, fold your hands behind your head. Time for that long overdue air-jam tribute to Tom Petty's "Free Falling"—cruise control. You're bound for glory, a genius, a prodigy. The future is bright, my friend. Put on your shades.

You're awake, staring up at a dark ceiling, the last night in your own bed. Scenes from *Animal House* and *Legally Blonde* playing over and over in your head. You envision friends, family, ex's, enemies huddled in dark corners whispering your name softly between fistfuls of Fiddle Faddle, tortured by your absence. You imagine your weekends immediately being booked with dinner-movie-coffee-date plans by handsome young males, job offers pouring in, ceremonies held, awards dedicated, benches—no, libraries—built in your name. Your clothes and books and CDs and eight pairs of high heels you'll never wear but don't want to leave with your little sister (the thief) all packed in big black garbage bags and prune boxes, piled up in the corner, waiting.

At last. The Day has come. You are a College Student. You've finally entered the world, the real world, the over-romanticized, over-glamorized collegiate world. You begin to uncover truths John Belushi never let on. You have to go to class. Reading is still a big part of your life. Learning? What? Direction, goals, a major, all have to be decided. Now. And you thought high school was hard. You find that such a large concentration of teens and twenty-somethings all trying to *find themselves* can be exhausting. Everyone is dyeing their hair and piercing their nose and getting tattoos, and they all wear Diesel jeans and spend their money at Urban Outfitters. They complain about rent and roommates and talk about their parents (either they love them, or they hate them and hope they die). And everyone plays guitar and everyone is *really into music*. They all pledge their allegiance to Bob Marley and Fallout Boy and Zeppelin and walk around wearing their Dark Side of the Moon T-shirts, headphones in their ears. And everyone is smoking and drinking or drunk, or they don't and they won't and never will (either/or, black and white, pick a side dammit). They use words like *exoneration*—always in the wrong context—everyone does it and it's the worst. And they all talk about politics and exchange rates and diplomacy and *oh our corrupt government* (they all hate the government). And everyone's heart is broken or breaking, they're falling all over love, in and out and all over it. Love and adore, or hate and abhor. No in between. Abandon all but the extremes. Supposed to make you more interesting, I guess, unique maybe. You'll see that it's really just the same kind of kids grouped in the same place learning the same things living the same kind of life saying the same stuff fighting the same battles with the same opinions and trying to be different in the same ways. It's annoying and tiresome, but the price you have to pay for that degree (not to mention thousands and thousands and *thousands* of dollars).

Try not to add to this hopeless demographic. Yes, yes, I believe education is vital, knowledge is power, learning is loving, school is cool, all that kind of crap, but if you can find a way around this insane sameness and still get the dream job—which, let's face it, you probably won't get even if you *do* go to college—attack. Pursue the alternative path, ferocious and foaming at the mouth. Get a library card or something. ❖

Seeing the Mode

Editorial/political cartoons can be immensely powerful. Indeed, David Wallis, editor of *Killed Cartoons: Casualties from the War on Free Expression* (Norton, 2007), quotes long-time *Washington Post* columnist

Art Buchwald as observing that "Dictators of the right and the left fear the political cartoonist more than they do the atomic bomb."

Here's a not-so-subtle cartoon. Look at how much work gets done in a simple drawing—and, importantly, how much opinion is conveyed in a single glance.

What do you think? To what degree do political cartoons present arguments in the ways we've been talking about? Does a political cartoon "establish a positive relationship with its audience"? Does a political cartoon consider the opposing argument? Do political cartoons use "loaded language"?

Clay Bennett/© 2002 The Christian Service Monitor (www.csmonitor.com). All Rights Reserved.

WRITER'S WORKSHOP

Using Models

Chapter 3 showed how to use models to open doors and inspire yourself to try experiments you'd otherwise never think to undertake. Nowhere is that more useful than in arguing, where our internal paradigm can be so constipated. Go read the newspaper and magazine columnists who have to hold readers' interest day after day or they don't get paid—read Maureen Dowd, Russell Baker, George Will, Thomas L. Friedman, Anna Quindlen, or anyone who writes a regular column in a major newspaper. Here's an inspiring model:

TWENTY GOOD REASONS TO CRY*

STANLEY BING

1. Your team has just lost the seventh game of the World Series.
2. Your stockbroker is arrested for insider trading, and you realize the guy never did one single unethical thing for you.
3. Your wife has run off with Marvin Hamlisch.
4. You decide to forgo your designer clip joint and have your hair cut by Rocco at the local barbershop. Six dollars and fifteen minutes later, you emerge with a kind of abrupt, vertical look currently sported only by military men and recently deinstitutionalized mental patients.
5. Indoor soccer.
6. You shave off your mustache and remember that you hate your face.
7. You forget to pre-order the vegetarian meal on TWA and, famished, eat two stuffed bell peppers in marinara sauce before you realize what you've done.
8. You spend $540 on a state-of-the-art compact disc player, only to find out the next day, in the current issue of *Audiophile*, that digital tape has suddenly become the decreed format of choice.
9. Twenty-four-year-old MBAs who earn in excess of a million dollars a year and complain their lives are empty.
10. Two weeks with your parents at their geriatric enclave in Sun City, Arizona.
11. You hear from your dermatologist that the only way to save your hair is to have injections of estrogen.
12. Your wife absolutely refuses to let you buy that personal helicopter you saw in the window at Hammacher Schlemmer.
13. In the course of a schmooze with a bright and frisky young woman you thought understood you, she inquires, "Woodstock? You mean Snoopy's little dog?"
14. Fatty corned beef.

Esquire, June 1987, p. 225.

15. You find yourself actually paying attention to Dr. Ruth Westheimer.
16. You don your seersucker suit for the first time since last summer and find that, while you can still button the trousers by forcing every bit of air from your lungs, the fly flares so radically your zipper shows.
17. In New York City today, the only legal place to light your post-dinner Monte Cruz is at home with your wife or in the middle of Central Park—and you don't feel all that safe in either location.
18. You enter a room filled with intelligent, dynamic, slender women, and realize that you will never know a single one except at exorbitant personal cost.
19. You are stuck on an elevator with Siskel and Ebert.
20. Your dog, Rags, with whom you shared every confidence and crisis for more than seventeen years, can no longer control his bodily functions. You make that last, inevitable trip to the vet. Afterward, you stand on the sidewalk in the bright sunshine, alone for the first time since your youth, wondering where life goes and, in your heart, knowing. ❖

Chico State student Katrina Nelson found Bing inspirational, so she wrote this:

EIGHT WAYS TO EARN COMMUNITY SERVICE
KATRINA NELSON

1. Cheer your friend on as loud as you possibly can as he leaps through the sprinklers, singing/screaming Jessica Simpson at the top of his lungs right before you realize the pack of Resident Advisers is walking directly ten yards behind you. You also might want to think about checking him in and making sure he doesn't go in the girls' bathroom.
2. When your clock shows four a.m., you shouldn't be getting that useless thing called sleep. You should be starting your casual trip to the dorm lobby. Once you finally make it there, quietly move all those green couches, side tables, and chairs you can into the elevator. Make sure it's packed up to the point where the elevator doors will barely shut. Once the doors close and the furniture is safely on its way to the next floor, take the other elevator back up to your room as if you were just coming back from a long, hard study session.

3. Throw out those boring yellow tinted lights in your room and grab a couple of black lights from the local Wal-Mart; it's open twenty-four seven so you don't have to ever worry about missing your chance. Then it's time to crank up your stereo, blaring "Sexy Back" so everyone can enjoy the wonderful sound of Justin Timberlake just as much as you. Don't forget to hand out party flyers to everyone on your floor and the one below you (so they don't feel left out).

4. Start a heavy argument with your roommate, who won't stop tossing and turning and complaining one too many times about your computer's noise when you just beat the record time for solitaire. Be sure to include very colorful words as you slam the door and stomp down the hallway to complain to your true friends who will understand where you're coming from. Don't worry, your RA (aka: your next-door neighbor) is bound to be wearing ear plugs, so there's no way she'll wake up to you this late at night.

5. Duct tape the door of your friend's room shut, not leaving any possible openings for her to crawl through. Be sure to attach one strand of it to that fire alarm in the hall, just in case she ever actually figures out a way to open that securely shut door. Her test at eight a.m. the next day really can't be that important, can it? After all, it is only finals week.

6. After you and your roommate somehow manage to destroy the table in your bedroom, perhaps in the heat of one of your fights, you have to find a new one fast. No money? No problem! Simply have a friend help you take the table from the recreation room up to yours. The Foosball Table will do if nothing else is available at the time. No one will ever notice it missing.

7. Take an innocent walk around 5th and Ivy with a group of your friends for a couple hours one night. When all of your lame friends decide they'd rather go to sleep than dance on the table with you, this might be your signal to start making that long journey back to the dorms. Once you finally get there, you might not be feeling too well. That's what the trash can right by the front desk is for, right after you give them your ID.

8. Welcome weekend: the best time of the year. Wait until just that right moment, when all the new freshmen are sprawled out across the lawn in front of the dorms watching the most intense part of the movie *Sin City*. Then take off in a dead sprint running by all the students and straight across that big screen with nothing but an umbrella hat on and a sign. It doesn't matter what the sign says because you'll be running too fast for anyone to read it. But since the RA gaining speed

on you might be able to read it, maybe write a valuable lesson you've already learned for surviving at college. ❖

Now it's your turn. Read the model essay below. Using it as inspiration, write an argument unlike one you'd think of yourself.

TIRED OF DEATH AND TRAGEDY? FIND RELIEF IN A NEW GALAXY

MARK MORFORD

You can take drugs. You can drink heavily. You can numb yourself with any number of whoopers and downers and zappers and nerve calmers, prescription and illegal and everything in between, thus rendering your psycho-emotional system moot and null and void and completely, happily unwilling to give much of a damn.

You can deny. You can reject. You can play dumb. You can ignore the news and shun the headlines and close your eyes to the bloody gruesome photos and go about your work and play in the park with your dog and read only *Us Weekly* and *Boing Boing* and pretend that all this horrible global tragedy, these hurricanes and earthquakes and various planetary abuses, the appalling death tolls and severed limbs and blood-drenched streets, they never really happen on the same planet you inhabit.

Sure, you're not stupid: Deep down you know they're swirling like a cold fire all around you, but you can't face them directly. You can't acknowledge too much, too deeply, too quickly, lest it burn your karmic tongue and rip you asunder and depress your spirit and make life just miserable as all hell. It's just too much to process.

I know how it is. You might say to yourself, just this month alone: "I cannot take any more, over 35,000 people dead from a massive quake in Pakistan and India and hundreds more buried alive in mudslides in Mexico and Guatemala as a result of Hurricane Stan, still more piles of dead in New Orleans and dozens (hundreds?) dying in unimaginably brutal ways every day in bombings and vicious warfare in Iraq, and that doesn't even include the everyday gunfire and the murders and the rapes and the busload of elderly people bursting into flames in Dallas, and the questions cannot help but emerge: Where to put all this bleak information? How to possibly sort through and find solace and hope? And by the way, what the hell is going on? Why so dark and violent and dour all of a sudden? What is happening to the world?"

It's tempting, it's understandable, to want to block it all out, to take only small doses of the horrors of the planet and shun the rest like a Republican shuns poor people. The world often careens at us hot and fast and mean, and when the atrocities pile up, our systems often automatically go into shock—they want shut down, recoil, and it becomes the most difficult thing of all to remain alert and compassionate and tuned in and remember that context, of course, is all you might have to get you through.

Context. Perspective. Do you need some? Would it be at all helpful in the wake of all this death and tragedy and a world that seems to be increasingly strained and riotous and overheated? Because a fascinating dose of context arrived just this week, as astonished astronomers noted a stupendous new (well, old) development in deep, deep space, the discovery of a rather shocking distant galaxy that appears to be much more well formed and dense and ripe than any astronomer would have guessed it could be, given its proximity to, you know, the dawn of time.

In other words, humankind has found yet another phenomenon—in this case, a massive, mature galaxy connected to a string of 300 galaxies so unimaginably vast it makes our little solar system, our entire Milky Way, seem like a grain of sand floating in a giant cosmic ocean (which, of course, is exactly what it is). They found another astounding and potentially world-changing wonder they cannot fully explain, one which, simply put, could alter our entire perception of how and when it was all created in the first place.

It's called HUDF-JD2 (for Hubble Ultra Deep Field) and it's officially the most distant galaxy on record, meaning it was formed when the universe was but a squealing, gurgling 800-million-year-old infant, and if it's as dense and mature as some scientists believe, then it throws all galaxy-forming theories into confusion, and you may take what Nigel Sharp, program officer for extragalactic astronomy and cosmology at the U.S. National Science Foundation, had to say as mantra, as gospel, as balm for your troubled spirit. It is this: "One of the standard problems with the universe is that it's large enough that unlikely things happen pretty often."

Write it on your hand. Scribble it in lipstick on the bathroom mirror. Tattoo it onto your tongue and then lick it onto your lover's tailbone because it is perhaps the most beautiful truism you will hear all year.

But this is not the important part. HUDF-JD2, per se, isn't what can provide a tiny bit of balm to your tragedy-overdosed, violence-numbed heart. The important part is how this major discovery is itself but a speck, a glimmer, a hint of a whisper of the vastness of Things We Still Don't Understand.

Which is to say, what we know of this world, of life, of death, of God, of time, of the cosmos, of all mankind's knowledge and all our experience and all our collected wisdom from millions of years sitting on this spinning water balloon still fits into a tiny thimble, a small Ziploc sandwich bag tossed into a massive churning shimmering sea of mystery and uncertainty and unquenchable weirdness.

There. Is that better? Does that give any solace? Can you step back and take the longer view and see the planet in context of the cosmic mystery, the Deep Unknown, with the never-ending parade of human tragedy merely part of a larger, bittersweet galactic circus, life merely a single line of obtuse poetry, and death merely a giant question mark? No? Try it again. Look at the stars. Look deeper. Remember, in space, no one can hear you scoff.

Personally, I suggest balance, a little bit of everything. Stay informed, read like mad, feel the world deeply, but shop and play and take your happy inebriants and have as much sex as possible. Study the news intently and donate money to charities and volunteer when you can and, if nothing else, quite literally hunker down and pray to whatever potent divine energy you believe in, even if it's just yourself, your own breath. Offer up healing and hope from your heart to the world, as pure energy, raw light, if at all possible.

And then sigh heavily and take off your clothes and drink a whole bottle of very good cold sake as you take a very hot bath, restlessly content in the knowledge that you're merely part of this vast cosmological uncertainty, that Earth itself is one of Nigel's "unlikely things" that, well, just sort of happened. Close your eyes, take a deep breath, check out the long view. Hey, it's the universe: It's not supposed to make sense. ❖

EXERCISES

1. Find an argumentative essay in *The Writer's Way* or elsewhere that uses an unconventional technique and use it as your model—write an argument that uses that technique. Attach a copy of the model to the essay, and at the bottom of the essay tell which technical feature you're imitating.

2. Write an anti-cliché—an essay that argues *against* a trendy belief people hold without thinking about it: argue that hunting is moral, machismo is beneficial to society, or exercise is unwise. For a great example, see "School Is Cool" on p. 271. *Don't make it a joke*—mean what you say.

3. Take an argument from A Collection of Good Writing and write a one-page essay answering the four diagnostic

questions we discussed earlier. How many of them did the essay address?

4. Do Exercise 3 using an argumentative essay you found outside *The Writer's Way*.

5. Do Exercise 3 using an argumentative draft of your own. Rewrite the draft, adding passages to address any of the four diagnostic questions you didn't address.

6. Write an essay using one of the following essays from Chapter 14 as a model:

    a. "Exactly How We Want It"
    b. "Why?"
    c. "School Is Cool"
    d. "Twenty Good Reasons to Cry"

Part Five

ACADEMIC WRITING

Chapter 15

WRITING IN SCHOOL: AN INTRODUCTION

Not as Different as You Might Think

It's easy to think that much of what we've discussed so far about writing has nothing whatsoever to do with writing in schools. Not so fast. While there are big and important differences, the basic ideas still hold true: your writing still needs to have a purpose, and you need to know, as specifically as possible, who your readers are.

Purpose

Often in academic writing, your purpose is simply to show your instructor that you understand the course material. In that case, your task is pretty straightforward. Keep in mind, however, that what really pleases most instructors is that their students not only understand the material but they can also take the ideas from it outside the classroom. For example, let's say you're writing a paper for an American Studies class that asks you to discuss the connections between the 1954 *Brown v. Board of Education* Supreme Court decision and the career of Elvis Presley (not as crazy an assignment as you might think). You could discuss how Elvis crossed racial barriers and combined traditionally white and black music in a way that wouldn't have been possible before 1954. That's probably what your teacher's looking for. But if you went beyond that and discussed, for example, how Eminem did the same thing fifty years later, you would be showing not only that you understand the course material but that you can also make connections to it *outside the classroom door.* You'd be surprised how happy that will most likely make your teacher.

In other types of courses, instructors are also looking for particular things, ideally explained in the assignment itself (see below). A first-year writing course, for example, might emphasize research, and the instructor would most likely be looking at the legitimacy and range of your sources, the degree to which you gracefully integrate them into your own text, the degree to which the material is correctly documented (usually MLA, in this case), and the way in which you draw insightful and meaningful conclusions from the sources. Now, while that might sound like a lot, it's actually fairly straightforward, too, with lots of models, advice, and instruction available—in addition to that which you most likely have discussed in class. For example, when making sure that your work is correctly documented, it's very easy to look at a handbook or website that tells you *exactly* how to do it.

Similarly, in some courses the purpose is to demonstrate in your paper that you learned something from and drew some conclusions from actually doing the writing—a noble purpose. Again, this isn't that difficult, since you're the one who did the work: it should be easy to show what you've learned.

But note how all of this is intimately linked to knowing who your reader is.

Audience

In order to write well in school, you need to understand your audience. Naturally, "the teacher" or "the professor" is your primary reader/evaluator, and in some cases he or she knows more about your subject than you ever will. For example, if you're writing a paper for a history class and your professor asks you to discuss the causes of the Civil War, she's looking for something very specific—most likely the very causes covered in her lectures and/or her assigned reading. So, of course, you give her that. Keep in mind, however, that she might be reading as many as a hundred responses to that same question, so imagine how most of the other ninety-nine students will respond and try to do something a little different. When I took American history in college, we were to discuss in our final papers some of the results of Manifest Destiny. I wrote a fairly conventional essay in which I discussed what I thought she wanted to hear, including how the settlers basically committed genocide on indigenous peoples as they moved west. When I looked at the paper and realized how generic it was, I wadded it up and round-filed it. Then I started over, writing about a trip I took to Arizona with my parents when I was a child and about some moccasins I bought as a souvenir, finding, when I got home, "Made in Japan" stamped on their soles. My point was the same, but my approach was different. She loved it, and she read it to the class as an example of what she thought was an excellent response to the assignment. Not only did she give me an A but when I'd see her on campus subsequent semesters she'd never fail to tell me how much she liked the paper.

Caution: Obviously, not all teachers/professors appreciate an original approach and some may in fact be put off by it, so you need to have a sense of whether that will work, which brings us right back, of course, to knowing your audience.

In other academic classes, such as first-year writing courses, professors often tell students that their audiences are their peers. Or they get more specific: fellow first-year students or even their classmates. The professor might go so far as to include as part of the assignment that the student choose her own audience. In that case, you're in great shape. You can choose to write for overweight red-meat-eating first-year male students at your university.

A word about level of formality. Students often come to college thinking that all academic writing is highly formal and that they need to use as many big words and to make their sentences as long and complex as they can. I've had students tell me that they learned in high school never to start sentences with "And," or never to use "I." And I think that's just crazy. Remember our first answer to almost all questions about writing? "It depends." Should you use first person? It depends. Can you begin a sentence with "And"? It depends. If, for example, the assignment asks you to examine several websites and discuss the degree to which they're appropriate for college-level research, then it might be fine to say, "I found one website that seems particularly relevant. . . ." I recently read a long, very thorough research paper by a student who discussed how the closing down of a large lumber mill pretty much destroyed the economy of the nearby town. Turns out the student had grown up in the town, and in her introduction and conclusion she talked about the differences she saw before and after the mill closed down. She could have done that without using first person, but her first-person observations made the paper both more readable and more credible.

Note: Don't confuse suggestions not to use "In my opinion" and "I believe" with cautions against using first person altogether. In those cases, the first person isn't necessarily inappropriate; it's just needless. If you're arguing that Led Zeppelin was overrated, you don't need to say, "In my opinion . . ." That *is* your opinion. So the suggestion to lose that phrase is probably a suggestion to tighten your writing rather than to make it more formal.

Often when students try to write in a voice that's too formal, they lose control. They'll use a thesaurus to find a "bigger" word and it won't be quite right. A couple of general rules: (1) Use a big word when it's the right word, not just *because* it's a big word.

On the other hand, there might be certain terms that you're expected to use to show you understand the course material. (2) If you do use a thesaurus, make sure you look up the meaning of the word in the dictionary to make sure you know exactly what it means.

Finally, remember that formality takes a number of different, well, forms. For example, while the voice in your paper might be fairly informal (first person, breezy tone, etc.), you can still use a formal (prescribed) documentation format. The student's paper about the closing of the mill was rather informal in voice but was documented perfectly, with dozens of in-text citations and a works-cited page that listed nearly twenty sources. However, some writing situations call for both: a formal voice, in which first person is inappropriate, *and* formal documentation. Ask your instructor if you're not sure.

A Brief Review

Sorry, but I just want to go over some of the stuff we covered earlier in the book, to remind you of the similarities between writing in the real world and writing in school.

1. You need exposure to learn how to write.

Chapter 1 says you can't write something until you've been exposed to lots of models and seen "how it goes." How much academic writing have you read? Unless you're a professor, the answer is probably "None." So ask your instructor for sample essays to use as patterns, or ask her to recommend a journal or two in the field whose articles you can browse through in the library.

2. You need motivation.

However hard it may be to find motivation when you're overworked, out of time, and writing on a topic you aren't fond of in a course you're being forced to take, you still need it. And fear or a need for a grade won't work well. How you learn to care is largely up to you, but here are two hints. Everything in the world is intellectually interesting to a thoughtful mind, and the true performer gets up for every performance, however small or cold the audience may be.

3. You need time to prewrite and revise.

Writing is supposed to be a multistage process allowing you to think, reflect, rethink, and revise repeatedly. School will rarely give you the time. *The single most difficult thing about writing in school is the lack of revising time.* There is no way to create extra hours in the day, so all you can do is learn to use the little time you have well:

> *Start thinking about the assignment from the moment it's assigned.* Even if you only have an evening to *write* it, you can *mull it over* for days with a part of your mind and jot down thoughts while doing work for other courses.
> *Plan to do at least two drafts.* Nobody's first draft is all that good.
> *Write an abstract before or after your first draft.* It will take five minutes and pay big dividends.
> *Devote thirty minutes or an hour to peer feedback with a respected reader.* Once you've drafted, another mind will take you farther faster than yours will.
> *Don't try to save time by not proofreading.* One grisly typo can shatter your reader's confidence in you. And remember, proofread from hard copy, not from your computer. You'll see things on the paper that you won't on your screen.

4. Topics are worthless.

This is doubly true in school, where writers regularly fall into the error of thinking that if they know what they're writing *about*, they know what they're doing. Never let yourself describe a writing project by stating its subject. Always press on to the meaningful questions: What are you saying about the subject? Why are you saying it?

5. Have a thesis.

In school writing, thesis is absolutely key—more important than purpose, even.

There is no way to make thesis making easy in school, but it helps to turn to three old friends: (1) Start thinking about the assignment from the moment it's assigned; (2) don't press for thesis too early—if you are going to arrive at an insight about *Hamlet*, it should happen near the end of your thinking process, not the beginning; and (3) ask yourself a question (What drives Hamlet mad? What is the effect of increased numbers of Hispanic voters on recent presidential elections?). A question helps you stay focused on the idea that you're seeking *an answer.* The answer will be a thesis.

The "should" often has little place in an academic thesis, because school writing often has little purpose beyond the accumulation of knowledge or critical analysis for its own sake. If your thesis is "Hamlet had good reasons for going mad" or "The North was no less racist than the South during the Civil War," and you can't see how you want anyone to do anything about it, that's OK.

6. More about audience.

Your audience in school is unlike any you'll encounter in the outside world, but you do have one, and the game is the same: understand how the reader thinks so you can predict her reactions and control them, in order to get what you want. In school you have a readership of one, one whose worldview is unknown and probably wildly different from yours, so predicting her responses becomes a Herculean task. But you have one advantage over the nonschool writer: The reader is standing right in front of you. So *ask her:* What does she want? What format does she like? Does she want you to include a paraphrase of the reading assignment? Can the assignment be done as a list, or does it have to be in paragraphs?

And you can make some intelligent guesses. If you try to imagine how a teacher thinks, you can put together a list of things that are likely to please her and get the grade you're after. Grading papers is a chore, so if you make grading yours painless and rewarding, your teacher will love you. Thus you should do the following nine things:

a. *Answer the question,* if one was asked. State the answer boldly, so it's easy to see, and put it up front.
b. *Follow directions slavishly.* Every teacher has something specific in mind when she gives an assignment. Doing something else, no matter how well you do it, misses the point.
c. *Waste not a word.* Make sure sentence 1 jumps right to the heart of the matter.
d. *Have a strong thesis,* and show the reader where it is.
e. *Highlight structure,* so the reader sees easily what's going on. If the assignment has asked you to do three things, use headings to show the grader where you're doing each one.
f. *Follow format.* Make the essay physically easy to read and to grade by having dark, clear print, a conventional font, and neat corrections, and by including all pertinent information— your full name, the course's full identification, the date.
g. *Use a colon title* (Chapter 8) to let the reader know at the outset which assignment this is and that you have a point.
h. *Be interesting.* Boredom is the paper grader's biggest enemy. Your mission, should you choose to accept it, is to rouse the grader from her slumber and make her glad she read your essay. Be funny, daring, provocative, dramatic, lively.
i. *Use a boilerplate structure.* Both because the grader wants to read you fast and because time is short, you may want

to fit your essay into one of two standard cookie-cutter structures:

Thesis and Defense	**Problem—Solution**
1. State your thesis.	1. Ask a question or state a problem.
2. Explain, defend, support, gather evidence.	2. Gather evidence and reason your way toward an answer.
3. Discuss implications of your discovery.	3. Arrive at an answer or solution.

7. Know your purpose.

You have several purposes. The first to come to mind is getting a good grade. To accomplish this, follow Rules a–i above. Next, since your teacher usually has a very specific purpose in mind for every assignment, be sure you know exactly what it is and make it yours. Ask if you're in any doubt. Finally, school has a short list of general educational goals you can assume are yours unless the instructor tells you they aren't:

Show you did the reading and understood it. This is the skill at the heart of most college assignments.

Use the course tools. The course has been teaching you a set of skills, a methodology, a philosophy, and a body of knowledge; put them to use. If you've spent the last weeks working with feminist theory, use feminist theory in your paper. If the course has been practicing statistical analysis, use statistical analysis in your paper.

Talk the talk. In the Guide to Studying, we talked about the importance of joining the club. Write to demonstrate your membership in the club of scholars. The primary badge of membership is talking the talk—using the jargon of the course. Every course, every discipline, has its argot. Literary criticism talks about symbols, subtexts, archetypes, genres, and deconstruction, for instance. At first, using a dialect that isn't your own feels like faking, but mimicry is key to learning, and using the new words is the only way to ever make them your own. Also, you need the jargon—it helps you say things easily. To talk about literature without words like "symbol" and "archetype" is like talking about cars without being able to say "tire" or "transmission." If the jargon doesn't facilitate your message making, you probably aren't using the course tools.

Note: This isn't contradictory to what we discussed earlier about not using big words just for the sake of using big words. In fact, this is using big words precisely *because* they're the right words. They're the words of the discipline, the language of the field of study in which you are working.

Perform a research-based analytical task. Academic writing seeks to teach you to do critical thinking and data-gathering research. So *don't* design essays where your feelings, opinions, or personal experience are the sole source: "I love my old rickety car"; "Nobody I know cares about popular music anymore"; "I'll never forget my raft trip through the Grand Canyon"; "There are no good men out there."

You can certainly use personal issues as a starting place, but redefine the task as an academic one. "My father's alcoholism tormented me when I was young" becomes "According to experts, what common psychological problems do children of alcoholic parents face?" "I think parents should stay home and take care of their small children instead of shipping them off to daycare" becomes "According to authorities in the field, how do children raised by stay-at-home parents and children raised primarily in daycare environments compare in terms of later mental health and success?" "I hate this short story—it's confusing" becomes "Why does the narrator in this story choose not to tell its events in chronological order?" Here are more such refocusings:

Personal essay	Academic essay
Infant circumcision is sexist.	Routine infant circumcision is brutal, has no demonstrable medical or health benefit, and should be discontinued.
Rape is a horrifying affront to women.	What are the accepted psychological theories on why people rape? What cultural factors produce a rape-prone society?
Nobody reads anymore.	How has the schools' approach to teaching reading changed in the last twenty years, and has it made any difference in students' reading performance?

You'll know you have an academic task when you ask yourself, "How do I know my thesis is valid?" and the answer is *not* simply "Because that's how I feel" or "Because that's what I believe," but is also

because that's what the experts say.
because the evidence and the research say so.
because that's the logical conclusion to be drawn from the facts.

Use citations. Citations (which we used to call "footnotes") are those little asides in which you tell the reader where you got a quote, opinion, or piece of information (Chapter 17). If you are having that dialogue with other writers, you'll have to tell your reader every time you use someone else's words or ideas by adding a citation. The more citations you have, the more you can rest assured that you're doing the academic thing.

Students can get cynical about citations, and nearly everyone has ponied up a faked bibliography to make an essay look more researched than it is. But if you think about it, whenever you write on an issue of interest to a discipline, your writing is making a contribution to an ongoing conversation. So wouldn't you want to hear what other contributors have been saying on the matter?

Avoid plagiarism. Plagiarism is using a writer's work without attribution and thus implying it's yours. You're plagiarizing if you use another's words, thoughts, facts, sequence of ideas, or anything else of value, without telling the reader where you found it. Since in the academy one's scholarship is the most valuable possession one has, and since academic writing requires constant use of other people's work, the danger of plagiarism is sky-high and the punishment Draconian: In any university with integrity, the penalty for plagiarism is expulsion.

The Internet has made plagiarism epidemic, for lots of reasons: The information on the Internet is being given away and doesn't seem to belong to anyone; an author's name is often hard to find; it lacks the "weight" of publishing—no editing, printing, binding, or bookstore shelving—so you don't feel you owe it anything; there's no visible place of origin; traditional citation format doesn't work. For more on avoiding plagiarism—and on documenting and paraphrasing properly and legally—see Chapter 17.

8. Write as a human being to human beings.

Writing as performance, writing to real people who are interested and involved in what we're saying, who need our help or want to be touched, entertained, amused—for most of us, that's where the payoff in writing is. Yet often, in school, all that seems to have little place.

There are two ways you can deal with this. First is to create an empowering fiction. Don't write to the instructor; write to an imaginary audience of real people who really want to know what you've learned and are looking forward to being entertained. They appreciate your wit. They want to be moved. Do this through the early drafts. Then, if you must, you can rewrite for school in the last draft, but you will have reaped the benefits of using the earlier approach.

But there is another solution. I once had a student whose writing was playful and personal and delightful to read. I told him, "I love this stuff, but you know you can't write like this for other professors." He said, "Odd that you say that. I've been writing like this for years, and every instructor has liked it but told me all the other professors wouldn't. I still haven't met the instructor who doesn't like my work, so I just keep doing it." If you try writing to your professor as if he were a real person reading you for pleasure, the fiction might come true—he just might shift gears, go along with you, and be grateful.

How to Read Writing Assignments

You'll find a huge range of types of writing assignments in school. In some, you'll have lots of freedom to choose your topics, purposes, and audiences. In others, you will be more confined by the demands of your instructor and the nature of the assignment itself. In a basic-writing or first-year composition course, for example, your instructor might ask you to write a simple narrative (about a significant event from your past, for example) or to respond to a brief quotation (for example, "Don't let your schooling interfere with your education"— Mark Twain). This assignment would probably come very early in the semester, and most likely the instructor would be using it to "diagnose" your writing: to look at how well you use specific supporting details, at your ability to acknowledge your reader, at your command of mechanics and convention. Some students like these kinds of prompts, because they're so open ended. Some students *hate* these kinds of prompts—right, because they're so open ended.

At the other extreme—and probably later in your academic career—you will run across assignments that ask you to do very specific things, usually incorporating lots of research (compare Frederick Douglass's and John Brown's views on abolition, or choose a major American corporation and discuss that company's environmental record for the purposes of potential "green" investors). Again, some students love these kinds of assignments, and some students hate them. Either way, though, and for all kinds of assignments, there are certain things to keep in mind.

Following the Advice of Woody Allen

One of my favorite lines from the great American philosopher Woody Allen is from his film *Love and Death*: "Eighty percent of success is showing up." In fact, I use this in my classes all the time, by way of explaining how to read an assignment. I tell students that if they "show up," that is, simply do all that the assignment asks of them, they are guaranteed at least to do moderately well. If the assignment asks that they include at least three citations, then, by God, include at least three citations. If the assignment asks for MLA documentation format, then use MLA documentation format. If the assignment asks them to attach an abstract, then attach an abstract.

Obvious? Perhaps. But I'm always amazed at the number of students who fail an assignment simply because they didn't "show up" or follow the instructions. So that's the first rule: *Read the instructions carefully, and do everything they ask you to do.* I recommend taking a highlighter to an assignment and highlighting everything that's required—and not just the due date. Then, before you hand it in, make sure you've done everything you highlighted. Chances are good you'll have completed Allen's "80 percent of success."

Instructions You're Likely to See on an Assignment— Highlight Them

Due date: Obvious, but hugely important.

Length: Some assignments ask for a specific number of pages, others for parameters (eight to ten pages). Give the instructor what she asks for. However, keep in mind that page requirements are *usually* provided to help you choose an appropriate topic and to suggest the degree to which your instructor expects you to explore that topic. Some, but not many, instructors will ask for a ten-page paper and expect exactly that. Most are more interested in what you have to say than in whether you can meet a precise page requirement.

Format: MLA? APA? Cover page? Letter of transmittal? Abstract? Some instructors specify margin width, type size, even font. That stuff's easy. Do it as assigned. (For more on documentation format, see Chapter 17.)

Audience: Often instructors suggest an audience for your papers (your classmates, the local community, etc.). Make sure you know whom the instructor expects you to write for. Sometimes instructors ask you to identify your audience yourself, perhaps in a simple sentence at the top of page 1. Do so.

Required sources/citations: Some assignments will specify a certain number of required citations, and sometimes there are requirements in addition to the *number* required. Does the assignment specify at least two nonelectronic sources? Real books? A personal interview? Do what it asks.

References to course material: Oftentimes instructors will ask that you try to tie in material from the course. Example: You're taking a film class and you have been assigned to choose a recent U.S. film to discuss. Earlier in the semester, the instructor showed *Casablanca* to the class, which he introduced with a lecture and then followed up by leading a lively class discussion. Try to bring to your paper relevant material from the lecture, the film, even the class discussion. It will show him that you have internalized material on which he is basing his course. Note: This suggests the importance of taking notes, sometimes even when doing so might not seem immediately useful.

Asking Questions

Instructors generally do the best job they can to make their assignments as clear as possible. That doesn't necessarily mean those assignments are going to make perfect sense to everyone. In fact, chances are pretty good that at least some of the class will have questions. If you're among them, instead of guessing what your instructor meant—instead of feeling your way in the dark and taking a chance on not "showing up"—meet with her. Tell her you're not sure what she meant by something and that you'd like clarification.

Important note: Don't accuse the teacher of being unclear, even if he is. Turn it around: "Now it's probably just me, but I'm not really sure what you meant by this passage about including only academic journals. Are online journals acceptable?"

It's also good to approach your instructor if you have an idea for a response to the assignment that might be "risky," or outside the assignment's parameters. Let's say your instructor has asked you to research and write about a woman who has had an impact on U.S. culture and has provided examples such as Susan B. Anthony, Betty Ford, and Hillary Clinton. But you have an idea: you think that Lucille Ball, as one of the first strong women on television, also had a large impact on U.S. culture. Would she be an acceptable topic for the paper? Maybe or maybe not, but you can easily find out by asking your instructor. He'll say either, "No, I want you to write about someone in politics," or, "Yes! That's a *brilliant* idea. I can't wait to see your paper." But ask whether your idea is appropriate *before* you do the work and turn it in. Otherwise, you might not even be "showing up."

A Final Word

I can't emphasize this enough: your instructor will probably be reading (and has most likely already read) dozens if not hundreds of responses to her assignment. Remember that. If the assignment is as straightforward as "Write about a significant event from your past," think about how many students are going to write about their parents' divorce, the death of a grandparent (or friend, or pet), or high school graduation. If you don't think you can bring something new to such a topic, try to be a bit more original. Write about finally getting asked to sit with the adults at a holiday meal, the time you realized that World Wide Wrestling was fake, or seeing true pain and poverty for the first time in the eyes of the young mother and child standing outside Target with the will-work-for-food sign.

Chapter 16

RESEARCH

A large part of academic writing is gathering and synthesizing data, so you need research skills. Data may be found in the field (interviews and questionnaires) or in the lab (experiments), but the two most common places to find it are in the library (books and articles), and on your computer screen (databases and websites). We're going to talk about how to use these last two.

Before we jump into the exotic world of research guides, abstracts, and keyword searches, let's get one thing straight: you don't have to reinvent the wheel. Thousands have gone down this road ahead of you, and many of them have left detailed instructions for you. Research assistance comes in at least five forms:

Your instructor. She works with the research materials in your field every day and can probably recite them off the top of her head for you.

Librarians. These wonderful people go to school for eight to twelve years just to learn how to help you find what you're looking for. Don't be reluctant to ask for help—they *love* this stuff.

Your library's support system. Any academic library should have student tours, free research guides in various disciplines (often called something like "How to Find Information on a Poem"), live seminars on topics like using the electronic databases, and online tutorials in research methods.

Websites and "help" programs. More and more these days, research is done online, and the virtual world is working hard to help you use itself. Scholarly databases are incorporating self-help tutorials, organizations representing academic fields are creating websites in how to do research in the discipline, and libraries are creating websites to guide you in using their collections.

Your classmates. Often the majority of the students in a class are working on similar research projects. Share your findings with one another. Point your classmates to articles and databases that you found useful (just as you would if you and a friend were both looking to buy new flat-screen televisions or laptop computers).

Using the Library

Think of the library as being made up of two parts: (1) the texts, those books, articles, and encyclopedia entries that contain the actual stuff you're looking for; and (2) search tools, instruments like catalogs, indexes, and bibliographies that help you scan the texts and find which ones have your stuff.

The Texts

Libraries traditionally divide their holdings into five sections: books, references, newspapers, government publications, and periodicals. You find your way around each by means of its own search tools.

Books are the part of the library we think of first. They reside in the *stacks*, and you find your way around them by means of the *main catalog*, which is probably electronic and accessed through a keyboard in the library's reference area or through your computer at home if you have a modem hookup to the university website. You can look in the main catalog under the author's name, the book's title, or the subject. Unless you seek a specific title or author, you'll be most interested in the *subject catalog*. You type in keywords, just as you do surfing the Web. You might consult the nearby *Library of Congress Subject Headings*, a big book that helps you use keywords the catalog recognizes. For instance, if you look under "Home Heating," it may tell you to type in "Heating—Home."

Books are the easiest part of the library to find your way around in, but they're a poor source of information, for two reasons. First, since it takes years to write, publish, and catalog a book, any information in the book stacks is at least several years old, so the information can easily be out of date. Never use a book as a research source without checking the publication date and deciding if it's too old to be relevant. Second, books are aimed at wide audiences, so they're usually broader in scope than a journal article, and you have to wade through lots of pages before you know if a book is going to have the information you seek. Use books when you want a broad introduction to a subject, like the history of England, but in more detail than an encyclopedia would give you.

One good thing about books is that they're physically present on the shelves and grouped by topic. So when you find one book that's helpful, the books on either side might be helpful as well. Always examine the books to either side of any book you take from the stacks. You can't always do that in a database.

Unfortunately, **reference sections** of libraries might be going the way of Edsels, dial telephones, and the Village People. The reference section used to be the place you went to find out how to say hello in Swahili or when Omaha, Nebraska, was founded, or to get a list of Beethoven's complete works. Not any more. Most such facts are now available online and *very* easy to find. Naturally, it's also easy to get the wrong information (see below for information on determining the legitimacy of online sources), so you need to be careful, but for the most part you can get current, accurate almanac-type information with the click of a mouse.

Having said that, I still recommend familiarizing yourself with the reference section of your library. Sometimes you'll run across information there that you wouldn't find online, largely because of the way the material is organized. As with books in the main catalog, reference materials are grouped by disciplines and topics, and you're likely to discover a resource you didn't even know existed right next to one you were looking for.

Newspapers usually have their own section in the library. The virtues of newspapers are obvious: they're up to date, the articles are about very specific topics, and they're written in plain English. But they have two major drawbacks. First, they're very hard to find your way around in, because they're almost impossible to index. Second, they're undocumented—you rarely can tell who wrote something or where the data came from. I suggest you use newspapers only if you're looking for something you know is there—if you know that the *Los Angeles Times* had a big article on your topic on page 1 on April 12 of this year—or if the newspaper has a good index. The move to electronic databases has helped here. It used to be that only newspapers like the *New York Times* and the *Christian Science Monitor* were indexed, but now even my local small-town weekly is.

Another use for newspapers is to provide historical context for a paper you're working on. Let's say you're writing a paper about your community's reaction to President John F. Kennedy's assassination on November 22, 1963. You could look at a newspaper published that day (either hard copy or microfiche; something from that long ago probably won't be electronically archived) to find out what the weather was like that day, what was playing at theaters, how much a loaf of bread cost—all of which would help both you and your readers imagine that day.

Governments produce a constant stream of publications on everything under the sun. These **government documents** are usually a world unto themselves in the library, a maze of pamphlets, fliers, commission reports, and the like, often without authors, dates, or real titles, often identified only by serial number, usually listed only in their own catalog and not in the main catalog. This section of the library, like the others, is converting rapidly to a Web-based format. As of 2006, for example, 93 percent of all new titles from the GPO (Government Printing Office) were available in electronic format. With each passing year, the percentage of paper publications shrinks and the percentage of virtual publications grows.

Using the government publications is an art. Often one reference librarian specializes in them; start with her help.

The **periodicals**—the magazines and journals—are by far the most useful section of the library for most researchers. The information is up to date, specific, and usually well documented and well indexed. If the library has a print subscription to a periodical, the very recent issues are usually out on racks where people can browse in them, but the older ones are collected—usually all the issues from a single year or two together—bound as books, and shelved in their own section of the stacks. More likely you'll access the articles through an online database to which your library subscribes. Soon all scholarly journals will be available only electronically, while libraries will probably continue to subscribe to hard copies of popular magazines.

Library Search Tools

The best article or book in the world is useless to you if you don't know of its existence. The academic world knows this, so it has developed an industry that does nothing but produce tools to help you find what you're looking for. All these search tools come in print form (books) and electronic form (websites and databases). There are four basic sorts: bibliographies, indexes, abstracts, and research guides.

A **bibliography** is a list of titles of works on a subject and publication details that tell you how to find them. Often indexes are called bibliographies, which may be confusing.

An **index** is like a bibliography except it's usually a multivolume, ongoing project, with a new volume every year or so. The 2008 volume lists publications in the field for 2007, which means that if you want to see what's been published over the last ten years, you may have to look in ten different volumes.

Bibliographies and indexes just list titles and information on where to find them, but an **abstract** will give you a one-paragraph summary of the work, which can save you from frequent wild goose chases.

The best of all is a gift of the computer age, the **full-text data-base.** This is a bibliography that contains the complete text of the articles it lists. When you find an entry that looks promising, you click on it and it appears on your screen. If it's useful, you can print it out right there—glorious! So you want to use full-text search tools when you can, abstracts as a next best choice, and bibliographies and indexes as a last resort. Any electronic database your library owns will tell you if it's full text always, sometimes, or never. Some databases are "full page," which means you're looking at a photocopy of the original printed page, and some are "full text," which means they merely scan and reproduce the written words, so you may not get graphics.

Search tools, like encyclopedias, have subjects, and they range from very broad to very specific. The broadest are bibliographies of all topics, like *The Reader's Guide to Periodical Literature*. It will tell you what has been published on your topic in any given year in any of several hundred popular magazines and journals. Use it if you want to know what *Redbook* or *Esquire* published on your topic.

Some search tools are devoted to broad academic areas:

The Humanities Index
The Social Sciences Index
Business Periodicals Index

Others are devoted to specific disciplines:

Music Index
Index Medicus
Biological and Agricultural Index
Child Development Abstract and Bibliography
Psychological Abstracts
Abstracts of English Studies

There are search tools in subdisciplines, like Victorian poetry, movie reviewing, and neuroenzyme chemistry. Often the leading journal in a discipline publishes a yearly index of work in the field.

A **research guide** does more than list entries; it's a real instruction manual on doing research in the field. It may summarize or critique the sources it lists, review the bibliographical materials available, give an overview of what's being done in the field, and even suggest fruitful new lines of inquiry. Research guides are sometimes devoted to very specialized topics: there's one on the minor nineteenth-century novelist Elizabeth Gaskell, for instance. If you can find a reference guide to your subject, and it isn't out of date, begin your research there.

The most underutilized research tool in the library is the special kind of index called a **citation index.** It lists every time one author or work has been referred to by another. That's all it does, but that's much more than it appears. When you find a work that is useful in your research, look it up in a citation index, and the index will in effect hand you a list of all other researchers who found that work useful too—in other words, a bibliography of everyone working on your research question.

Researching from a Terminal

With each passing year, the search tools we've been talking about and the sources they help you find are less likely to be print and more likely to be electronic and accessed through a terminal. A good electronic search tool, or "search engine," can search the majority of the entire World Wide Web—over 550 billion documents—in about ten seconds and give you a list of what it found in order of usefulness. It lets you call up the full text of the sources in seconds, tells you what the call number of the journal is if your library has it, arranges for a fax of the article to be sent to you immediately if your library doesn't have it, and prints out anything it can access or saves it to your computer or diskette. Most libraries will let you do all this from home via modem. Electronic search engines are often updated *daily*. They can reduce research time for a typical term paper from weeks to hours, and you will learn to love them.

If you're uncomfortable doing electronic research, ask for help. Reference librarians now spend most of their time helping people find useful indexes, databases, and full-text articles. Additionally, most academic libraries have tutorials on how to do effective electronic research. Go to your library's website and look for a "Help" or "Tutorial" link.

Databases

There are two kinds of places your keyboard will take you: databases and websites. Databases are more useful to you in school, because that's where most of the serious research is published. A database is essentially the old periodicals section of the library in digital form. It's typically available only by subscription, so your library will buy rights to use it and you will access it through your library's website, often using a password. The database may be an index—a list of entry titles— or it may be an abstract, in which case you get paragraph summaries of entries. But more and more databases are *full-text*, meaning you can call up the complete text of an entry at a mouse click.

Your library may offer you a choice among fifty databases. Which ones should you use?

Ask the librarian. Tell her what you're working on and ask her to recommend a database. She'll steer you to the most user-friendly, comprehensive one available at the moment.

Start with full-text databases only. They'll cut your work time by about 90 percent. If and only if what you need isn't there, use the abstract indexes next and the plain indexes as a last resort.

Choose a degree of breadth. Each database covers a certain territory. Some, like Academic Search, survey all academic fields. Some, like Wiley Interscience, are devoted to broad areas like science or the humanities. Some are devoted to single disciplines or issues like literature or feminism. Some are indexes to individual journals or newspapers. The more you know what you're looking for, the more focused a database you want.

Look at the time frame. What years does the database cover? In the old days, the problem with bibliographical tools was they were often months or years out of date. Now we have the opposite problem: since the data is so vast and is coming in constantly, databases often chuck older information before it's really old. Many databases only contain entries from the last few years. And some databases, believe it or not, contain no entries from the most recent few years (usually two). Depending on your project, such databases may be useless to you.

Use more than one database. No database searches all available documents on a topic, so if you want to be thorough you'll use several of them.

Choose a level of sophistication. Some databases cover only cutting-edge academic and professional articles. Some cover popular magazines. Some cover newspapers. Pick one that talks on your level. If you're writing on the politics of radical mastectomy, there's no point in trying to decipher the *Index Medicus* when *Newsweek* or *Redbook* will speak your language.

Once you're inside, you order a database to search in one of two ways. You can do keyword searches, the way you do in an Internet search, where you pick a word or two central to your project and ask the search to retrieve every entry that uses those words. Just as often, you'll want to work from the topic *index* at the beginning of the database, select a topic ("English literature" or "sports"), which will lead you to a list of journals in the field, and then search individual journals by the keyword method.

Websites

Websites are different from the articles in databases. They're on the World Wide Web; they have URLs (Internet addresses, like www.amazon.com); they're usually free to anyone with an Internet connection. There is no editorial control, so they range in credibility from serious academic publication to Debbie-cam trash. Databases are little more than the old academic world of journal articles made digital, but websites are the new frontier, with an MTV sensibility.

By far the most important thing to remember about using the Web is that no one screens what you're receiving in any way, so you'll have to judge the worth of a site. Any psychopath can create a website and distribute his ravings, so never assume that the content of a site has any inherent credibility whatever.

You search the Web in four ways: via subject directories, search engines, subject gateways, and website links. **Subject directories** are like indexes: they begin by presenting you with a list of topics or subject categories: sports, current events, health. You choose a topic and follow the directions. Yahoo! is the most famous subject directory. Even though everyone calls it a search engine, it isn't. Subject directories are usually run by editors, so the quality is usually higher but the coverage smaller, since editorial judgment takes time.

Search engines (Google, Yahoo!, etc.) are what everyone thinks of when they think of electronic searches. When you log onto the Internet you probably get a string of them across your screen, and you need only click on one and ask for a keyword search. If they're not there, type in the URL: www.google.com, for example. No search engine searches all of the Web, each engine stresses different subject areas, and each engine uses a different search logic. Therefore, it's worth your time to duplicate your search in a few of them. Because search engines are run by computer programs, not people, they can't think and will give you tons of dross along with the gold. Some search engines are better than others. Google seems to be the best right now, but ask your librarian for a recommendation.

Subject gateways are little known and harder to find, but they're the most academically minded search tools. They're directories devoted to narrow fields, typically run by editors who are specialists— thus the quality is very high. If you can find one, start your research here. Find them by looking at your library's list of research tools under a topic like "Anatomy" or by asking someone in the field, like your instructor.

Once you've found a search tool and gotten to the keyword stage, you're ready for the moment of artfulness: designing the search parameters. When people first use search tools, they're excited by the fact that a ten-second search can turn up 10,000 "pages" (as sites are called on the Web). Soon they realize that this fecundity is a curse. You don't want 10,000 pages; you want the five useful ones. The trick is to design a search that calls up as few pages as possible without missing any important ones.

Here's how novices do it wrong: You're writing a paper on Tiger Woods, the golf pro, so you type into the search engine *Tiger Woods golf pro*. You get back a list of every page with any one of those words used prominently, all fifty million of them, including all references to tigers, wood, golf, or professions. Here's how you do it right: You learn the database's search language, a short series of instructions about how to conduct searches, instructions communicated by words and symbols: most commonly +, −, "", *and*, *or*, *not*, *, and capitalization. With many search engines, typing in + *"Tiger Woods"* + *"golf pro"* will bring up only those pages with *both* the complete phrases "Tiger Woods" and "golf pro." commonly, five minutes spent learning two or three rules in the search language can reduce a hit list from 100,000 to 4. Languages differ from one search tool to another, and each tool should have a help page with the necessary tutorial. If you can't find one or get help from a librarian, consult www.lib.berkeley.edu/TeachingLib/Guides/Internet/Strategies.html.

The most powerful search tool on the Web, and the easiest to use, turns out to be none of the three we've seen so far; it's the **links** contained within websites. Almost every site on the Web has several links to related sites—the virtual equivalent of a recommended reading list. If you can find one useful website, its links will probably give you several more, and each of those will give you several more. Sometimes the links are *hyperlinks*, highlighted keywords throughout the website text that automatically take you to other sites; sometimes they're listed in a "Related websites of Interest" list at the end of the site or in the main menu.

Evaluating the Credibility of Your Sources

Because so much information (and noninformation) is available both in hard copy and online, you must be vigilant about determining what's credible and what isn't. Most libraries' tutorials include guidelines for making sure that a source is current, credible, and valid. I like the one developed by Sarah Blakeslee and Kris Johnson at my library (Meriam Library at California State University, Chico)—and not just because of the unusual acronym.

The CRAAP Test

The **CRAAP Test** is a list of questions to determine if the information you have is reliable. Please keep in mind that the following list is not static or complete. Different criteria will be more or less important depending on your situation or need. So, what are you waiting for? Is your website credible and useful, or is it a bunch of . . . ?!

Currency: *The timeliness of the information.*

When was the information published or posted?
Has the information been revised or updated?
Is the information current or out of date for your topic?
Are the links functional?

Relevance: *The importance of the information for your needs.*

Does the information relate to your topic or answer your question?
Who is the intended audience?
Is the information at an appropriate level (i.e., not too elementary or advanced for your needs)?
Have you looked at a variety of sources before determining this is one you will use?
Would you be comfortable using this source for a research paper?

Authority: *The source of the information.*

Who is the author/publisher/source/sponsor?
Are the author's credentials or organizational affiliations given?
What are the author's credentials or organizational affiliations?
What are the author's qualifications to write on the topic?
Is there contact information, such as a publisher or e-mail address?
Does the URL reveal anything about the author or source (examples: **.com**, **.edu**, **.gov**, **.org**, **.net**)?

Accuracy: *The reliability, truthfulness, and correctness of the informational content.*

Where does the information come from?
Is the information supported by evidence?
Has the information been reviewed or refereed?
Can you verify any of the information in another source or from personal knowledge?
Does the language or tone seem biased or free of emotion?
Are there spelling, grammar, or other typographical errors?

Purpose: *The reason the information exists.*

What is the purpose of the information? to inform? teach? sell? entertain? persuade?
Do the authors/sponsors make their intentions or purpose clear?
Is the information fact? opinion? propaganda?
Does the point of view appear objective and impartial?
Are there political, ideological, cultural, religious, institutional, or personal biases?

Chapter 17

USING SOURCES

Since in academic writing you're constantly using other people's texts to support your case, a large part of the art consists of smoothly weaving other people's words and thoughts into your own paragraphs. There are three ways to do that: summary, paraphrase, and quotation. Let's look at them in order of difficulty, hardest first, and in order of desirability—summarize most, paraphrase next most, and quote least.

Summary and Paraphrase

Summarizing is another word for abstracting (Chapter 6). Professionals summarize a lot, often reducing a large article or report to a single sentence. You read David Rakoff's wonderful 3,500-word essay "Streets of Sorrow" (*Conde Nast Traveler*, November 2006) and you summarize it this way: "Despite the fact that Hollywood destroys the dreams of most who come seeking fame and fortune, those dreams are still worth having." When you summarize like that, you can include several different sources in a single paragraph.

Paraphrasing is saying someone else's content in about the same number of your own words. It's what you do when you tell a friend what another friend told you. David Rakoff writes, "People have been coming out West with stars in their eyes for so long, and for just as long, some have returned to where they came from, their hopes dashed. But if the fulfillment of one's dreams is the only referendum on whether they are beautiful or worth dreaming, then no one would wish for anything." I might paraphrase, "According to David Rakoff, like all those who came West only to return home, their dreams destroyed, we must continue to dream, to continue to wish for things." Notes: (1) You see how my paraphrase loses the urgency, the grace, and the overall power of the original, which is why sometimes it's better to quote a passage, or parts of a passage—see below. (2) It's important that even when paraphrasing, you acknowledge the source of the original; if not, you're plagiarizing. See Quotation and Documentation, below.

Why paraphrase when it's easier to quote? For at least three reasons: (1) You don't want your paper to be simply a list of things other people have said. (2) Your audience is probably different from the original audience. You might be taking a quotation from *American Film*, a journal for serious film scholars, and using the material in an article for high school English teachers who use film in their classes. (3) Oftentimes, paraphrasing helps you understand the original. In fact, when you put a passage into your own words you internalize it in a way that you don't when you simply quote.

Considering the following quotation from *All Music Guide*:

> "U2 started out as a Dublin pub band and began earning recognition after the band won a talent contest sponsored by Guinness in 1979. This led to the release of a three-track EP, *U2–3*, that topped the charts in Ireland and won them quite a following" (Erlewine 336).

Now you could simply change that around and put it into your own words or you could make it your *own*. I look at that, and I think, Hmm, rock band, pubs, Guinness, contest, and so I would do something like this:

> *It seems only natural that a relatively unknown Dublin pub band would get its big break by winning a talent contest sponsored by an Irish brewer. According to Iotis Erlewine, that's exactly how U2 first got noticed, when they won a Guinness-sponsored talent contest, leading to a recording contract, a successful first record (U2-3, with just three songs), and, subsequently, a devoted following in their native land (336).*

My version is longer, but I don't think it's "wordier"—still pretty tight writing, thank you very much. But it's mine now; I've brought something to it that I think makes it work as well as the original in other ways.

Remember too that when you're paraphrasing, you need to **change the original in two ways**:

- You must change the *language* of the original, or, as your teachers used to say, "Put it into your own words."
- You must change the *structure* of the original. That is, you need to change the way the original sentence or passage was phrased.

Read the original below and the paraphrases that follow. Which are plagiarism, and which are acceptable?

> Original: "Good grades in English may or may not go with verbal sensitivity, that is, with the writer's gift for, and interest in, understanding how language works."
>
> *(John Gardner, On Becoming a Novelist, 3)*

1. *People may or may not do well in English classes depending on how sensitive they are to language, or to their talent or interest in making sense of language (Gardner 3).*
2. *According to John Gardner, a writer's sensitivity to language, or her gift for or interest in understanding how language works, may or may not have a bearing on the grades she gets in an English class (3).*
3. *According to John Gardner, it's difficult to know why students do well in English classes. It may have to do with how sensitive they are to language—whether it's natural talent or just interest in the subject (3).*

What do you think? Plagiarism? Number 1 keeps the structure of the original. And in fact, it keeps a lot of the original language as well. Verdict? Plagiarism. Number 2 changes (reverses) the structure but keeps too much of the original language. Plagiarism. Number 3? This one changes both the structure *and* the language. This one's acceptable. Note that all three document the original correctly: if there's no signal phrase ("According to John Gardner") or the source is otherwise unclear, then it must be identified in the parenthetical, by the author's name and page number (MLA format). If the source is identified or otherwise clear, all that's required is the page number.

Quotation

Why and When to Quote

Quoting is good because it constantly reminds you that you need to back up your claims. But it's easy to quote too much. Instead of thinking and writing, you are simply transcribing the thinking and writing of others. So limit your use of quotations. A paper should never be more than one-fifth quotation by volume. Never quote a passage just to reproduce what it *says*. Rather, quote only when the *words themselves* are important. Quote only the few words you absolutely need: as a rule of thumb, *be reluctant to quote an entire sentence.*

How to Quote

Students like quoting entire sentences and passages because they're easy to punctuate:

> Hoffmeister captured the essence of Lang: "When the dust has settled and we can see him standing clearly before us, we see that the real Lang is not really comic, but tragic."

If you must do this, *don't connect the quote to your previous text with a period or a comma:*

> Wrong: * Everybody knows that drinking and driving don't mix. "Alcohol confuses the mind and slows down the reflexes."

> Wrong: * My opinion is that they think in another frame of mind, "I've got mine, to heck with you, Jack."

Instead, add a conjunction:

> Everybody knows that drinking and driving don't mix, *since* "alcohol confuses the mind and slows down the reflexes" (Willard 34).

Or use a colon:

> My opinion is that they think in another frame of mind: "I've got mine, to heck with you, Jack."

Or interpolate a phrase like "He says" or "Hernandez put it like this":

> My opinion is that they think in another frame of mind. They say, "I've got mine, to heck with you, Jack."

If the quotation takes up more than three lines of text, indent the entire quotation and leave space above and below it.

Quoting whole sentences is wasteful, however, so we aren't going to do it, which is why you must learn to punctuate a quoted phrase within your own sentence. The trick is *to make the quotation match the grammar of its surroundings.* In other words, the passage must make logical and grammatical sense with or without the quotation marks. So make sure the quotation has the same number, tense, and person as the text around it. If the sentence is in past tense, the quotation will probably have to be in past tense. Here's a quotation that goes awry:

> Wrong: * When George sees his mother, he doesn't know "how I can tell her of my pain."

To check yourself, read the sentence without the quotation marks and see if it makes sense:

> Wrong: * When George sees his mother, he doesn't know how I can tell her of my pain.

You can solve the problem in two ways:

1. *Use less of the quote:*

   > When George sees his mother, he just isn't able to tell her about his "pain."

2. *Rewrite the quotation slightly to make it fit.* Surround the changes with square brackets (not parentheses):

   > When George sees his mother, he doesn't know "how [he] can tell her of [his] pain."

Documentation

Why and When to Document

Scholars care greatly about the sources of your insights and your information. The daily paper or *People* magazine almost never tells you where its facts come from, because readers are far more interested in the information than in where it came from, but to a researcher reading your academic writing, your facts are only as good as the place where you got them and your conclusions only as good as the facts they're based on. Scholars call telling the reader where you found the information *documentation, citation,* or *referencing.*

What needs to be documented? There are things that come out of your own head—personal feelings, opinions, memories. Those things don't need documentation. Everything else you write or say needs documentation, since you owe it to some outside source. You heard it somewhere or read it somewhere or saw it somewhere. Those things aren't yours; they belong to the people who told them to you. You must give the owner credit in a citation.

There is one exception to all this: you don't need to document data that're common knowledge or easily verifiable. If you claim that Tierra del Fuego is at the southern tip of South America, you needn't document it because your reader can verify the fact in any atlas. But if you assert that Tierra del Fuego has tactical nuclear weapons, you'd better tell the reader where you found out. Thus all quotations must have citations, since it's never obvious where a person's words came from.

Document for two reasons. First, you must have accountability. If your reader doesn't know where the information came from, he can't evaluate your sources or see if you're using them well, and thus he can't trust you. Second, you must avoid plagiarism, the number one pitfall of the research paper.

Students are often shocked by how rabid their instructors are about documentation; they say, "But if you do that you'll be documenting every other sentence!" That's quite rare, actually, except perhaps in a highly technical or literary dissertation. Keep in mind that your job is to explore what others have said about your topic, to make connections among them, to synthesize them, and to draw conclusions. Think of it this way: a research paper that would need documentation for "every other sentence" is little more than a bibliography with excerpts. Instead of having someone read your paper, you might as well just refer him to your sources. What you want to do instead is "own" the citations, make them your own, as in my paraphrase above about the origins of U2's success.

How to Document

Let's assume you've just quoted from one of your readings and you want to tell the reader where the quotation came from. We used to cite via *footnotes* at the bottom of each page. That format is extinct, killed by its own incredible inefficiency. Taking its place are several citation systems specific to individual disciplines. We'll practice the two most common formats: MLA citations, which are used by most of the humanities, and APA citations, used by most of the sciences.

Both of our citation formats use brief information in parentheses in the text as a kind of shorthand cue to bibliography entries at the end of the paper. You write, "In fact, Earth has been invaded three times by aliens ( )," and between those parentheses you put just enough information to let the reader find the fuller information in the bibliography. The two systems give different cues, and consequently they format the bibliography differently as well.

MLA citations. The Modern Language Association has established a citation system used by scholars in literature and allied fields. It puts in parentheses the author's last name and the page number. That's all—no punctuation, no "p.," no nothing:

```
In fact, Earth has been invaded three times by
aliens (Smith 12).
```

This tells the reader to look through the bibliography until she gets to a work by Smith; there she'll find out the author's full name, the work's title, the publisher, date of publication, and anything else she needs in order to find a copy of the source herself.

In any of these citation systems, the basic rule is to put in parentheses the minimal information the reader needs to find the bibliography entry. So if your text tells the reader the author's name, the parentheses don't have to:

```
Smith showed that Earth has been invaded three
times by aliens (12).
```

But if there is more than one Smith in the bibliography, you'll have to tell the reader which one you mean:

> In fact, Earth has been invaded three times by
> aliens (J. Smith 12).

And if Smith has more than one title in the bibliography, you'll have to tell the reader which one you mean by including an abbreviated version of the title:

> In fact, Earth has been invaded three times by
> aliens (Smith, Aliens 12).

It's often easier to include that sort of information in the text itself:

> Jolene Smith, in Aliens Among Us, argues that Earth
> has been invaded three times by aliens (12).

If you're working with plays, poems, long works divided into books, or any text where the page number isn't the most useful way of directing the reader to the spot, give her whatever is. For a play, give act, scene, and line numbers; for a poem, give line numbers; for a long poem divided into books, give book and line numbers:

> Hamlet blames himself for his "dull revenge"
> (4.4.33).

> The people on Keats's urn are "overwrought" (42)
> in more than one way.

> We're reminded by Milton that Adam and Eve don't
> cry for very long when they leave the Garden of
> Eden (12.645).

Hamlet's line occurs in Act 4, scene 4, line 33, Keats's comment in line 42 of "Ode on a Grecian Urn," and Adam and Eve's tears in line 645 in Book 12 of *Paradise Lost*.

When you find yourself in a situation not quite covered by the rules, just use common sense and remember what citations are for: to get the reader to the bibliography entry. If the work has no author, you'll have to use the title as a cue:

> In fact, Earth has been invaded three times by
> aliens (Aliens Among Us 12).

If the title gets bulky, it's cleaner to put it in the text:

> "Studies of UFO Sightings in North America, 1960-
> 1980" offers strong evidence that Earth has been
> invaded three times by aliens (12).

Or use a short form of the title, if it's unambiguous:

> In fact, Earth has been invaded three times by
> aliens ("Studies" 12).

How to format the MLA works cited list. In the MLA system, at the end of the paper you make a list of all the sources you've cited and title it "Works Cited." Each source is listed once, and the sources are in alphabetical order by authors' last names. The sources are un-numbered. The first line of each entry is unindented, but all other lines are indented five spaces. In the entry, you include all informa-tion the reader might need to locate the source itself (*not* a particu-lar page or passage in the source). Here's a typical entry for a book:

```
Smith, Jolene. Aliens Among Us. New York:
     Vanity Press, 2007.
```

Here's a typical entry for a magazine article:

```
Smith, Jolene. "Aliens Among Us." UFO Today 14
     Jan. 2007: 10-19.
```

The title of the article is in quotation marks; the title of the whole volume is underlined (or in italics). All information about volume numbers, issue numbers, seasons (for example, the Fall issue), days, months, and years is included. The page numbers are the pages the article covers, not the pages you used or referred to in the citations.

APA citations. The American Psychological Association has a citation system that is used by many of the social sciences. Sometimes called the name/date or the author/year system, it gives the author *and the year of publication* in parentheses, and usually omits the page number:

```
In fact, Earth has been invaded three times by
aliens (Smith, 2007).
```

APA encourages you to put the author's name into the text, put the year in parentheses immediately following the name, and put the page number (with the "p.") at the end of the sentence if you choose to include it:

```
According to Smith (2007), Earth has been invaded
three times by aliens (p. 12).
```

How to format the APA references list. Because the APA scheme asks the reader to find sources by author and year, you must structure the entries in the bibliography (which the APA calls References instead of Works Cited) so the year of publication im-mediately follows the author:

For a book:

```
Smith, J. (2007). Aliens among us. New York:
Vanity Press.
```

For an article:

> Smith, J. (2007, January 14). Aliens among us.
> UFO Today, pp. 10-19.

There are lots of little ways in which this format differs from MLA's, beyond the location of the year. For instance:

1. Only the author's first initials are used, not the whole first name.
2. Only the first letters of titles and subtitles and proper nouns are capitalized, but, just to make things hard, names of periodicals (like *Science Weekly*) are capitalized conventionally.
3. Titles of articles or chapters, which have quotation marks around them in MLA style, have none here.
4. APA uses "pp." before the page numbers for magazine articles, but not for articles in professional journals (no joke!); MLA never uses it.
5. APA indentation is the opposite of MLA's: indent the first line of the entry only.
6. MLA uses punctuation differently, in several little ways.

In an author/year scheme, if you have several works by the same author, list them in chronological order, the earliest first. Distinguish between items in the same year by assigning letters: 1990a, 1990b, and so on. If the source has no author, begin the entry with the title and alphabetize it as if it were an author.

Making Sense of It All

As soon as you start making citations, you realize you have a thousand unanswered questions about format. Do you write the date of a magazine "December 2," "Dec. 2," "2 December," or "12/2"? Do you underline record album titles or put them in quotation marks? If you have four authors, do you list them all or just list the first and write "et al."? Don't try to memorize answers to all such questions; instead, remember four principles:

1. *Use common sense and blunt honesty.* If you're entering something weird and you're not sure how to handle it, just tell the reader what it is. If it's a cartoon, write "Trudeau, Gary. 'Doonesbury.' Cartoon," then the usual newspaper information. If it's an interview, use "Interview" as your title. If it's a private conversation or a letter, write "Private conversation with author" or "Personal letter to author."
2. *Err on the side of helpfulness.* When in doubt about whether to include information—a government pamphlet's serial number or a TV show's network—put it in.
3. *Be consistent.* Once you do it one way, keep doing it that way.

4. *Get a style manual or research guide, or bookmark an online guide and use it frequently and carefully.* Citation format is pure convention, so you can't use logic to figure out what's right. On the other hand, because the formats are all conventional, all the manuals and guides and websites will have the same rules and information but might be organized differently, with some going into more detail/explanation than others. Check out several current ones (that include online citation information), and find one that you like. MLA publishes the *MLA Handbook for Writers of Research Papers*, and the APA publishes both *Concise Rules of APA Style* and the *Publication Manual of the American Psychological Association.* Additionally, numerous websites—many sponsored by well-known universities—offer free access to formatting information (just search the phrase "MLA format," for example, and you'll get lots of hits). Further, it's quite likely your own school's library has its own citation-format page or links to ones that it endorses. Go to your library's website and look for a link to "Documentation format," or something similar.

Citing Online Sources

Electronic research has created a monstrous headache for all writers using citations. Consider for a moment the key elements of a traditional citation: author, title, publishing date, place of publication (city and publisher), and page number(s). A Web source may well have none of these. Whichever of them the source does have can change overnight, since most electronic texts can be updated and altered to any degree at any time. Citing such ephemera can feel like writing on the surface of a rushing river. To keep your head above water, obey the following general rules:

1. See if the source itself gives you citation instructions. More and more, encyclopedias and other sources online include a header that begins with something like "Cite this article as . . . " You can just copy it down.
2. Unless otherwise instructed, use the traditional citation format as a template and make the electronic citation conform to it as closely as possible. For instance, if there is no title for the piece, ask yourself, "What is the nearest thing to a title here?" and put it in the title's place. Personal e-mail isn't titled, but it usually has a subject line (a.k.a. the "re" line) when it appears in your mail cue, and that will serve.
3. The less bibliographical information you have on a source, the less you should use it at all. Even online, a work of integrity tends to have an author with a real name, some sort

of page-numbering system, a publication date, and a permanent existence in some stable archive. If your source has none of these, maybe you shouldn't be taking it seriously.

4. Print at least the first page of any electronic source you use—it will preserve the reference data across the bottom or top.
5. If you use an electronic version of a print source (like a newspaper article from a database), do not cite the print version—acknowledge in your citation that you used the electronic form (since the page numbers are different, for one reason).
6. When making a parenthetical reference to an Internet source that has no author (which is happening more and more frequently) remember the parenthetical's main purpose: simply to point your reader to your Works Cited or References page. So find a keyword that will appear on that page and use it in the parenthetical. Example: You're citing a sentence from Junior's Juke Joint (a personal favorite website; you'll recognize it by the bullet holes in the pages . . .), which does not identify its author. Just quote the sentence, and then use a keyword from the name of the site, like this:

> *"If you're hanging around a Delta juke joint and you notice somebody sipping a clear liquid from a plastic milk jug, the liquid probably ain't water. Ask them for a sip; it's wonderful stuff" (Juke).*

7. Perhaps the most important rule of all: *never include the URL in the body of your text, even in parentheses.* There's little that's more annoying, or that makes a writer look lazier or more uninformed, than a twenty-seven-character URL right in the middle of an essay or research paper.

And when building bibliographies, obey the following guidelines specific to each of our two citation formats:

MLA citations. An entry for an electronic source contains the following information, in this order, when available:

1. Author's name
2. Title of work—using the subject line for e-mails
3. Print publishing information, if the work originally appeared in print
4. Title of website, database, periodical, and so forth
5. Name of editor, compiler, or maintainer of site
6. Version number or volume and issue numbers
7. Date of publication or latest update
8. Name of subscription service or name of library used to access file
9. Name of list or forum

  10. Page or section number
  11. Name of site sponsor
  12. Date of access
  13. URL

See models below.

  APA citations. List the following elements in this order, when available:

  1. Author
  2. Date of work or date last modified
  3. Title
  4. Information on print publication
  5. Type of source, in brackets: for instance, [Online], [Online database], [CD-ROM]
  6. Name of vendor and document number, or "Retrieved (date) from the World Wide Web:" and the URL

See models below.

Model Citations

Here are templates for common bibliography entries, in MLA and APA format.

A book with an edition number and multiple authors:

MLA: Tremaine, Helen, and John Blank. <u>Over the Hill</u>.
         10th ed. New York: Houghton, 1946.

APA: Tremaine, H., & Blank, J. (1946). <u>Over the
         hill</u>. (10th ed.). New York: Houghton Mifflin.

A book with an editor:

MLA: Blank, John, ed. <u>Over the Hill</u>. New York:
         Houghton, 1946.

APA: Blank, J. (Ed.). (1946). <u>Over the hill</u>.
         New York: Houghton Mifflin.

A book with an author and an editor or a translator:

MLA: Blank, John. <u>Over the Hill</u>. Ed. Helen Tremaine.
         New York: Houghton, 1946.

APA: Blank, J. (1946). <u>Over the hill</u>. (H. Tremaine,
         Ed.) New York: Houghton Mifflin.

MLA: Blank, John. <u>Over the Hill</u>. Trans. Helen
      Tremaine. New York: Houghton, 1946.

APA: Blank, J. (1946). <u>Over the hill</u>. (H. Tremaine,
      Trans.) New York: Houghton Mifflin. (Original work
      published 1910).

A government pamphlet:

MLA: United States. Dept. of Commerce. <u>Highway
      Construction Costs Per Mile, 1980–1990</u>.
      #32768. Washington: GPO, 1991.

APA: U.S. Department of Commerce. (1991).
      <u>Highway construction costs per mile,
      1980–1990</u>. (DOC Publication No. 32768).
      Washington, DC: U.S. Government Printing Office.

Anonymous article in a well-known reference work:

MLA: "Alphabet." <u>Collier's Encyclopedia</u>. 1994 ed.

APA: Alphabet. (1994). <u>Collier's Encyclopedia</u>.

Anonymous newspaper article:

MLA: "Remembering the Horror." <u>San Francisco Chronicle</u>
      11 Sept. 2007: A1.

APA: Remembering the horror. (2007, September 11).
      <u>San Francisco Chronicle</u>, p. A1.

Television show:

MLA: <u>Company's Coming</u>. ABC. KZAP, San Francisco.
      13 Oct. 2006.

APA: <u>Company's coming</u>. (2006, October 13).
      San Francisco: KZAP.

Computer software:

MLA: <u>The Last Word</u>. Computer Software. Silicon
      Valley, CA: DataBase, 2002.

APA: The Last Word [Computer software]. (2002).
      Silicon Valley, CA: DataBase.

Lyrics from a record album or compact disc:

MLA: The Ruttles. "Company's Coming." <u>Live Ruttles</u>.
       CD. RCA, 1964.

APA: The Ruttles. (1964). Company's coming. On
       <u>Live Ruttles</u>. [CD] New York: RCA.

World Wide Web journal article (these model citations have been taken verbatim from Nick Carbone's *Writing Online*, 3rd edition, Houghton Mifflin, Boston and New York, 2000):

MLA: Lewis, Theodore. "Research in Technology
       Education: Some Areas of Need." <u>Journal of
       Technology Education, 10:2</u>. Spring 1999. 2
       Aug. 1999 <http://scholar.lib.vt.edu/
       ejournals/JTE/v10n2/lewis.html>.

APA: Lewis, T. (Spring 1999). Research in
       technology education: Some areas of need.
       <u>Journal of Technology Education, 10:2</u>. Online
       journal. Retrieved August 2, 1999, from the
       World Wide Web: http://scholar.lib.vt.edu/
       ejournals/JTE/v10n2/lewis.html

Personal e-mail:

MLA: Russell, Sue. "E180 Fall 1999." Email Interview
       with Author. 10 June 1999.

APA: The APA discourages listing in the reference list any source that can't be accessed by the reader. Cite personal e-mails in the body of the text.

Database:

MLA: U.S. Census Bureau. "Quick Table P-1A: Age and
       Sex of Total Population: 1990, Hartford-
       Middletown, CT." 1990. Lkd. Home page at
       "Population and Housing Facts"/"Quick Tables."
       U.S. Census Bureau, American FactFinder.
       10 June 1999 <http://factfinder.census.gov>.

APA: U.S. Census Bureau. (1990). Quick Table
       P-1A: Age and Sex of Total Population: 1990,
       Hartford-Middletown, CT. [Online, follow links
       Population and Housing Facts, then Quick Tables].
       <u>U.S. Census Bureau, American FactFinder</u>. Retrieved
       on June 10, 1999, from the World Wide Web: http://
       factfinder.census.gov

EXERCISES

1. You've written a term paper citing the following sources. Make two end-of-paper bibliographies, one in the MLA citation system and one in the APA.

   a. A book called *Mystery Train: Images of America in Rock 'n' Roll Music*, by Greil Marcus, published by Flume Press in New York City in 1997.

   b. A book called *The Best American Travel Writing, 2005*, edited by Jamaica Kincaid, published by Houghton Mifflin Company in Boston in 2005.

   c. An article titled "Google's Moon Shot," written by Jeffrey Toobin, in *The New Yorker*, February 5, 2007. The article runs from page 30 to page 35.

   d. An essay called "Dancing with Dylan," by Wendy Lesser, in a book called *The Rose and the Briar: Death, Love, and Liberty in the American Ballad*, edited by Sean Wilentz and Greil Marcus and published by W. W. Norton and Company in New York in 2005. The essay begins on page 317 and ends on page 325.

   e. An anonymous editorial called "What Was He Thinking?" in the *San Francisco Chronicle* on February 2, 2007, on page 7 of Section B.

   f. A personal e-mail sent to you by Stan Bimee, with the subject line "Song Allusions in Stephen King Movies," sent on January 27, 2006, and received by you the same day. Stan's e-mail address is stantheman@sbc.csuchico.org.

   g. An anonymous article called "Redneck Pig Roast," at www.deltablues.net/roast.html. No author, no page numbers, no dates.

   h. A YouTube clip of Paul McCartney, George Harrison, and John Lennon doing the famous "Pyramus and Thisbe" scene from *A Midsummer Night's Dream* on an old British television variety show at www.youtube.com/watch?v=Y8obSjg8IXw.

2. Imagine that the following sentences each cite one of the sources in exercise 1, sentence *a* citing source *a*, sentence *b* citing source *b*, and so on. Add parenthetical citations to each sentence in each of our two citation formats. For example, the first sentence with a citation in MLA format might look like this: "Marcus claims that Elvis Presley is a metaphor for the American experience and represents both the best and the worst of our society (12)." Invent page numbers as you need them.

a. Marcus claims that Elvis Presley is a metaphor for the American experience and represents both the best and the worst of our society.

b. In her introduction, Kincaid writes, "The Travel Writer doesn't get up one morning and throw a dart at a map of the world, a map that is just lying on the floor at her feet, and decide to journey to the place exactly where the dart lands."

c. Toobin writes, "Google intends to scan every book ever published, and to make the full texts searchable, in the same way that Web sites can be searched on the company's engine at google.com."

d. Bob Dylan's songs have more to do with traditional dance than most people realize.

e. San Francisco mayor Gavin Newsome is in deep trouble after news of his affair with an employee leaked to the public.

f. "Stephen King is both a musician and scholar of pop music, and his stories that have been made into movies make effective use of music."

g. "Since they have nothing to do the rest of the day but stand beside the fire and season the pig and turn it every once in a while and, since it's a cold winter morning, that's a damn good time to pass around a bottle of Old Stumphole 90 proof sour mash. At lots of pig roasts, the fellows who started the pig to roasting are sound asleep at eating time."

h. At a time when the Beatles were the darlings of the pop world, they could get away with anything and in fact be quite successful even as comic Shakespearean actors.

3. Write two unacceptable and one acceptable paraphrase of each of the following. Share them with your classmates, discussing the degree to which both the language and the structure of the originals were changed.

> While jazz matured in a climate of segregation, and rhythm and blues out of the inequality that fueled the civil rights movement's push for racial integration, the newer form of black expression, known as hip hop, took shape during the 1970s and 1980s as the American economy was being deindustrialized.
> *(Richard Crawford, America's Musical Life: A History, p. 848)*

> Throughout the inhabited world, in all times and under every circumstance, the myths of man have flourished.
> *(Joseph Campbell, The Hero with a Thousand Faces, p. 3)*

Chapter 18

THE ACADEMIC RESEARCH PAPER

A research paper is a large—ten to thirty pages—project that gathers information primarily from written materials. It's often called a term paper if it's due at the end of the term, as the culmination of the semester's work.

Setting Out

The very idea of a research paper strikes terror in the hearts of many students, or at least makes their eyes glaze over. Fear not, though: they're not that bad. You just need to rearrange your thinking a bit. First of all, keep in mind that research itself is not a bad thing, and it's not exclusively an academic thing. In fact, it's something you probably do every day. Thinking about buying a new laptop? Switching over from hardwire to wireless? Thinking about where to go on spring break? Whether to get a flu shot? Wondering about that exchange program to London? Trying to decide between economics and history as a major? A Honda Civic or a VW Jetta? A new snowboard?

Research, my friend, research.

That's right. You wouldn't go into any of those decisions or purchases blind, would you? So you research. You ask your classmates about their experiences with their Dell laptops and their Powerbooks. You read consumer reports about Civics and Jettas. You demo some snowboards.

Second, remember that the paper itself has a purpose, which means of course that it has a reader. You're doing the research and then putting it together for the benefit of a reader, who will make some use of it. He'll find out from reading your paper whether a flu shot is a good idea or what to look for when purchasing a snowboard.

Of course, chances are you're not going to be writing a college research paper on snowboards—although, then again you might be. More likely, your instructor will ask you to choose a topic and submit the paper at the end of the term. If you're lucky, the assignment's parameters will allow you to find something that you're truly interested in so that the research you do is useful to you and the paper you write is engaging to a reader. Here are seven things to keep in mind to increase the chances of that happening:

Like all good seeds, a term paper is a task to be performed. It is a question to be answered, or a thesis to be defended.

Your paper has an audience, a potential reader whom you can describe in detail.

Your paper is useful to the reader. He's going to go out and do something with it: choose a heating source for his new house, set up a compost pile, select a treatment for his disease. The audience whose needs you care about the most is you, so try to ask a question whose answer *you* can use.

You'll know the moment the project has ceased to be useful to someone: when you find yourself copying down information from a source just because it's "on your topic," with no sense of how you're going to use it or why it matters. When that happens, stop and ask yourself again who's going to use your work and how they're going to use it.

The task is achieved primarily through information gathering, not by expressing your opinion.

The subject is something you know enough about to ask intelligent questions. If you write about something you're totally ignorant of, you'll be almost forced into hiding your ignorance, writing on topic instead of task, pointless information gathering, and plagiarism. The good project is one you know enough about to know what still needs knowing. Let's say you're thinking of buying a new computer. Certainly you know quite a bit already, in terms of what you want to use it for: word processing, e-mailing, online research, burning CDs, watching DVDs, taking it with you to class. There are a lot of computers that have these capabilities. How much memory do you need? Which ones offer the best tech support? Which ones offer the best warranties? Which ones are the easiest to upgrade? Which ones have the best screens for viewing DVDs? These, and probably others, are all questions you'd research before making your purchase.

Your project does something no other source has quite done for you. If you find a book or article that simply does your task, beautifully and finally, you're out of business. You must find a new task, or you'll have nothing to do but plagiarize the source.

Approach the problem in two ways. First, write about what's new. Study the latest advances in a field, before other writers have worked them over. Don't write about how to buy a mountain bike; write about the advantages and disadvantages of the new generation of mountain-bike air-suspension forks. Second, narrow the audience. If you write on alternatives to fossil fuels, a host of writers will have been there before you. If you're writing on the comparative virtues of different kinds of home heating for someone who's building a small cabin in Trinity County, California, considering the area's peculiar wood fuel supply, power company rates, and local building codes, and your reader's floor plan and budget, it's unlikely that it's been done. If you write on anorexia, everything seems to have been said already; but if you write to freshmen anorexics attending college away from home and talk about the special pressures of that environment on that particular personality type, you're more likely to find new ground to break. And narrowing the audience will make it easier to remember that this work is something someone will *use*.

The task is neither too big nor too small. "The term paper must be twenty-five to thirty pages," the instructor says, and you just know what's going to happen. Either you'll pick a topic that runs dry after eight pages and you end up padding and stretching, or to prevent that you'll pick a gargantuan topic like U.S. foreign policy and never finish the background reading. How can you find the task that is the right size?

First, any *topic* is too large, because the amount of information on any topic is endless, however narrowly the topic is defined: there's an endless stream of information on Russia, but the stream on Moscow is equally endless, and so is the stream on the Kremlin. Second, any almanac-type question is too small: "How many people in this country actually escape prison via the insanity plea?" Interesting question, but after you write down "On the average, thirty-five a year," the report is over.

Beyond that, any task that fits our other criteria will prove to be the right size, once you master the skills of Chapter 7 for making a prompt expand or shrink as the need arises. You don't define a thirty-page task at the outset. Rather, you pick a task and begin; as you read and write and think you say, "This is getting to be too much—I have to cut back," or "I'm getting to answers too quickly—I've got to enlarge my scope." And you shrink or expand to suit. If my sailboat chartering versus leasing versus club joining paper proves too much, I can write about the pros and cons of chartering only; if it proves too little, I can write about all possible ways to get into sailing, including crewing for other boat owners, or discuss the cost of sailing, including insurance, maintenance, and hardware options. If I'm writing on how effectively the Food and Drug Administration monitors drug testing and marketing and that proves too large, I can write on whether the FDA dropped the ball on NutraSweet; if it proves too small, I can write about whether federal regulatory agencies generally do their jobs and whether they do more harm than good.

Getting Things Organized

Term papers are largely exercises in handling data avalanches. You need a system for handling bits. Bits are pieces of information: facts, figures, quotes, thoughts from you, titles of works to be read. You need to be able to find a bit in your notes, cluster and recluster bits quickly, tell whether or not a bit has been used in the report yet, and cite the bit in the final draft. Here's how.

Up front, decide whether to gather data via computer or by hand. There are advantages either way. The computer's advantages are that it encourages you to think in terms of *filing* from the outset, and it makes reshuffling bits easy, via copying and pasting. Further, depending on your topic, what you find online might be far more current and relevant than anything you could find in a book or journal. When my older daughter was ten, she was diagnosed with scoliosis. Of course, my wife and I wanted to read all we could about it and, being sort of old-school, asked the doctor to recommend some books or journal articles. "Don't even bother," he said. "Books and journal articles are so long in production that they're out of date by the time they're published. Go online. Read the results of *current research*."

There are drawbacks to online research, though. For example, you can see only one screen's worth of data at a time, so you lack an overview, and it can be hard to find individual items. Also, much of your note taking will be done while you're in the library, so you'd need a laptop computer.

Record all bibliographical data as soon as you begin to take notes. If it's a book, write down the authors' full names, the complete title of the work, the publisher, and place and year of publication. If it's a periodical, record the volume number, issue number, and date. Record the page number(s) where the things you're taking notes on appear, and absolutely everything else you might need to find it again later, including the library call number or URL. It's tedious, but five minutes now will save you an hour when you need the information a month from now.

Invent a system for keeping files of bits you've used in the report and bits you haven't. You must be able to look at a dozen bits and say, "Those seven I've used; those five I haven't." But don't check off the used bits by deleting them or throwing them away—keep your data intact so you can rethink it, use it elsewhere, and proofread it later. Make photocopies of hard-copy sources and use highlighting pens.

Invent a cueing/categorizing system for your notes. You need a way of labeling your notes so you can tell what they're about without rereading them. Some people use keywords: when they've taken notes on an article, they head the notes with a few keywords (or phrases) identifying the article's main issues. If you're writing on alternative heating sources, you might read an article hostile to wood-burning stoves and end up with a list of keywords like "wood-burning stoves," "air pollution," "shrinking resources," and "health hazards." If three weeks later you want to deal with the health hazards of indoor open fires, you simply make a stack of all note cards bearing the "health hazards" keyword and your data is ready to go. Computers help by making it easy to copy and paste a fact or quotation in ten or twenty different categories.

Build cubbyholes—physical or electronic sites to house notes according to topic or keyword. If you're not using a computer, get a lot of manila folders or shoeboxes.

Never let the bit and its bibliographical data get separated. As you move a quote or a stat from cubbyhole to cubbyhole, keep all info on where it came from attached to it.

Don't forget to brainstorm. As you strive to control the data avalanche, don't get so organized that you forget the lessons of the earlier chapters: Writing and thinking are messy, recursive businesses, and you need a lot of loose time to wander and discover. Don't take too much control. Especially don't try to do one task at a time. Writing is multitasking, and you do a creative task best when you're busy doing others. For instance, don't resolve to do the background reading, then draft, because both reading and writing are ways of thinking, and each will propagate the other—read and write simultaneously and continuously throughout the term paper process.

Format

Since a term paper is bigger than an essay, the format may be more elaborate, with several elements that shorter papers usually don't have:

> *A title page,* on which you give the title, your name, the date, and usually the course name and number and instructor's name
>
> *A table of contents*
>
> *Appendices,* where you put the raw data the average reader won't want to read
>
> *Graphics*—pictures, tables, graphs—either in appendices or throughout the paper
>
> *A list of illustrations* following the table of contents, if you have graphics throughout the work
>
> *A letter of transmittal* on the front, addressed to the receiver of the report, saying in essence, "Here's the report"
>
> *An abstract* before page 1, summarizing the paper for the reader who only has a minute
>
> *A bibliography* or Works Cited list at the end
>
> *Section headings:* "Introduction," "Conclusion," "Discussion," "History of the Problem," "Three Possible Solutions," "Recent Advances"

There are models of most of these features in the sample term paper following. Use those models as templates unless your instructor has her own format.

Don't fall in love with format for format's sake. Many beginning researchers make the mistake of getting too fancy with formatting (like a Powerpoint presentation that's all flash and no substance). Use formatting to make the paper easier for your reader to make sense of, not to impress him.

Graphics

Graphics—tables, graphs, illustrations, photographs—can really improve your paper's effectiveness. They can put complicated data into easily understood images. They can provide concrete evidence of a point you're making (the way women were typically portrayed in 1960s television sitcoms, for example). In addition, they simply give your reader a break from the text. And with computers' increasing ability to download images, combined with computer programs that easily translate raw data into tables, it's not difficult to end up with a very professional-looking presentation. Some things to remember: (1) Images *are* easy to download, but that means it's also easy to plagiarize. You must acknowledge your sources. (2) Graphics are there to clarify, oftentimes to put what you've said in words into one easily graspable image— for example, a look at how well students do on reading tests based on their parents' income level. News magazines like *Time* and *Newsweek* are masters of that art, so study their graphics for lessons in effective presentation. Here are four principles to follow.

Graphics are not self-explanatory. Be sure to tell the reader exactly what he's looking at and what it means. Title the graphic informatively, label its parts clearly, and explain whatever needs explaining, in footnotes below the graphic or in the report's text right above or below the graphic.

Avoid overload. A graphic's power is in its ability to dramatize and clarify a point or show the relationships between a few bits of data. If you try to make a graphic do too much, its power is lost. Better three graphics making three points clearly and forcefully than one spectacularly ornate graphic making three points at once and obscuring all of them.

Number all graphics, unless you have only one. That way you can readily refer to the graphic by saying, "as shown in Figure 1."

Express ideas as drawings. We understand pictures better than numbers, so whenever possible express your data as a drawing, not as columns of numbers—use figures instead of tables, technical writers would say.

Let's pretend we're reproducing the results of an agricultural experiment on the relationship between fertilizer application rates and plant growth. The experiment took five groups of identical plants and gave each a different amount of fertilizer, then measured the growth after a month to see what dosage produced the most. Here we have the data expressed in a table:

Group #	1	2	3	4	5
(mg/gal):	(10)	(20)	(30)	(40)	(50)
Growth (in inches)	1.2	3.1	5.0	-1.1	-3.7

Here we have the data expressed in a figure:

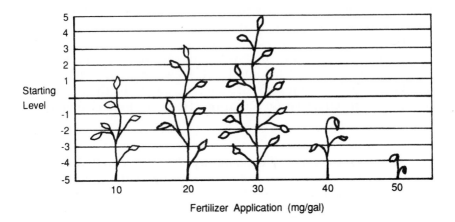

Fertilizer Application (mg/gal)

Isn't it easier to see the point in figure form?

Two Model Research Papers

Here are examples of two quite different research papers.

Nicolas decided on his topic rather late, after abandoning two that he just couldn't get fired up about. He'd read a little about lobotomies and then saw a television documentary on John F. Kennedy that mentioned almost in passing sister Rosemary Kennedy's lobotomy. He simply wanted to know more. An excellent paper resulted from his research.

Nicole was very interested in how women have been portrayed in television sitcoms, knew enough about the subject to get going, but still had lots of questions to ask and experts to consult in order to make her points convincing. Note how, while she takes her subject very seriously, she obviously had some fun writing the paper—and how that translates into wonderfully readable prose.

A CURE OR CONTROL: THE LOBOTOMY

NICOLAS S. DANSCUK

The Abstract

A lobotomy, or psychosurgery, is a procedure in which sections or regions of the brain are removed in an attempt to regulate the performance of the brain resulting in changes in mental characteristics. It was thought that by severing the nerves that gave rise to ideas and emotion you would diminish creativity and imagination. Through the late 1800s and early 1900s lobotomies became a widely accepted procedure when dealing with patients in psychiatric wards. It is estimated that by 1955 more than 40,000 men, women, and children in the United States, and thousands more around the world, had undergone a form of psychosurgery that left their brains irreparably damaged. But is there more to the story than this? What if rather than treating the patients with a cure, the lobotomy was a means of controlling patients? It was reported that in some military hospitals after World War II there were so many patients that they resorted to lobotomies just to keep some form of control over the situation. It is also mentioned that some young girls were sent to have lobotomies performed to "cure" their promiscuous ways. In fact, Rosemary Kennedy, John F. Kennedy's sister, had a lobotomy performed on her because "it would help her and calm her mood swings that the family found difficult to handle at home" (Johnson). Today the procedure has been almost completely discredited and looked down upon in the Western world.

Introduction

In a famous Monty Python skit a man goes to a brain specialist (a common man) complaining that his brain hurts and asking for help. The brain specialist examines the man's head and comes up with the conclusion, "It will have to come out!" If it were only this simple. This skit refers to a lobotomy, which during the early to mid-1900s was very popular and looked at as an acceptable procedure to treat ailing patients with mental disorders. But is there more to the story than this? What if rather than treating the patients with a cure, the lobotomy was a means of controlling patients? Whether it was controlling violent behavior, promiscuous activity, or disorders as a result of trauma, the lobotomy was referred to as a quick and easy way to "cure" these abnormalities. To many it was seen as being easier and more cost efficient to deal with someone in a "vegetated" state of mind— a body with very little mind or personality left—compared to an individual who could harm themselves or others.

What Is a Lobotomy?

A lobotomy, also known as psychosurgery, is a procedure involving surgically removing parts or regions of the brain, mainly the prefrontal lobes, with the goal of removing the "troubled thoughts within" ("Psychosurgery"). Originally it was believed that by severing the nerves that were the foundation of ideas you would reach a state of emotional flattening which would disrupt imagination and creativity, the idea being that these are the human mental characteristics that are troubled (Zimmer). It has been known since early civilizations that the brain was the source of thought and, as a result, of evil as well. However, for centuries brain surgery consisted of little more than drilling holes into someone's head to relieve pressure and release this evil (Miller).

Brief History of the Lobotomy

The first recorded experimentation involving a lobotomy was in 1890 when a superintendent of a psychiatric hospital in Switzerland, Dr. Gottlieb Burckhardt, drilled holes into the heads of six of his patients and removed sections of their frontal lobes ("Adventures"). After the surgery there seemed to be an altering in behavior between four of the patients with varying degrees of success; two patients died (Miller). Egas Moniz, a Portuguese doctor, also experimented with cutting regions of the frontal lobes on 20 patients who were chronically psychotic.

He also noted that this procedure had a "calming" effect on these patients and set out to share his findings ("What's the Worst?"). Ironically Moniz received the Nobel Prize in 1949 and to this day remains the only person to do so in the field of psychology ("Adventures"). These pioneering breakthroughs in medicine paved the way for future psychiatrists and physicians.

One of these pioneers, Dr. Walter Freeman, changed the era of lobotomies and made a number of advancements, creating the procedure that we are familiar with today. In 1935 Freeman attended a conference of neuroscientists in London and was intrigued by what he witnessed. In attendance were two chimpanzees brought by John Fulton from Yale University who both had their entire frontal lobes completely removed, which radically altered their behavior (Zimmer). He called this procedure a lobectomy, which literally means the removal of lobes ("Psychosurgery"). Those in attendance were amazed at what they saw and the discussion on the significance of such a procedure raised a question that all participants had on their minds: "If the frontal lobe removal prevents the development of experimental neurosis in animals and eliminates frustrational behavior, why would it not be possible to relieve anxiety states in man by surgical means?" ("Adventures"). Freeman became fascinated with this new technique for treating psychiatric patients and made it a goal to master this so-called lobectomy. Even though he was a neurologist, he had no qualifications as a surgeon so he called upon his colleague James Watts to perform the procedure as Freeman directed his movements. While Watts inserted the rods into the persons through the side of their head, Freeman would stand in front of the patient and direct Watts to either move up, down, in more, etc. After practicing for a week on brains that they acquired from the morgue, Watts and Freeman operated on their first live patient ("Adventures").

On September 14, 1936, a 63-year-old woman from Kansas who was faced with the decision of either entering a mental institution or going under the knife was brought to Freeman's attention ("Adventures"). She suffered from an agitated, depressed, and fearful personality, which was exactly what Watts and Freeman were looking for.

When they awoke her from the surgery, she displayed a sense of calm, which was in direct contrast to how she was before the procedure. Watts and Freeman were thrilled with the results. However, after a week the woman began to behave strangely, talking incoherently, and showing little emotion toward her surroundings ("Adventures"). This was but a minor setback in their practice. Within the next six weeks the two surgeons proceeded to operate on another five patients.

It became a process of performing the procedure, seeing the patient's results, and then making adjustments from one patient to the next, almost like a guess and check method ("What's the Worst?"). One technique created by Freeman that became very popular was the "ice pick" lobotomy. In this procedure an ice pick was inserted above each eye through the eye socket and into the brain ("Adventures"). This procedure was praised because of its ease and its time-efficient manner. Rather than a two-hour surgery, a patient could be in and out of the operating room in 20 minutes. Freeman even went as far as to try and set records for how fast and how many lobotomies he could perform. In 1952 he performed 228 lobotomies over a two-week period, even going to the extreme of operating on two patients at the same time ("Adventures"). Over time Freeman became so satisfied and confident with his results that he actually went on to make a propaganda campaign to encourage its use. Many physicians, and even the media, embraced the lobotomy as a quick and effective way of treating those who suffered from chronic mental conditions (Zimmer).

It was not until the 1960s that lobotomies began to lose their appeal. The introductions of chlorpromazine and other neuroleptic medications made the procedure obsolete ("Adventures"). The brutality of the procedure began to raise questions in those who saw that little was done to cure patients.

Cure or Control

As lobotomies became more popular and widely accepted as a way for treating those who possessed chronic mental conditions, the criteria for who would receive a lobotomy got less and less extreme (Zimmer). People getting them were no longer the most violent or untreatable; rather they were beginning to be used on those who broke the law or even someone who didn't listen to his or her parents. As it turned out, even those who seemed better only showed fewer symptoms; lobotomy did not cure mental illnesses at all. It was a way for doctors or psychiatrists to control society. The following are the stories of different individuals who had a lobotomy performed on them as a means to control their mental state.

Howard Dully's Story

"I've always felt different . . . wondering if something's missing from my soul." These are the words of Howard Dully, a 56-year-old man who today recounts his past being a young boy and having a lobotomy performed on him ("Dully's Lobotomy"). As he looks back to the days of his childhood and discovers why this procedure was carried out, he finds information that calls into question whether it was done to cure his mental state as a child or to control a normal, rambunctious kid.

After losing his mother at age five, Howard's stepfather remarried a woman named Lou who despised him. Howard claims that she hated him and would do anything she could to get rid of him ("Dully's Lobotomy"). In Howard's research he found notes of Dr. Freeman in which he recounts Lou Dully's meeting regarding her stepson. Freeman wrote: "Lou Dully came in for a talk about Howard. Things have gotten much worse and she can barely endure it. I explained to Mrs. Dully that the family should consider the possibility of changing Howard's personality by means of transorbital lobotomy" ("Dully's Lobotomy"). According to Freeman, Lou Dully saw her stepson as defiant and savage looking, one who didn't react to either positive or negative reinforcement, and a child who got lost daydreaming (Vertosick). To many these would seem like rather common traits for a young child, who may be slightly disobedient.

However, to Mrs. Dully this was not normal, and psychosurgery was the only treatment.

After the procedure Howard's personality drastically changed. When told about what had been done to him after the surgery Freeman noted that he took it without any emotional reaction whatsoever, sitting quietly with a slight grin. The power was now entirely in the hands of Lou Dully. The procedure had not left Howard a "vegetable" but it did change his ways of obedience. It was in turn her way of "controlling an individual."

Rosemary Kennedy's Story

Growing up, Rosemary Kennedy, John F. Kennedy's sister, was a beautiful young woman whom all the men adored. She desperately wanted praise and loved to be in the spotlight. However, there was one thing that stood in her way of fame: she was painfully slow, and some even characterized her as mildly retarded.

Her father, Joe Kennedy, was appointed by FDR just before WWII broke out in Europe as the ambassador to the Court of St. James.

During this time such a position was regarded as the most important diplomatic position any American could hold ("Rosemary Kennedy"). As a result the Kennedy family and name would move into the highest circles of British society. Although no one mentioned Rosemary's disability, family members knew that she was different from other girls in some way. One of the main problems was that Rosemary was too good-looking as well as being very promiscuous, two characteristics that did not go well together (Johnson). Often at night Rosemary would sneak out and embark on acts that "the priest says not to do" (Bly). Surprisingly during its height, a lobotomy was a common suggestion when it came to dealing with girls of this nature. The family did whatever they could to protect her from potential suitors, because if word slipped out of her condition it would be looked down upon by such an elite society ("Rosemary Kennedy").

Searching for a way to control his daughter and keep his prestige, Joe Kennedy sought the help of a doctor who was experimenting with a new type of brain surgery to treat mental abnormalities, Walter Freeman (Johnson). Freeman discussed the procedure with Mr. Kennedy, highlighting all the positives, the only drawback being that part of her head would have to be shaved ("Rosemary Kennedy"). Not long after their discussion his daughter was wheeled through the operating room doors and the procedure began. Freeman and his colleague drilled a hole in her head and with a tool similar to a small spatula began digging. They continued to remove brain matter until Rosemary could no longer perform simple mathematics or carry on a conversation. When her condition was observed after the procedure she was said to have "fallen into an infant-like state, only traces left of the young woman she had been" (Bly).

After the procedure Rosemary was placed in a series of private mental institutions and the procedure was not talked about by family members. Joe Kennedy rarely spoke of his daughter in fear that his reputation would falter as a result (Bly). His goal was not to cure his daughter; his goal was to control her and he found a way to do so through means of psychosurgery.

World War II Soldiers' Stories

Images of screaming, disemboweled teenage soldiers and dismembered corpses, losing friends on a regular basis and wondering if you will be next provoked mental scars that traumatized veterans when they returned home from the front. Post-traumatic stress disorder plagued many soldiers for years, some to the point of being admitted to mental hospitals for treatment. During World War II it was estimated that more than 504,000 troops were lost from the battlefield because of psychiatric-related collapse ("Adventures"). With many of these troops being admitted to mental hospitals and the lack of a quick treatment to treat many of the mental disorders, the number of patients began to swell well over the treatable number. Doctors frantically searched for a technique that would allow for soldiers to be dealt with in an efficient and timely manner; they found it in the lobotomy. It also helped doctors control the violent behavior that some of the soldiers exhibited which could potentially harm others. Rather than paying for the patients' stay at the medical ward, soldiers were given this procedure and then sent home to their families. Oftentimes their family members were not told of the procedure.

Conclusion

When the word *lobotomy* is used today, images of Ken Kesey's *One Flew Over the Cuckoo's Nest* flash into the minds of most people. Its accounts of shock therapy and lobotomies as a means to control the ward's patients are chilling representations of this procedure and its true nature. As we have seen in Howard Dully's and Rosemary Kennedy's stories, the lobotomy was a procedure that allowed others a means of controlling those that did not fit the "mold" of society. Today the procedure has been almost completely discredited and is looked down upon in the Western world. This is not to say that its practices still do not continue elsewhere in the world or even to a select few patients in the United States. In fact, today medication is looked at as the dominant form of treatment with psychiatric patients, yet in some cases lobotomies are still used as a last resort.

Works Cited

"Adventures with an Ice Pick." *Lobotomy.info.* 10 Dec. 2003. 12 Nov. 2006 <http://lobotomy.info/adventures .html>.

Bly, Nellie. "Joe Has His Daughter Lobotomized." *Y Ted K.* 1 March 2000. 16 Nov. 2006 <http://www.ytedk.com/ lobotomy.htm>.

Johnson, Christine. "Rosemary Kennedy and Lobotomy." *Psychosurgery.org* 8 Jan. 2005. 15 Nov. 2006 <http:// www.psychosurgery.org/2005/01/rosemary-kennedy- and-lobotomy.html>.

Miller, Allison Xantha. "Better Living Through Lobotomy: What Can the History of Psychosurgery Tell Us About Medicine Today?" *Stayfreemagazine* 21. 16 Nov. 2006 <http://www.stayfreemagazine.org/archives/21/ lobotomy.html>.

"My Lobotomy: Howard Dully's Journey." *NPR* 16 Nov. 2005. 15 Nov. 2006 <http://www.npr.org/templates/ story/story.php?storyId=5014080>.

"Psychosurgery." *Wikipedia: The Free Encyclopedia* 11 Nov. 2006. 20 Nov. 2006 <http://en.wikipedia.org/ wiki/Psychosurgery>.

"Rosemary Kennedy." *Fatboy.* 16 Nov. 2006 <http://fatboy .cc/Rosemary.htm>.

Vertosick, Frank T., Jr. "Lobotomy's Back." *Discover* 18. 10 (1997). 20 Nov. 2006 <http://www.discover.com/ issues/oct-97/features/lobotomysback1240/>.

"What's the Worst Ever Idea on the Mind?" *British Physiological Society* 9 Aug. 2006. 17 Nov. 2006 <http://www.bps.org.uk/publications/thepsychologist/ extras/pages$/2006-news/whats-the-worst-ever-idea- on-the-mind.cfm>.

Zimmer, Gene. "Lobotomy & Brain Damage: Psychiatry's Legacy." *SNTP.* FTR. 16 Nov. 2006 <http://www .sntp.net/lobotomy/lobotomy.htm>.

LUCY, YOU HAVE SOME 'SPLAININ' TO DO

NICOLE BENBOW

The Abstract

I Love Lucy revolutionized society when it hit the airwaves in 1951. Lucille Ball was the epitome of the stereotypical housewife. However, since the time when that first episode began, America's thinking has not changed much. To this day, there are subtle and elaborate hints that are constantly telling women that they do not belong in the work force, but in the kitchen cooking and cleaning. For better or worse, women are fighting a battle against the portrayals of famous television sitcoms and the ideals of what women's roles should be.

Riddle: A father and son go out fishing for the day. On their way back, they are broadsided in their car and both are in critical condition when they are wheeled into the closest hospital. The doctor, just about ready to operate, looks down and notices the patient. The doctor says, "I cannot work on this patient; this is my son!" How is this possible?

Introduction

A large heart appeared on the screen, and the familiar theme song to *I Love Lucy* began. The black and white screen cannot take away from the large redhead that filled up the screen. Without fail, a smile would form on my face and I would begin to bob my head and hum along with the theme song. My fifth grade homework, chores, and other activities soon forgotten, I sat engrossed on the couch to watch half an hour of one of my favorite shows. Time has passed since then, and I see Lucy in a new light. She is still an icon and the epitome of clean-cut humor, but things have changed. I no longer laugh when Ricky belittles Lucy for being a "crazy" woman, or smirk when Fred and Ricky think that Lucy and Ethel have it easy staying at home all day. I find myself drawn to the way women were treated in those old days, and even more transfixed that society's wayward thinking has not changed much since 1951. Classic television sitcoms tend to depict the same story over and over again. Women belong inside cooking, cleaning, sewing, etc., while men are supposed to be out working and bringing in the money.

History of the Problem

Show after show illustrates this misconception about women's roles. On the TV hit *I Dream of Jeannie*, Jeannie must always be nice so that her "master" will not send her away. In *Leave It to Beaver*, Mrs. Cleaver always had a bright phony smile on her face; it was such a phony smile it made you wonder what Mrs. Cleaver was really thinking about. Most likely, she wanted to shed her uncomfortable skirts, dresses, and pearls for a nice pair of capri slacks like Mary Tyler Moore did on the *Dick Van Dyke Show*. In fact, Mary Tyler Moore had to fight tooth and nail to be able to wear pants on screen. According to Vince Waldron, author of *The Official Dick Van Dyke Show Book*, her decision "may not seem like a particularly radical choice today, but Mary Tyler Moore's insistence on wearing her own form-fitting slacks on television was little short of revolutionary in 1961" (128).

Since television made its debut, women have been seen and cast as the caretakers. When women did step outside the house and get jobs or become interested in the business world they were usually ridiculed on many television shows. On *I Love Lucy*, Lucy was in charge of paying the bills. To determine which one she would pay she would spin them on a lazy Susan. Ricky sees her do this and just shakes his head at her absurdity. "Her acts of rebellion—taking a job, performing at the club, concocting a money-making scheme, or simply plotting to fool Ricky—are meant to expose the absurd restrictions placed on women in a male-dominated society." However, in episode after episode she could still be seen cooking Ricky's breakfast every morning (Anderson).

Discussion

Even the hit TV shows of today do the same thing. On *Desperate Housewives*, only a handful of women have jobs. Susan writes children's books (note that her office is at her home). Lynette is the working mom, and there have been several episodes where she has taken the brunt from family, friends, and strangers for not taking enough care of her family and working too much.

Two nights ago I sat down to watch several television shows and started jotting down things that I noticed. From a news program, a reality television show, and a television sit-com, and all the commercials that came in between, there were several things I noted. Why was it that sports broadcasters rarely spent any time covering women's sports? Sports like NFL, NASCAR, NBA, and MLB all got the broadcaster's time and attention. However, sports dominated by females of the same sport got limited coverage. Why is it that women were always seen in commercials advertising items like vacuum cleaners, kitchen utensils, and cleaning products while men are seen more often next to rugged trucks and in suits? The answers are simple; these misconceptions are based on the depictions that women should stay at home and be the perfect Mrs. Cleaver.

The patriarchal society is founded on the concept that the male is the head of the household. This idea has been around for decades and will continue to be the dominating force. In today's world, women are actually the majority of the population, but are treated as the minority. There is a huge underrepresentation of women in politics, sports, and corporate executive positions. Could it be because we constantly depict media images of women not being capable of being independent over and over again?

About two weeks ago I saw a Dove commercial that rocked my mind. The commercial is called "Evolution," and whenever you get some free time, go to YouTube.com and watch it. The commercial is less than two minutes long, and it completely challenges the ideals of what beauty is and what we label as right. Women are constantly being showcased on television as needing to be beautiful stay-at-home moms that love every minute of driving their kids to soccer and planning elaborate dinners for their families, and Dove wanted to push the limits of what they consider the new evolution of beauty.

The joke about the college professor is something that always fascinated me too. A college professor wrote the words "woman without her man is nothing." The professor then told the students to punctuate the sentence correctly. The women in the class wrote, "Woman! Without her, man is nothing!" The men in the class punctuated the sentence to be "Woman, without her man, is nothing!" It is a simple joke that is made to bring laughter to a subject as simple as punctuation. However, the sad truth of the matter is that those classic women of the fifties really did rely completely on the men. They were helpless women who stayed at home and did as their husbands asked. It was not common for a woman to have a job, so her say in any matter was what she chooses to cook for dinner each night.

The book *Mass Media in a Changing World*, by George Rodman, discusses the golden age of television and its lasting effect on society. He wrote,

> . . . critics point out that the golden age wasn't golden for everyone. Lucy wasn't the only woman who was portrayed as incompetent outside of her traditional gender role. Programs such as *Father Knows Best* and *Ozzie and Harriet* portrayed women as stereotypical housewives whose husbands made all the important decisions. Even when female characters ventured out of the home, as Lois Lane did in *Superman*, they were usually subordinate to men. (263)

This same book goes on to include the top ten most influential shows of the time. *I Love Lucy* landed in the top spot. *I Love Lucy* changed what people were talking about and had the entire country on the edge of their seats for the episode when Lucy gave birth to her first child.

San Diego State University communications professor Martha Lauzen conducted an annual study of television content. She found that nowadays the higher the number of female creators, actors, editors, etc., working on a show, the more likely the program will be "moved around and surrounded by programs not getting high ratings or shares" (Lauzen). Women are still not taken seriously when it comes to important topics like what is aired for the world to see and watch night after night.

In Michiko Kakutani's article "Books of the Times: A Feminist Eye Studies Portrayals of Women," she discusses the book *Where the Girls Are Growing Up Female with the Mass Media*, by Susan J. Douglas. According to Kakutani, Douglas views many Disney heroines as sweet, beautiful women who need rescuing by a prince and "the wicked stepmothers and queens are 'older, vindictive' women, who have 'way too much power for their own good, embodying the age-old truism that any power at all completely corrupted women and turned them into monsters.'" (1). Every Disney movie I have ever seen goes along with this concept that when a woman gets power things go bad. Malificent and Cruella de Vil will forever be on Santa Claus's bad list for their evil deeds.

I can remember when the country band the Dixie Chicks was on top of the world. Their albums sold by the millions and their concerts were sold out. The main singer, Natalie, made a comment about how she was ashamed that President George Bush was from Texas. Whether or not you thought the comments were made in good or bad taste, these women had every right to express their opinions on the subject. However, the backlash these women experienced as a result of the statements that one of them made was phenomenal. Fans that had supported them for years were stomping on their CDs or burning them in protest. Tickets sales dropped dramatically and their latest CD fell off the top album list immediately. Emily Robinson, one of the band members, felt that much of the anger stemmed from the fact that they were an all-female band speaking their minds. In the *Playboy* (December 2005) issue she was quoted as saying, "It's way worse. A guy would have been an outlaw, the Johnny Cash or Merle Haggard of his generation. . . . Read the stuff on the Internet: 'Just tell that bitch to shut up.' They don't want to hear mouthy women to begin with. Forget about its going against their political grain." Oh, no, are you telling me that there are really women out there that speak their minds on hush-hush topics—how revolutionary!

Women have proven that they are equals when it comes to men. Nevertheless, women take a backseat to men. Lucille Ball, a woman who was seen as an icon, was put under great inquiry in newspapers and gossip columns when she and Desi Arnaz divorced. People could not believe that the characters on TV were not really in love in real life, and I guess they could not believe that women did not "belong" in the kitchen either.

Real women everywhere are still captivated by the idea that they need to be reliant on the man. Dr. Nick Neave, an evolutionary psychologist from Northumbria University, published the article "Sorry, but Women Are Dependent on Men." He reports:

> One might argue that it's only natural for today's women in their 30s or 40s to feel dependent on a man. After all, the vast majority were raised by mothers who by and large didn't have careers and were forced to rely financially on their husbands. Yet study after study proves that today's women in their 20s are just as insecure.

Studies have shown that photographs and movies leave a much longer and more lasting impression than just captions or words. Millions of people tuned in to watch shows that showcased the woman-stays-at-home sitcoms, like *I Love Lucy*. These images influenced people more than any speaker, newspaper, or article could. Seeing the same kind of images over and over makes people believe that they must be true. Albert Bandura created the social learning theory that states that an audience's attitudes are shaped by what they learn through others' behaviors. Another theorist invented the Gerbner's Cultivation theory that is based on the philosophy that when people see the same thing over and over again it changes their beliefs.

I will admit that the episode that has Ethel and Lucy going out and getting jobs still makes me laugh so hard my stomach aches afterward. Who knew that watching these two try to package candy would be so funny? What is unfortunate, though, is that when the ladies try to go out and get a decent job they fail miserably. Once again, the show was subtly hinting that women did not belong in the work force.

Conclusion

Lucille Ball did pave the way for many female actresses in the entertainment business, but she also created the stereotype that women need to be the perfect wives that stay home all day. Lucille Ball was even quoted once as saying, "Women's lib? Oh I am afraid it doesn't interest me one bit. I've been so liberated it hurts." No doubt Lucille Ball had no idea that her acting would change this country and shape some of the basic ideals of women today. She was a young woman who was born to act; she played a character when she became Lucy Ricardo. Her hopes and dreams for the future were not to sit at home and discover recipes and dust every spec of the house. She was a woman who was capable of great things, just like every other woman.

Answer to the riddle: The doctor was not a grandfather or stepfather (as many others suspect if my Principles of Sociology class is an indication), but is actually the son's mother! Women's roles are not usually seen as being strong, independent, reliable, and smart, and it makes it hard to cast a woman doctor into the scenario.

Works Cited

Anderson, Christopher. "I Love Lucy." *The Museum of Broadcast Communications.* 28 Oct. 2006 <http://www.museum.tv/archives/etv/I/htmlI/ilovelucy/ilovelucy.htm>.

"Dove Evolution." *YouTube.com.* Dove. 6 Oct 2006. 1 Nov. 2006 <http://www.youtube.com/watch?v=iYhCnojf46U>.

Google Images. Google. 2 May 2003. 10 Nov. 2006 <http://www.totallycool.net/DixieChicks2/IMAG0002.JPG>.

Kakutani, Michiko. "Books of the Times: A Feminist Eye Studies Portrayals of Women." *New York Times* 14 June 1994. 30 Oct. 2006 <http://query.nytimes.com/gst/fullpage.html?res=9400E1DF1F3AF937A25755C0A962958260>.

Lauzen, Martha. "Statistics on Women Directors." *Movies Directed by Women* 26 Aug. 2001. 29 Oct. 2006 <http://www.moviesbywomen.com/marthalauzenphd/ceiling.html>.

"Lucille Ball Quotes." 30 Oct. 2006 <http:// library.thinkquest.org/CR0215629/lucillequotes_.htm>.

Neave, Nick. "Sorry, but Women Are Dependent on Men." *Daily Mail* 4 Dec. 2006. 11 Dec. 2006 <http://www.dailymail.co.uk/pages/live/femail/article.html?in_article_id=420513&in_page_id=1879>.

"The Playboy Interview: Dixie Chicks." *Playboy* Dec. 2005. 10 Nov. 2006 <http://www.playboy.com/magazine/interview/>.

Rodman, George. *Mass Media in a Changing World.* New York: McGraw-Hill, 2006.

Waldron, Vince. *The Official* Dick Van Dyke Show *Book: The Definitive History and Ultimate Viewer's Guide to Television's Most Enduring Comedy.* New York: Hyperion, 1994.

Part Six

A COLLECTION OF GOOD WRITING

Here are some wonderful essays, divided into five groups: personal essays, informative essays, argumentative essays, academic essays, and five published essays on food. I hope you enjoy them and are inspired by them. Read them, use them as models, learn from them. After each one, I offer a brief discussion.

Personal Essays

YA GOTTA GET A GIMMICK

MEGAN SPROWLS

"Megan, I don't see your name anywhere. Where is it?"

"It's right here, next to—oh no."

"What? Who's ... Mazeppa?"

"You don't want to know, Jaime. You don't want to know."

In all reality, Mazeppa was the shield-carrying, gladiator-belt-wearing, trumpet-bumping burlesque dancer I had been cast as in Sondheim and Styne's musical *Gypsy*. She was a horror. She was crude. She was racy. She was a stripper. She was everything I feared.

She was my savior.

I've always carried around a few pounds that I didn't really need, and during my early high school years, my mind had somehow developed a sort of "funhouse mirror" complex which made me think I was a lot larger than I actually was. I decided that I would be able to hide my pudginess by draping myself in baggy jeans, extra large T-shirts, and the biggest possible sweatshirts I could find. I was keeping my true self enclosed under layers of cotton and polyester. I was wearing this exact outfit when my director held up the costume I was expected to wear. It was a black bikini embellished with puff paint and sequins, the highlights of which were two strategically placed tassels.

"Megan, are you okay? You look a little pale."

"Parker, I can't wear that. I just can't. I'll die."

"You can wear bicycle shorts."

"What about the stomach part, Parker? The audience isn't going to want to see *aaaall* of this."

"I guess you can wear a leotard if it makes you feel better."

"Yeah, it would. A lot."

Crisis one was averted. The next day, however, was our first choreography rehearsal. I walked into the theater with a knot twisting and tightening in my stomach at the prospect of having to bump and grind. The choreographer beckoned me onto the stage and I slowly trudged up the stage steps, my worn jazz shoes making a scuffing sound on the stone. Biting my lip, I stepped center stage and prepared for my dance instructions, fiddling idly with the strings on my dance pants, hoping the choreographer would somehow see how uncomfortable I was and take pity on me. She didn't. I bumped and grinded my way across the stage at least twenty times that day, my face flushed with embarrassment the entire time, mostly at the part where I was required to bend completely over and stick my head through my legs with my bottom facing the audience.

I didn't know it at the time, but playing Mazeppa and being forced to confront some of my greatest fears about my body had slowly begun to change the way I looked at myself. Gone were the sweatshirts, the baggy jeans, and the large T-shirts. In their place were cute blouses and Arizona jeans. I began to take pride in my appearance and paid more attention to my hair instead of just pulling it into a ponytail. However, there was still one problem remaining: I had no idea how the audience would react to me playing a burlesque dancer.

Opening night finally arrived and all too quickly intermission was over. I zipped up my knee-high black boots and gave myself one last look in the mirror. I didn't recognize the creature I saw staring back at me. From the three-inch-heel boots and the gladiator-style skirt to the black leotard stretched taut over the flab I had tried so desperately to conceal and the dark red lipstick to the heavily lined eyes, and the gladiator helmet overflowing with purple feathers, I was a completely new person. My transformation was complete: I was no longer the shy, unkempt looking girl I had been a year prior. I had blossomed into a beautiful butterfly after being faced with adversity and took flight as I grew into my femininity.

My breath caught in my throat, I grabbed my trumpet and slowly walked backstage to where my entrance was. Nerves I hadn't felt in years suddenly multiplied by the thousands and settled into my stomach. My hands were shaking. I couldn't do this. I couldn't do it. They would laugh at me. I would be a laughing-stock. Oh, was that my cue line? Cringing inwardly, I burst forth from the sheltering wings of the theatre and stormed on stage, expecting to be booed off. Instead, I heard a very different noise: A whistle. First one, then another. Was that a cheer? Another whistle! I was almost smiling when I opened my mouth to begin my lines. Energized by the audience's response, I performed my dance to the best of my abilities and, from what I hear, "stole the show."

A good actress learns something from every part she plays. She takes something away from being another person and the character becomes part of her, almost as if she were infused into her soul. I thought Mazeppa was a curse, but it turned out that she was the catalyst I needed. I still have my low points, as does everyone, but most of the time I feel that sassy, spunky, take-no-crap-from-anyone character living inside of me. As my song said, "Kid, ya gotta get a gimmick/If you wanna get applause." After playing Mazeppa, I finally had a gimmick: Myself. I was going to show myself to the world instead of hiding behind clothes and bushy hair. If they didn't like me, well then that was just fine, but at least I was out there. I know none of this would have happened if I hadn't sucked it up, gritted my teeth, confronted my fears, and become a stripper who bumped it with a trumpet.

> *This is a great example of a writer having fun not only with language but with her own childhood perceptions of herself. Remember, we don't like to be preached at. We like people and writers who don't take themselves too seriously. And the language! Just listen: "She was a horror. She was crude. She was racy. She was a stripper. She was everything I feared. She was my savior." Megan leads us one way and then all of a sudden switches directions— with a one-sentence paragraph. Beautiful. And it certainly breaks rules ("Don't use lots of short sentences in a row"), doesn't it? She's even having fun with her title, with all those "g's." And that ending: ". . . who bumped it with a trumpet." Good stuff.*

BIGGER IS BETTER

MORGAN F. HEUSCHKEL

Like many people in this country, I drive my own car. Well, perhaps "car" is a misnomer. I actually drive a boat. A land yacht. It's a 1984 Mercury Grand Marquis—four-door, beige, and big enough to require its own zip code. Ten years ago, I would have laughed at the mere thought of driving such an oversized behemoth. But things have changed. I have changed. I'm almost embarrassed to say it, but I actually like my car. I really like my great big American car.

    I certainly didn't start out that way. I had spent most of my youth being driven around in small imports, like the Nissan and Mazda owned by my parents. Both were most sensible and economical cars. Then, at age 23, I inherited my grandmother's Grand Marquis (I guess when you're a grandparent you can drive what you want). I balked, even in the face of this unconditional generosity. "Drive this . . . this tank?" thought I, while my friends zipped around town in their Volkswagens and Toyotas. Never! But drive it I did.

It took some getting used to. At first I got agoraphobia sitting in the front seat, and it took half an hour to scrape off the bumper sticker that read "Retired and Loving It!" I had one or two minor "incidents" before I fully learned the Mercury's perimeters. But, please, don't tell my mother—I blamed any and all body damage on irresponsible, anonymous drivers backing into the car in the parking lot at Penney's while I was shopping for blouses. However, I can now parallel park in places like San Francisco with such grace and acumen that bystanders often burst into spontaneous applause. No, really. And soon I found myself warming to the Creature.

For one thing, the Merc had some undeniable practical virtues. It could seat six without even blinking, and was obscenely comfortable. It had a stereo like a concert hall and automatic everything—windows, seats, mirrors, brakes, steering, you name it. The suspension practically levitated over speed bumps and potholes and did ninety miles per hour like a walk in the park, albeit a very fast one. And I'm safe. Thirteen years ago safety features like anti-lock brakes and air bags weren't the relatively standard additions they've become today, so the Mercury went without them, but it more than made up for them by surrounding me with two tons of solid beige steel and at least twelve feet of breathing space between me and either the nose or the tail of the car. Garbage trucks bounce off me.

But the matter went beyond pragmatics. I began to relish the unapologetically un-P.C. nature of the car. In this age, when smoking has the same social cachet as baby seal slaughtering, the Mercury has three (yes, three) sets of lighters and ashtrays. My mother's '92 Mazda didn't even come with a lighter. And mileage? While I never did any formal number crunching on the subject, a rough estimate places the car's mileage at around eleven miles to the gallon, under the most optimal of conditions (say, the hand of God pushing you down the freeway). If you're used to driving and being driven around in smaller cars, it can take a while to get used to being behind the wheel of a car with such . . . presence. There is much to be said for what a big car can do for your self-image. It is not coincidence that many larger American cars are reminiscent of armored personnel carriers. While tooling down the road, imagine that you are A Most Powerful Person. What would you do to solve the budget crisis? How about that nasty little mess in the Middle East? Go on, give those kids at the bus stop a presidential wave and a flash of your famous smile. Chomp on a big see-gar. There, feels good, doesn't it? Try getting that sense of empowerment from a Hyundai.

I began to notice that smaller, more economical cars were no longer attractive to me. While eyeing the ads in magazines and newspapers, I would pass over the colorful spreads on Sentras, Accords, and Tercels, and home in on the layout for the new Oldsmobile Cutlass Sierra. On the street, El Dorados and Impalas would sing to me. And when I got to borrow a friend's 1982 Cadillac Brougham de Ville for a week while he was on vacation, I thought I'd died and gone to heaven. Azure blue, with wondrous lines and a body in pristine condition, this monster and I spent a glorious week touring the countryside. Replete with leather interior, four built-in lighters, and every button, knob, and gadget known to man, the Cadillac showed me that there were even bigger, more luxurious fish to fry than my little Grand Marquis.

Sure, people can call cars like mine "gas guzzlers," "space hogs," and "boats," but are theirs the voices of economic and ecological practicality, or the green-tinged song of jealousy? Tired and grumpy from years of bumping knees, noses, and elbows in the cramped interiors of their "practical" cars, these people turn their ire on us, the drivers of luxury liners, in an attempt to salve their pride. Might I suggest, good people, that you put aside your indignation and mistrust and consider taking a drive on the wide side? Borrow your Aunt Ethel's yellow Cadillac for a week and discover the joys of driving big. Sit behind the wheel of that cavernous expanse of leather and steel and knobs and dials, of foot wells roomy enough to make a basketball player giggle and a trunk so big you need a miner's helmet to see it all. See if your heart doesn't melt just a little.

> *This is a personal essay that, despite the fact that it's de-cidedly "me-oriented," connects to a reader. It's funny, and it's fun, and you don't get the sense that Morgan is full of herself or trying to teach us anything—partly be-cause, like Megan does, above, she acknowledges that there might be just a slight gap between her perceptions of herself and others' perceptions of her. And she's fine with that, in a lighthearted way. It's also fun because she's ex-aggerating, and we know it, and she knows we know it. And she's got a great eye for detail (she "shows"): four-door beige 1984 Grand Marquis, shopping at Penney's for blouses, Aunt Ethel's yellow Cadillac, the "Retired and Loving It!" bumper sticker, for example. Additionally, she brings up issues we can all relate to, like the cost of gaso-line, the "nasty little mess in the Middle East," and the difficulty of parking in big cities (San Francisco).*

HAMMERHEAD AT THE TRAIL'S END

RAEN WILLIS

Gold can be found in unlikely places. Lovers of live music know this. They prowl the clubs, and even the streets, waiting for lightning to strike. It's blind luck, really. But you have to put yourself out there.

Wednesday night at the Trail's End, a small working-class tavern in a small town, Oregon City, just outside of Portland. There are dozens of such neighborhood taverns in the Portland area, corner pubs, where absolutely nothing has been spent on the ambience and it's all about the music. The place feels convivial even when there are only four or five people in the house and one of them's the bartender and one's the waitress.

Wednesday night is blues jam night—a very mixed bag. Anyone who wants to play gets to, either sitting in with the house band, or with other musicians who drop in, or a combination of both. Like Forrest Gump's chocolate box, you never know what you're going to get. We head over, expecting nothing. It's a cold midweek night in early March and the rain is coming down, so it's no surprise that the crowd is small—there are as many musicians milling around on the stage as there are patrons in the audience, but these working-class jazz buffs are loyal and enthusiastic.

We're surprised to find that the entire second set has been given over to some guy none of us has ever heard of, named, of all things, "Hammerhead." No last name. We joke about the name. It doesn't look promising. We get into the house band, just four guys unknown outside of a twenty-mile radius who light it up nightly at the Trail's End—Ray Davis's smooth, inventive lead guitar, Scott White's hard-kicking bass work, Jeff Alviani's inspired, mobile keyboard, all resting on Tom Drew's solid percussion. You never heard of any of them. Mark Knophler's Sultans of Swing in the flesh.

Hammerhead arrives, his overcoat flapping around his gaunt six-foot-five frame, long grayish-black hair hanging around a sculptured and eloquent face. He strides to a table and folds himself down. His body language speaks of a long and intimate association with alcohol or something worse, and the fight to put it behind him. He orders what looks like a club soda.

He unfolds from the chair and steps up on the stage with his band. He starts with the downbeat, and right away his harmonica playing is molten yet controlled. He has our attention and our respect.

But what gets me is his vocals. When he starts singing, I know immediately it's the real deal. There are plenty of competent blues singers, but this is something else—like Paul Butterfield, with that slurred-to-dead-center in his phrasing, the rich, shadowy voice that honors the sadness and the struggle to endure that is the blues. You can't learn to do what Hammerhead is doing. You can practice and hone it and be mad to have it, but somehow you have to live it or you don't ever get it this deep. It isn't decorative or pretty—it's got more important things to do. On the up-tempo songs it's a dancy slide of pocketed sensuality, and on the slow ones it's a cinder-cone rising from seething hurt.

When the set is over, Hammerhead gives the stage over to the jammers who have been filtering in over the last hour. They start to play—some good vocals, guitar, and alto sax work. The guys are working hard and having fun, but it's just pretty good, and I need the magic right now. I get up to leave and approach Hammerhead on my way out. He's facing the wall next to the stage, attending to his harp. I walk up behind him and touch his elbow to get his attention, tell him how much I loved what I'd heard. His guardedness instantly softens, and he thanks me kindly. Then I walk out into the rainy dark. I've never heard of Hammerhead since.

> *This essay gets quite a bit of work done. While on one hand it's a straightforward description of Hammerhead— and the "small working-class tavern" where he's playing—it also actually has an argumentative edge, beginning with its first sentence. Then by the end, Raen's moving into some very interesting territory, based on what he's just described. Here he suggests that musicians work hard and make great art but are largely ignored and then forgotten by American culture, which is tragic.*

GRADUATION THEATER

MARIE ROW

I'm forty-one years old. I've had a long time to envision this scene. I've imagined it with several different scripts. The most common image that surfaces, though, is where I give a little rendition of Bette Davis's "I did it myself" speech.

She said that, once, on a talk show. She shared an imaginary Academy Award speech with the audience, one where she stood in front of the podium, held up the award, and said, "I did this myself." Instead of rattling off a long list of thank you's to who was there, who had helped, who had supported et cetera, et cetera, she departed from tradition by simply and clearly claiming the trophy as her own. She was quite brazen and bold about the whole thing, in her Bette Davis daring and defiant way.

That's usually how I imagine myself on my graduation day, following in the footsteps of this actress renowned for her vivid portrayals of diabolical schemers and eccentric heroines. I am reminded that I do not want to meekly walk up shrouded in my black gown, smiling, and shake an administrator's hand, only to grasp my diploma, pose for the camera, and then retreat to my section to search for my folding chair. I want to take that diploma and declare to the world that it is mine because I earned it. I want to use that spotlight to thank the person really responsible for my success. I'm dedicating my diploma to me. I did this myself.

I did it when my grandmother voiced, "I never thought I'd see the day" when I pressed on beyond high school, to my stepmother's secret delight. I did it when my step-cousin stated, mildly surprised, that I didn't seem at all mentally handicapped as I had been described. I did it after it was helpfully suggested by my relatives that trade school was the height of challenge that I could handle. And I did it after Dad declared as fact that no one my age makes it through college.

I did it after my husband announced that it would be best for all concerned if I'd stay home and tend to him and our soon-to-arrive son. I did it after my divorce, when my boyfriend felt it would be good for the relationship if I continued working a slightly lower-paying, lower-status job than his, one that would guarantee that I never threatened the unchanging and comfortable status quo. I did it when I completed my Associate of Arts degree, and my cousin relented and agreed that we had better have a celebration, seeing as how, for me, it was probably the end of the line.

I did it attending three different colleges as my family moved seven times. I did it while mothering three children and holding seven jobs to support them. I did it pregnant. I did it at night after work when the kids were asleep. I did it by attending a new University while one son started high school and another started pre-school. I did it when I was unemployed. I did it the November the refrigerator broke down, and when the car finally gave out along the side of the road during finals. I did it after the Lancaster earthquake left me host to the spore *Coccidiodes immitis*, also known as Valley Fever. I kept doing it after I lost my home. I kept doing it after I had survived the modern cures for breast cancer, and after my daughter died and was placed in a small desert grave.

I did it when I was exhausted, scared, and lonely.

After ten scholarships, transcripts patched together over twenty-one years, and a 3.85 grade point average, I have finally done it. I am going to receive that elusive Bachelor of Arts diploma. And when it comes to the thank you's, well, Bette, move over. I am prepared to take my place.

> *This essay draws its power from its willingness to defy convention: "I will not say what I am expected to say." Any time you do that you run the risk of being disliked, and Marie risks coming off egotistical or hostile. But she triumphs over those risks, proving in the meantime that in any situation there's always something new, personal, and powerful to say—even in a valedictory address, the world's most tired set piece.*

HOW TO TALK TO YOUR KIDS ABOUT DRUGS

ROSA LEVY

If you get to that day when you have kids and they grow up a little and they want to know about drugs, do you tell them? Do you tell them all of the things you did, starting at age sixteen, when you met Suzie and Jenn and started drinking and smoking cigarettes and driving around in your car all night or sitting down by the river talking about boys and sex (which you had never had then, but it wouldn't take long—your friends were always bragging that they had slept with so many and teasing you that you hadn't, and you felt small and silly even when you drank beer and drove your car fast and stopped going to school for a while)? Will you tell them how drinking made you sleep with boys who were mean to you, how you would go to anyone then, how your mother (good, smart, bewildered mother, who always taught you to make your own way, never thought you would be mean and dumb and waste your life and mind and body as if they were a worthless burden to you) waited up for you at night afraid that you had died and then screamed "I don't know what you are turning into" and you screamed back that you hated her because the last thing you would ever be able to do was admit that who you were turning into was somebody you hated too? And maybe if you told your kids this story when they were young enough that they still had that kind of perfect adoring love for their parents then later when they got mad and mean they would remember that story and not want to lose themselves or you, even if it is only for a little while.

There are other stories too, increasing in depravity (or at least intensity)—do you tell those? How at the first college you went to you met Megan and Mark and started to smoke pot and then drop acid and eat those bitter little mushrooms but it was an intellectual, spiritual experience then or so you all liked to say and so you would take acid and look at trees and talk about books and ideas and lie in the park twirling perfect flowers over your head and go to concerts in dark halls with day-glow amoebas crawling the walls and the music exploding through you and it always seemed like everyone should be hallucinating, like you had discovered the true Tao of life, but that there is a lesson here too because it ended with flunking out of college, with a dull head and sad-achy, realizing that another year or so had passed and you still didn't know how to make yourself happy by working and making stuff that lasts and that every time you fail even a little bit you remember it, so that the next time you try to do something your past reminds you how easily you gave up before? So maybe your kids will look at you and see all that wasted time, and how the drugs never did open you up so much as divide you into pieces of people and that sometimes you still have to collect the pieces off the floor and stuff them into clothes and try to walk around like you are whole, hoping nobody can see the places where you are coming apart.

Do you tell the last tale, the one that hurts the most, which you probably shouldn't tell them because most days you can barely tell it to yourself, because there are some things that can be forgiven and some that can't, some that hang around and hover at the edges of sleep, smack you awake and gasping knowing that whatever you do, you were once this person capable of these things and that knowledge never goes away? So do you tell them how you were married and somehow you didn't want to be married any more so you started to sleep with Eddie, and Eddie sold but mostly used cocaine, and somehow you started doing it with him in his bedroom in his mother's house while she slept and how for ten minutes at a time you got to be this superstar in your own life, and how the two of you moved on to amphetamines and would get high and walk all over the city, laughing and talking about life as if it were this curious, trifling thing and ordering food in restaurants and walking out without eating it and figuring you must be the smartest people in the world to have discovered something so easy and fun that hurts no one and they say isn't addictive? Or about the inevitable divorce and how you began begging money from all your friends until they ran from you and all you cared about was getting high, until finally you went to Europe to escape everything, especially yourself, who you hated for ever thinking there was a way out of living besides getting up and facing yourself every day unblinking, and drugs, which you hated for taking sweet people and smart people and good people and destroying them by telling them that horrible lie that living a life that is sometimes quiet and disappointing and ordinary isn't good enough, that you need a life where you get to be a superstar? Maybe that is the thing to tell them, the one thing, and maybe you don't even have to sacrifice yourself, maybe you can just tell them that there are ways to escape your life for a minute or two and that these ways can feel incredible for a minute or two but the loss is that you trick yourself into believing that there is a way out of the work and drudgery that sometimes is life, and that if you trick yourself too many times you may not remember how to look at life on a spring day and see the sun shining and feel all the wonder of that growing and not need anything to make you feel how beautiful and perfect that moment is.

> *I always tell my composition students to take risks in their writing, especially in early drafts, which they can run by readers to see if those risks are paying off. If you're not sure what "taking a risk in writing" means, read this one. Talk about risks! It's a personal essay and an argument at the same time. It seems to be rambling talk, but it's a very hard kind of thing to write. Our reaction to Rosa keeps getting more and more complex, because her view of herself is so multifaceted. She describes her weaknesses with so much skill that we both accept her self-loathing and admire her for her courage. And what courage this essay has! Not only the courage to discuss the author's sins in the raw without sentiment, but also the courage to take the reader on an exhausting roller coaster. And notice that while it's utterly fresh and original, it's a redressing of two of the oldest clichés in essay writing: "Just say no to drugs" and "Don't make the mistakes I made as a youth."*

THANKSGIVING

LAURA KATE JAMES

I sit next to her on the cold concrete steps of our front porch—our exhale hangs in the frigid air, mine of vapor, hers of smoke—we watch the scarce late-night traffic pass. "I forgot how little happens here," she scoffs, as if the idea of a small town should have been ixnayed at the first draft of civilization. It's November already and three months have elapsed since I've seen her. Even the jeans she's wearing are foreign to me, ones I've never borrowed. Her fingernails are painted black. Black like her hair, colored with cheap dye that cost her little more than eight dollars at Fred Meyer. Black like her hooded sweatshirt advertising Lewis and Clark College in white Old English style lettering. She brings the butt of her cigarette to her lips and inhales quietly. I watch her do this and she knows it. She flicks her thumb and bits of ash fall on her shoes. Smoke issues from her mouth.

I rest my chin on my knees and survey our street. A solitary lamp. A few parked cars. Our cousins' house, two doors down. The mailbox at the end of our driveway with the flag shaped like a hummingbird. The grass she and I used to run across in our swimming suits with the sprinklers on. The walkway leading up to where we sit now. Her weekend baggage waiting patiently to be brought inside.

"There's enough to keep me entertained," I answer, though it's nothing near the truth and she knows. She's lived there too.

She laughs. "It's just so weird to be back here again, you know?" No. I don't know. This is my home. I don't have anywhere else to be like she does. I wrap the yellow scarf higher around my nose and mouth and pull my green jacket sleeves over my knuckles. It's cold sitting next to her there. And quiet. Already we have exhausted the subjects of Portland and school on the drive home from the airport and I have little else to say.

She takes another drag and throws the remains of her Marlboro onto the damp and browning lawn, littered with leaves. "How are things with the parental unit? Is it annoying? Being their center of attention and all?" I shrug. She lights another. "You don't *have* to sit out here," she says, noting my apathy. "You're gonna smell like smoke." I shrug again, and look at my shoes. Too many days have inserted themselves between us, and the familiar companionship I knew in our childhood has dissipated like the smoke in the mist that hangs in the glow of the streetlight. She offers me a drag; I fill my lungs with smoke.

> *In its own minimalist way, this is a beautiful piece of writing. Note that while on one hand it's pure description, it still manages to convey a tone and a sense of how the author feels about what she's describing. Laura Kate uses short sentences (and sentence fragments) as well as attention to the tiniest of details ("ash falls on her shoes") to suggest a sadness and weariness beneath the surface of the writing. This would be an excellent essay to model. Try to describe a meeting with a friend using the same rhetorical devices that Laura Kate uses here.*

THE DOS AND DON'TS OF GETTING OVER THAT SUMMER-BETWEEN-HIGH-SCHOOL-AND-COLLEGE FLING WITH A BOY WHO HAPPENS TO BE ONE OF YOUR BEST FRIENDS AND IS NOW GOING TO A DIFFERENT COLLEGE THAN YOU ARE

MEGAN SPROWLS

Imagine, for a moment, that in your senior year of high school you met the most gorgeous guy you've ever seen in your life and he turned out to be . . . for lack of a better word: perfect. But due to your lack of luck in the love department, your newly found soul mate ends up being your best friend. Summer rolls around and on the night of your commencement from high school, you sit with your chum on the front steps of his beautiful Victorian house. The night is balmy and the first stars are beginning to appear. Chirping crickets provide a musical background as you confess your love for him and find out that (gasp!) he feels the same way. Great, right? Well, not quite.

The next day he goes to camp for the entire summer, so nothing can come of it. Yet you spend every Saturday with your cell phone glued to your hand in the off chance that he might come home and call you. Then, one night, it rings. He's home. So you gather up all your friends, grab a cake, and drive to his house. That's right. It's his surprise birthday party. Fifteen people roaming around with no chance of being alone. Yet through a stroke of luck (and some deliberate planning on your part) you end up being the last one to leave. You murmur a soft good-bye but he says nothing. Instead, he pulls you onto the couch with him and you spend the next two and a half hours with your lips locked together as you try to suck each other's face off.

After your glorious night of PG-13–rated bliss, he goes back to camp for another month and doesn't call you. Just like a man. The next time you see him, he says nothing about what happened and you don't bring it up because you're at the county fair and once again surrounded by friends who can't seem to take the hint. You drive him home at the end of the night and park your car in front of his house and immediately get out to say goodbye to him. No words come and instead you latch yourself on to him, your arms encircled around his waist in a Kung Fu death grip.

As he hugs you back and you listen to the steady beat of his heart, a nightmare suddenly flashes across your eyes: The next time you see him there could very well be a beautiful, blonde, big-breasted bimbo hanging on his arm. This could be your last chance to have him to yourself. Gathering up all your courage, you break your grip on him, stand on your tiptoes and pull him down to you for what you know will be your last kiss. He doesn't resist and instead pulls you closer to him. Eventually you both settle on standing with your foreheads pressed against each other's in complete silence—you trying to memorize everything about this moment and him thinking God-only-knows-what. Soon, it is time to go. You have one final embrace. This time your head is positioned directly over his heart. It's racing now. He breaks away, turns, and goes into his house leaving you alone in the dark with an empty car and an even emptier heart.

Five minutes later, you lie on your bed, numbly staring up at the darkened ceiling. In five hours, you will get in your car and drive a hundred miles north and he will drive a hundred miles west. You roll over and hug your pillow. As tears slip out of your eyes, you think to yourself, "Oh crap. Now what?"

- **DO** cry. It's a perfectly healthy emotion and even though it makes your nose run like a fountain and your eyes look like you've been smoking something, you'll feel better after you're done. Well, maybe you should cry a little more just to be sure.
- **DO NOT** keep licking your lips to see if they still taste like his. They don't, and now you have to buy Chapstick because you've managed to make them raw and chafed.
- **DO NOT** scream out his name in the middle of campus while you're moving in because you see a guy who looks a little bit like him. All you will get is very strange looks from people.
- **DO NOT** go up to the look-alike after he doesn't respond to your call and confront him about how he could be so rude. All you will get is a restraining order.
- **DO** keep in touch with him. After all, he is your best friend and just because you're at college doesn't mean you can't talk, right?
- **DO NOT** scream obscenities at your cell phone when it doesn't connect to his on the first try.
- **DO** try calling him back.
- **DO NOT** let your paranoia take over and start to think that in the 48 hours he's been at that hippie school he's turned into the biggest man whore in the planet and is now sleeping with anything that moves and has boobs when he doesn't pick up the phone.
- **DO** leave him a message.
- **DO NOT** joke about him suddenly turning into the biggest man whore on the planet and sleeping with anything that moves and has boobs while you're leaving him a message.
- **DO** realize what an ass you just made of yourself.
- **DO NOT** call him back and leave him another message telling him that.

- **DO** tell your roommate the story. That way when you're sobbing in the middle of the night she won't think you're a psycho.
- **DO NOT** gather the rest of the girls from your floor and tell them the story because you think that they should be "informed."
- **DO NOT** use senior pictures given to you to help illustrate the story as you tell it to the girls on your floor.
- **DO** leave him messages on MySpace or Facebook to let him know you still care . . . but not in a creepy, stalker-type way.
- **DO NOT** make lists while looking at Facebook of all the new female friends he is adding from his hippie college and plot ways to eliminate them should they get between him and you.
- **DO** listen to your other friend when she tells you that, for your own good, you should take his name out of your cell phone, off your instant messenger list, off your MySpace, and take down all pictures of him in order to cleanse yourself from him.
- **DO NOT** add him back to your cell phone, put him back on your instant message list, put him back in his #2 spot on MySpace, and put back up all the pictures of him the very next day because you miss the sight of his adorable face.
- **DO NOT** be disappointed when he doesn't come home to go see a football game the exact same weekend you do. Even though you may not think so, calculus midterms *are* important in the grand scheme of things.
- **DO NOT**, however, run around the football stand screaming and jumping up and down when he calls you at half time to tell you he's on his way home and he'll meet you at Denny's after the game.
- **DO** feel free to run and leap into his arms when you see him in the Denny's parking lot. This is the first time you've seen him since you've gone to college, after all.
- **DO NOT** forget to check and make sure you don't lock your keys in your car in your excitement to see him. When your dad has to drive to Denny's at 12:30 in the morning to give you the spare key, he won't find it half as amusing as you do.
- **DO NOT** break down into tears as you're driving home from Denny's because you miss him already.
- **DO** decide that you're sick of crying and that you're going to stop.
- **DO** stop.
- **DO** realize that maybe . . . maybe you just had a breakthrough. Could you possibly be getting over him?

- **DO NOT** try to then convince yourself that maybe you don't *want* to get over him. You know you have to.
- **DO** continue the healing process of getting over him. Keep in touch: instant message him, call him every once in awhile, and see him if you are home at the same time. You may not ever be a couple, but at least you will always be friends. You will always . . .
- **DO** look at the cute boy who just passed you in the hallway and interrupted your internal monologue. Boy, does he have a nice—

Imagine, for a moment, that in your senior year of high school you met the most amazing guy you've ever met in your entire life and he turned out to be . . . for lack of a better word: perfect. The perfect best friend. He spends hours with you in his hot tub talking about college, his hopes, his dreams, and his future. You both plan Denny's trips with the rest of your friends and spend the entire time doing things that could probably get you kicked out if you hadn't made friends with the manager and all the wait-staff. He talks to you when you call him in tears at one in the morning and gently talks you down by getting in a fight with you about whether or not there are penguins in Hawaii and almost convinces you that he can, in fact, speak Eskimo. You tell him that you think he should learn to speak Polar Bear. You both laugh and then realize that you need to go to bed. He says goodbye and is about to hang up when you say his name. He waits and, biting your lip, you whisper, "I love you" into the phone. There is a pause, and then he whispers, "I love you too." Immediately you hang up the phone and spend the next twenty minutes dancing around your room. Because it's true: you do love him. It's a deep love felt between really good friends that can't really be explained.

However, just because you love him in this way doesn't mean you can't occasionally have the urge to pin him up against a wall and do naughty things to him.

- **DO NOT** actually do that . . .

. . . unless you have a really good excuse.

This is the perfect piece of writing to take us from personal essays to informative essays, because it's a little bit of both, isn't it? What Megan's done here is turned a lesson that she has learned from personal experience into a sort of tongue-in-cheek instructional manual—you don't have to read too deeply to see that the "you" to whom she refers is

really the "I" of her own experience. And I think she suc-
ceeds marvelously, even though those instructions really
only amount to a list of things that went wrong for her. So
how is it an "informative" essay? I think it is in the bigger
picture. She's not really saying "leap into his arms when
you see him in the Denny's parking lot"; she's asking read-
ers to think in larger terms about their long-distance
relationships.

Informative Essays

SCRATCH THAT ITCH

BENNETT LINDSEY

You feel that burning, untamable desire again. You know you
shouldn't do it. It will only make it worse. You try to think
about something else. You rock back and forth in your chair.
Finally you give in and scratch that mosquito bite. For a brief
moment, you experience pleasure akin to orgasm—then you realize you've only made the problem worse. Now the bite hurts
twice as much and in a few minutes it will be swollen and infected. Luckily, there is no need to ever go through this misery
again. There are several simple preventatives that will encourage those vile bloodsuckers to keep their distance or minimize
the damage if the preventatives fail.

Everyone's favorite bug repellent is a spray can of chemicals, like Off! Unfortunately, these products are sticky and
gooey and stink and are generally carcinogenic. The better they
work, the worse they are for you. The most effective, and therefore the most lethal, is DEET (diethyl toluamide). You can buy
bug repellent that is 100% DEET, or any smaller percentage—
just read the ingredients label. It's wise to carry DEET on trips
into serious mosquito country, just for those emergencies when
nothing else works and your back is to the wall.

But there are less toxic, less repulsive products. Any bug
spray that is citronella-based is safe to use, feels OK on the skin,
and is effective enough to keep off all but the most voracious
bugs. There are two schools of thought on the smell. Some consider it aromatic; others hate it. Wear it to an outdoor concert
and you'll find out which group your neighbors are in. Citronella
in any form works, so you can use citronella candles on your
picnic table. Other plant products that produce smells that
mosquitoes don't like are tea tree oil, eucalyptus oil, and any
citrus juice.

You can protect yourself over the long term by altering your diet. Mosquitoes bite you because they like the way your sweat smells, and that is largely a product of what you eat. To take yourself off the mosquito menu, avoid refined sugar and alcohol and consume foods rich in thiamin (vitamin B1): brewer's yeast, molasses, and wheat germ, all of which are good for you in other ways. Or simply take a vitamin B pill. The old wives' tale that garlic keeps vampires away turns out to have a grain of truth in it—ingesting garlic or rubbing it on your skin turns mosquitoes off. You can add it to almost anything you eat, and it will only cost you your social life. Mexicans, who have learned to cope with mosquito swarms of Biblical proportions, swear by the tequila diet—after a couple of Tequila Sunrises your problems will be gone, or at least you won't be conscious of them anymore. Anything that smells good—perfume, hair spray—is to be avoided.

You can bathe in chlorine—mosquitoes don't like the smell any more than people do. A dip in a heavily chlorinated pool should do the trick. Or you can smoke. It's horrible for you, so if you don't want the cancer you might consider hiking with a friend who has the habit and just standing downwind. A campfire will have the same effect at night without the health hazards.

If none of this seems appetizing, wear clothing. Modern outdoor clothing is so light and breathable that you can wear it on even hot summer days. You can even buy mosquito-net hats from outdoor catalog companies, if you don't mind the fashion statement. But determined mosquitoes will bite right through thin cloth, so you may end up bug-spraying your shirts and pants. Or you can hang your clothes in that evening campfire. And choose dull-colored clothing—mosquitoes like bright colors.

If the barricades fall and you do get bitten, there are several things you can do to minimize the damage. As with all bites, begin by washing the area. Then apply one or more of the following lotions or poultices: baking soda, goldenseal, tea tree oil, walnut oil, Vitamin E oil, charcoal, a slice of onion, or good old calamine lotion. Take lots of Vitamin C. And don't scratch! Your mother told you the truth: if you pick at it, it will never get well.

This is a straightforward informative piece of writing. Its usefulness is obvious and low-key. Bennett wisely doesn't try to make more of it than it is; he just organizes the information well and adds a lightly amusing, pleasant tone. And he's framed the essay core with a funny opener and a good punch line.

THE SPROUT ROUTE

WINSTON BELL

You take nutritional supplements. You exercise and eat well-balanced meals. You've even started doing more of your grocery shopping at the health food store. What's missing from your program? Home-grown sprouts. Sprouts are the richest source of whole-food nutrition on the planet, and by far the easiest to grow on your own.

Sprouts are nutritious because they're alive when you eat them. Living foods supply something you can't get anywhere else: enzymes, living organisms that break down food so the nutrients can be absorbed. When you eat living foods, the enzymes needed for digestion are included in the food, but with cooked, aged, or processed foods, your body has to add enzymes from its own limited supply. As enzymes are depleted, your body loses vitality and numerous health problems arise. Living foods are also a rich source of essential nutrients—proteins, vitamins, minerals, sugars, and oils.

The easiest and most practical way to get living foods onto your plate is by growing your own sprouts. You don't need to be a scientist or even a gardener. Sprouts demand very little care, so they're perfect for the person with limited time or space—in other words, all of us. It's simple: soak the seeds, rinse them, and watch them sprout. It takes a few minutes a day, and you don't have to wait long to enjoy the fruits of your labor—a seed will germinate into a mature sprout in one to seven days. And sprouts reduce your time in the kitchen, because you don't cook them.

Sprouts are cheap. You can buy seeds for a couple of dollars per pound. That pound will grow into many, many pounds of wonderfully healthy food. And the materials for your sprout farm are cheap and never have to be replaced.

Cooking with sprouts is easy. Just throw them into almost anything you're making, as little or as much as you like. You can start in the traditional way, by adding them to sandwiches and salads, but soon you'll want to think outside the box. Sprouts can be used in juices, yogurts, cheeses, dressings, breads, and desserts. Eventually you can base your entire diet on sprouts, since living foods can provide your body with everything it needs.

Sprouts have many advantages over those other healthy staples, raw fruits and vegetables. If you buy your fruits and veggies at the store, they are already days old and most of their enzymes and nutrients are gone, since foods retain their life force for only three days after harvest. And if you try to grow them yourself, the commitment of time, money, energy, and space is enormous—vegetable gardening isn't a sidelight, it's a career. Sprouting takes almost no space, and since it takes place indoors, you have no problems with weather, irrigation, pest management, soil conditioning, or disease control.

You can buy sprouts in the store, but you want to grow your own, for lots of reasons. First, the sprouts you buy in the grocery store are old, so a lot of their enzymes and nutrients are history. Second, growing your own means you can experiment with different varieties and combinations, which will give your body a wider range of nutrients—your local store probably only stocks one or two kinds of sprouts. Third, seeds are much cheaper than sprouts. And fourth, sprouting is fun.

So what do you need? First, seeds. Buy organic seeds in bulk at the health food store. For a well-balanced diet, grow more than one kind of sprout. You can sprout almost any kind of seed, but start with the seven traditionals: almond, mung bean, sesame, sunflower, alfalfa, and wheat. Next, buy some wide-mouth canning jars and non-toxic screening material at the homeware store. Cut the material into circles, put water and seeds into the jars, put the rings from the lids over the jar mouths (throw away the flat part), and screw the rings down tight over the mesh. Now all you need to do is rinse the seeds two to four times a day and harvest your sprouts when they are a few inches long. You'll probably want to buy Ann Wigmore's *The Sprouting Book*, which will give you more detailed instructions, lots of nutritional information, and delicious recipes.

> *Part argument, part informative essay, "The Sprout Route" succeeds in many ways. The writer is confident and passionate but not preachy, just taking us through the process step by step. He's very aware of his readers and what they know and want, and he's likable as a writer—so easy to agree with. Finally, he has the courage to avoid a traditional/conventional conclusion, letting the piece simply end where it wants to.*

THE LAST STOP FOR AMERICA'S BUSES

JOHN MERCER

After waving off my friends, I just stood there, dwarfed by the enormous message towering over me: "International Border, Welcome to Mexico." Taking a deep breath, I tossed my duffel bag over my shoulder and headed for the bus station. It was here that I was forced to make my first decision. A large blackboard displayed the names of various cities in alphabetical order. To the right of each name were times and prices. "Primero and Segundo," I read, thinking to myself, "First and second class . . . I wonder what's the difference?"

Mexico, like all countries, has its own system of bus transportation. To help you get started, I've summarized the functions of the four bus classes below. With a little time and a lot of patience, you'll soon be busing your way across Mexico like a local.

The woman at the counter was helpful and fortunately spoke a little English. First-class buses have toilets, air conditioning, and fewer stops; second-class buses don't. Naturally, considering a thirty-six-hour bus ride, these items are no longer luxuries; they're necessities. Within fifteen minutes I had bought my ticket and boarded the bus for Guadalajara, first class . . . or so I thought. An hour later, I was fidgeting in my seat after four unsuccessful attempts at the restroom door. I remember thinking, "The poor bastard must really be constipated"; then I remembered I was in Mexico and knew that wasn't possible. Someone finally stopped me and explained the facts: the restrooms don't work; they never have worked; they never will work.

The same can be said for the air conditioning. In all fairness, the first-class bus does have fewer scheduled stops; however, due to the lack of facilities, it's always making those necessary unscheduled stops. Realistically, there's only one reason to travel first class: You won't normally find the crowds that plague the cheaper second class.

I probably wouldn't have ever tried a second-class bus if it hadn't been for the first-class bus strike which left me stranded in Puerto Escondido. Preparing myself for the worst, I was pleasantly surprised. Although the buses are uglier and lack the maintenance of the first, passengers have the comfort of knowing the drivers are first-rate mechanics. Second class has more scheduled stops, but they have little effect on arrival times. Like the tortoise racing the hare, the bus sputters along at a consistent pace, seldom far behind in the end. The atmosphere is pleasant, probably due to the open windows and fresh air.

It was this favorable impression of second class that led me to try third class, and for this I'll always be grateful. The third-class bus stations are separate from the previous two, and are normally found in the sections of towns best avoided by people with white faces. However, for those of you who have the time and aren't easily discouraged, you may find the heart of

Mexico lies along the paths they forge. They're almost free, because they're government-subsidized. If you're in a hurry or trying to get someplace, forget it. But if you like the thought of listening to Bob Marley tapes through distorted speakers while traveling in a modified school bus so old it may have taken your grandparents to school, stay seated—you're in for a ride. The routes are treacherous, sending the bus bouncing and rattling up and down roads without signs to places without names. Along these roads, most of which are dirt, you will come face to face with people who have spent their entire lives camping out. I remember their stares, looking at me like someone might look at moldy food discovered in the back of the refrigerator. I suppose the story of the man with the white face who was seen on the bus that day may still be told at night by the fire or among the women doing wash at the banks of the river. I will always remember the people and places I found while riding the third-class bus.

The fourth and last class of buses are the city buses. They're the cheapest way to tour a city without getting lost. Like all city buses, they spend the day doing laps. So don't hesitate; jump on, toss the driver a C-Note (about five cents U.S.), and relax.

> *Here's a nice example of basic information enriched by a lively and complex personality. To John's simple informative message he adds the dramatic* in medias res *introduction, the narrative structure, and rich physical details ("listening to Bob Marley tapes through distorted speakers"; "I suppose the story of the man with the white face may still be told at night by the fire . . .").*
> *He portrays himself as a slightly inept gringo falling into this wisdom against his will. That helps with a problem all informative writers face: the reader's fear of the unknown. John is saying, "I blundered my way through, so you can do it."*

WHY FALLING IN LOVE FEELS SO GOOD

JUDY KRAUSE

After a few years of marriage, I realized I had married the wrong person. We had nothing in common. All the magic was gone. So I got divorced, and have deeply regretted the time I wasted in the marriage and the pain the divorce caused my kids and family.

Why did I make the mistake in the first place? How could I have been so blind? I was a typical young American adult when I married. My parents had been married thirty years to each other. I wanted to be married. And I was in love. Surely that was the sign. If I was in love, that must mean he was the man for me.

I was making the same mistake that thousands of Americans make every year. Perhaps if I'd known just a little more about the physiology of love, I'd have done a better job picking a partner, and my children wouldn't have had to live in two homes. If we teach our children more about love, perhaps the astronomical divorce rate in this country will come down a little.

The simple truth is, Nature programs us chemically to select the wrong partner, or at least the first partner. I discovered this while reading a wonderful book about women's physiology and psychology, *A Woman's Book of Life*, by Joan Borysenko, Ph.D., where I learned about the relationship between the infatuation stage and one's ability to pick a mate. Here's what happens. When a human meets a member of the opposite sex, her old reptilian brain makes a few quick checks to see if he would be a suitable mate: Is he strong, is he healthy, does he smell right? If the old brain is satisfied, it orders her limbic system to kick in, where a neurotransmitter called phenylethylamine, or PEA, is released. She doesn't realize what is going on, but she's in mating mode, and with one look of interest from the lucky guy, her infatuation mechanism takes over.

PEA gives you those wonderful "in love" feelings—the wild euphoria, the skyrocketing libido, and the self-esteem you've always craved. Suddenly the world is wonderful, you're wonderful, the other person is wonderful. Suddenly you can stay up making love until the wee hours with your boyfriend and go to work the next day looking fresh. Suddenly you are understanding, generous, tolerant, and loving toward everyone. PEA makes you unable to reason, you know it, and you like it—what did reason ever do for you? And then PEA gives you the big lie: It says to you, All these wonderful feelings are proof that your new partner is the one. You feel this good because he is so right for you. And you'll always feel this way.

It's all a lie, because PEA remains in your system for about six months after meeting Mr. or Ms. Momentarily Right—then it leaves, and you return to earth, and you see your partner for the first time without the benefit of chemicals. Who is that person? And did you really promise to spend the only lifetime you have with . . . that?

This system worked well when we lived in caves, people needed to mate constantly to provide fresh population reserves, humans lived until they were thirty, couples stayed together long enough to raise the children, and smell was a fairly good indicator of partner potential. But times have changed, and Mother Nature hasn't caught on. With divorce rates at about 50% in this country, wouldn't it be great if we told each other, and especially our kids, what's really going on? If we published the knowledge that it's a chemical we're in love with, not a person, that the chemical's sole purpose is to mislead us into a committed relationship we'll regret, and that it doesn't last, we could be on our guard.

How do we spread this information? The perfect vehicle already exists—sex education classes in high school. Let teens know about the infatuation stage and PEA. Tell them their feelings are marvelous and to be celebrated and enjoyed, but they are unique to a 3–6 month period and are in no way something to base life-long decisions on. They will learn that choosing a life partner should be done after the infatuation stage has passed, or at least calmed down. If young people hear this, maybe the next generation of children won't consider living between two homes a normal lifestyle.

> This essay has a great sense of what Chapter 12 calls the "argumentative edge"—it's saying loudly, "I think you need this information—it will save your life." It reminds us that informing is not a boring recitation of facts; it's tossing the reader a life preserver. Its sense of "should" is so strong that a case could be made for putting it in the argumentative essay group.

Argumentative Essays

WHY I NEVER CARED FOR THE CIVIL WAR

SHAWNI ALLRED

I got mostly A's and a few B's all through high school and have managed, for the most part, to do the same in college. I'm sure that most people, when they hear that, are thinking, "That means she's really smart." Well, I'm not stupid, but I don't know near as much as people think I know. I just learned how to pass tests. I got an A in history, but I couldn't tell you where the first battle of the Civil War was fought. I got an A in geometry, but I couldn't in a million years tell you the area of a circle. There are many things I "learned" that have vanished from my memory, thanks to some flaws in the teaching system.

The setup is always the same. The teacher lectures, and the students take notes. I'm thinking of one class in particular, a history class. We went from the Pilgrims to Harry S. Truman in twelve weeks. I was bored out of my mind. I tried so hard to care about the soldiers in the Civil War, but with the teacher outlining the lecture on the board and citing facts as though he were reading from a cookbook, my passion for them was lost. As a result, I remembered what I needed to remember to pass the test, but then it was gone.

The tests reinforce the problem. Comprehensive, timed tests encourage short-term memory. The students, knowing all along their grades will rest heavily on tests, study for the sake of passing the test, not for the sake of learning. They stay up late the night before, cramming as much information into their minds as they can. And it works. They pass the exams and get rewarded. Unfortunately, that A or B is often only a measure of the student's ability to cram.

Is this what we want education to accomplish? To teach students how to cram? Or to teach them to remember the Civil War like it was a recipe? I hope not. I hope the aim is to teach students information they will remember, that means something to them, information they can teach others and use themselves for the rest of their lives. The first step to improving the quality of education is for educators to agree that these are their primary objectives. From there, the solutions to achieving these goals are exciting and endless.

Controlled discussions could be used in place of lectures. For example, if my history class could have had us sit around in a circle and bounce ideas off one another, I might have gotten to the heart of what the Civil War was all about. We could have asked each other questions like, Why did we allow slavery? How do you think the slaves felt? What would you have done if you were one of them?

Even more creative is the idea of using experience as the basis for learning. A friend once had a class where the students acted out the Salem witch trials. Some were judges, some townspeople, some witches. He says he'll never forget that part of history. Another friend had a philosophy class where students walked into strange classrooms and stood inside the doorway until they felt the stares of the other students, in order to understand what Sartre meant by "the Look."

Finally, we could grade, not on timed tests, but on class involvement, homework, and maybe take-home exams. Students would feel they were being rewarded for getting involved in their education, not for becoming experts in test taking.

The question remains whether teachers are willing to step out of old ways of teaching. Some already have. It's because of one teacher I had in the fifth grade that I remember the names of the micro-organisms that live in a drop of pond water. We went to the far end of the playground and scooped up the muddy green water all by ourselves and took it back to the classroom to look at it under a microscope. There were paramecia, volvoxes, and amoebas. I remember.

> *This is a wonderful example of how you can effectively use narrative and personal experience in argument papers. Note again how the details work—in this case in her conclusion, especially, which just makes her point even more emphatic. She remembers.*

A MORAL VICTORY?

ANGELA COOP

In 1984, a group of white male police officers brought suit against the city of San Francisco, alleging that they were the victims of reverse discrimination. They maintained that they had been passed over for promotion in favor of less qualified women and minority officers because of the city's affirmative action policy. The U.S. Supreme Court has recently refused to hear their case.

This action is seen by some as a victory for women and minorities, but, if the allegations are true, isn't it really a loss for us all? The law prohibiting discrimination is intended to ensure equal opportunity for everybody. No group is exempted. It doesn't mean equal opportunity for everybody except white males.

I'm not a white male, but I've been married to one for fifteen years, and I've seen a lot through his eyes. My husband is a mechanical engineer. He's a professor now, but he worked in industry for seven years, and he had a consulting business for six years while he taught, so he has a good understanding of his place in the professional world. Unfortunately, reverse discrimination is nothing new to him. It's a fact of life. Employers are forced by federal equal-opportunity quotas to give preference to Hispanics, blacks, and women.

My sister is also an engineering professor. Although she teaches in the same system with my husband, her experience has been vastly different. Basically, what she wants she gets. It's that simple. It has to be that way, because the quota system makes her a sought-after commodity, and her employer can't afford to lose her.

It took my sister a long time to appreciate the injustice of this. For years, she felt like she deserved everything she got, even though other professors actually quit working in her department because she was treated so favorably. Somehow she felt like she was rectifying the problem of sexism in the workplace, a goal so virtuous as to be worth any cost.

When I talked to my sister last week, she was excited because her department was interviewing the wife of one of my husband's friends. The department doesn't actually have an open position, but the University has funding for a certain number of faculty who meet "specific criteria." As luck would have it, this woman, who normally wouldn't be considered because of her lack of experience, is black. She's irresistible!

We feel an awful sense of collective guilt in this country for what we've done to women and minorities, and we should. We've behaved inexcusably. Affirmative Action policies were developed in an attempt to make up for those past injustices. But do we really think we can right past wrongs by creating new ones? It's said that those who forget history are condemned to repeat it. I would never propose that we do that. But I think it's time to forgive ourselves and move on.

> *Note how this essay moves through its material with complete sureness but no sense of thesis plop or wooden outline. It's an anti-cliché essay, or was when it was written, and it sets the reader up for the surprise thesis nicely in the first paragraph by inviting the clichéd response. The conclusion is a lovely lesson in how to end without summary restatement.*

THE GOOD MOTHER

KAREN ARRINGTON

If you're raising a child and it's going beautifully, you can pat yourself on the back for doing a great job. But it's possible there's another explanation. And if you find yourself sitting in judgment of mothers who appear to be doing the less-than-perfect job, don't convict too quickly. You may find in a few years that you've been condemning yourself. It happened to me.

I had my first child when I was twenty-three. I sailed through my first initiation into motherhood with flying colors, approving nods from elders in grocery stores, and rave reviews at family reunions. My son was bright, sweet, mature, and well-behaved. He was creative, clean, not spoiled, and nicely dressed. He was a testament to my superior mothering skills—what else could it be?—and I was quite proud of a job well done. I was set apart from those stressed mothers in supermarkets barking short-tempered commands at their out-of-control offspring and receiving cool glances from the other moms.

I couldn't understand how mothers could be reduced to tears by small children, or how they could have trouble asserting their parental authority. Spanking, of course, was out of the question, and any civilized and competent parent would refrain from this medieval atrocity. It was obvious to any onlooker that my majoring in Child Development and working in the mental health field had paid off. I was the one other mothers asked for advice. And after twelve years of motherhood, I could walk the talk. Or so I thought.

I had my second child when I was thirty-six. The tempo of my life was very different. The nightly feedings weren't as easy to accommodate to, and I had to return to work after only six weeks. Determined to offer this child the same amenities as I had my first, I dutifully split my lunch break in half so I could tear home to nurse him. My sitter shook her head in amusement, or amazement, and said that I had brought new meaning to the term fast food.

Ryan was born May 5, and he grew curls that flipped up over his ears resembling horns. I had joked that he was my little Taurus, my bull, and indeed when pressed or angry he would drop his head and lower his eyebrows, stopping just short of pawing the ground. But he was a beautiful, happy, and very sociable baby, and I was still giving my arm a work-out patting myself on the back.

Then he turned two. At this point, his crying took on a new velocity and pitch that would after a time leave his brother and me grimacing with our hands to our heads. However cute at first, his stubbornness was relentless and began to pose major problems. When opposed, he would become inconsolable, his crying escalating.

I was, however, resolved to be the capable, intelligent mother equipped to shape this young one's psyche. When the going gets tough, the tough moms get going. I consulted psychologists and counselors. I read more books on parenting the strong-willed child. And I attended parent meetings where parents and authorities shared experience and advice.

While I was seeking out better methods to form Ryan's personality, I didn't realize how much he was reshaping mine. I found myself resorting to yelling, snapping, and even—unbelievable—spanking. I had become the recipient of the chilly and disapproving glances in the grocery store aisles.

Ryan changed every concept that I held about myself as a mother and a person. He changed my views about parenthood, children, and personality. He showed me that children are not simply empty slates awaiting impression; they are active participants in their environment, making their own imprints on the world, evoking response from their caregivers. I have had to redefine my goals as a parent, and recognize that infants are born with distinct personalities intact. My job is to guide what is there by nature, not create the perfect person with my superior nurturing skills. I have less power than I thought. And all those simple absolutes about who I am—I'm not a spanker, for instance—now seem open to debate and dependent on context.

Now that I am pursuing a teaching career, these discoveries have gained a new relevance. As a teacher, I expect to put my best foot forward and bring students along in their learning in every way available to me. But, as with Ryan, I can't determine what my students will walk away with, what mark they will leave, or who they will be. Their own personalities will make those choices. I can do a good job and the results might not show it. That is important to know, because to bank on your own image as Super Mom or Super Teacher is to set yourself up for a devastating reality check.

My enlightenment has also changed my relationship to my peers. I listen to students in my University classes loudly voicing their oh-so-sure opinions on all subjects and passing judgment on others, including parents, from their unassailable position of ignorance. At family gatherings, my outspoken in-laws and cousins do the same. I once might have joined them, but now I look and listen longer before I speak. I sit back more quietly, and, if not more wisely, then surely more humbly.

And now when I meet disheveled mothers in the supermarket vocalizing shrill, ignored refrains to their progeny, I don't automatically react with silent pity for the kids, as I once did. I'm slower to assign blame, and I ask if my condolence for those unlucky children couldn't be better replaced with compassion for mothers who may find themselves struggling to understand and cope with the complex little people who have graced their lives.

> *This essay earns our deep respect. Karen speaks to us from a deep and gutsy place. She's saying, "I had my own simplistic, idealized view of myself handed to me in pieces, and I'm going to relive the pain of that in public so you can share in the wisdom I gained." Sometimes writing is good because the writer is good— honest, daring, generous. We should appreciate the gift.*

RESCUE DOGS: THE BEST OPTION

DANIELE SMITH

Coming home to a dog is one of the best feelings in the world. Dogs wait all day for you to return home, just to run up for the chance to worship the ground you walk on. When it comes to loyalty and absolute selfless friendship, dogs are the best by far. However, just like there are many options as to which pet to get, there are many options as to where to get the pets. If you are looking to buy a dog, getting one at a shelter is better than purchasing a pedigreed dog. When you get your dog from an animal shelter, you spend less money, you have the assurance that the shelter dedicates time to the friendliness and health of the animal, and you do something for your dog in return for the love they bestow upon you: you save their life.

For various reasons, dogs purchased from an animal shelter cost less. Statistically, these dogs are not purebred dogs; the dog is not the offspring of certain expensive breeds, and they do not come with "papers." For these reasons alone, purchasing a dog from a shelter costs hundreds of dollars less. Jacque Lynn Schultz, Companion Animal Programs Adviser, lists the costs of a shelter dog in her article "Counting on You," which total a little over $300, including spaying or neutering, initial vaccination, a wellness exam, items for the dog, and training. When I got my Australian-shepherd mixed dog, Gypsy, she cost only $75, and though we put a deposit down on her surgery, we got it back once she had been spayed. Good shelters provide this service free as an investment in order to prevent future strays; plus, "fixing" extends the life of the pet.

Another article from a site owned by Best Friends Pet Care, Inc., "Purebred vs. Mutt—the Pros & Cons," confirms that "purebreds can be very costly, running anywhere from several hundred dollars to over a thousand dollars." Additionally, there is the possibility of future costs; the owner could end up paying much more money in hospital bills due to the genetic conditions inherent in purebreds. Best Friends Pet Care, Inc., goes on to state that "[purebreds] are more prone to health problems, many of which are often due to overbreeding. These can include immune system diseases, skin diseases, bone and joint disorders, sudden heart disease, eye diseases, epilepsy or seizures, cancers and tumors, neurological diseases, and bleeding disorders." Any one of those problems can run up veterinarian bills in a way only six-figure incomes can heal. Plus, the fact that purebreds are more delicate adds to the worry of the owner concerning the health of the dog. Mixed-breed dogs don't have these problems as a whole and with good care of the dogs, their health problems run few and far between. I have has my dog for over five years now, and she has not had to be taken to the vet due to illness once.

Along with rescue dogs being cheaper in the short term and long run, people running the shelters also have a tendency to provide more care and attention to a dog before it goes to a new home. Shelters make sure that their animals are socialized and can happily live with people. No such guarantee on the pedigreed. Pedigreed dogs and dogs from a pet store might come from bad breeders who breed their dogs in "puppy mills." Norma Woolf's article "Just What Is a Puppy Mill?" defines them as places that mass-produce purebred dogs, and may mistreat their dogs, as the owners have too many to properly care for. A licensed breeder of dogs would provide them with better care, but again, that would cost much more. Shelters rely on volunteers to socialize and provide care to the animals, and those sorts of animal lovers are readily available. The San Francisco SPCA website states that volunteers give the dogs "love, companionship, attention, exercise and training," along with aiding events such as "dog play groups" and "field trips." Quite possibly the best example of pre-care to the animals is the fact that volunteers will "teach basic skills that will help dogs find a home more quickly and stand them in good stead throughout their life" and "assist at public dog training classes offered at the SF/SPCA."

Even with all this extra attention, some people are skeptical about getting a dog at a pet shelter because although a lot of dogs were strays picked up on the streets, there are still quite a few of the animals that had been given to the rescue shelter by their former home. These people think that the dogs given up have something wrong with them. However, from my experience of going to the pet shelters and reading the reasons (they have the reasons the animal was put up into the shelter printed on a profile of the animal outside their kennel), most people put up the dogs for minor reasons. The most common reason I found was that the animals had simple-to-fix problems, like they barked a lot, or weren't properly toilet trained, or maybe were too hyper. I know from experience that these problems are usually easily fixed through simple training or proven prevention methods. Some people just couldn't financially support the animal, or had children that they were afraid to have the dog around. Another reason is that the people were moving, and couldn't take the animal with them. There are some incredibly bad reasons people put animals in shelters, too: I have heard cases of some people giving up their dog because they were going on vacation, and it was simply cheaper to get a new dog upon their return than pay for the kennel costs. The above reasons are valid things to consider when getting any dog: whether or not these things would bother you, because they are problems even with pedigreed dogs.

Another problem people see with getting a kennel dog is that most of the dogs at an animal shelter are adult dogs. Most people simply want puppies because they are adorable, but a lot of other people think in terms of money, and getting the most value in years out of a dog. However, there are many advantages to getting an older dog. It's very likely that older dogs have training to some extent, or at least it is more likely over puppies. Puppy behavior like teething or urinating due to excitement is also not a problem with older dogs. Additionally, older dogs are usually more mellow than your average puppy, much less excitable, and therefore also better around children. The saying "You can't teach an old dog new tricks" is also not necessarily true. It gets harder for older dogs to learn, just like an older person, but it is not impossible. I didn't get my dog as a puppy, but we trained her after getting her, and even later into her life I taught her new tricks like balancing a treat on her nose until I say "go."

However, above money and above the sort of care an animal receives, the best reason to rescue a dog from an animal shelter is that you save the lives of animals. Animal shelters can only hold animals for so long before they have to euthanize the pets to make room for more; if the animal is there for a long period of time, they are considered by the shelter to be "unrescueable." A lot of people know that animals are euthanized in pet shelters, but they fail to realize that even if they only rescue one pet, they save multiple lives. In the article "Pet Adoption Is the Loving Option!" Pia Salk writes: "Adoption saves more than just the life of the pet you adopt.... If you adopt from an animal shelter, you're making room for another dog or cat, or you're allowing other dogs or cats at the shelter to be kept for a longer period of time." Breeders who manufacture good purebred dogs in a healthy environment usually have no problem in selling their puppies, and would probably not euthanize unsold dogs if the issue ever arose. Therefore, acquiring your dog at the animal shelter is the right thing to do. Plus, you still receive the best companionship money can buy.

The choices you make regarding acquiring a pet are totally your own, and there are many more facets to the issue to be considered. If you breed animals or want to participate in a pet show, a purebred dog is surely the way to go. If you want the extreme temperament of a purebred guard dog, or the specific abilities of a bred hunting dog, these qualities could be found in a mixed breed. My mixed dog is an excellent guard dog that

easily recognizes friends and family but is very protective
against strangers, even though she is not even a fraction of the
"traditional" guard dogs, like pit bulls. If you need to be certain, you could still get a purebred. However, for the same doggy
loyalty and companionship at a fraction of the price and twice
the "feel-good" quality from saving a life, the best option by far
is to acquire a rescue dog.

Works Cited

"Purebred vs. Mutt—the Pros & Cons." Best Friends Pet Care,
    Inc. 10 Oct. 2006 <http://www.bestfriendspetcare.com/pet_
    facts/purbred-mutts.cfm>.
Salk, Pia. "Pet Adoption Is the Loving Option!" Humane America
    Animal Foundation. 10 Oct. 2006 <http://www.1-800-save-
    a-pet.com/>.
Schultz, Jacque L. "Counting on You." Petfinder. 10 Oct. 2006
    <http://www.petfinder.com/journalindex.cgi?path=/public/
    adoptshelterdogmonth/1.15.20.txt>.
"Volunteer Opportunities at the SF/SPCA." San Francisco SPCA.
    10 Oct. 2006 <http://www.sfspca.org/volunteers/volunteer
    .shtml#dogwalk>.
Woolf, Norma B. "Just What Is a Puppy Mill?" Canis Major Pub-
    lications, 10 Oct. 2006 <http://www.canismajor.com/dog/
    puppymil.html>.

*This essay showcases two of the requirements of the
successful argument paper. First, it's a very small, and
manageable, topic. It's not about abortion or euthanasia
or the legalization of marijuana. It's about rescuing dogs
from a shelter. Simple. Second, it's got a very small audience, whose concerns and counterarguments the
writer can address fully. This isn't for everyone. It's not
even for animal lovers. It's for people who are looking to
buy a dog. Remember, the narrower your audiences, the
better you can know them.*

AIDS HITS HOME

JEFFERSON GOOLSBY

I got the bad news about my fifteen-year-old nephew a couple
of days after he was told the bad news himself. My brother—
his dad—was visiting us down in the valley and told the rest of
the family. It was hard to believe. My nephew seemed so young
and healthy, the star of the high school basketball team in a

small mountain community of two thousand people where everybody knew everybody. It couldn't happen to him. That's what we all said. Yet it had. The AIDS epidemic had reached this small, remote town in full force.

Was he HIV positive? Not at all. In fact, he was a virgin. But a group of well-intentioned educators from the big city decided to be "pro-active" and drove up to my nephew's town and planted the fear of HIV and AIDS in the hearts and minds of all the local school kids. They even brought along an HIV-positive gay male to bear witness to the looming devastation. AIDS had come to this town in all its horror. Not the disease—just the propaganda.

It reminded me of when I was twelve and had inflicted on me my first sex education course, though anti-sex education would have been a more suitable title. After we boys were mysteriously segregated from the girls, my flustered male teacher threaded up a peculiar filmstrip showing outline drawings of a flaccid penis. For no specific reason, animated arrows indicated that something called "semen" would flow from the "scrotum" and exit. After this meaningless film, unrelated to anything I called life, we were shown something with more impact. Two guys who worked in an auto garage were talking. One spoke of how it hurt when he "urinated." "You've got VD!" said his buddy in horror; "Venereal disease."

Sex and VD. Semen and disease. Hand in glove. Back to back. As inevitable as the turn of the seasons.

Thirty years later, the words are different but the pattern is the same. When an American child approaches the age of sexual activity, our schools enter a crisis management mode and quickly tell him or her, "If you have sex, disease will follow." It used to be that if you masturbated, you'd go mad. Now the stakes have been raised: if you have sex, you'll die. The educators told my nephew that a single sexual exposure could result in infection; there was no cure; death was almost inevitable; not even a condom could totally, absolutely, with complete certainty guarantee protection from the scourge. Run, run for your lives! By what unknown logic a sexually active gay male supported this argument was not entirely clear.

I wistfully recalled the sex education I had witnessed while living in Sweden. There, sex education begins at age five. Sex is viewed as a healthy, wonderful, natural human activity. When children reach a sexually active age, they are calmly and accurately informed of health risks. No horror shows. No foretellings of doom. No revolting videos of deformed genitals.

What sort of people would consider it rational to teach young people at almost zero risk that sex can kill them? What sort of person would take pleasure in turning sex into a thing of fear and dread? I think we know what sort of people do this, and their numbers seem to be growing.

Is the chance of dying of AIDS real? Yes, as is the chance of dying from flash floods, airplane crashes, stranger abduction, lightning, poisonous jellyfish, and esophageal obstruction. How great is the risk? For my nephew, the risk approaches zero—much less than the risk of death by lightning, inconceivably less than the risk of death by car collision. He is much more likely to die from heart disease caused by the margarine on his breakfast table. Certain, very limited groups of people living highly specific lifestyles and practicing highly specific behaviors are at risk. By all means, put the fear of god in them if you can. But nobody in my nephew's town has AIDS. Even here at our local campus, where 14,000 college students frolic, most of them with sexual abandon, every year, there has been exactly one single HIV diagnosis—ever.

But we don't tell young people that if they practice anal sex with multiple partners or share needles they are at risk. We don't tell them that 95% of HIV or AIDS patients are gay men. We tell them that every young person in the room is hanging by a thread—fall victim to your base appetites and have sex, and die. And we don't show them videos showing the horrid remains of people struck by lightning or detail the agonies of a person dying from the deadly sting of a poisonous jelly fish.

Why is this so? Because it isn't about disease or risk or protection; it's about keeping young people from having sex, by telling any lie we think might work. It's about brainwashing a young man so that when he looks across the room and sees that sweet, pretty girl sitting there, he sees images of sickness and wasting instead of, lord save us, pleasure and joy. And it's a lie. Why do we do it? Why do we do it?

> *This is an anti-cliché essay that demonstrates a lot of guts. Sex is such a difficult subject to handle that few of my students ever touch it. Jeff gets it just right—no smirking, no squirming. And what a lovely little trick opening. I'll bet you fell for it hook, line, and sinker—just like I did.*

Academic Essays

"GALAXY QUEST" AND THE USES OF LITERATURE
ANTOINE LAVIN

"Galaxy Quest," the 2001 hit science fiction movie comedy, works on many different levels. It is a parody of science fiction television, a subtle commentary on our culture of celebrity, a moving tale of personal redemption, and a complex, carefully worked out exercise in plotting. But in addition, it offers an answer to questions that English majors get asked often: "What's so important about movies and TV? Isn't it all just entertainment?"

Everybody can see that "Galaxy Quest" is affectionately teasing the TV series "Star Trek" and its annual conventions and obsessive fans. These fans know the floor plan of the USS Enterprise, both Kirk's and Picard's, by heart and argue about the home life of the lava monster in Episode #42.

It's also a study of the American worship of celebrity and the horror of being "washed up." In the story, the actors in the original TV series "Galaxy Quest" were once stars, but the series was cancelled many years ago, and now they squeeze a living out of humiliating appearances at mall openings and annual "Quest-Cons." At these depressing gatherings, they are forced to face their uselessness and has-been status again and again.

It's also a retelling of the ancient myth about discovering your best self. Jason Nesmith (played by Tim Allen, doing a hilarious take-off of William Shatner), the actor who played the captain in the original "Galaxy Quest" series, is a drunk full of self-pity when the movie begins. He is approached by an alien race called the Thermians, who have been monitoring old "Galaxy Quest" reruns from space and naively think that the transmissions are "history." The Thermians ask "Commander Taggert" (Nesmith's character's name in the old series) to lead his crew on a mission to rescue their people from the evil space villain Sarris. Thinking it is some kind of public appearance, he accepts. He is terrified when he discovers what is really going on, but he finally discovers that he can be a space captain. He does have the makings of a hero inside him.

The movie is also fun to watch just because the plot is so well put together. The best example of this is the character of Brandon, the ultimate Trekkie nerd who appears again and again throughout the movie trying to engage "Taggert" in conversations about trivial technical problems from old episodes, like exactly how the dilithium crystals were wired to the thruster tubes to re-ignite the engines in Episode #12. Brandon appears to be in the movie only to represent the Trekkie mentality, but it turns out that he has a larger role to play. The Thermians give "Taggert" a communicator. Brandon, being a good Trekkie, has his own fake communicator, which looks just the same. Taggert and Brandon collide and exchange communicators by accident. When Nesmith needs key information about the layout of the space ship in order to defeat the bad guys, Nesmith uses his communicator to call Brandon. Brandon then gets his fellow nerds together and their expert knowledge of the ship's layout saves the day.

These four reasons make the movie outstanding all by themselves. However, the movie has something more to offer.

It also teaches us something about being human and experiencing literature, and how the two are interrelated.

The Thermians tell us that in their past history they had constant wars and bloodshed. Then they began receiving the transmissions of the Galaxy Quest "history." The world of "Galaxy Quest" is full of fairness, equality, and peace, like the world of "Star Trek." There is no racism or war. The Thermians decide to model their society to be like the world of "Galaxy Quest," so they imitate everything they see, including all the sets, costumes, etc. The result is a world of perfect kindness, honesty, and brotherhood. They don't understand lying, for example. Cooperation is the norm. The Thermians also literally become human in form. They use image projection so they can appear as human to the human crewmembers.

We are invited to laugh at the Thermians and their naïve misinterpretation of TV images. However, beneath the joke lies an important theme. What the Thermians are doing is learning to be good, kind, and civilized by watching TV. They see an idealized, goody-goody image of human behavior, they embrace it as their ideal, and so they try to make the ideal come true in their own lives. They succeed completely. Everything they make while imitating the TV show works: the space ship, the beryllium sphere that powers the ship, the communicators, etc. There is no logical way this can happen, since there is no way to invent the technology, but if we see their success as a symbol for the way humans use literature, it makes sense. In the real world, the Thermians cannot really make a space ship that flies, but humans can read a book, see the image of a hero or saint, and choose to live their lives according to that model.

In fact, the human race has been doing exactly that since the beginning of history. Literature is a model humans use to inspire them to live the right kind of life. People read about (or watch) Gilgamesh or Perseus or James Bond and they say, So that is how I am supposed to live my life. Or, so that is how I am *not* supposed to live my life. Consequently, the character and his world become real, as the world of Galaxy Quest becomes real when the Thermians make it real. The world of James Bond becomes real when a generation of American males read the James Bond books or watch the movies and spend the rest of their lives trying to dress, walk, and talk like Bond.

Each of us is like the Thermians. We are lost, we don't know how to behave. We don't know how to get along with each other. We don't know what life is supposed to look like. The males don't know what it means to be male. The females don't know what it means to be female. Therefore we follow the Thermian plan. We experience literature. There we select models, and dedicate our lives to imitating them. We define ourselves as cowboys, swashbucklers, *femmes fatales*, war heroes, daring spies, damsels in distress, or faithful wives. By magic, it works. Whatever we choose, we become. The world of imagination becomes real because we will it to be real. Just like the Thermians, we project an artificial image of ourselves and live in the projection.

The power of this magic is amazing. The Thermians literally remake their world. Literature is always doing this. In England in the nineteenth century, Lord Byron wrote poems about a Satanic character called the Byronic hero, and the next few generations of literary people in England spent their lives acting the part and seeing the world as the Byronic hero saw it. In America in the Fifties and Sixties, two generations of young people devoted their lives to acting out the role of Holden Caulfield in *The Catcher in the Rye* or James Dean in "Rebel without a Cause."

Now we can answer the question we started with. What is so important about movies and TV? They are the templates we use to construct the fantasy we call our lives. We can choose any fantasy we like. The consequences of our choice are enormous. Generations of American men have paid the price for choosing as their template the Gunslinger, and generations of American women have paid the price for choosing as their template Cinderella. The Thermians chose their template wisely, so they lived in peace and harmony. What choices are you making?

> *This essay makes two interesting and very worthwhile assumptions: (1) that popular art (movies, TV) is complex, artful, and deserving of serious examination; and (2) that literary criticism is about big, important things. Antoine goes far beyond the typical student pose of "I'm saying these things about this movie to be saying these things about this movie." He has something very important to tell us about how we live our lives. That movement from the specific subject (the movie) to large life issues is at the heart of most good academic work.*

SOME ALTERNATIVES TO BURNING RICE STRAW

JAIME RAYNOR

In California a controversy has raged for years over whether or not to allow rice farmers to burn the straw left over after harvest. The California Air Resources Board and most California citizens don't want the farmers to burn, because burning pollutes the air and makes many residents of agricultural areas suffer from allergies. The farmers argue that they must burn because burning is cheap and gets rid of molds and diseases that wreak havoc on the rice crop.

The State Government is currently trying to find a solution to the problem. At present their only solution is to compromise and let the farmers burn a fraction of their straw but not all. This is only a temporary solution. If farmers are allowed to burn only 20% or 25% of their fields, they are still polluting the air and people are still getting sick. A satisfactory, long-term solution is still being sought. Senate Bill 318, which regulates the amount of rice straw that can be burned, mandated a committee to explore the different ways to put rice straw to use or get rid of it in ways that don't involve burning.

At first glance, burning can appear both necessary and justifiable. Rice crops are highly susceptible to diseases, and even large amounts of pesticides have been found ineffective in controlling them (Why Par. 2). And rice burning is hardly the only culprit in California's pollution problem. When interviewed, rice farmer Lyle Job argued, "I don't understand why the government wants to restrict us when all the agricultural burning—wheat, corn, oats, and others, not just rice—is only 2% of all the pollution in the air. Cars pollute the air more than agriculture does, and the government doesn't tell drivers they can only drive their car 10,000 miles a year."

Despite these arguments, there are presently several methods in place which provide workable alternatives to rice burning. Many of these methods have been used by enlightened rice farmers for years with success, while others are very new.

Lundberg Family Farms in Richvale, California, has been growing organic rice using non-polluting technology for years. Most simply, Wendell Lundberg explained in a personal interview, when a rice field gets diseased Lundberg's simply lets the field go unplanted for a year. Another alternative is to rotate crops. That way when a field becomes infected, a crop can be grown that isn't susceptible to the disease for a year.

Rice stubble can also be worked back into the soil instead of burned. The Lundbergs crush the stubble with huge rubber rollers, then work the stubble into the soil with a chisel (Straw Par. 4). All these procedures cost more than conventional burning, and many farmers are therefore resistant to them, but they work and the gains to our health and air are worth the cost.

Ecologically friendly ways of handling rice stubble have other benefits. The Lundbergs flood their fields after working the straw into the ground. This gives migrating birds such as geese, ducks, and swans a place to rest in mid-migration. It also benefits hunters in the area, because the time when the fields are flooded is around the same time when hunters are getting ready for duck and pheasant season. The flocks of birds actually help decompose the straw by trampling it (Straw Par. 4), while their excrement provides "natural fertilization" for the crops, which the Lundbergs call "vital to the soil building program" (Soil Par. 4).

Traditional farmers who embrace these new methods are going to have to adopt a larger view of the agricultural cycle. The Lundbergs explain, "Most farmers consider the soil to be merely an anchor for the plant's roots, and treat it as a sterile medium in which they attempt to control growth, weeds, insects, and diseases with chemicals and burning" (Soil Par. 1). The Lundbergs view the soil as a living organism (Soil Par. 1). For instance, they plant nitrogen-fixing legumes as a cover crop during the winter after the rice season is over (Soil Par. 2). The nitrogen from the legumes helps grow better rice without the Lundbergs having to resort to polluting chemical additives.

If farmers don't want to go to the expense of plowing rice straw into the ground or letting fields lie fallow for a year, there are other ways to avoid burning. First, straw can be bailed like hay and used as a construction material. Second-generation rice farmer Rick Green is using baled rice straw to build houses (Sirard IB3). Green explains his methods in this way:

> The straw is set upon a concrete base, placing it out of contact with the ground and moisture, its worst enemy. Once the straw is stacked two bales high, a metal plate is placed across the top to cinch down the bales. At eight feet, stucco is poured over the project, making it look like an adobe wall.

The resulting walls are fifteen inches thick and have an astounding insulation rating of R-53, according to Green: "When it's 105 degrees outside, the inside of the house is about 70 degrees," he says (all Sirard IB3).

Building houses out of rice bales is currently still more expensive than using lumber, but only because we pretty much give the lumber companies our forests for free. Since rice straw is almost limitless in supply, a waste product, and annually renewable, doesn't it make more sense to use it and save the trees we have left?

Another way to market rice stubble is to bury people in it. Hard as it may be to believe, Will Maetens has begun selling rice straw coffins (Gabrukiewicz B3). A six-foot, eight-inch coffin of compressed rice straw costs only $375, compared to conventional coffins, which run anywhere from $2,000 up. This is a great idea for those who are not so well off, who want to be buried in a more natural way, or who like the idea of becoming one with the earth.

A third way of marketing rice stubble is to turn it into fuel. The city of Gridley in Northern California recently secured a letter of intent from BC International of Boston to construct a plant in their town, at a cost of $60 million, for the conversion of rice straw to ethanol (Gonzales E1). This may prove to be the best solution to the burning problem so far. If it works, it will not only solve the problems associated with rice burning, but will also help solve our energy problem and create needed jobs in economically depressed rural areas.

With all these alternatives to burning, and more on the way, it seems that burning is unnecessary. The alternatives may cost a little more now, but as industries like rice home building and ethanol become established, that should change. And even if it doesn't, the benefits of these alternatives are so many and so great, for the farmers and the community, that I feel the time has come for rice farmers to give up their old ways and turn away from burning.

Works Cited

Gabrukiewicz, Thom. "Businessman's Rice Straw Coffins Designed for Ecologically Correct." *Sacramento Bee* 8 Dec. 1997: B3.

Gonzales, Anne. "Pesky Rice Straw Could Fuel New Business for Gridley." *Sacramento Bee* 28 Sept. 1997: E1.

Job, Lyle. Personal interview. 1 Nov. 1998.

Lundberg, Wendell. Personal interview. 31 Oct. 1998.

Sirard, Jack. "Rice Farmer Constructs Walls of Waste." *Sacramento Bee* 22 June 1998: IB3.

"Soil Enrichment." *Lundberg Family Partnership with Nature.* 1 Dec. 1998 <http://www.lundberg.com/partnership/soil.html>.

"Straw Incorporation." *Lundberg Family Partnership with Nature.* 19 Oct. 1998 <http://www.lundberg.com/partnership/straw.html>.

"Why Burn Rice Straw?" *Rice Disease: How an Old Flame Burns Them Out and Protects Our Crop.* 17 Oct. 1998 <http://riceproducers.com/whyburn.html>.

This essay has a fine sense of its own importance. Jaime is saying, "I'm not writing this just to fulfill an assignment. Hey, people are choking to death out there on that smoke, and there are lots of things we can do about it!" It's also about an issue close to home—Jaime and his readers are actually breathing that stuff.

JACK KEROUAC: ON THE ROAD AND OTHERWISE

LAURA KATE JAMES

> *And before me was the great raw bulge and bulk of my American continent; somewhere far across, gloomy, crazy New York was throwing up its cloud of dust and brown steam. There is something brown and holy about the East; and California is white like the wash lines and emptyheaded—at least that's what I thought then. (Kerouac 89)*

Jack Kerouac was born in 1922 in Massachusetts. Mother, father, sister—brother died young. Grew up, went to school. To Columbia, Columbia to play football, they paid him too. A year or so of college, went mad, dropped out, joined the Merchant Marine then the Navy. Then back to New York to write for a spell. And then to the road, the holy open road, and our story begins.

Da Beats: According to Jack Kerouac

> *The only people for me are the mad ones, the ones who are mad to live, mad to talk, mad to be saved, desirous of everything at the same time, the ones who never yawn or say a commonplace thing, but burn, burn, burn like fabulous yellow roman candles. . . . (Kerouac 8)*

Such were the Beats, these "mad ones," writing and speaking and singing, taking root in the foreign soil of the American-post-war continent. After the bomb was dropped, the US dove into a period of paranoid conformity, influenced by McCarthy and the like. Quiet submission and support of their government was demanded of the American people, along with a Cleaver-esque lifestyle and attitude; toe the line for God and Country, they were told. Feared were the free thinkers, the creative ones, speaking out and doing what they pleased. This counterculture, this bohemia that never yawned, sprouted and grew up like weeds among the roses of American ideals (Martinez 68). And they called it a Beat Generation.

Kerouac, a "key figure" in planting these seeds, coined the phrase "Beat," meaning "beaten-down" and "beatific," both miserable and holy (Zott 63). This new genre, mindset and breed were manifested in Kerouac, Ginsberg, Burroughs, Huncke, and Homes—poet saints—and a few other madmen who sought freedom from conformity and mainstream literary molds through their spontaneous and chaotic prose (Sterritt 7). With each turn of the pen they moved further and further away from the demands of the 1950s society and led thousands into the new lands they were discovering. Their writings and interactions were water to the sleeping seeds and called the weary ones to life.

Men and the Music

> *I got sick and tired of the conventional English sentence which seemed to me to be so ironbound in its rules, so inadmissible with reference to the actual format of my mind as I learned to probe it in the modern spirit of Freud and Jung, that I couldn't express myself through that form any more. . . . —Jack Kerouac (Weinreich 2)*

Jack Kerouac lived a full rich narrative that was punctuated by three things: two friends and a trumpet—each having significant pulls on the direction of his writing. Sticking close to Allen Ginsberg and Neal Cassady and living on a steady diet of bop jazz and booze, Kerouac channeled his surroundings through his pen and out of it filtered his own unique style and beat. His muses:

Allen Ginsberg

Ginsberg, a pillar of Beat Literature, served Jack as Loyal Friend, Critic, and Fellow Beat, one who helped first give shape to the genre that Kerouac fit into. In 1956 Ginsberg published his "revolutionary" poem *Howl*, a highly controversial political and social statement that was brought under intense legal fire soon after publishing (Munger). It was the solitary rain cloud in the scorching political/social climate that gave shade and water to Kerouac's work, allowing it to dig down its roots and grow up into the defining oak that it was destined to become (Zott 64). Together, Jack and Allen's symbiotic writings created a niche in the literary environment, goading each other on, refining their talents and styles in a tireless game of bigger and better.

Neal Cassady

Cassady served as Divine Inspiration and Hero (Dean Moriarty) of Kerouac's novel *On The Road*. A madman who published hardly a thing—famous for personality rather than talent (though he was talented)—Neal Cassady was Kerouac's golden god, a "street cowboy" that Jack was bent to emulate and capture in words, a friend he chased across the map (Sher).

Kerouac says of their meeting, "with the coming of Dean Moriarty began the part of my life you could call my life on the road" (Kerouac 3). Their correspondences put Kerouac on the path toward his spontaneous narrative prose, inspired and encouraged by Cassady to venture from his Thomas Wolfe influences and blaze his own trail across the English plains (Weinreich 18). Without Neal Cassady the history of the world would be dramatically altered: (a) Dean Moriarty wouldn't exist, (b) Kerouac's novel wouldn't exist, (c) the road itself might disappear, (d) Jack would still be a slave to proper verb usage and such grammar things, and (e) "Further" would be left without a driver in 1964.

Jazz

> [He] hopped and monkeydanced with his magic horn and blew two hundred choruses of blues, each one more frantic than the other, and no signs of failing energy or willingness to call anything a day. The whole room shivered. (Kerouac 202)

In the '40s, Kerouac and his posse witnessed and worshiped a new wave of jazz—musicians like Miles Davis, Charlie Parker, Dizzy Gillepsie and Slim Giallard shook the genre with their quivering horns and unpredictable beats—the birth of bebop; they went mad for it (Sterritt 51). Mused by the improvised harmonies and extempore of bop music, Kerouac developed his own style that reflected its creative spontaneity. His goal was to reproduce in words the tenor man's blow of a sax, exhaling sentences until he said what he wanted and emptied his lungs, period (inhale), then blow again—he called it "breath separations of the mind" (Swartz 10). The most illustrative *On the Road* passages are those that recount Sal and Dean's endless nights in jazz joints, dancing and digging the tenor man blowing on the bandstand, "shaking and swaying," lungs pulling from the bottom of his feet, vibrating the low notes "Mu-u-u-u-sic pla-a-a-ay!" into the microphone so all the glasses jumped and bounced in the booths, ice rattling (Kerouac 198–199). Bop became a drug to Kerouac, it affected and hypnotized him. Each yawp of those magic horns pulled and tugged at the spirit of his writing.

On The Road

> "You boys going to get somewhere, or just going?" We didn't understand his question, and it was a damned good question. (Kerouac 22)

Jack Kerouac wrote his legendary *On the Road* in three weeks, or so he told Steve Allen. He was determined to keep his novel true, sure that his spontaneous writing would produce the purest upheaval of his soul, so was his habit of writing in one sitting on long rolls of teletype paper his thoughts uninterrupted by the ending of a page ("Kerouac," *The Steve Allen Show*).

Sur la Route or *On the Road*, as essential as it was, had mixed reviews to say the least. A novel published in 1957 about a nomadic young man abandoning traditional American life for the road, chasing after madmen, engaging in all sorts of drunken squalor and tea-smoking good times, was rejected by middle-class Stepford America, seen as "objectionable." People held up the book, pointed to the cover and said, "Here is proof that today's youth is going straight to hell" (Zott 64). It was embraced by others as a "major" work of the times, by the generation that named Kerouac its "avatar." *They* held up the book, pointed to the cover and said, "Here is the holy word, here is *it*, this is what I live by" (Millstein).

On the Road gave voice to the weary masses, the social deviants, Kafka's cockroaches; it—in its 310 pages—captured the creed of a million American madmen. Of this, Kerouac said to the *New York Journal*, "It is not my fault that certain so-called bohemian elements have found in my writings something to hang their peculiar beatnik theories on" ("32479"). The purpose of *On the Road* was to record Jack's glorious life on the road, his quest for meaning and all those who were a part of it. But it grew far beyond its original goals into the social statement of the decade, it was a damn good hook to hang those hippie hats on.

Kerouac died young in an alcoholic pit of squalor. At the end of his life he left over twenty books recounting his holy quests, but no evidence that he ever really found what he was looking for.

Works Cited

"32479. Kerouac, Jack." *Columbia World of Quotations.* New York: Columbia University Press, 1996. 9 Nov. 2006 <www.bartleby.com/66/79/32479.html>.

"Kerouac." *The Steve Allen Show 1959.* YouTube.com. 11 Nov. 2006 <http://youtube.com/watch?v=kQZ9Lv5pwwk>.

Kerouac, Jack. *On the Road.* Cutchogue, N.Y.: Buccaneer Books, 1975.

Martinez, Manuel Luis. *Countering the Counter Culture: Rereading Postwar American Dissent from Jack Kerouac to Tómas Rivera.* Madison: University of Wisconsin Press, 2003.

Millstein, Gilbert. "Books of the Times." *New York Times* 5 Sept. 1957. *New York Times on the Web* 8 Nov. 2006 <http://partners.nytimes.com/books/97/09/07/home/ kerouac-roadglowing.html>.

Munger, Kel. "The Beat Goes On." *Chico News and Review*. Chico, Calif.: Chico Community Publishing, 2006. 16 Nov. 2006 <http://www.newsreview.com/chico/Content?oid= oid%3A246393>.

Sher, Levi A. "Jack Kerouac." *LitKicks: Jack Kerouac*. 19 Sept. 2002. 3 Nov. 2006 <http://www.litkicks.com/BeatPages/ page.jsp?what=JackKerouac>.

Sterritt, David. *Mad to Be Saved: The Beats, the 50's, and Film*. Carbondale: Southern Illinois University Press, 1989.

Swartz, Omar. *A View from* On the Road: *The Rhetorical Vision of Jack Kerouac*. Carbondale: Southern Illinois University Press, 1999.

Weinreich, Regina. *The Spontaneous Poetic of Jack Kerouac: A Study of the Fiction*. Carbondale: Southern Illinois University Press, 1987.

Zott, Lynn M., ed. *The Beat Generation: A Gale Critical Companion*. Detroit: Gale, 2003.

Suggested Reading

Amran, David. *Offbeat: Collaborating with Kerouac*. New York: Thunder's Mouth Press, 2002.

Foster, Edward Halsey. *Understanding the Beats*. Columbia: University of South Carolina Press, 1992.

Holton, Robert. On the Road: *Kerouac's Ragged American Journey*. New York: Twayne Publishers, 1999.

"Kerouac's On the Road." *NPR: Present at the Creation*. National Public Radio. 9 Sept. 2002. 8 Nov. 2006 <http://www.npr .org/programs/morning/features/patc/ontheroad/>.

Theado, Matt. *Understanding Jack Kerouac*. Columbia: University of South Carolina Press, 2000.

Watson, Steve. *The Birth of the Beat Generation: Visionaries, Rebels, and Hipsters, 1944–1960*. New York: Pantheon Books/Random House, 1995.

What I really like about this piece is how it's written in the spirit of her subject. That is, it's about writers who broke rules, forged new ways of using the English language. Lived their lives that way. So Laura Kate breaks rules herself—look at those sentence fragments—and in so doing underscores the points she's making. The result is a kind of nonacademic academic essay. A very successful one.

Five Essays on Food

*People have been writing about food for as long as they have
been writing about love and war. Records from ancient
China, Egypt, and Rome all include observations and trea-
tises on diet—on planting, hunting, harvesting, food preparation, and even specific recipes and etiquette suggestions—and
of course on food-and-drink "pairing," to use a modern term.
It's a fascinating way to look at our past and who we are as
human beings. (For an anthology of centuries of food writing,
see Mark Kurlansky's* Prime Cuts, Ballantine Books.*)*

*Currently, food writing is enjoying a sort of renaissance,
with a proliferation not only of cookbooks but of food-related
memoirs and essay collections. I'm concluding* The Writer's
Way *with five pieces of food writing that I think you'll enjoy
and that I hope will inspire you (1) to realize that there are
topics for essays all around us; (2) to write better and more
passionately yourself; and (3) to try to fully appreciate even
the smallest fine moments of your own life.*

M.F.K. FISHER ON BACHELOR COOKING

B is for Bachelors . . . and the wonderful dinners they pull out of
their cupboards with such dining-room aplomb and kitchen chaos.

Their approach to gastronomy is basically sexual, since few
of them under seventy-nine will bother to produce a good meal
unless it is for a pretty woman. Few of them at any age will
consciously ponder on the aphrodisiac qualities of the dishes
they serve forth, but subconsciously they use what tricks they
have to make their little banquets, whether intimate or merely
convivial, lead as subtly as possible to the hoped-for bedding
down.

Soft lights, plenty of tipples (from champagne to straight
rye), and if possible a little music, are the timeworn props in
any such entertainment, on no matter what financial level the
host is operating. Some men head for the back booth at the corner pub and play the juke-box, with overtones of medium-rare
steak and French-fried potatoes. Others are forced to fall back
on the soft-footed alcoholic ministrations of a Filipino house-
boy, muted Stan Kenton on the super-Capehart, and a little sup-
per beginning with caviar malossol on ice and ending with a
soufflé au kirschwasser d'Alsace.

The bachelors I'm considering at this moment are at neither
end of the gastronomical scale. They are the men between twenty-
five and fifty who if they have been married are temporarily out

of it and are therefore triply conscious of both their heaven-sent freedom and their domestic clumsiness. They are in the middle brackets, financially if not emotionally. They have been around and know the niceties or amenities or whatever they choose to call the tricks of a well-set table and a well-poured glass, and yet they have neither the tastes nor the pocketbooks to indulge in signing endless chits at Mike Romanoff's or "21."

In other words, they like to give a little dinner now and again in the far from circumspect intimacy of their apartments, which more often than not consist of a studio-living-room with either a disguised let-down bed or a tiny bedroom, a bath, and a stuffy closet called the kitchen.

I have eaten many meals prepared and served in such surroundings. I am perhaps fortunate to be able to say that I have always enjoyed them—and perhaps even more fortunate to be able to say that I enjoyed them because of my acquired knowledge of the basic rules of seduction. I assumed that I had been invited for either a direct or an indirect approach. I judged as best I could which one was being contemplated, let my host know of my own foreknowledge, and then sat back to have as much pleasure as possible.

I almost always found that since my host knew I was aware of the situation, he was more relaxed and philosophical about its very improbable outcome and could listen to the phonograph records and savor his cautiously concocted Martini with more inner calm. And I almost always ate and drank well, finding that any man who knows that a woman will behave in her cups, whether of consommé double or of double Scotch, is resigned happily to a good dinner; in fact, given the choice between it and a rousing tumble in the hay, he will inevitably choose the first, being convinced that the latter can perforce be found elsewhere.

The drinks offered to me were easy ones, dictated by my statements made early in the game (I never bothered to hint but always said plainly, in self-protection, that I liked very dry Gibsons with good ale to follow, or dry sherry with good wine: safe but happy, that was my motto). I was given some beautiful liquids: really old Scotch, Swiss Dézelay light as mountain water, proud vintage Burgundies, countless bottles of champagne, all good too, and what fine cognacs! Only once did a professional bachelor ever offer me a glass of sweet liqueur. I never saw him again, feeling that his perceptions were too dull for me to exhaust myself, if after even the short time needed to win my acceptance of his dinner invitation he had not guessed my tastes that far.

The dishes I have eaten at such tables-for-two range from home-grown snails in home-made butter to pompano flown in

from the Gulf of Mexico with slivered macadamias from Maui—
or is it Oahu? I have found that most bachelors like the exotic,
at least culinarily speaking: they would rather fuss around with
a complex recipe for Le Hochepot de Queue de Boeuf than with
a simple one called Stewed Ox-tail, even if both come from
André Simon's *Concise Encyclopœdia of Gastronomy*.

They are snobs in that they prefer to keep Escoffier on the
front of the shelf and hide Mrs. Kander's *Settlement Cook Book*.

They are experts at the casual; they may quit the office
early and make a murderous sacrifice of pay, but when you arrive the apartment is pleasantly odorous, glasses and a perfectly
frosted shaker or a bottle await you. Your host looks not even
faintly harried or stove-bound. His upper lip is unbedewed and
his eye is flatteringly wolfish.

Tact and honest common sense forbid any woman's pen-
etrating with mistaken kindliness into the kitchen: motherli-
ness is unthinkable in such a situation, and romance would
wither on the culinary threshold and be buried forever beneath
its confusion of used pots and spoons.

Instead the time has come for ancient and always interesting blandishments, of course in proper proportions. The
Bachelor Spirit unfolds like a hungry sea anemone. The possible object of his affections feels cozily desired. The drink is good.
He pops discreetly in and out of his gastronomical workshop,
where he brews his sly receipts, his digestive attacks upon the
fortress of her virtue. She represses her natural curiosity, and if
she is at all experienced in such wars she knows fairly well that
she will have a patterned meal which has already been indicated
by his ordering in restaurants. More often than not it will be
some kind of chicken, elaborately disguised with everything
from Australian pine-nuts to herbs grown by the landlady's
daughter.

One highly expert bachelor-cook in my immediate circle
swears by a recipe for breasts of young chicken, poached that
morning or the night before, and covered with a dramatic and
very lemony sauce made at the last minute in a chafing dish.
This combines all the tricks of seeming nonchalance, carefully
casual presentation, and attention-getting.

With it he serves chilled asparagus tips in his own version
of vinaigrette sauce and little hot rolls. For dessert he has what
is also his own version of riz à l'Impératrice, which he is convinced all women love because he himself secretly dotes on it—
and it can be made the day before, thought not too successfully.

This meal lends itself almost treacherously to the wiles of
alcohol: anything from a light lager to a Moët et Chandon of a
great year is beautiful with it, and can be well bolstered with

the preprandial drinks which any bachelor doles out with at least one ear on the Shakespearean dictum that they may double desire and halve the pursuit thereof.

The most successful bachelor dinner I was ever plied with, or perhaps it would be more genteel to say served, was also thoroughly horrible.

Everything was carried out, as well as in, by a real expert, a man then married for the fifth time who had interspersed his connubial adventures with rich periods of technical celibacy. The cocktails were delicately suited to my own tastes rather than his, and I sipped a glass of Tio Pepe, properly chilled. The table, set in a candle-lit patio, was laid in the best sense of the word "nicely," with silver and china and Swedish glass which I had long admired. The wine was a last bottle of Chianti, " 'stra vecchio."

We ate thin strips of veal that had been dipped in an artful mixture of grated parmigiano and crumbs, with one of the bachelor's favorite tricks to accompany it, buttered thin noodles gratinés with extra-thin and almond-brown toasted noodles on top. There was a green salad.

The night was full of stars, and so seemed my eager host's brown eyes, and the whole thing was ghastly for two reasons: he had forgotten to take the weather into his menu planning, so that we were faced with a rich, hot, basically heavy meal on one of the worst summer nights in local history, and I was at the queasiest possible moment of pregnancy.

Of course the main mistake was in his trying to entertain a woman in that condition as if she were still seduceable and/or he still a bachelor: we had already been married several months.

—from *An Alphabet for Gourmets,* 1949

PASTS AND REPASTS: A MEDITATION

HENRI BOURRIDE

The preparation and distribution of food necessarily brought the whole family together, the fathers apportioning to their children the results of the hunt, and the grown children then doing the same to their aged parents. These gatherings . . . were little by little extended to include neighbors and friends. Later, when the human race had spread out, the tired traveler came to join in such feasts, and to recount what went on in the far countries of the world. Thus was born hospitality, with its rights sacred to all peoples, for one of the strongest

laws is that which commands respect for the life of any
man with whom one has shared bread and salt.
                              (Jean Anthelme Brillat-Savarin)

Bread and salt. Two ancient commodities, and two words that take us from the dining table into our distant past. Salt, from the Latin "salarium," a Roman soldier's "salt allowance," or "salary." And bread . . . which too will take us back to Rome, and to our words "companion" and "company": In Roman times, a *companio* was one with whom you broke bread—or *pan*.

Henri's been thinking about company lately. While on one hand it's time for scarves, great coats and long, ruminative afternoon walks along windswept avenues, it's also time to start thinking about the holidays. Stews simmering on stoves and turkeys and prime ribs roasting in ovens. Champagne chilling in refrigerators. Dinner parties, feasts, merriment. Tables set for eight, ten, even twelve. And, of course, good drink.

Jean Anthelme Brillat-Savarin, the father of food writing, was a French lawyer interested in archaeology, astronomy, chemistry, and gastronomy. He published his classic book, *Physiology of Taste, or, Meditations on Transcendental Gastronomy*, in December of 1825, two months before he died. The book has never been out of print. In 1949, it was translated into English by America's greatest food writer, M.F.K. Fisher. Anyone interested in philosophy, history, poetry, dreams, aging, Jesuits, eels, marriage, fasting, drinking, Latin, gluttony, music, oysters, fondue, or the "erotic properties of truffles" would be well advised to pick up a copy.

Aphoristic in nature—in fact, the first chapter is titled "Aphorisms of the Professor"—Brillat-Savarin's book manages to argue both that we take the subject of food far too seriously and at the same don't take the subject seriously enough. The book is wildly funny—at a New York restaurant Brillat-Savarin, visiting from France, drinks with two Englishmen, one of whom, passed out at the table, comes around long enough to attempt to belt out "Rule Britannia" before passing out again and then being taken to the door, along with his equally inebriated companion, "feet foremost."

Yet the book also reminds us how difficult it is to distinguish among the different kinds of nourishment we need to carry on the intricately complex relationships we have with each other, with eating and food, and with ourselves. Food, love, sex. Who hasn't substituted one for the other? As Brillat-Savarin writes, "Taste is the sense which puts us in contact with savorous or sapid bodies, by means of the sensation which they cause in the organ destined to appreciate them. . . . [I]n eating, we experience a certain special and indefinable well-being, which arises from our realization that by the very act we perform we are repairing our bodily losses and prolonging our lives."

Dinner parties—with friends, companions, parties that continue with drink and conversation long into the night—give us the opportunity to confirm our connections, however tenuous, to each other, and to better understand our places among the earth's other creatures—animal and vegetable—which, Brillat-Savarin reminds us, supply the bounty of our tables.

Last Sunday I set two extra places at my own table. Napkins in napkin rings, place tags, dinner and salad plates, silverware, water tumblers, wine glasses. When I sat down, alone, I raised my glass in toast: to H. and G., so far away and still so close, and to my many companions, in the far countries of the world and from the strange course my life has taken. Then I took a long drink of Bordeaux, and broke a baguette in thirds.

"The pleasures of the table are for every man," Brillat-Savarin wrote nearly two centuries ago. "[T]hey can be a part of all our other pleasures and they last the longest, to console us when we have outlived the rest."

ON THE ROAD TO MOROCCO

CHRISTOPHER KIMBALL

Many of our family vacations are best remembered through a glass darkly, years after the fact, when the family album fails to remind us of the moments best forgotten. But every once in a while, one of our family vacations actually bears fruit—the sweet variety, not an unripe tropical specimen. In March, we flung caution to the wind and decided to trek through the Sahara Desert in Morocco, near the Algerian border. Three planes and 24 hours after leaving Boston, we ended up in the streets of Marrakech, trailing the donkey cart that held our luggage through the narrow streets of the old city on the way to our *riad*, a small hotel that was once a private home.

I am not one to tour palaces and other architectural monuments—just give me something good (and unusual) to eat. This, of course, is no mean feat when you are traveling with young children and local guides who prefer to steer their clients to the most European eateries. (Yes, you can order spaghetti Bolognese and pizza in a tourist café fronting the major plaza in the old city.) But Marrakech did eventually come through in the food department. Fresh-squeezed local oranges; yogurt lightly sweetened with rose water; the local flatbreads; coconut cookies; lamb tagine with fresh almonds; skewers of ground, spiced lamb; and *pastilla*, a thick pancake-style pastry filled with ground meat, spices, and nuts.

The next day we piled into two Land Rovers and headed southeast, through the High Atlas and down toward Ouarzazate. By the afternoon, we had left the paved road behind and were on a track that wound around old mud and wattle towns built into the sides of bleak mountains, with serpentine river valleys, lush and green, below. (Locals take the bus to the end of the line, where they switch to donkeys. The animals are arranged in a stand much like taxis.) The day is a confused memory of fiercely handsome Berber children, goatherds and shepherds, and donkeys fitted out with metal "roof racks" that let them transport huge loads of forage.

The next day, at the tail end of sunset, we finally made our way into the desert and to our campsite. El Hussein, the sprightly 72-year-old camel driver, was waiting (he had walked three days to meet us) along with his four camels. (As warm-blooded creatures go, by the way, camels are quite intelligent. They drool rather than spit, their legs fold up like lawn chairs when they sit, they enjoy a good rub behind the ears, and their huge feet spread out like yeast dough as they plop them on the sand.) The next morning, after a breakfast of flatbread, oranges, and coffee, we set out over the dunes, mostly walking, with rest periods taken on camelback.

The desert is not just a sandbox. The landscape varies wildly from the classic dunes of *Lawrence of Arabia* to towering black mountains, parched white lakebeds, scrub, thousands of small white and blue flowers (which, owing to my inaccurate translation of our guide's conversational French, I erroneously call "Monkey's Onion"), and seas of rock and thorn. Far on a mountainside, we see dozens of goats grazing and a goatherd standing still in a dark *djellaba* (robe) on top of a ridge. Two young boys cross our path in the middle of nowhere and stop to chat. We come across an abandoned Berber beehive oven used to make bread. (The bread is cooked over coals on top of a perforated metal shelf.)

That evening, I sit on the top of the largest dune near our campsite and watch the sun dissolve into a far haze. On the next peak, a man is kneeling and praying to Allah. A small village is visible off to the east, toward Algeria. I count 17 hand-sketched trees in and around the swirl of dunes. I can hear the murmur of the local Berber dialect spoken by the cook, Hussein, and our guide, Muhammed, punctuated by exuberant expressions of "Inshallah." An hour passes, the sun is ebbing, and I sense that I am sitting above a vast pool of time, as if the days and weeks have fled the rest of the world, swirling to a stop on this flat sun-drenched landscape where there are no shadows. I was told that the Berbers are still a nomadic people. How else does one live in this timeless landscape?

And then, on the third day, it happens. The simple, well-prepared food. The loose robes and headdresses. The hours of walking and storytelling. The front-and-back rhythm of the camels. The hot, sweet mint tea. The intense flavor of a cool, sliced orange after lunch. There is so little here that each thing becomes important. Each gesture, each bite of food, and each sip of water matters. A fig, a date, a handful of nuts . . . we learn to enjoy the small things.

We make our way to Fez, a city more cosmopolitan than Marrakech. We spend a day walking the bazaar and discover live snails, a camel's head, brightly colored vats of soap, dyed silk, fruit, mint, fish, live poultry, leather goods, brass and copper pots, sweets, street food, hole-in-the-wall bakeries . . . the senses are overwhelmed. We depart before sunrise, hefting duffel bags through dark, narrow streets. I leave with the taste of perfumed oranges, rose water, mint, almonds, saffron, preserved lemon, cinnamon, cumin, and coconut still lively on the tongue. But it's the vast, unfiltered memory of the desert that beckons, as if I were leaving home for a foreign land. The sun is rising, but, in my mind's eye, it is sinking, there is a call to prayer, men in hooded djellabas face Mecca, and there is finally time to consider every grain of sand.

COOKING MY WAY TO MEXICAN

CAROLYNN CARREÑO

On New Year's Day of what would be the last year of his life, I visited my dad in his house overlooking the river valley in Tijuana, Mexico. His fourth wife, Grace, was reheating some of the turkey and *mole* left over from a party they'd had the night before, and casually asked me if I knew how to make *mole*. I laughed at the very idea of my being able to whip up the famously complex sauce of chocolate, chiles, and about 30 other ingredients. "Shame on you!" she said to my dad. "Every Mexican girl should be taught to make *mole*." She called me over to the stove for my first Mexican cooking lesson and it was then, as I toasted sesame seeds in a dry skillet with Grace coaching me over my shoulder and my father sitting at the kitchen table behind us, that I first understood that I might find the key to my Mexicanness here, in the kitchen.

All my life, you see, I had felt like a phony Mexican—a cultural amputee, feeling around for a part of me that wasn't there. I was born in Tijuana, but when I was three my Mexican father and American mother divorced. I moved to San Diego with my mother and sister, where I traded in my Spanish for English, changed my name from Carolina to Carolynn, and passed as an all-American kid. Growing up, when teachers and classmates asked about my last name, I'd drop the "I'm half Mexican" for the shock value. People naturally found it hard to believe that this freekle-faced girl with her strawberry-blond hair in Pippi Longstocking braids could possibly be Mexican. But nobody found it harder than I did.

When I got older and began to appreciate what it meant to be from another culture, though, I began to want Mexico for myself. I took Mexican history classes in college and spent a summer studying Spanish in Guadalajara. I spent more time with my dad and the two children he had with Grace. But all that these efforts accomplished was to make me feel like even more of an outsider. I'd never be a real Mexican-American girl, a girl who was American out in the world but came home to a loving *abuelita* stirring a pot of beans on the back burner; who drifted effortlessly back and forth between Spanish and English and joined a three-generation assembly line to make tamales at Christmas. A girl like that would feel, deep down, what it meant to be Mexican.

As curious as I was about the whole Mexican thing, though, I had never pursued the relatives I supposedly had in Mexico City. So it was a surprise when, some years after the *mole*-making experience, when I had moved from California to New York, I came home to my Greenwich Village apartment to find a message in a strong Mexican accent on my answering machine. The voice identified itself as José Carreño and claimed to be my uncle. Would I like to meet him? After a few awkward phone conversations, José came to the city and took me out to dinner.

"You must go to Mexico City," he told me. Then, perhaps sensing this would seal the deal, he added, "My mother is a wonderful cook." He spoke of her specialties—toasted corn tortillas dipped into a rich black-bean sauce and drizzled with creamy white cheese; and *tinga*, a shredded-meat dish so delicious that the mere mention of it made him homesick.

"Do you think your mother would teach me how to cook these things?" I asked, feeling that having a project might make plopping myself down in a house full of total strangers—even if they were, technically speaking, family—less intimidating.

"I don't see why not."

Three months later, I was standing in front of a high metal gate in the southern quarter of one of the world's most populous cities. I rang the bell and out burst three exuberant women—my aunts—plus a short, sturdy, older woman in an apron with her cropped gray hair combed back. This, it turned out, was Josefina, José's mother. She led me straight inside, where my aunts, talking in Spanish all at the same time, sat me down and started bringing out bowls and platters heaped with food: rice, guacamole, soup, tortillas, grilled meats, a cactus salad.

Early the next morning I found Josefina, as I would every morning, in her galleylike kitchen, puttering from the stove to the refrigerator to the *licuadora* (blender) and back to the stove in a sort of moving meditation. She prepared breakfast for me and the four children and two grandchildren who live with her, then started straight in, showing me how to make real Mexican guacamole. No tomato, no cilantro, no lime juice, no fancy knife skills—just a very ripe avocado, a little onion, and some salt all smashed together in a *molcajete*.

For the next five weeks, Josefina explained and demonstrated and patiently answered my stream of questions. She first showed me, then let me finish the job at hand so I'd know how to do it by myself. I first tore and toasted various kinds of dried chiles. Standing close beside me at the stove, she didn't seem worried that I would overcook them until, suddenly, she whisked the comal from my hands and off the heat a split second before the chiles burned.

A foot shorter than me, Josefina had to reach up to the pot to stir or to bring the wooden spoon to her mouth so she could check the seasoning. She was so confident in her knowledge of how things should taste that she reached for whatever was missing—salt, vinegar, or another pinch of chile—without apparently giving it a thought. I, meanwhile, stood by her side, clumsily peeling one poblano pepper for every four of hers, notebook and pen at the ready as I insisted on attaching measures and reason to the things she did so perfectly by instinct.

"Wait, Josefina. Why are we adding more oil?" I asked.

"Because it needs it."

"But how do you know?"

Josefina smiled sweetly, paused to think, then explained, "If you don't see *ojitos* [little eyes] of oil on top of the dish, it needs more."

By the end of my trip, I had words like *hervir* (boil), *mezclar* (mix), and *hornear* (bake) rolling off my tongue as if I were a true Mexican. I also knew now that just about all Mexican sauces are made by puréeing together peppers, tomatoes, tomatillos, and chiles. That there is no such thing as a standard "chile powder," but rather many types of dried chiles, each with a distinct flavor, that have been toasted and then ground together. That to bring out their flavors, fresh peppers get charred over an open flame and tomatoes are roasted on a hot comal.

The fact that I could comfortably use the word *comal* in a sentence and toast an avocado leaf with some degree of familiarity was more rewarding than I could possibly express. But beyond acquiring these skills—and learning, through Josefina, dozens of my Mexican great-grandmother's recipes—was the fact that the door to my own Mexicanness had been opened, the door I had to walk through in order to become who I wanted to become. To arrive, finally, in my own life.

A LETTER FROM NEW ORLEANS: SOME HEROES AND THE FOOD ON THEIR TABLES

LOLIS ERIC ELIE

I am writing to you from my usual desk, only now there is plywood to my right, covering the broken window. The ceiling above me is dry, though there is a stain where rainwater dripped through my 170-year-old roof. Behind me is a small patch of moldy Sheetrock. I must preserve it as evidence to show the insurance adjuster, if he ever comes.... As you have gathered, I'm lucky. My fence is horizontal, my car is drowned, but in New Orleans as it exists since Hurricane Katrina, I am one of the fortunate ones. I know that you are hungry for news of your favorite people and places. Much of the news is good. The French Quarter, the Garden District, and many of the other places you have visited escaped with relatively little damage. Mardi Gras will still take place, at the end of February, though the planned eight-day celebration will be four days shy of the usual duration. Jazz Fest will take place at the end of April. But with its fairgrounds so badly damaged, no one knows exactly what it will look like. The most devastating images you have seen were primarily from newer residential areas of the city, far from our historic architecture and legendary restaurants. If you confine your movements to these places, life can have that elusive quality we so long for these days: normalcy.

Right after the storm, our chefs were among the first responders. John Besh, the former Marine who commands the four-year-old kitchen at Restaurant August, was cooking red beans and rice for emergency personnel in Slidell, across Lake Pontchartrain from the city. Paul Prudhomme, unable to cook at K-Paul's Louisiana Kitchen, in the French Quarter, set up his kitchen equipment in a tent outside his suburban spice factory. Nearly 30,000 relief workers got their own relief from army-issue meals-ready-to-eat in the form of fresh salads, chicken Creole, and made-from-scratch desserts. "We're not firemen. We're not policemen. The only thing we could do is feed people," Prudhomme said.

Food is identity. We New Orleanians eat our share of typical American fare, but we are not fully ourselves unless we are serving and eating the food that defines us. Louis Armstrong often played "Struttin' with Some Barbecue," but he always signed his letters "Red beans and ricely yours." Emergency measures may have dictated a limited menu, but we were determined that such measures would not endure for long. By early October, very few New Orleanians had returned to the city, but chefs had more options. "We didn't want to just open and serve the easy stuff like hamburgers and chicken fingers. We wanted to bring back the cuisine of New Orleans," said Dickie Brennan, the owner of Bourbon House, Palace Café, and Dickie Brennan's Steakhouse. The opening-day menu at Bourbon House was dressed to impress: Soft Shell Crab Po' Boys, Shrimp Chippewa, Gulf Fish Pecan, and Bread Pudding.

Our food, which has long served as both our sustenance and our emblem, is the bedrock on which we are building our recovery. It has been the local restaurants, not the national chains or even the deep-pocketed fast-food places, that have bounced back first. Even three months after the storm, it was a lot easier to find a po' boy than it was to find a Whopper or a Chicken McNugget.

JoAnn Clevenger, owner of the Upperline, in the Garden District, understands her expanded mission. She is the philosopher queen of our restaurateurs. "I think that just one restaurant opening gives people hope. Optimism can be contagious." Clevenger believes our population will return. And she and other restaurateurs got an unexpected boost from another phenomenon. When people returned, they didn't dare open their reeking refrigerators. They just taped the doors shut and placed the appliances on the curb with the trash. Lacking functioning home kitchens, people went out in search of food and fellowship. "My restaurant is now a gathering place," Clevenger said. "It might sound Pollyannaish but it is cheerful. I watch the people in here night after night run to another table to see each other. They run!"

I started dining at the Upperline in the 1980s. As I enter this night, I'm immediately struck by the contrasts of old and new. These layers tell their own Katrina story. The warm hug of Clevenger's greeting is timeless, but the carpet smelled of storm decay, she tells me. It was discarded in favor of the terrazzo floor it covered. Her eclectric art collection still crowds the walls, but familiar pieces, moved in advance of the storm, have been rearranged in unfamiliar places.

In the kitchen, chef Ken Smith aims for a balance of home and haute. The arrival of a signature dish—roast duck with ginger peach sauce and sweet-potato french fries—makes me feel at home and at ease. The bacon-blessed richness of the Cane River country shrimp is cut by a crisp grit cake. As I taste it, I am anchored in a moment of prehurricane bliss.

Clevenger gives you the determination to make it all work, and so does Jay Nix. A contractor by trade, he bought the Parkway Bakery in 1996 because it was next to his house and he feared that a liquor store might replace the business that had baked bread and served po' boys since the 1930s. Inspired by that history, Nix renovated the place and taught himself the restaurant business. He had been serving nostalgia on French bread for less than two years when Katrina hit. In December, he was still cleaning up. But he was also plotting his return. "I tell you what. New Orleans is coming back through people's stomachs and their appetites. If you've been following it, it's the restaurants that are getting people excited."

Willie Mac Seaton is determined, too. She had been cooking great soul food in relative obscurity until last year, when she was recognized at the James Beard Foundation Awards as one of America's Classics. The audience, moved by the slow resolve of her 88-year-old gait and the sincere sparseness of her acceptance speech, cheered and cried. She promised them that whenever they made their way to the Crescent City, she would be there.

She is 89 now. The shotgun double house that is both home and restaurant was flooded. The furniture, the fixtures, all lost. But she had a plan. Her son Charlie serves as sous-chef, purveyor, and handyman. He would get the place ready. It didn't seem to occur to her that, at 71, Charlie might not be the ideal candidate. She still hopes to open, but where will she find the money and manpower to do so? The owners of Gautreau's, Dooky Chase, Garbrielle, and Commander's Palace would also like to return soon, but they, too, face costly repairs.

All true New Orleanians, born or transplanted, have a Creole spirit. Our joie de vivre, we have long joked, marks us as redheaded stepchildren in the vanilla American mainstream. But what was once humor is now a dreadful cloud. We worry that our nation will not help us rebuild our homes and levees.

We live and we cook now with an intensity that reminds the world and ourselves of what will be lost if New Orleans is lost. The day Restaurant August reopened, red beans and rice were on the menu. And the Friday lunch menu boasts a down-home seafood and sausage gumbo among John Besh's decidedly non-traditionalist offerings. "I've got something I've got to get off my chest, and here it is," he said. "I don't want to serve a damn thing here unless it has roots that stem from all those crazy bloodlines that built New Orleans."

To understand us now, you must learn the most popular phrase of our new lexicon. We speak of "pre-K." It has nothing to do with early childhood education and everything to do with that long-ago period before the hurricane. This reference point precedes the answers to such questions as "Do they have valet parking?" Post-Katrina, the storm is invariably the main topic of our conversations. But, as in pre-K days, breakfast talk is spiced with anticipatory statements about where one will go for lunch or dinner. No restaurant is more talked about than Donald Link's Herbsaint. Meatloaf remains on his lunch menu as a vestige of those days immediately after his October opening, when he sought to serve comfort food. But it is his chile-glazed pork belly with beluga lentils and fresh mint and his banana brown-butter tart that now dominate discussions of his restaurant.

Fears were raised a year and a half ago when chef Thomas Wolfe bought Peristyle from the popular Anne Kearney. Would the hearty fare from his self-named restaurant across town run roughshod over her meticulous, classic creations? The answer is that, both pre-K and post-K, Wolfe has proved adept at serving dishes as elegant as those Peristyle diners had come to expect.

Two restaurants that were scheduled to open around the time of the hurricane simply altered their debut dates and moved forward. Uptown, Alberta serves elegant bistro food. An hour's drive across Lake Pontchartrain in Abita Springs, Slade Rushing and Alison Vines-Rushing have transplanted the award-winning food they created at Jack's Luxury Oyster Bar in Manhattan to an environment closer to their Mississippi and Louisiana roots. At the Longbranch, their bacon-topped reinvention of Oysters Rockefeller may be the most exciting new dish I've tasted, though the smoked lamb rib served alongside the rack of lamb with wilted romaine and tomato jam has had my taste buds dreaming.

These days, you feel more a part of the restaurant family than before. You know that some of the cooks may well be doubling as dishwashers and that dress codes have been relaxed. Cuvée still requests attire befitting the opulence of its gold-leaf ceiling and its wine list. Chef Bob Iacovone is aiming for lushness, as is evidenced by his opening salvo of foie gras crème brûlée. But post-K fine dining means jeans are acceptable, though not encouraged. Of course, the waiter will still swap the standard white napkin for a black one that won't get light lint on your dark pants.

Once you leave the restaurants, you are often confronted with stark reality. Many neighborhoods are still empty; many streets unlit. This is already a long letter. I didn't intend it to be. But it has taken me this many words to explain to myself what I want you to understand about my hometown. Despite the pronouncements that our beloved city is too dangerous, too hurricane-prone for human habitation, we fully intend to rebuild. Put simply, this place, above all others, is where we wish to live.

Red beans and ricely yours,
Lolis

Text Credits

Henri Bourride, "All Rise." *Chico News and Review*, February 17, 2005. Reprinted by permission of the author.

Henri Bourride, "Pasts and Repasts: A Meditation," *Chico News and Review*, November 13, 2003. Reprinted by permission of the author.

Carolynn Carreño, "Cooking My Way to Mexican," *Gourmet* magazine, June 2006. Copyright © 2006 Conde Nast Publications. All rights reserved. Originally published in *Gourmet*. Reprinted by permission.

Jon Carroll, column on bullfighting, *San Francisco Chronicle*, April 17, 2006. Copyright 2006 by *San Francisco Chronicle*. Reproduced with permission of *San Francisco Chronicle* in the format Textbook via Copyright Clearance Center.

Neva Chonin, "Nothin' But a Tween Thang," *San Francisco Chronicle*, July 23, 2006. Copyright 2006 by *San Francisco Chronicle*. Reproduced with permission of *San Francisco Chronicle* in the format Textbook via Copyright Clearance Center.

Lolis Eric Elie, "A Letter from New Orleans," *Gourmet* magazine, February 2006. Reprinted by permission of the author.

M. F. K. Fisher, "On Bachelor Cooking" from *An Alphabet for Gourmets* by M. F. K. Fisher. Copyright © 1989 by M. F. K. Fisher. Reprinted by permission of North Point Press, a division of Farrar, Straus and Giroux, LLC.

Christopher Kimball, "On the Road to Morocco," from *Cook's Illustrated*. Reprinted with permission from the July/August 2005 issue of *Cook's Illustrated* magazine. For a trial issue of *Cook's* call 800-526-8442. Selected articles and recipes, as well as subscription information are available online at www.cooksillustrated.com.

Mark Morford, "Tired of Death and Tragedy? Find Relief in a New Galaxy," *San Francisco Chronicle*, October 14, 2005. Copyright 2005 by *San Francisco Chronicle*. Reproduced with permission of *San Francisco Chronicle* in the format Textbook via Copyright Clearance Center.

Oscar Villalon, "The Semi-Sweet Science, *San Francisco Chronicle*, December 3, 2006. Copyright 2006 by *San Francisco Chronicle*. Reproduced with permission of *San Francisco Chronicle* in the format Textbook via Copyright Clearance Center.

Tom Wolfe, excerpts from *The Right Stuff* by Tom Wolfe. Copyright © by Tom Wolfe. Reprinted by permission of Farrar, Straus and Giroux, LLC.

AUTHOR/TITLE INDEX

Essays by Author

Essays by Title

SUBJECT INDEX

abstractions, 89–94
  avoiding in personal writing,
    209–213
  concretizing, 91–94, 215–218
  using examples with, 234
  See also concretions
abstracts, 115–123
  descriptive, 119
  evaluating, 120–122
  examples of, 118
  guidelines for creating, 119–120
  as organizational tool, 106, 119
  from outlines, 105
  for prewriting, 64
  for research papers, 326,
    329, 336
  as search tool, 298
  transitions and, 115–118, 120,
    122–123
Abstracts of English Studies, 299
Academic Search, 301
academic writing, 282–294
  audience for, 283–285, 287–288
  documentation in, 283, 290,
    309–318
  examples of, 402–413
  format for, 196–197
  guidelines for, 285–291
  level of formality in, 284–285
  openings in, 150

originality in, 294
purpose in, 282–283, 288–290
quotations in, 307–309
reading assignments for, 291–294
as research-based analytical task,
  289–290
summarizing and paraphrasing in,
  305–307
talking the talk in, 288–289
thesis in, 286–287
time factors in, 285–286
See also documentation; research;
  research paper
accuracy, of information, 304
active voice, 92–93
adjectives
  compound, 189–190
  tone and, 82, 84
adverbs, as connectors, 117
agreement
  pronoun, 179–181
  subject-verb, 179
Allen, Woody, 292
alliteration, 156
All Music Guide, 306
American Film, 306
American Graffiti, 203
American Psychological
  Association. *See* APA citations
analogies, 234, 248